DOWN UNDER
over easy

How I Couch Surfed
My Way To a
Less Expensive Holiday

*For everyone at Wascana.
Keep up the good work!*

By Joan Trill

Joan Trill

Published by:

FriesenPress
Suite 300 – 852 Fort Street
Victoria, BC, Canada V8W 1H8

www.friesenpress.com

For information on bulk orders contact:
info@friesenpress.com or fax 1-888-376-7026

Distributed to the trade by The Ingram Book Company

To Jason and Jenna and the rest of my family and friends, who first encouraged me to go on the adventure and then to write about it.

TABLE OF CONTENTS

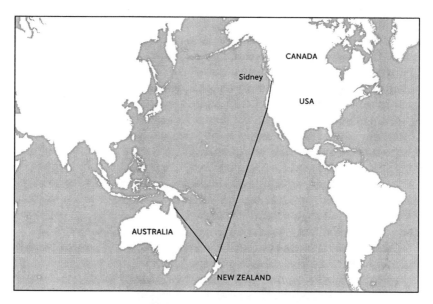

IN THE BEGINNING

The bodies were scattered with reckless abandon. A young female on the couch, a couple lying heaped in an oversized chair, more bodies strewn across the floor in various positions of repose. Who of us has not crashed at a friend's house? Too tired, too far from home, too wasted to wend our way to the familiar confines of our own beds, most of us have stayed at a friend's place for a night or two on short notice. I had just never imagined that at the age of fifty-eight I would once again be crashing in a similar manner - but this time it would be with strangers, friends I had not yet met. I always read the travel section of our local newspaper and this Sunday was no different. My eye and mind were caught by this unique travel opportunity called couch surfing.

Couch Surfing is a free (yes, free!) internet-based, international organization that connects a worldwide network of travellers and hosts. Their mission statement; "At Couch Surfing International, we envision a world where everyone can explore and create meaningful connections with the people and places they encounter. Building meaningful connections across cultures enables us to respond to diversity with curiosity, appreciation and respect. The appreciation of diversity spreads tolerance and creates a global community." Their slogan is 'Participate In Creating a Better World One Couch at a Time'. I went to the website that day and joined. While there is no registration fee, contributions are accepted with twenty-five dollars recommended. I decided to contribute to help with the costs of maintaining the website.

I became familiar with the website and looked at about twenty profiles of couch surfers from all over the planet before I filled in the details for my own profile, then put it on the couch surfing website.

Now why on Earth, some of you may ask, would anyone in their right mind want to stay in a strangers home? Who knows what they might be like? What if the couch is occupied by a Great Dane and a Golden Retriever both gleefully snoring and slobbering in your face all night long? What if your hosts have strange habits such as sitting down at the table with the family at meal times? What if they live at the end of a country road with no electricity and no running water? What if . . . ?

What indeed. It turns out that I did stay at the end of several country roads and many families sat down at the table for meals and there were geckos running wild on the walls in one place, and a lot of pets were involved, but it was precisely these unknowns that make couch surfing such a blast! You never know exactly what you're getting into and that's part of the fun. Once you have either hosted or surfed at someone's home you can leave a reference on each other's profile. These are most valuable when looking for a place to stay.

Now why on Earth, some of you may ask, would anyone in their right mind invite total strangers to stay in their home? What if these guests are axe murderers or thieves? What if they smell bad? Pick their feet? What if your guests want to stay up past your bedtime and play loud music and what if they don't like my dog? (Please go back a paragraph and read the answer)

These are valid concerns. Answers can be found in the person's profile on the couch surfing website. Part of my couch description says that I have a Fox Terrier who will be your shadow. Emma thinks all company is there for her playing pleasure. Obviously, if you are allergic to, or simply do not like dogs, you should skip right over my profile and find somewhere else to stay. If you don't want to sleep on a couch or on a double air mattress in my office, skip my profile. If you don't want to stay in the small town of Sidney, skip my profile. If you want to smoke in my house, skip my profile. But if you want to stay in a friendly and comfortable place and feel welcome, then read my profile again, have a look at the references people have left for me, then decide if mine might be a place you'd like to stay. When someone asks to stay with me I read their profile and check their references too.

My first couch surfing experience was hosting a young couple from Holland. The greatest number of members are young, in their twenties, but there are lots of like-minded people of all ages and I found it relatively easy to find someone to stay with. About a month before their arrival I received an email from Dore and Michel saying that they were interested in surfing my couch. There is a section on the website that you fill out and it is forwarded through a safe email link so your private email address remains hidden. The dates they wanted to stay here worked out for me so I responded with a "Yes, those dates work for me." We corresponded over the next four weeks and I gave them my phone number the day before they were due to arrive. Their travel plans had changed along the way, so they arrived a day earlier than they had first planned on, but by corresponding I knew of this change well in advance. They stayed two nights, this being agreed upon after their arrival. I find it a good idea to agree to host or ask to stay for one or two nights, thus allowing flexibility to the visit's length. It is easier to add to a stay than to ask someone to leave early. They found a lot to do here and other than to sleep, were in the house for only a few hours over the two days. So while we didn't get a lot of time to talk to one another, it was very easy to host them. Though food is not necessarily part of the arrangement, I offered them breakfast each day. After two days they left to explore more of Vancouver Island returning six days later to stay another two nights before travelling to Vancouver to sell their van and catch a flight home. Again, they were courteous and mindful in keeping me abreast of their itinerary. I think it is important to contact your host if there are any changes to your plans; it is just common courtesy.

My second experience was hosting three people from Vancouver. They had taken the ferry to Sidney and were on their way to visit friends on Salt Spring Island which is one of many beautiful Gulf Islands near Victoria. The ferry schedule precluded them from getting a ferry from Sidney to Salt Spring Island the day they arrived, so they surfed with me then caught a ferry to their destination the next morning. They were fully self sufficient having brought their own linen and food.

Hosts offer a wide variety of options. The closest I came to sleeping on an actual couch was spending a night on a futon. I spent a night in a garage based guest room and a night in a travel trailer, the rest were in separate bedrooms. I had my own sleeping bag which I used occasionally, but most hosts provided linen too.

Members use the website to contact other surfers around the globe to arrange accommodation or simply a meeting. There is no obligation to host other people, but it is generally expected that everyone will offer a place to stay if it is possible. In Hawaii, my daughter, Jenna and I spent a great afternoon with Leila on Maui. Leila has a tiny place and so does not host surfers overnight. We already had a place to stay so met Leila for lunch one day. After lunch she drove us around some beautiful places that tourists know about and then special places off the beaten track, including a walk through a first growth Hawaiian forest. It was wonderful to have a local guide. No money is exchanged for couch surfers, but we bought Leila lunch as a gesture of friendship.

There is a website for Down Under / Over Easy too that offers links and pictures.
Simply go to www.downunderovereasy.com

To check out couch surfing, go to www.couchsurfing.com

To find my couch surfing profile place your mouse over the Surf/Host heading then click on the following: Basic Search, Definitely has a couch - go down the page to World and click on: North America, then Canada (country), then Sidney (city) – then down the page a bit, click on List Surfers on Next Page. I should pop up on that list.

NEW ZEALAND

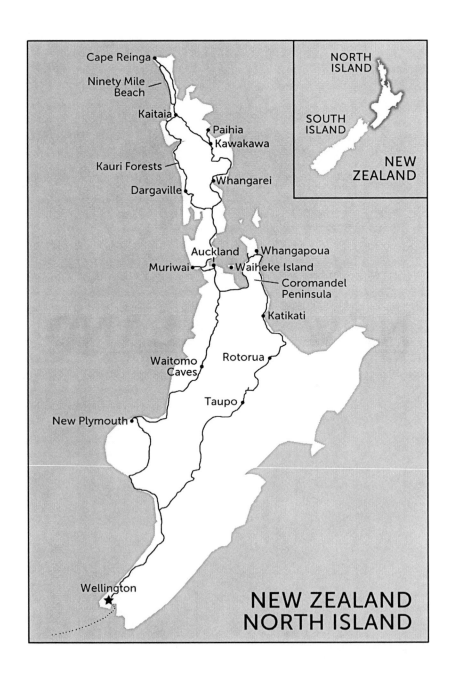

Cape Reinga
Ninety Mile
Beach
Kaitaia
Paihia
Kawakawa
Kauri Forests
Whangarei
Dargaville
Auckland
Whangapoua
Muriwai
Waiheke Island
Coromandel
Peninsula
Katikati
Waitomo
Caves
Rotorua
Taupo
New Plymouth
Wellington

NORTH
ISLAND

SOUTH
ISLAND

NEW
ZEALAND

NEW ZEALAND
NORTH ISLAND

SOUTH OF THE EQUATOR

Andy had already backed down the steep driveway once in order to build some momentum for his second attempt. I was still trying to come to terms with the fact I was in New Zealand after being home in British Columbia some twenty-one hours earlier.

"What the heck am I doing?" was the often asked question on the long plane ride south.

What indeed. No one had tried to talk me out of setting off alone on a three month adventure to New Zealand and Australia. Family and friends were bemused, but also happy for me to be taking the long-dreamed of trip. My doctor had told me that I would have to have my right knee replaced before too long – it might last four more years or perhaps only two. With surgery on the horizon, I knew that I wanted to make this trip while I was still able to walk around fairly well. I had decided to embark on this trip only eight weeks earlier. Opportunity met preparedness and I leapt at the chance.

To make it economically viable, I would be couch surfing where possible and otherwise staying in hostels. My luxury would be renting a car. A car equates with a lot of freedoms: freedom to go exactly where and when I wanted, freedom to stop along the roadside and take a picture of yet another tree, beach, rock, freedom to zip down to a picturesque cove, to climb to a lookout with ease, something my body, in particular my knees, simply would not allow.

The first part of my journey was a flight that took me from Victoria to San Francisco where I had an interesting incident with a security dog. The terribly cute beagle was walking amongst a group of us passengers sniffing away, just doing his job. He came to my bag, sniff, sniff, sniffed and sat down, an indication that I had something in my bag that he had been trained to detect.

"Ma'am, do you have any food in your bag?"

"Yes, I have some peanuts."

"Do you have any fruit in your bag?"

"No, no fruit."

The beagle's nose said otherwise. The female security officer unzipped my bag and asked the same question again. Nope, still no fruit in my bag. She began to unpack the bag, asking the same question again. No, still no fruit.

"The only fruit that has ever been in this bag are a few bananas and apples from a trip in Hawaii three months ago." Having seen the bottom of the bag she now seemed convinced that I wasn't smuggling forbidden fruit and she and the dog went on their way. I found this security incident quite amusing. On my trip to Hawaii I had left my Swiss army knife in my fanny pack and it passed through security five times without being detected and here in San Francisco a dog had stopped me for what must have been just a few Hawaiian banana molecules left somewhere in my duffle bag. Go figure!

I had an hour and a half to wait for my flight to Auckland which I passed by getting a drink and walking around the shops – but no buying, not just three hours into my trip!

The flight from San Francisco to Auckland would take twelve and a half hours and would carry me roughly ten thousand five hundred kilometres over the Pacific Ocean. It seemed rather daunting, I mean twelve hours, that's a lot of time stuck in my seat in a big metal tube with a few hundred strangers. I needn't have worried at all about how to pass the time. I had never been on a plane that offered a personal entertainment system so I was like a kid in a candy store. (Actually a big kid who loves to watch movies and TV). I was delighted to find eighty movies to choose from and episodes from twenty or so TV shows, several episodes each, from animation to nature, New Zealand travel shows and video games. There were several newly released movies that I had been meaning to watch and now with nothing but the night sky to see out my window I was given the perfect opportunity. With a few TV offerings, a few meals and seven hours of sleep the half day passed by quickly and efficiently.

"Ladies and gentlemen, we are now on our final approach to the Auckland airport. Please see that your items are secure and your seatbacks and tables are in the upright and locked position."

Here I was, first time in the southern hemisphere. I had left home on Monday afternoon and after only nineteen hours was in Auckland. That is just amazing to me. Of course I soon realized that it was Wednesday down under. Tuesday had simply vanished as we crossed the International Date Line. I knew that I would get the day back at the other end of the trip.

After clearing customs around five in the morning it was great to walk out the doors and see my name on a sign held by Andy. Andy drives for the North Shore Shuttle Service in Auckland. He efficiently loaded me, his only fare, and my two small bags into the shuttle and we were soon heading north. We bypassed downtown Auckland and went over the Harbour Bridge to North Shore. For budget minded travellers, the airport shuttle service is the best way to get to your destination. They offer door to door service and you pay less than for a taxi. You most likely will share the shuttle and so you get the added bonus of meeting new people and seeing more out of the way places in the area as you make their stops. Unless of course, yours is the first stop, then you don't see anything extra.

So it was, at this very early hour, how we found ourselves at the bottom of Mike and Heather's driveway in Beach Haven North. I had met Heather and Mike seven years earlier on a five day bus tour in Greece. They had since travelled through Vancouver twice, once coming over on the ferry to Sidney for the day and once my daughter, Jenna and I went to see them in Vancouver for lunch and a bit of sightseeing. For several years, I had been telling them I was going to travel to New Zealand. Now here I was, the only thing separating them from me was an incredibly steep driveway. Andy made a noble run at it but was turned back as the tires on the right side came very close to dropping off the edge and onto the neighbour's driveway. So he had to retreat once, but now he had a good idea of the ideal runway path and he tackled it again. The second attempt was a complete success. I was really here. There stood Heather and Mike in their pyjamas, smiling a warm kiwi welcome as we came to a halt at the top of the driveway. After saying farewell to Andy and getting settled in my room, Heather Mike and I had breakfast on the front deck enjoying their fantastic view over the waterway below us.

"Joan, have you ever had Vegemite?"

"Vege what? I don't believe I've ever even heard of it. What is it?"

"It's a spread that we put on toast or crackers and sometimes use as a pastry filling."

Doesn't that sound harmless to you? It did to me. Of course, I was already making a comparison to jams. (You Don't Know What You Don't Know)

"Sure, I'd love to try it."

Then I saw the look they gave each other and Mike broke in to a huge grin. Hmmm, that seemed a little suspicious to me. They told me that vegemite has quite a unique and somewhat strong flavour - I might not like it and I should put only a tiny bit on a corner of toast to try it out. They said it is an acquired taste and that Kiwis like it because they have been brought up eating it. Little warning flags went up in my head, but I mean really, how bad could it be? Well, let me tell you something – it could be really bad! I sniffed it first – a strong aroma of brewer's yeast came from the thick, dark brown spread that hunkered down on the corner of my toast. With two pairs of eyes intensely watching my face and both of them now smiling in anticipation I brought the morsel closer, closer to my mouth. Then I went in for the bite. To my uninitiated palate the very salty and yeasty taste offered no pleasure at all.

"Oh my gosh – what have you given me?"

Of course, they just laughed at me now. I finished the rest of my Vegemite toast corner.

"Thanks Heather and Mike. That was truly very interesting and I can see why it has to be an acquired taste if you are not used to it. I don't think I want to take the time to develop a taste for it. Do you have some kiwi jam?" Yes, they had jam.

After breakfast we all got in the car and headed east towards Auckland. It was a school day for Heather – she teaches French at Rangitoto College and Mike had some work-related meetings to attend. After a fifteen minute drive they dropped me off at Devonport, a small suburb of Auckland, which is on the north shore of the harbour across from downtown Auckland. Ten dollars bought me a return ticket and what a good deal that turned out to be. It only takes twelve minutes to cross to the other side of the harbour but during that time I was able to see some of the best views of Auckland's central business district. Auckland's skyline is punctuated by Sky Tower. It's like a hypodermic needle with the observation levels two thirds of the way up, then the slender communication tower rising beyond that. It seemed to be twice as high as other buildings downtown. At three hundred twenty-eight meters, it is the tallest free-standing structure in the southern hemisphere. I headed for it as soon as I got off the boat. I always try to find the highest observation point when in a new place as it takes so much longer to get oriented to new surroundings at ground level. My street level view was limited to the closest buildings that formed a canyon around me - so much cannot be seen or even imagined. Even though it is the tallest structure downtown, it was most often hidden by other buildings. Fortunately I have my father's good sense of direction and it didn't take long to walk to its' base.

There are three glass-fronted elevators at Sky Tower. I entered one and was whisked away, ascending, watching ground level rapidly recede. It took forty seconds to reach the main observation level at one hundred eighty–six meters above ground level. I left the elevator and walked into the sky.

A city's skyline is its fingerprint. Paris is instantly recognized by the sight of the Eiffel Tower, New York by the Empire State Building. You don't hear about people taking pictures of the 'groundline' in a city - but the skyline, that's a whole different story. Standing next to the windows and having a chance to see everything from an eagle's eye view allowed instant orientation. The city was perfect Lego architecture, of a play set not yet invented. The buildings stood ramrod vertical but had different footprints. Most were a collection of rectangular dimensions but always arranged in slightly different configurations. Some were eight-sided, some six-sided, some triangular in shape. They varied in height from four to over forty stories. The color was generally white to ivory but there were a lot of other finishes as well. Several were clad in glass and reflected and became hidden in their surroundings, camouflaged, yet standing out.

One shone like bronze glass. White letters on a blue and red roofed building marked the YM and YWCA. Other lettering; Rendevous, Duxton Hotel, DDB, www.iag.co.nz, 0800newcops told of what was in some of the buildings. There is a great deal of diversity in the buildings that comprise a city. Such diversity can only be appreciated when viewed from on high such as in Sky Tower.

One thing I especially loved about being up in Sky Tower was that I had the opportunity to look at rooftop gardens and patios. I had the chance to see where people got to relax and have a coffee break or eat lunch.

The view extended for over eighty kilometres on this particular sunny and clear day; from this vantage point I was able to get completely oriented to Auckland and the surrounding countryside, waters and islands. While I was up there, I planned where I would go to next – a large downtown park several blocks from the tower.

There were several large television monitors set up on the observation deck that I hadn't really paid attention to when I first arrived. After walking all around the observation deck and soaking in the spectacular views of Auckland I turned to the monitors. They displayed the Louis Vuitton Yacht Race – a race I had never heard of before, but apparently quite important in yachting circles. The top ten teams in the world were here for this racing series. Races were held over the first two weeks of February with two boats facing off at a time. It was being broadcast live from; you guessed it, the waters near Auckland. I asked about the race and was directed to look to the northeast. Some two kilometres away I could see two yachts vying for position against one another. I was very happy to have my binoculars with me. It was great having the race on the monitors as there was commentary about the boats involved, the strategies employed and red and yellow lines drawn to explain tactics - so much information that made the race understandable for me, the uninitiated.

At night the Sky Tower would be illuminated with red lighting as this is the color used when there are races associated with the America's Cup. The tower is lit up in various color combinations to support different causes: pink for breast cancer month, red and green for 'Kidz First' Children's Hospital at Christmas, green for St. Patrick's Day, to mention a few.

I looked at the information they offered for an opportunity to jump from the tower. "Sky Jump is one of New Zealand's most thrilling tourist attractions and one of Auckland City's 'don't miss!' experiences. Sky Jump can be described as Base Jumping while attached to a wire - just like a movie stuntman. You'll fall very fast (approximately 85kph) for around 11 seconds, and then come to a very smooth landing in the plaza below." It sounded like a blast, but I decided to be just an observer.

I was busy watching the yachts when a jumper leapt off just above me and was brought to a halt just out in front of the main observation deck. When you jump, you are lowered about five meters where you are stopped and held, hanging, for a photo opportunity before the final drop.

Dressed in a bright blue and yellow jumpsuit and in a full body harness, the helmeted girl was looking upward and waving to a camera above, saying hello and goodbye and getting ready to be released. And then she was gone! I stepped closer to the side and through the glass floor over the drop zone observed her plunge. Boy, she got small very quickly and it was only seconds before she touched down on the target below. She was all smiles and gave a wave and thumbs up from the landing area.

One option is to buy a two- jump package. I was told of one fellow who almost died of a heart attack when doing his second jump! Apparently no one told him that on the second jump there is no initial stop for photos near the top. When he passed that point and kept falling, he thought that something was wrong, oh so terribly wrong! You can imagine the rest - what an adrenalin rush that must have been!

Two hours had flown by when I finally made my way back into the elevator. Again, the change in perspective was rapid and dramatic as I passed back down to ground level.

Next, I headed off to the east, towards the park I had seen from above. I passed a huge Extreme Slingshot ride that carried three people at a time, seated in a spherical structure that consisted of three seats with lap and shoulder harnesses surrounded by roll bars. They sat side by side, two boys and one girl, holding on to the catch bar in anticipation of their ride. With the release of the sphere, they shot skyward, suspended by two huge bungy cords that took them first up then down, then up then down, several times until finally they slowed and were brought safely back to their starting point. Their faces were lit up with scary delight!

Albert Park is situated on a ridge and the entrance I had chosen was at the bottom of the hill. At this location I found a delightful spot to take a rest. I took a seat on a bench with my back towards the hill and found myself sitting under the branches of huge trees that shaded and cooled the area. It was then that I noticed the two rock 'poles'. Some imaginative person had come up with the idea to gather twenty-five large rocks for each pole. The rocks, averaging just over a meter in diameter, were fairly flat, as if you had taken a marshmallow and gently squished it between your thumb and finger. Holes were drilled through the center of the rocks, a metal pipe passed through them and they were stacked in formation to a height of about ten meters. From the top of each, water cascaded down the rocky surfaces, sending out a fine cooling mist that drifted through the area. It was just a nice place to escape the heat and hustle and bustle of downtown Auckland. Having enjoyed the peace of the area for fifteen or twenty minutes I got up off the bench, straightened my knee and got it to a working stage once more and headed into the park.

I climbed up the steep footpath to the top of the ridge and in to Albert Park. There is a huge flat area at the top of the ridge, where I found an abundance of flowers, statues, artwork, memorials and a large Victorian fountain. It was similar to some parks back home in Victoria with red and pink snapdragons standing in tight formation by the thousands, blue and yellow irises, pansies of many persuasions with their little blue and yellow 'faces' following the sun, lanky bluebells, orange, yellow and white poppies – just thousands of aromatic blooms arranged in beds of glorious hues. There is a beautiful floral clock, which was constructed in 1953 to commemorate Queen Elizabeth II's first visit to New Zealand.

Statues abound - Queen Victoria is cast in bronze to mark her sixty year reign. She stands with hands clasped in front of her, gazing slightly up and to her left as if still watching over this Commonwealth country. The Boyd statue is of a beautiful young woman draped in a gown and represents Love Overcoming Hate. There is a memorial statue to Auckland journalist, George Reed, another honours former governor of New Zealand, Sir George Grey. Many other statues give recognition to the people who have served in the armed forces and who have lost their lives in battle.

My favourite things were the trees. There are many old trees from around the world that grace the park: oak trees, Mexican palms, Moreton Bay figs from Australia and a tree of special magnificence, an Ombu, a native of Argentina. The Ombu tree has intriguingly twisted branches with a massive root system that emerges above the ground as the tree matures. The roots were like separate logs radiating from the multi trunked specimen. They were almost a meter in girth and were smoothed from hundreds of people standing and sitting on them. There were many nooks and crannies that looked perfect for animal homes.

I think the most interesting sculpture is the Throwback sculpture, crafted in 1988 to commemorate the one hundred year anniversary of the Auckland Art Gallery which is located in the park. It looks like a giant protractor or huge capital 'D', stuck in the ground at one end with the straight edge leaning slightly as does the Tower of Pisa. Walking around it, I was able to frame different views of the park through its open middle.

There are a lot of dark green benches upon which to sit and ponder the wonder of it all – sitting there I seemed far removed from the city that surrounds this island retreat. Stainless steel water fountains abound and were in regular use by park visitors.

I left the park along a path that was somewhat of a tree tunnel with leafy branches arching overhead. So I stepped out of Albert Park and was once more on the streets of the city. Heading north, I wandered back to the ferry terminal, taking in storefronts and people watching along the way. Before too long, I was back on the ferry to Devonport and once again enjoyed the fabulous views of the skyline of Auckland. At Devonport I walked along the main street for a half hour or so, before crossing the street and making my way to the waterfront park. The park was being well used with people strolling, playing, walking dogs, cycling, swimming in the pristine bay and watching boats and people. Mike picked me up from here late in the afternoon.

We returned home where the three of us had another pleasant evening, sharing photos of their recent trip to Hawaii. I also watched the news with them. The main story of this early February day and of previous weeks and weeks to come were the immense and devastating forest fires that were raging in south-eastern Australia. Hundreds of homes had been lost and the death toll stood at thirty-five; by February 24, that number would rise to two hundred ten. Witnesses told of whole towns being on fire, even the roads were burning. Wildlife and their habitats had been turned to ash. With temperatures reaching forty-seven Celsius and no rain in sight the fires were unable to be controlled. Meanwhile in northern Queensland and along the north-eastern shore of Australia, people were dealing with record-setting rainfall and flooding. If only things could have been evened out . . . .

The next morning I finally rolled out of bed after a thirteen hour sleep, refreshed and ready for my second day in New Zealand. Heather didn't have to work as she shares her teaching position with a colleague so we would spend the day together.

Muriwai Beach is about a half hours drive from Mike and Heather's home. We drove out to the regional park where we parked the car and headed out along a path towards the water. We were now on the west coast of New Zealand on the Tasman Sea. I could smell them before I saw them. Heather and I had reached a viewing platform above the colony of gannets – hundreds of them - a sizeable colony perched atop towering rocky pillars and cliffscapes. Sitting down they appear mostly white, a black 'racing' stripe running along the bottom edge of their folded wings. They have a distinctive orangey-yellow head and black pin striping along their beaks and around their blue eyes. When they flew I could see that about half their wings are black and the end of their tails are also black. I thought they were very striking. Space is at a premium for the twelve hundred pairs of gannets that nest here each spring. Like a white polka-dotted tapestry on a brown background the gannets were pretty evenly spaced over the large flat area just below us. Squawks and pecks at each other let territorial boundaries be known. Each bird had to carefully negotiate air space when taking off and landing, manoeuvres that took them precariously close to the open beaks of their neighbours. Hundreds of fluffy chicks kept busy flapping their wings in preparation for flight. In a few weeks they would be mature enough to leave their lofty home. They would have one chance to make it – when they stepped off the cliff it would be 'fly or die'. Heather told me that the young would then fly across the Tasman Sea to Australia, returning several years later to nest at this same colony. Just off shore there are two vertical towers that serve as parts of the colony as well. There were gannets everywhere, soaring out over the ocean; setting off on fishing trips to return later with delicacies for their almost-mature chicks. We watched the birds for about twenty minutes; observed hundreds of take-offs and landings, saw chicks being fed, watched boundaries be settled upon, worried for chicks that were so very close to the edge of oblivion. It was marvellous.

This vantage point also gave us other spectacular views. Just below one of the bird-covered towers is Flat Rock, a huge platform that was being used at the time by several fishermen. The rock fishermen have to be wary of the tides, currents and the waves that might come and sweep them off the slab and into the water below. Heather said that people have died at the site; five were swept out to sea in 2005. There has been a safety campaign to encourage the fishermen to always wear life jackets. Nowadays Alex Chu always wears one – he lost a friend here in 2005, while managing somehow to hold on to the rocks and save himself.

Up the coast on our left the hills plunged steeply into the ocean with no beaches possible. To our right stretched Muriwai Beach, its black sand marking the border between the sand hills on the right and the surf on the left. This is where Heather was taking me next. We got back into the car and drove down to a new parking area. Black sand absorbs the sun's rays and becomes very hot so we kept our sandals on until we got to the water where they were quickly removed. The dark color of the sand made me think the water should be cold but it was very pleasant to wade through - it gets heated as it comes in over the warm sand. It wasn't very busy but there were others enjoying the beach: walking, playing in the sand, surfing and just relaxing. I watched a young boy and girl digging in the sand with their bright yellow and red plastic shovels. They looked more like they were playing in mud than in sand – quite a contrast to those playing on lighter colored beaches. Heather and I waded north for about twenty minutes. It was wonderful and warm as we waded along, a light breeze blowing. We turned and headed back to the car after this first experience of mine with the Tasman Sea.

From here we headed south into the Waitakere Ranges. This is a heavily forested chain of hills that cover almost forty thousand acres to the west and south of Auckland. The area has been protected since 1895 as the Waitakere Ranges Regional Park "for the conservation of native flora and fauna". I loved the fern trees the most because they were new to me. Heather pulled off Scenic Drive and into the parking lot for the Elevation Restaurant. We walked through the restaurant and out on to its large deck. The panoramic view offered spectacular views of Auckland, the Waitakere Ranges, and both the east and west coasts of New Zealand. We had refreshing lemonade and just sat back and enjoyed the view and each other's company. It was great! We had a lovely tour and returned home around dinner time. We prepared another nice meal of barbequed sausages and chicken accompanied by salads.

The next day I returned to the Devonport ferry terminal and caught a ride out to Waiheke Island, the gem of the Hauraki Gulf Islands, a twenty-five minute ferry ride. The draw for me was Sculpture on the Gulf. This is a biennial outdoor sculpture exhibition placed on a two kilometre long public walkway near Matiatia Harbour, the gateway to Waiheke Island. When we were nearing the island, I could already make out several of the sculptures placed on the trail. After disembarking, I caught a ride on the shuttle bus to the beginning of the walk. The path hugs the hillside of Waiheke Island above the water and the sculptures are partly chosen for their visual and physical connection and interaction they have with the environment. The coastal scenery is incredibly beautiful and the sculptures enhance the location. The sculptures are placed on headlands and in tiny valleys and offer delightful discoveries at every turn. My favourite was a group of eight life size Meerkat soldiers, each dressed in combat gear, complete with helmets, weapons and flak jackets. They were "Special Forces on Patrol". At a cost of $37,500 they will not be coming to my yard any time soon – or later.

Another sculpture was a corrugated metal "Water Tank" on a low platform. This brick red tank was about two meters in diameter and three meters tall. In its watery interior were suspended several commonly found objects: a fishing lure, pieces of seaweed, a plastic jellyfish, all gently bobbing about as a pump circulated the water. Portholes of various sizes allowed a look into this imaginary underwater world and for $35,000 you could have it in your own yard. The water tank will not be coming to my yard any time soon – or later.

So I trekked along the artist's path interacting with other people, taking pictures and just enjoying the unique placement of these sculptures, twenty-nine in all, beside the sea and under clear blue skies.

It was hot on Waiheke Island, about thirty-two Celsius, and there was little shade on the sculpture walk. The narrow path had no level stretches, always going up or down and at one particular section, descended a bazillion steps - my knees would have appreciated my trekking poles! I'm so glad that I had the foresight to come prepared with my water bottle. At paths end I bought a cool beverage for the short walk back to the parking lot where the bus would take me back to the harbour to catch the ferry. It was a great experience.

Heather, Mike and I had one last evening together before I set out to explore their country. Mike and I spent some time pouring over my New Zealand map, mapping out possible routes and highlights. With his keen advice, I added a trip to Ninety Mile Beach at the northern end of the island.

PAHIA

To rent a car, a credit card is required. Such a simple statement, but not always simple to do. I had arranged for my rental car a month before my trip began. I wasn't really prepared for my son's email that pounced from my inbox in the very first hours of arriving in Auckland.

"Mom, it is urgent that you contact VISA immediately as your card security has been compromised."

Not the way to start a vacation, not the way to start a vacation at all! But, what could I do but call VISA. Here is what transpired. Somehow, my card's number had been taken by parties unknown and VISA cancelled the card on the spot. When the fellow asked if I was going to be in any one location for more than five days so they could courier a new card to me, I told him that wouldn't be happening any time soon. It was arranged that the new card would be mailed to a couch surfing host in New Plymouth sometime over the next ten days and should be waiting for me at that address. Fortunately, I had my bank debit card so I was able to get cash at most ATMs.

Back to the car rental. I had been explaining to the agent the credit card saga, who seemed to ignore the tale until her machine said that the card was no longer valid (imagine, that – just like I had been telling her). Friends to the rescue. My dear hostess, Heather, had the car put on her credit card for me and signed for the rental agreement. Fortunately, the card is not charged until the end of the contract so by the time I dropped the car off in Wellington, I had my new card and simply put the charges on it. (Travel Luck)

While at the rental agency's office in Auckland I had arranged to drop off my rental car on the Wellington side which is on the north island and exchange it for another in Picton which is on the south island. I was making this exchange as taking a car across on the ferry on a return trip basis would cost almost three hundred dollars. As a passenger I would be paying sixty-three dollars each way. The young Hertz agent assured me everything was set for the exchange. I had changed the length of my stay on the south island and was dutiful in explaining the change of dates to the agent

"Everything is all set" she assured me.

"Don't you want to know the new dates of my travel and when I'll need the car on my return to the north island?" I asked.

"No, it doesn't really matter ", she assured me again.

"Well, I think it actually might matter. You see, I have changed my travel plans and will be staying four more days on the south island" I told her once again.

"No, it doesn't really matter" she assured me again.

Well, let me tell you, I wasn't really surprised to later find that it really does matter, it matters a lot! At any rate, I finally had my car, bade fare well to Heather and Mike and set out on my own – sort of. Mike had come up with the idea to follow them out of downtown Auckland, north over the Harbour Bridge and on to the main highway. This was a very nice way to get out of Auckland. Some five kilometres later, we waved our goodbyes as they turned off to their place and I continued north. This was a great stress reducer. If you get discombobulated in a city's traffic and you don't have friends to lead you out of town you can always flag down a taxi and hire them to lead you out of town.

Driving on the left side of the road came naturally somehow. Of course I had been following Mike and then was on the open road. I just had to keep my right shoulder to the center line and I was okay.

And there I was, driving alone in the car through the gorgeous country side of New Zealand. I had been a single mom since my kids were three and seven and had taught special education, science and math in high school. My daughter, Jenna, has bi-polar disorder which took us on a seven year long, life and death odyssey. There are not sufficient words to describe that journey here – that is another book. Jenna got better over the years as she spent time in the hospital then a series of supported living arrangements. I talked with her, her doctors, support personnel, her brother, Jason, my doctor and my psychologist, Tina. Would Jenna be okay if I went on a trip for three months? Everyone said "Go!" so I hurtled through the 'open door' several months later.There is no way I would have embarked on this long-dreamed of trip had she not been so well.

To be alone was surreal. No responsibilities to anyone else, a clock, a schedule, work, looking after a house and yard. No one to care for but myself.

Driving was very therapeutic. I didn't even turn on the radio for the first five days as I just wanted all to be quiet and non-disruptive. And so my little white car insulated me from the past. It was a vehicle to a freedom I had yearned for but wasn't familiar with. The New Zealand countryside is comprised of rolling hills carpeted in green grasses, crops, plants and trees. I settled into the rhythmic wending of the highway amongst the geology of the land and entered that peaceful world of solitude.

Several hours and a few hundred kilometres later, I approached of Whangerei, a city of just under fifty thousand people and gateway to the Northland of the island. Finding a park alongside a marina was relatively easy and proved to be a great place to have a picnic lunch. I had made a sandwich and added fruit, nuts and a bottle of ginger beer to complete my meal. The temperature was in the high twenties, and once again, I thought how lucky I was to be here in the New Zealand summer. There was a children's playground that was protected from the harsh rays of the sun by a series of fabric canopies arranged over the play area. I spent my time people watching and just enjoying my anonymity and the peaceful surroundings that come from parks and marinas.

I had stopped at the information center and picked up the free Whangerei Walks brochure and now drove to the Kauri Park. Soon after parking the car, I was walking over a bridge across a stream and onto the well maintained forest trail. The noise was the first thing that caught my attention. The sound of millions of cicadas spattered at the forest with an incessant noise; imagine millions of crickets. The forest closed in quickly over the trail and I was soon immersed in the kauri trees. The incline was so gradual that I didn't really notice the ascent. This was a tree top walk, a walk cleverly designed and skilfully executed in a very nonintrusive way. The serpentine boardwalk carried me higher into the trees, where a unique perspective made me appreciate the flora and fauna of this beautiful little park. I stopped at various places along the way and just enjoyed being alone in nature. I continued around the loop and found my way back to my car to continue on my northward journey for the day. It had been a perfect break from driving, but now it was time to move on.

Not too much further along the road I parked again and took a short walk to the twenty-six meter high Whangerei Falls. A beautiful fall, the water cascades in a narrow column over the edge of an old lava flow. As I do at all waterfalls, I isolated a small body of water at the edge of the fall and followed it as it cascaded down the cliff into the pool below. I repeated this observation several times, counting the seconds it took for the water to make its journey. Then I closed my eyes and listened to the water as I replayed my falling water 'video clip' over and over in my mind.

For the next two hours the road turned inland, away from the ocean. Then it turned east to the coast again and to Paihia, a coastal town in the Bay of Islands. The Bay of Islands features in the top twelve of the one hundred and fifteen ranked travel destinations by National Geographic magazine. It is the cultural center of New Zealand and a world renowned tourist destination. I was really looking forward to my time in the area. With a sub-tropical climate the winters are mild and weeks of sunshine and warm evenings mark the summer with January and February the hottest months. Under clear skies the temperature was thirty Celsius on my arrival. The area is an aquatic paradise, a truly amazing playground teeming with wildlife and natural wonders to be shared and enjoyed by the whole world.

The area was favored for Maori settlement. It was an area of first contact with explorers such as James Cook and Dumont D'urville. The whaling industry brought ships to the area. Whalers and seal hunters traded with the Maori, Kororareka (modern day Russell) became the center of trade in New Zealand. Firearms became one of the main trade items of the era.

Conflicts arose between Maori and Europeans, between whalers and sealers and missionaries. In 1832, James Busby was appointed as British Resident. His job was twofold, to keep British commerce safe and to stop unjust British actions against the Maoris. He gathered twenty five Maori chiefs and Europeans in Waitangi and chose the country's first flag.

Busby wasn't pleased to find that the following year 40,000 acres of land in the area had been bought by a Frenchman. In order to prevent the French takeover of New Zealand Busby again organized northern Maori chiefs to sign a declaration of independence, ratified in 1836. King William IV recognized the United Tribes of New Zealand and agreed to act as protector of the new state.

Several years later concerns were raised on several fronts: Maori tribal wars, lawlessness and the fact that a private firm, The New Zealand Company wanted to formally colonize New Zealand. The Colonial Office advised that a British colony be established and in January 1840 Royal Navy officer, William Hobson arrived to establish the constitutional steps to do so. His task was to negotiate a voluntary transfer of sovereignty from the Maori to the British Crown. On February 5, missionaries arranged for a large gathering of northern chiefs on the front lawn of Busby's house where Hobson read a number of proclamations: the boundaries of New South Wales would include New Zealand, Hobson would be appointed as Lieutenant Governor of New Zealand and the third related to land transactions. These proclamations were debated for hours on the lawn in front of Busby's house after which the Maori chiefs crossed the river and continued deliberations late into the night. While some chiefs opposed the treaty others were accepting of the Crown. The following morning, forty-five chiefs were ready to sign and this was arranged to happen. The founding document of New Zealand, the Waitangi Treaty was signed on February 6, 1840 giving the Maori possession of their lands, forests, fisheries and other valuable lands. They ceded their governorship to the Queen and now had the privileges and rights of English citizens.

I arrived in the small coastal town of Paihia in the late afternoon of February 6, and headed for the information center. This was the busiest day of the year in Paihia, as it is Waitangi Day. The staff made several phone calls on my behalf and managed to find a bed in a hostel, a few blocks away.

So, my first hostel. What was I expecting? A very good question. I was expecting to be the oldest person staying there – I was. I was expecting the twenty some-things to be loud and partying – they weren't. Alcohol and drugs are not allowed on the premises of any of the hostels I stayed at. I was expecting that I might be ignored by these young travellers – I wasn't. I was expecting that I might be one of the first ones up in the morning – I wasn't. A lot of expectations for a totally unknown experience – well not entirely unknown. The last time I had stayed in a hostel was when I was twenty and I was back packing around Europe with my best friend. Now a baby boomer at age fifty-eight, I was at the other end of my travel age, the time when my children have grown and left home, the time when I was retired. I checked in and unlocked the door to my dorm for the night. There were two sets of bunk beds – I claimed a bottom bed. Two other girls came to the room a few hours later to share the room. I made a simple supper and spent a pleasant evening walking on the beach at sunset and then talking with a few people at the hostel.

The next morning, I felt very privileged to be driving my own car. As I watched many young backpackers on foot walking on the paths along the waterfront of Paihia, laden with their gear, I could only marvel that I had been able to do the same at their age. The car was an enabler. I drove around the streets of Paihia, stopping here and there to take photos or just to be there in the moment and soak it all in. I was able to drive the three kilometres to Haruru Falls and walk downstream along the cliff top taking in the sight of the falls and the sandy beach where I would paddle to that afternoon. I drove to the Waitangi Treaty site and was able to see where this significant treaty had been signed one hundred and sixty nine years ago. I could imagine the gathering of people on the hill just north of Paihia and appreciated being on location. Because I had the car I was able to stop at a nearby park and watch as father and son flew two huge, multi-colored kites hundreds of feet in the air.

Next on my itinerary was a half day kayak trip, which would take me along the shore of Paihia and up the tidal estuary of the Waitangi River. I found the kayak site, parked my car, and ate lunch on the beach nearby. It was also nice to have some time to sit and relax and begin reading the John Grisham novel Jenna had given me for Christmas.

I made my way over to the kayak shed at the appointed time and was met by the youthful crew, who were working that day.

"Hi. Welcome to Coastal Kayaks. My name is Adam and I'll be your guide for today."

"Adam, what province are you from?"

"Manitoba. How did you know?"

"Your Canadian accent – or rather a lack of an accent to me - gave you away."

It turns out that Adam is a young Canadian who was working as a guide in New Zealand. I would run into a lot of young Canadians doing similar jobs while on my journey. Back home at Whistler, British Columbia, a few months later I met a lot of young people from New Zealand

and Australia working at the resort. So there is a grand exchange of youth going on around the world, a perfect age to travel and work.

I have been kayaking back home a few times so I had a basic under-standing of the art of paddling and how to get into and out of a kayak. But this had been quite a few years and many pounds ago. Being overweight changes the dynamics of motion, and this was never truer than when en-tering and exiting a kayak. Sea kayaks have a rudder which is controlled by foot pedals. So the first order of business is to enter the kayak on land and adjust the foot pedals to the individual. I sized up the dimensions of the cockpit as my kayak sat there on the sandy floor of the shed. Would it be large enough? Having a basic grasp of physics, mini alarm bells sound-ed, as I noticed the kayak was on a slope with the bow pointing uphill. This would increase the difficulty when exiting the kayak.

Adam by my side, I straddled the kayak and sat down on the deck just behind the cockpit, my hands on either side of me. Next, I lifted my legs and placed my feet inside the kayak just in front of the seat. Then lifting with my arms I moved forward and with gravity helping, lowered myself into the seat. My bare feet found the pedals too close to the seat, so Adam reached in and adjusted them for the length of my legs. This part of the procedure had gone fairly well. Now it was time to get out of the kayak by simply reversing the steps. I placed my hands on the side of the cockpit and pushed up and backward slightly. I could not bend my legs at this point so was relying totally on the strength of my arms. I'm proud to say that I managed to get up and out of the cockpit and sit on the back edge of the cockpit. My straightened legs were still together and under the deck of the kayak. It was at this time that things went awry. That slight incline my kayak was sitting on worked with my momentum and gravity, and I began a slow backwards roll. I mean, this was a backwards roll that you see on funniest video shows all the time. A roll from which there is no es-cape. A roll from which there is no chance of recovery. An embarrassing roll. A roll for everyone else to laugh at. All this flashed through my head at lightning speed and quickly I found myself on the sandy floor of the kayak shed none the worse for wear. What could I do? I laughed along with everyone else, stood up and brushed myself off. The worst part of the trip was over.

The other members of our group were soon outfitted and we took the kayaks down to the ocean. Three couples shared double kayaks, Adam, another man and I each had single kayaks. We didn't use spray skirts, as the waves were not very high that day, so the cockpits were wide open. I watched the first kayak head out into the small surf and noticed that some water did indeed enter the cockpit. This person was much lighter than me, so I knew that I would be sitting lower, and probably get wet. While the first kayak had ridden over the waves mine plowed straight through them and I got soaked from the waist down. Ah, the joys of kayaking! I didn't really mind as the water was comfortably warm. As Adam had instructed, our group paddled out about one hundred meters off shore and rafted up to wait for everyone. Rafting up is when you line up side by side and hang on to the kayaks next you to form a small flotilla. It took about ten minutes for our six kayaks to be joined in this manner. Adam was the last to join the group. He gave us a few more instructions then we put our blades in the water and began pulling.

We headed north along the waterfront of Paihia on this beautiful summer day. I was paddling in paradise with the crystal-clear waters, blue skies and green islands dotting the bay. We settled into a steady rhythm as we made our way the one and a half kilometers to the estuary of the Waitangi River. Once we had paddled under the bridge and into the inlet, the water was very calm which made paddling easier. Kayaking means that you are sitting at water level so it is a very 'up close and personal' experience. We followed the winding river that was bracketed on each side by small hills. There were a lot of birds in the area: flying, fishing, and gathering in trees to watch our passage. When we paddled close to shore, we could see hundreds of tiny fish who make their home in the roots of the plant life where they find food and safety from predators.

After an hour of paddling we could see Haruru Falls, our trip's furthest point. We pulled in to shore a hundred meters to the left of the falls, disembarked (I didn't roll out this time) and had a stretch, a swim and some tea and cookies. After this break we paddled over to, in front of and into the horse shoe shaped falls – at least the front of the kayaks nosed under the falls and were pummeled by the water. Numerous pictures were taken by Adam with each of our cameras. Maori legend says that a water monster lives in the pool at the base of Haruru Falls. We didn't have any encounters with said beast, just perfect weather and company.

While we had paddled down the middle of the estuary on our way to the falls our return trip took us to one side and through a mangrove forest. I had always wanted to see one of these forests but hadn't imagined that I would someday be kayaking through one. You see, in the Rocky Mountains, the trees stay high and dry and I'm sure I had never even heard of mangrove trees in my youth. These trees live in a harsh environment that would kill most species of trees, the inhospitable tidal zone between land and sea. They rise out of the water on a multitude of stilt like roots forming spectacular forests that help prevent erosion. The trees adapt to their watery environ by extending aerial or breathing roots to the surface from their submerged root systems. They provide an excellent habitat for small fish and marine life, providing them with shelter and food in the tangle of underwater roots. Many different birds live among the branches of mangrove trees such as egrets, ibises, finches and herons. We paddled slowly and silently through the shallow waters of this magical area. The only sound came from the birds, the dripping of water off our paddles and the occasional rubbing of our kayaks on branches.

After exiting the mangrove forest, it was only a short paddle back to the bridge. We saw a group of youngsters lined up on the bridge taking turns jumping off into the water below. Adam told us to paddle towards the right side of the bridge and then at the last second turn and paddle under the left side. No questions asked, we did as instructed. As we passed under the bridge, the boys who had been on top of the bridge plunged down in spectacular cannon ball fashion one after another. If we had taken the right hand route we would have been soaked! Adam was happy that we had 'deked' them out this time. The wind had picked up and the water was quite rough so most of us elected to pull out at this point and get a ride back to the kayak shed in Paihia. Once again, I got out of my kayak with the limited skill and grace that a rather large person with a bad knee can muster. I was wet, but not because I had tumbled into the ocean. We were all wet – it's just something that happens when paddling a kayak. We piled into the van for the short ride back to the other boat house where we had started our trip. A few minutes later we disembarked and helped take the kayaks in to the shed, hung up our gear and said our goodbyes. It was a fabulous way to spend four hours in this marine paradise.

I left Paihia around four thirty and turned west to head out to the other coast of New Zealand. A ten minute drive south of Paihia there is the small town of Kawakawa. While there are glow worm caves and an historical railway associated with the area, perhaps the biggest draw is a public toilet house designed by world renowned artist Frederick Hundertwasser. It is apparently the most photographed toilet in New Zealand and I know that the eighteen pictures I took are seventeen more than I took of any other on my trip. Now, why, you may ask, would I take so many pictures of a loo? Because it is a unique conglomeration, an assembly of and by the people, of very simple and unique tiles, glass and grout along with the requisite plumbing that toilets require.

Well, I had never imagined a toilet such as this one! The front of the building projects over the sidewalk with differently shaped vibrant pillars of blue, yellow, ochre, green, brown, red and purple supporting the grass-covered roof. This is not a simple grass roof, but one planted with ornamental plants with their lush Troll Doll hair lolling over the edges of the structure like so many napping giants down for a sleep. The undulating tile and brick floor is soon apparent as you step nearer. There are six tiles of varying sizes with ladies patterned on them on the wall on the right side of the building and six tiles with men on the other to mark the appropriate entrances. There are artistically wrought iron gates that can be closed and locked across the halls when the toilet is closed. This is a perfect example of Hundertwasser's trademark organic style.

Not only was the toilet designed by Hundertwasser, he also helped with some aspects of the construction. College students created ceramic tiles. An old Bank of New Zealand was the source for the bricks used in its construction. Young and old people from the community helped erect the unique structure complete with a living tree, copper handwork, a grass roof, ceramic pillars, gold balls and individual sculptures.

When I entered I was treated to a hall tiled with muted earth tones on the floor while the walls were mainly white, interspersed with vividly coloured tiles cut in various shapes and sizes. I wondered if Martha Stewart would think this was 'a good thing'. Personally I think it's a great thing. There were a lot of single tiles created by a variety of artists making up an eclectic mosaic of wonder. To walk in this loo is to walk on an undulating floor of mosaic tiles that do not meet the walls at right angles but rather curve into the wall.

The windows feature light that shines through green, blue, brown and clear bottles. Beneath one sink swims a sperm whale. New Zealand's fern pattern adorns each side of the facility in a dark forest green.

Documentary teams from France and Japan have been attracted to this project and visitors number in the thousands. If you are on a bus tour of the northern island chances are that you will stop to visit the loo here - to see it and to do whatever it is you may need to do. This project has made an economic imprint on the town's business sector as I, like many other visitors, wandered through some of Kawakawa's stores and bought a few things. The Hundertwasser toilet has won several awards including the 'premier' certificate award in the Creative Places Awards contest in 2000. It's just a very unique toilet, both practical and quite an attraction for a little town on the northern island.

After this unique stop, I headed for the Tasman Sea side of the island. The landscape was of hills and valleys, all beautiful to look at in their green attire. The road was good, but very windy in parts. I emailed my daughter that she would have some serious competition playing Mario Kart as I was getting so much real life practice – she laughed at the thought!

AUPOURI PENINSULA

My second night in a hostel was in the small town of Kaitaia, the town that services the Aupouri Peninsula, the pointy finger part of the north island. I had come here on the recommendation of Mike and Heather who said Ninety Mile Beach is the main attraction. Through the hostel owners, I arranged an all day sand safari for the next day. Taking a tour was the only way to go for me, as my rental car was not allowed to be taken off main roads, down quicksand creek beds, over rocky terrain, and speeding along a Tasman Sea beach. But that's exactly what our four wheel drive vehicle would do over the course of the eight hour day!

Terry was our driver and guide for the day. I was picked up at nine, joining other passengers already on board. Soon our bus was full with twenty adventurers. Lines and clumps of trees were separated by open grasslands on the rolling hills of the peninsula and an ocean view was never far away. Cattle dotted the fields in this farmland of the north. Very pleasant scenery all in all.

Our first stop was Gumdiggers Park. Our guide, Mark was slender and wore dark grey slacks, a navy shirt and a brown and blue baseball style hat. He had a stylish goatee and kind, brown eyes that danced as he talked. The gum diggers' village has been re-created at this digging site which is over one hundred years old. Living conditions were harsh with the diggers having only the smallest of makeshift shelters framed with branches and roofed with a canvas overlay. Beds were branches that had been lashed together and then layers of burlap were placed on top. The gum store had long saw blades, cross cut saws, burlap sacks, sieves, shovels, picks and garden forks that hung on the walls.

Mark talked at each of the holes in the area. Kauri trees produce the gum at points of injury to protect themselves, much as we form a scab over a cut. This occurs primarily in the root and crown systems. The diggers would excavate one end of a tree then set off to find the other end some meters away. Thus, the area is not one long excavation, but a series of straight sided holes dug meters apart and averaging a few meters deep.

The working conditions made the living conditions look great by comparison. Imagine digging through layers of rain soaked swamp mud, heavy mud, mud that covers your body with your glistening eyes the only truly clean spots. The mud is insanely compact and heavy and must be cleared from above, then from around the huge, entombed, ancient trees. Then the gum has to be distinguished, rescued from its hiding places and brought to ground level where it is cleaned and then readied for shipping. Imagine doing this with rain pouring down and pooling in the recesses you have made with your shovel and sweat equity. Imagine doing this with the overpowering summer sun beating down for weeks on end. This was the life of a gum digger. But there was money to be made and it was a means for farmers to support their families in the winter months. The gum has been harvested for two hundred years. Maoris had used it for starting fires, as chewing gum and for tattooing purposes. It was prized by Europeans to use in top quality varnishes. The kauri trees that the gum comes from are from 14,000 to 150,000 years old, buried in layers from cataclysmic events that are still being studied. Were they laid flat by tsunamis, volcanic activity or hurricanes?

We continued on the main road that splits the peninsula. From the elevated road, Terry pointed out our lunch spot, a small rather straight beach a hundred meters below. We drove down to the picnic area where we shared the site with a few other people. Lunch had been packed in several coolers which were now carried out from the buses storage area. Generous sandwiches, beverages and deserts were consumed sitting on benches, logs and the grass. We also had time to stretch our legs and go for a walk down to the water and along the sand. The beach was a perfect stretch running between vertical rocky volcanic outcrops that plunged in to the sea. The waves crashed in with regularity as they always do providing a white contrast against the turquoise of the ocean.

Not long after leaving our lunch site we arrived at Cape Reinga. We disembarked at this northern tip of New Zealand. The lighthouse could easily be seen about a kilometre from the parking area at the end of an ever-sloping, downward, meandering path. We were left on our own to make the trip to the lighthouse and back. Although it was 28°C an ocean breeze helped keep it cooler. The reddish, finely ground, gravel base 'smooshed' softly beneath my sandals, the wind blew in my hair and my knee protested at the decline. It didn't take any pictures when I was heading to the lighthouse, which would leave me a good excuse to stop frequently on the way back uphill. As lighthouses go, it is short and resembles a stout silo, painted white, with black for the frames around the skinny windows and for the dome. It would be at the far end of a lighthouse line-up, the short end. The headland provides sufficient altitude for it to be seen from far out at sea. The dome is topped by a lone, black, pivoting arrow serving as the weather vane.

This is where the Pacific Ocean and Tasman Sea meet. It is not a calm meeting , but one full of action, like two rival gangs bumping into each other and sizing each other up. The ocean looked like an incredibly blue prairie sky with a swath of slender clouds, slashing diagonally across the center. These 'clouds' were the clashing of the waves, where the two ocean currents run headlong into each other and fight for unclaimed territory. I smiled at the magnificence of it all.

Looking from the lighthouse I could see a lone tree jutting from its rocky foothold on the side of the headland. It is not a big tree, perhaps eight meters tall, a tree that has somehow survived clinging to the rocky face in this windswept and salt-sprayed habitat. It is a Pohutukawa tree. It is thought to be eight hundred years old: an ancient tree, a spiritual tree. Maori legend says that their spirits pass through this tree on their way to Hawaiiki, the land of their origin.

Near the lighthouse there is a signpost, which marks distant cities in faraway lands, one of which is Vancouver, British Columbia, at eleven thousand two hundred twenty-two kilometres distance (I live about fifty kilometres from Vancouver). I was also three thousand eight hundred twenty- seven kilometres from the equator and six thousand two hundred eleven kilometres from the South Pole. How cool is that? Who needs a GPS?

Turning from the oceans I headed back up the path, making photo stops along the way. What an area of contrasting features! From clashing oceans and rocky outcrops, to tall sand dunes and sandy beaches, from the cool blues of the water to the earth tone browns and blacks of rocks and the lush multi-greens of grasses and foliage that covered the hillsides.

Even though it was hot and the hill a good test of stamina, I had no trouble getting back to the parking area. Slow and steady pace - it worked for me and my knee.

For the next part of our adventure we would be leaving the hardtop road and driving down Te Paki stream. Yes, a stream bed. This is a place where rental cars don't go, where only four wheel drive vehicles should pass. This route is a connector between the main road and Ninety Mile Beach both of which are considered part of the road system of New Zealand. Terry had driven this route many times before and took us down this road with familiar bravado. The ride was fairly smooth with us rolling slightly from side to side more than having any vertical jolts. It was important to keep moving because if the bus stopped in any one spot the water was likely to wash the sand away and the bus would sink. If you have ever stood still on a sandy beach and had the waves come rushing around your feet you'll know what I mean. And if you haven't ever done that, it's time you got to an ocean and tried it.

We rolled and meandered along this wet, sandy roadway, with tall Pampas grass and reeds marking the shoulder in places and the low edges of sky-high dunes in others. Terry parked the bus at the base of one of the sand dunes. We disembarked, walked to the rear storage area of the bus and took hold of the sand sleds that Terry was passing out. It was time to put our stamina and fun quotient to the test as we tried out sand tobogganing. All of us know that there is a price to pay before the fun of careening downhill, whether it is on skis, snowboards, cardboard or sleds. And this price was trudging several hundred meters uphill as there are no chairlifts or gondolas here in the dunes. Of course this was no ordinary hill, but a huge sand dune which is so incredibly hard to walk up. I relegated myself to avid photographer. With my knee protesting at every step, I walked one third of the way up the dune and set myself up in a position to take some great photos. The one-man red and blue sleds were carried to the top of the dune, and then clutched by their riders as they pushed off and made a fairly rapid descent. Invariably, the riders were bucked off with a somersault or two at the end of the run. The two most hardy, young males of our group, made four runs before they packed it in.

From the sand dune, it was only a short five minute drive until we got out to Ninety Mile Beach. The first thing Terry told us was that Ninety Mile Beach is not ninety miles long. He said that the most common story for the misnomer has to do with the distance a horse could travel in a day, that being about thirty miles. It took missionaries three days to travel the length of the beach so they called it Ninety Mile Beach. It is in fact, only fifty-five miles long. But what a fabulous fifty-five miles it is!

It was low tide. We had a hundred yard wide, sandy superhighway, which smoothly passed beneath our wheels at one hundred ten kilometres an hour. We only slowed when we passed through one of the several streams that carved into the beach as they made their way to the ocean. With the Tasman Sea on our right and the sand dunes on our left I just sat back and enjoyed the unchanging expansive vista.

Terry stopped the bus at several points for photo opportunities. One of these was at the remains of a car that had been engulfed by waves and sand so that only the top third of the rusted body was exposed. This brought back forty year old memories of a car that suffered a similar fate at Long Beach near my home. A young man had driven his car on to the beach as we had done. But he drove too close to the ocean and hit a soft spot in the sand. Soon the first wave sloshed around his tires and the car began its to sink into the sand. We helped him retrieve personal items from the car but there was just nothing anyone could do to save his car once the ocean had begun it relentless takeover.

We also stopped opposite a huge triangular shaped rock that rose from the sea several hundred meters off shore. It resembled a shark's fin, but a big one at around fifty meters tall. A hole had been weathered through by water and wind which now formed an arch. I wondered how many more years it would be before the pounding surf would complete the job and the arch would crash into the ocean.

All too soon Terry turned the bus to the left and up the 'The Ramp' near the village of Waipapakauri. This is the access point at the south end of the beach. We made our last stop at Ancient Kauri Kingdom which is a show case for beautifully crafted kauri wood items. The center piece is an incredible winding staircase carved inside a huge fifty tonne section of an ancient kauri tree. Information at the Kingdom says that 'the tree grew for 1087 years before it toppled in the swampy area where it lay for another forty -five thousand years. It was extracted in 1994 and taken to Kauri Kingdom where it was cleaned and situated in the center of what was to become the Kauri Kingdom show room which was built around the log. It took five hundred hours to carve and polish the staircase which is enjoyed by 100,000 visitors each year.' I had it all to myself when I walked up then down the staircase. I sat on the stairs and marvelled at the age, size -3.6 meters across, 11.3 meters around, 5.1 meters tall - and incredible polished beauty of the wood. I had someone take my picture on the staircase then took their picture for them.

There is a huge variety of skilfully crafted kauri items in Kauri Kingdom. Incredibly little wood is wasted in the making of fine furniture as the smaller waste pieces are used to make a myriad of other striking items, such as bowls, trays, kitchen tools, clocks and salt and pepper shakers. If Kauri wood was a gem, it would be an opal. When polished it has an opalescent quality about it. The soft grain and honey colors shimmer and shine as you walk by and call out to be touched, to marvel in its incredible warmth and beauty. Kauri wood is unique in the world. Living trees are protected as their ancestors are revealing their inner beauty.

I was dropped off at my hostel at five, just in time to make supper after which I did a laundry and talked with other visitors. A lady was walking her two pups past the hostel so I went over to them and petted them for awhile. I really miss the constant activity of my dog, Emma – but it was nice to have a break from her too. It had been a very interesting and enjoyable day!

DARGAVILLE

This day marked the seventh day of my journey. The goal was to travel just over two hundred kilometres from Kaitaia to Dargaville. I was excited to be driving south to Dargaville as I would be travelling through the Kauri Forest, home to giant trees of historical significance. Also, tonight would be my first time being a guest as a couch surfer. Just south of Kaitaia I turned off the main road and headed west to the ocean. I was rewarded with a great viewpoint at the south end of Ninety Mile Beach, so now I had seen its entire length.

There are some very special considerations when driving in New Zealand. The prime one for me of course was to stay on the left side of the road. The road of the day was always posted at one hundred kilometres per hour unless you were going through one of the zillions of curves. I can't recall more than a few stretches of road that I had time to accelerate to one hundred before I had to slow to forty, no twenty, no ten kilometres per hour for a curve. The shoulders were pretty much non-existent with lush foliage rising right next to the asphalt as if to challenge its right to be there at all. The road marking was always a dashed line, a line that says, back home at least, that it is safe to pass. Well, no, it was rarely safe to pass as vision was almost always restricted. It seemed to me that between the curves, most drivers in New Zealand try to attain that one hundred kilometre per hour speed, as if it's a personal challenge. You never know who's coming around the next corner, or on whose side of the road they might be! Mario Kart training - look out Jenna – I think I can beat you!

Hokianga Harbour extends inland from the Tasman Sea for thirty kilometres. I had taken a short ferry ride across the estuary and then driven along the south side of the harbour to where it meets the sea. There is a short hill top walk that took me through a tunnel of wind-swept low-lying trees out onto a cliff top viewpoint. The north and south shores at the opening of the harbour are extreme opposites! On the north, a huge sand dune with sparse vegetation glides down to the shore. On the south side, rocky outcrops plunge near the vertical down to the shore. There is a lot of vegetation on the south side with hardly any exposed areas until the cliff's edge is reached. It was another warm (29C) and humid summer day and it was nice sitting on the lone, single board bench having the ocean breeze blow through me.

A short distance south of Hokianga Harbour winds an eighteen kilometre stretch of road that runs through a Kauri forest sanctuary. This forest is the highlight of the west coast. Kauri trees do not taper as they escalate skywards. They do not look like towering Douglas Firs or Redwoods. They exit the ground looking like a gigantic stalk of broccoli, parallel sides unfettered by branches until they reach a point where foliage bursts from the top of this column like a huge puff of green popcorn. And they are very large trees, second only to Redwoods in size.

Near the north end of this reserve, I pulled into a parking area to visit the largest living Kauri tree, Tane Mahuta, Lord of the Forest. It was an easy walk and took only a few minutes to reach a large wooden deck that expands from the narrow path to offer a viewing area for this largest tree. As soon as I approached the deck, I noticed the silence. There were a few other people at the site, but it was strangely hushed. Even the children were quiet as they gazed skyward at The Lord of the Forest; it is an outdoor cathedral where homage is paid to one of the miracles of nature. Tane Mahuta is just over fifty meters tall and has a circumference of just less than fourteen meters. He is as tall as a half football field and it would take eight adults touching fingertips to give him a group hug around his trunk. His age has been estimated between twelve hundred and twenty-five hundred years. Thirty minutes passed easily for me as I sat and pondered the existence of this forest and of other similar places I had visited – the Redwoods in California and the Douglas Firs near my home in Canada. Trees are magnificent living things. They stand in one place for their entire lives, living in conditions they have been dealt with, taking in carbon dioxide and letting out oxygen for us. They provide habitats for many of the world's land-based creatures – the world cannot exist as we know it without them. I love and appreciate trees for all they do for our physical and spiritual existence. I walked to the second viewing area and spent a few minutes there, alone with Tane Mahuta, before turning and heading back to the car somewhat refreshed.

A bit further south, the Kauri Walks car park was reached. There is no set fee for parking here but there is a sign which indicates that theft has been a problem and recommends a two dollar payment to a park attendant who was on site in his truck. I made the donation and bought some piece of mind. This walk was physically easy, along a wide, well-maintained path through the lush forest. The twenty minute walk took me past a lot of Kauri trees, the most impressive of which is the Father of the Forest. Although he stands twenty meters shorter than the Lord of the Forest, his girth is two and a half meters larger. Nearby is an impressive group, The Four Sisters, who have fused together at the base.

The bark of a Kauri tree is fairly smooth. Large 'flakes' fall off the trunk like so many thousands of jigsaw puzzle pieces and lay piled in great heaps at the base of the tree and act as one form of protection for the root system. The bark looks like a pock marked desert landscape of worn mountains in rusty reds where bits have recently fallen and darker shades of purple and greys where older pieces stay intact. I took my time with the trees and documented my visit with a lot of pictures. I returned to my car an hour later and continued on my southward drive through the forest. And that is how I got to the town of Dargaville on the west coast of New Zealand.

Current Mission: *"To share our space and cultural experiences in this country. To hear and tell stories about travel and lives lived."*

These are the first words in the profile of couch surfers Donna and Jerry who live in Dargaville on the North Island. I knew I would have a quiet place to stay when I called from town to get directions and was told to drive up Mount Wesley Coast Road and come to the second to last house on the right. Finding their home was easy. Jerry was in the garage as I pulled into the large gravel driveway. Jerry, a pony-tailed, lanky fellow, was wearing shorts, work gloves and boots. He sauntered over to me, "Welcome darlin," and gave me a hug. I immediately felt right at home.

We walked into the garage. Jerry was heating water in a double boiler saucepan on a portable propane stove. From the top of the saucepan was a six foot long piece of ducting about six inches in diameter and crowning it all, the saucepans' lid.

"This doesn't look like ordinary supper preparations, Jerry", I noted.

"No, indeed, it isn't. It's one of my projects. I have a piece of wood I'm steaming and once it's flexible enough I'm going to bend it into a circle in an attempt to make a drum. Don't know if it'll work or not, but I'm giving her a try."

And so I was introduced to the ingenuity of Jerry. Jerry and Donna had come to New Zealand from Newfoundland, Canada eight years earlier. I have liked every person I had ever met from Newfoundland and Jerry and Donna were no exceptions. They bought a raw piece of land in Dargaville, and since that time have constructed a beautiful homestead. The concrete blocks that form the walkway to their home are embedded with small pieces of stained glass. Partway along the walk, a gorgeous flowery stained glass rendition of birds of paradise, that Donna had made, welcomes visitors. The vaulted knotty cedar ceiling in the living area and many windows give a sense of being in the outdoors. The white walls reflect the light and give it a spacious appearance. Jerry built all the kitchen cabinets which include a huge free standing cabinet that can be rolled into different locations. A black, wood burning stove, set between the kitchen and living room areas provides their heat.

Donna drew the house design and construction plans in consultation with Jerry. She is the organizer of the house. Donna propagates seeds, works in their gardens, pays bills and organizes social affairs. Jerry makes the projects a reality. She will sometimes come up with an idea and arrive home to find "that Jerry has created it or come up with a prototype ... he's great that way."

Stepping out on the deck was I was in one of their gardens. Strawberries grew in pots placed down the sides of the stairs. Vegetables and flowers flourished in beds along the house. Jerry and Donna rely on rain water and have a huge cistern next to the house. Jerry has set up the plumbing so the gray water from the house goes immediately out to the vegetable and flower gardens. When I had a shower that evening I was very conscious of the water supply and had a 'navy shower'. I got in the shower, got wet, turned off the water, shampooed my hair and washed, then turned the water back on to rinse - very efficient as a water saver.

They have berry bushes and fruit trees on their property and summer and winter vegetable gardens. They are very self-sufficient and have short and long-term plans for themselves and their hillside haven. The view from their deck is of green rolling hills and pastures that faded into the distance. In their nearest field there were forty or more black and white Holstein calves roaming around and doing their social thing. Jerry showed me to my bedroom, where I quickly settled in then we did a tour of the property. Every fifteen minutes or so Jerry and I would go out to the garage and make sure that there was still water in the double boiler.

Donna got home from work a short time later and I immediately liked her. Donna works as a part-time Community Occupational Therapist working out of the small local hospital here and visiting people at home. Not too long after her arrival we all went out to the garage. It was do or die time with the steamed wood. My job was to stay out of the way, which I did admirably. When dealing with steamed wood, timing is critical. As soon as the wood is removed from the steamer it needs to be bent, otherwise, it would cool too quickly and there would be no chance of making a wooden circle. Donned with gloves they worked together to turn off the stove and remove the wood from the duct. With all the strength he could muster, Jerry began bending the wood over his knee. It yielded somewhat, but after only a few seconds, it snapped!

Jerry took it all in stride, laughed and said "Well that didn't work!" The three of us went over new strategies for next time: making the wood thinner, narrower, letting it steam longer . . . . I knew Jerry would figure it out in the long run and would make his drum, that's just the type of person he is. Some months later I learned that Jerry was successful in making his drum, an Irish Bodhram. Success came by cutting very thin layers of local rimu wood and steam-bending them. Then the layers were glued and clamped together in a circle. Drum number three is in the making.

Jerry is the house cook. He went out into the gardens and picked fresh vegetables that he turned in to a sumptuous dinner for the three of us. After the meal we took a walk up the road, enjoying each other's company and the tranquility of the evening. Over a period of six hours, only four cars passed the house. It is a very relaxing place. After a nice evening together I enjoyed a wonderful sleep and arose refreshed the next morning to continue my journey. I consider myself so very lucky to have had such a positive first experience as a couch surfer with Donna and Jerry.

This is the reference that I left for them on their profile. 'Jerry and Donna have a great home and property that they have built and dug out of the land over the past few years. They are a very green couple and use their resources wisely. They are a wonderful and interesting couple who are welcoming and caring. Their place is very quiet and peaceful and the view over rolling pastures and farmland is spectacular. Thanks so much for allowing me to be part of your experience!'

They left this reference for me. 'Joan had tea and spent a night with us and left quite early in the a.m. so didn't get a lot of time to get to know her. She is however pretty low-key and flexible and easy to have around. And thanks, Joan, for being our evening dish washer!'

KAURI FORESTS

Today I would cover about three hundred seventy kilometres which meant for an easy day of driving. The Kauri Museum would be my most interesting stop along the way. The museum is in the tiny town of Matakohe, population four hundred, about an hour south of Dargaville. This museum is one of the most captivating I've ever visited. Anything there is to know about Kauri trees and the industry surrounding them is on display in an array of meticulously crafted reproductions and original items.

A huge life-size mural and historical photographs show how these giant logs were hewn from the forest and transported to sawmills by teams of bullocks. The power of fifty-six teams of bullocks was replaced in 1929 by a Caterpillar, the Cat 60, which is on display. There are more saws on display than in any hardware catalogue. And these are huge saws; saws large enough to fall the second largest tree species in the world. There is an actual running sawmill that has been relocated to the museum. The original machinery includes a massive band saw, with seven foot diameter wheels, slicing through a two meter kauri log. The machinery is driven by slow-moving electric motors. It is so realistic and believable that I had an urge to talk to the workers before realizing they were only mannequins. The mannequins in the museum are based on actual people who lived in the area and worked in the industry with their faces made from imprints of descendants of the people who first came to the area. They look like the original people, carry the names of these inhabitants and can been seen working at their actual jobs. Steve and Bob are shown in a swampy area using long metal rods to probe the mud in their search for gum.

One room is dominated by the biggest slab of wood I've ever seen – twenty-two and a half meters long, four and a half meters high. It is the world's largest kauri slab. There is also a huge cross-section of a kauri log where over nine hundred growth rings mark historical events from the time this tree was a seedling until it was harvested by an eight foot chain-saw in 1960.

One area is a re-creation of a lovely six room home, which dates from about 1800. This is a fully furnished area, which has lifelike mannequins engaged in everyday pursuits.

Imagine having a coffee table crafted from wood that is over 35,000 years old! This slab was 'marred' by incredibly beautiful, shimmering irregularities that were outlined in dark brown. This was just one of the many hundreds of fascinating wood products that were available in the shop.

There is a large mural that I especially admired. The plaque describes it as 'Kauri Story - Kauri Bush: Bush Working: A New Farm, Scenes in marquetry using wood veneers by Mary Wilkinson, framed in Kauri by Mal Wilkinson'. More than a meter tall and several meters long, three different scenes have painstakingly been created in fine detail in shimmering soft natural tones that ripple across the landscape.

I was delighted to find a cozy seat that was carved into a huge swamp log. I love the two pictures of me first on the spiral staircase at Kauri Kingdom and second, nestling contentedly inside this second, large tree.

My final stop was downstairs in the Gum Room. 'Examples of exquisitely beautiful polished kauri gum are on display at The Kauri Museum.' Special pieces were polished and carved to make extremely beautiful collection pieces. The museum has the largest collection in the world on display 'Kauri gum is a resin which bleeds from the tree. If the bark is damaged or a branch is broken by the wind, the resin bleeds out and seals the wound. This prevents rot or water getting into the tree. It can build up into a lump which goes hard. As the tree grows the bark is continually shed. The gum is forced off and falls onto the ground around the tree. This had been happening for millions of years before mankind started to use it. There were vast quantities of gum in the ground. Kauri gum was collected from the ground by picking up the exposed pieces on the surface. As this disappeared gum diggers probed in the ground with gum spears to find the gum, then dug it up with spades. Kauri gum was used by the Maori people for cooking and lighting because it burns very easily. It was also used as a pigment to make the dark colour in tattoos and as a chewing gum.' kauri-museum.com

Happy with the time I had spent adoring the Kauri Museum's treasures I got in to my car and drove south through Auckland and beyond for two more hours to Waitomo. Once again I first visited the *i* center. I was a bit familiar with some of the attractions in the area as I had started researching my trip in late November. I purchased a cave tour ticket for the next morning and called and reserved a hostel dorm for the night. It was a domestic night for me: doing a laundry, catching up on emails and driving back to the nearest town to use an ATM to get some cash.

WAITOMO

One of the most unglamorous, uncoordinated things I could ever imagine doing is squidging[1] into a black wet suit on a sunny New Zealand day with the temperature in the mid thirties. No water nearby, nope, no ocean, no lake, no river, not even any sign of rain.

Why, you may ask, would I be putting myself through this inconvenient truth of trying to cram my Rubenesque body into a wetsuit?

Well, I would answer, because I want to journey underground in a subterranean labyrinth of caves and look at glow worms, and I want to do it in the dark, with a bunch of strangers, while floating in a cold creek in an inner tube.

Just over two hours south from Auckland, the Waitomo region is home to a collection of unforgettable sightseeing attractions, including Black Water Rafting, Ruakuri Cave, Aranui Cave and the world famous Waitomo Glow Worm Caves. Underneath the Waitomo region stretch fifty kilometres of caves and unique limestone formations. These caves are part of a unique karst limestone landscape sculpted by water into blind valleys, sinkholes, springs, arches and fluted rock outcrops. This was a must see destination for me. I had found out about the caves on the web in December and decided that I would experience the Black Water Rafting trip and participate in The Labyrinth Tour. They describe this tour as 'Waitomo's original and amazing underground cave-tubing experience that is known and talked about all around the world.' On a three hour trip you work your way through tight squeezes, take leaps of faith over cascading underground waterfalls and float serenely down river as you enjoy the glow worm show on the vaulted limestone galleries up above. Blackwater Rafting is a unique cave tubing experience offering fun, mystery and adventure.'

The glow worm goal seemed far removed from me as I struggled with my wetsuit. Through and series of contortionistic wriggling and the help

---

1 A compound word - an ungainly procedure when a combination of squeezing and wedging are applied to a task

of another lady on the tour, I was finally encased in black neoprene. Did I mention that it was in the mid thirties? We gathered for our first group photo, a line of naive ninjas looking about as dangerous as black gummi bears.

With the heat building in our wet suits we clambered into the van for the next part of the tour. A short ride later we disembarked into a dirt parking lot. Ahead of us we saw three towers of inflated car inner tubes. Our instructions were to find a tube that fit our butt. This was done with some laughter and tube tossing at one another until we each had a suitable circle of rubber. Our second group photo was taken from a rear vantage point, each of us holding our tubes strategically over our backsides.

The walk to the creek was a short one, culminating in a small wooden platform projecting some seven feet out and above the small creek below.

"The reason you have to learn to jump backwards into the water is that there are two waterfalls in the cave. They are too dangerous to climb down. The safest way is to jump backwards with your inner tube"

What had Brad just said? He wants me to what? Jump backwards? Over a waterfall, no, two waterfalls, in a cave? A dark cave?

I looked at the platform then noticed a second, somewhat lower platform about four feet above the water. I was somewhat relieved when he asked for a volunteer to be first to jump off not the higher platform but this lower one.

I was ready to forge ahead, but a younger girl was the first to go. Then, I found myself at the end of the platform, back to the water, balanced on the balls of my feet, heels hanging over the edge of the boards, my inner tube gripped firmly over my backside.

One, two, three and I jumped off, plunging into and fully under the water. It was absolutely fabulous! Remember that we had been encased in our hot wetsuits for about a half hour now. The cold water offered immediate relief from the wetsuits stifling confines. I had landed correctly in my inner tube and was now bobbing along merrily to the little landing beach. I rolled out of my inner tube and made my way back to the platform where the last of our intrepid group was taking the plunge. We all passed through this initiation, so it was back into the van with our inner tubes for the short drive to the cave itself.

As the rest of the group disembarked, I was looking around for a nice cave opening, resplendent with steps, lighting and perhaps a railing to hold onto. No such opening was apparent. Brad directed our gaze a few yards away along the cliff side to a narrow slit in the rock face. From this distance it looked impossibly small for me to wedge my way through, but as we drew closer I could see that it widened to over a meter and was about three meters high.

I went first, tube in hand, leaning on the walls for support as I made my way down and through the rocky trail and into a small chamber in the cave. We all gathered for group picture number three, taken by our second guide, Jed, all of us hoping our final photo would show the same number of adventurers.

The next ten minutes were spent walking down the creeks' uneven bed, getting used to the enveloping darkness of the cave, carrying my tube and trying to keep my balance over the uneven terrain. There were several places which required stooping over and turning sideways to jiggle through so I was glad I'm not too claustrophobic. My headlamp offered limited illumination but was all I really needed.

We gathered again and Brad told us about the monstrous eels that live in the cave. Then he shone his light into a nearby pool in the creek and introduced us to Mort, a four foot long eel who appeared from the dark waters. He didn't seem to mind as one by one we entered his pool and gingerly made our way past his home. We got to a spot where it was finally deep enough to sit in our inner tubes and float along in the darkness. It was time to turn off our headlamps and look upward. We were rewarded with the blue light of thousands of tiny glow worms on the ceiling.

"Basically, what we're looking at is the snot and feces from a bunch of cannibalistic maggots." Jed explained that it is not glow worms that hang from the cave ceilings, but rather their larvae. When the larvae hatch, they make a nest of silk and then hang a group of threads about thirty centimetres long. The threads are covered with mucus and waste and are sticky. A chemical reaction leads to the blue glow that attracts prey where they become trapped then devoured by the larvae. If there is nothing at hand to eat, the larvae will eat others of their kind. The larvae stage lasts around nine months and then change in to a mosquito-like insect. This adult stage only lasts a few days; they mate, the females lay eggs and then die. The cycle repeats itself.

The quietness of a cave is almost absolute. The only sounds were the water flowing and our breathing with the occasional whispered 'wow' or 'cool'. Sight was the only sense I utilized for a time, just floating with the current and enjoying this natural phenomenon overhead. It reminded me of lying out on the dock at our lake side cabin when I was young. With no light pollution and the clear air of the Rocky Mountains it allowed for an exquisite view of the heavens. In this cave it was easy to imagine I was looking not at insects but at new universes many light years away.

We came to a narrow spot in the cave and had to wade through thigh deep rushing water along the creek bed for a short time. At the next floating opportunity we made a long chain by holding the feet of the person behind you; this formation was of course, called 'The Eel'.

The increasing noise of rushing water signalled the first waterfall. I got to watch as two people stood backwards on the edge of the fall, inner tube strategically placed and jumped backward into the black abyss. My turn found me ready to go on the count of three and away I jumped. After the initial question of "I wonder if I'll hit my head of that jutting overhand I saw on the edge of darkness?" I just went with the fall, plunging under the cold water once again.

"Whoo Hoo! Let's do it again!"

We continued, floating all the time now, sometimes with our headlamps on, sometimes in the still darkness when we would get to an area of glow worms. At one point I could see light entering from above. We stopped under the hole and Jed told us this was a tomo, a hole in the ceiling of the cave. The particular one we were looking at was sixty-five meters above us. That's how far underground we were. Looking up, that's a lot of rock.

The second waterfall was pure fun!

Brad had us pull over to the side of the cave and gather one last time at the cave wall. The water was six meters deep beneath us and he instructed us to turn off our head lights. The blackness was absolute; vision not possible even on a microscopic level and Brad and Jed began to give our last set of instructions for the final part of our trip.

"To avoid hitting your head, be sure to lean exactly like this . . . . When you get to the large green rock on your left reach out like this . . . ."

All useless instructions in the pitch black of the cavern.

"The last game we play is called get out of the cave in the dark on your own."

In total darkness, one by one, we released our hold on the cave wall and drifted off into the 'Belly of the Beast'. Flowing with the current we made our way, hitting walls, rocks and on occasion, a fellow traveller. And so we came back to the natural light of the world, one at a time from our labyrinth experience. This part of the trip had taken about six or seven minutes and I would have been quite happy to have continued for a longer time.

We emerged from the cave very near the spot where we had picked out our inner tubes. We took our tubes and stacked them back on the poles to await the next group. Then it was back in the van to return to base and squidge out of that black neoprene cocoon. I found it actually harder to take off my wetsuit than it had been to put it on; another lady and I helped each other with some tugs to free our legs and feet from its clutches; it felt so very good to be unencumbered once again! Then we all had a shower to warm up before getting into our dry clothes. The last part of the adventure was a nice lunch of soup, bread and salad. I bought some pictures that were put on a DVD and left the building. It was a great way to have seen the cave, to have been engulfed in the cave, to have really been part of it. I highly recommend it to anyone who wants to add a little adventure to their Waitomo experience. Caves are an incredibly inspiring natural wonder and to travel through a cave by unusual means was amazing. For Christmas, my brothers, John and Geof, had given me cash which I earmarked for a Waitomo tour; they gave me one of my trip highlights. So thanks again to my brothers for that memorable experience.

My next venture was to the Glowworm Caves. We gathered on benches in a covered area until our young Maori guide, Liza met our group. After a climb along a path up to the opening of the cave, we passed through a narrow door, along a passage, and then began our descent down an old tomo shaft. The word 'wai' means water in Maori and 'tomo' means shaft or hole. We had a good vantage point of the tomo, enlarged over thousands of years by water. When there is sufficient rain, the waterfall appears in the cave. Soon we were at the Banquet Chamber, the second level. This is a place that early cave visitors stopped to eat. On the ceiling of the cave I could see the sooty evidence that smokers were among these visitors. Liza then led us to a large formation, the Pipe Organ. The formation is composed of stalactites and stalagmites that do indeed look like the pipes of a church organ. Liza told us that not all visitors get to see the Pipe Organ due to the dangerous build-up of carbon monoxide at times.

Next we went down to the lowest level and stood in the Cathedral. It's a beautiful cavern that's eighteen meters high. Church pews provided seating for us as Liza told us about the features. Due to its size, shape and rough surface, the Cathedral has wonderful acoustic qualities and has been used for concerts as well as weddings and other functions. Liza asked if any of us wanted to sing; there were no takers. My children, Jason and Jenna had told me several times that singing is not one of my talents.

We made our way to the jetty for the conclusion of our tour, a boat ride. The boat was an open rowboat style with several aluminum benches running from side to side. The eleven of us found seats and we pushed off from the pier. There were no paddles, oars or motor. The power was by Armstrong. That is to say that Liza's strong arms would provide the power to propel the boat along its route. A series of ropes had been hung from the grotto's walls. Hand over hand, she pulled us silently over the water. We looked up and were rewarded with the shimmering, glimmering of thousands of tiny glow worms on the ceiling above us. It was just as magical as in my first cave of the day.

We docked at a second jetty ten minutes later and said our goodbyes to Liza. She left in the boat, pulling hand over hand to return it for the next group of tourists and slowly faded away in to the darkness.

I really liked this forty-five minute tour. The tour covered two hundred fifty meters, so it wasn't a long trek, but it had many gorgeous features to behold. It was so very different from my morning adventure. Photography isn't allowed in this cave so I bought postcards as I did for all the caves I visited.

I went back to my car and drove five minutes up the road to my third cave tour of the day. It is named for the local Maori man who discovered the cave ninety-nine years ago in 1910, Ruruku Aranui. Our guide met us under the roof of a small shelter near the parking lot. Sporting a smile and dressed in khaki shorts and a matching short sleeved shirt, Dan would be our leader. After a brief introduction we set off through the forest on a path that soon began to climb. I know this is counter intuitive, but most of the caves I visited began with a climb. It took about fifteen minutes to make our way along the hill side to the Aranui Caves' entrance. We followed Dan inside where we gathered for our first information stop. Aranui cave is a dry cave; there is no water to add to, or form new features. Because there is no water, there is no life deep in the cave. But here, near the opening, there live a lot of wetas. Wetas are an insect that instantly reminded me of crickets, but these were much larger. Lanky is a good work to describe these long legged, long-antennaed creatures. There were hundreds of them living in the nooks and crannies of the cave walls. They venture out of the cave at night where they find food. Dan assured us that the wetas do not live deeper in the cave. As in all caves, walls were not to be touched as oils from our hands will stain them. I was happy to hear that photography was allowed in Aranui Cave.

The intricate lighting system that has been installed is controlled by a series of switch boxes. Dan turned on the first lights. They weren't too bright from our vantage point. We walked along the path – ahead it seemed to abruptly end and fall in to a great hole, no guard rail in sight. Parents, hold on to your children. That's one thing I liked about New Zealand, you are expected to have common sense and be able to look after yourself. You know what I mean: don't go near the edge of the cliff in the cave to look over. At home: don't ski out of bounds. When we got to the edge of the rather large hole, a narrow set of stairs could be seen on the left hand side. They had a hand rail running down the right hand side otherwise, I'm sure many people would have taken a tumble over the side and in to the abyss. Single file – as there is no other way to descend – we carefully made our way down to the cave floor.

The limestone formations were incredibly beautiful! It was just a magical place for me. There were the usual stalactites and stalagmites but each and every one is a unique sculpture of nature. At one stop we looked up forty meters along a tumble of rocks that have been layered by marvels of nature. It was so easy to imagine people, plants and animals carrying on lives in this natural diorama. There were huge folds of rock, as thin as curtains draped from the ceiling. Limestone straws hung from the ceiling in many places – imagine that – hollow rock formations – to cool! One short stalagmite rose from part way up a wall. It was shaped like three large marshmallows, was shades of orange and when Dan put a flashlight behind it we could see a fire-like glow.

When we came to a fork in the path, we climbed a long set of very narrow stairs to our left. All the stairs were very narrow – so narrow that I'm sure if I had sat down, I would have had wobbly parts hanging over the sides. There were always handrails along the stairs and often along the path to help with balance and to keep us from tipping into the walls. At every turn there was some new scene to stand in silent wonder at, to take a picture of, and just to marvel at the creativity of it all. Wanting to stay at this terminus of the path, I dallied for a time and let the others get ahead on the return part of the trip. By the time I found my way back to the bottom of the stairs, I was temporarily 'misplaced' from my group and so missed the sharp turn to the left to go up the other path. I continued by myself, back along the main path, all alone now – just me in the cave. There were no sounds in the cave- no animals, no water- just absolute quiet as I held my breath so as not to disrupt the feeling. I stood in silent awe and tried to wrap my mind around where I was standing - deep in the earth, in an artificially lit space, limestone formations a silent testament to the power of time. It was very surreal and mystical – I loved being alone. I soon figured out that everyone else was lost so went back to find them. We met at the bottom of the stairs; they were coming down from the right hand side – the fork in the path that I had not yet taken. They passed me one by one and once the stairs had been cleared, I made my way to the right. I am so glad that I had come back as this path led to some of the neatest places in the cave.

I met Dan as he was last to clear the area, making sure that everyone was out before he hit the lights and the cave plunged back into utter darkness. Dan came back to the end of the path with me and pointed out various formations before we turned back to the larger part of the cave. We stopped a few minutes later near the top of the stairs and started talking. The rest of the group had been trusted to find their own way out of the cave and back down the trail to their cars. So it was just the two of us and neither one of us had to hurry off. We talked of travel, nature and cave geology – then our conversation took a turn to physics and 'weird' science including atoms, quarks, the infinity of the universe and even astral projection. He told me about his son, Derek, who has the ability to see auras around living things and has a sense for things past when in certain situations. Then Dan told me about his life-changing experience.

"Do you believe in astral projection? Well, here's an interesting story for you. My buddy and I were driving in my truck. A huge semi truck was approaching us and there was also a cyclist on the road. There were only two things that could happen: we were going to be forced off the road and over the bank or the cyclist would be struck by the semi and we would all go over the bank. There was nothing we could do – we leaned back in our seats, hung on for dear life, yelled and waited for the inevitable. A split second later, we were just coming up to the same corner, but there was no sign of the truck or the cyclist. It was if we had been snatched from the accident and taken through time and deposited at the same place a few critical seconds later. We pulled over to the side of the road and I asked him what the heck just happened? He said "What happened? Sure as hell, don't ask me, 'cause I don't have a clue!" So we just looked at each other for awhile in stunned silence before we pulled back out on to the road."

What a cool story to hear anywhere, but here in this wondrous cave, it seemed plausible to me. (You Don't Know What You Don't Know).

That just added to the mystery of Aranui Cave. We walked back to the entrance, turning off the lights on the way. When we got back to the car park I thanked Dan for the private tour and for sharing his story. His ride, Liza, from the Glowworm Cave, had been waiting for him for over half an hour. It was to be the best cave tour on my trip. So farewell to Dan, Liza and Waitomo Caves.

NEW PLYMOUTH

After the days' underground adventure I drove two and a half hours south to New Plymouth. This is dairy country so the landscape was green and dotted with black and white Holstein cows. I knew I was getting closer to New Plymouth when I could see the strikingly beautiful Mount Taranaki on the horizon. If you have seen The Last Samurai, you have seen Mount Taranaki as it doubled for Mount Fuji in the movie. It is a symmetrically shaped volcanic cone that dominates the area rising 2518 meters from its surroundings. "In the Maori language Taranaki means 'Gliding Peak', a name that ties it to the legend of how it came to be in its current location. Unrequited love saw Taranaki move from the central plateau, carving the Whanganui River in the process and filling the channel with his tears." (www.nz.com)

Activities abound year-round on Mt. Taranaki. Many roads and trails are used to take locals and visitors up, down and around the mountain on foot, bicycle and in motor vehicles. You can sign up for a professionally guided climb to the summit. In winter, skiers enjoy careening down its slopes. So it is a mountain for all seasons.

Using directions that my host had sent, I soon found the home of Barbara and Craig, who had been couch surfers for a year. We are of a similar age and I liked their profile. I had contacted them in December to see if I might be able to stay with them in February.

Barb's philosophy - "I want to help travellers in my country so that one day somebody will be able to help me when I travel. "

I felt very welcomed by Barbara and Craig from the moment I landed on their deck! They also had an envelope for me from VISA. As you may recall, my VISA had been compromised on the first day of my trip. They said they could have a new card in New Zealand in five days so I arranged for the new card to be sent to Barbara and Craig's address for me to intercept. It had arrived only that morning (eleven days later – not five) and had been delivered even though the street name was misspelled. (Travel Luck)

True to her profiles' personal description, Barb is keen to show visitors 'around our scenic area.' After supper, she took me to beautiful Pukekura Park. There is a cricket oval that is nestled at the base of a hillside where international games were held. As the boundary is not large enough for the modern game, it is no longer used for international matches. Barb told me that the oval was used as a movie set in filming The Last Samurai. This is the location where Tom Cruise was seen issuing instructions to the Japanese soldiers he was training. The park has ferns and many different trees and plants from around the world that I appreciated even as dusk settled around us. There is a wonderful lake in the park where people can hire boats and float away daytime hours. The park also features fountains and well maintained walking trails that pass over bridges and meander through its fifty-two hectares. Barbara proved an excellent and knowledgeable guide. It was a lovely way to spend the evening.

Barbara and I returned home to find Craig still watching the same cricket match as when we left him a few hours earlier so I thought it was a good time to learn about the game. Craig's first words to me were that cricket is a sport that may go on for as long as five days, and still no one is sure who won. I found it intriguing to say the least and definitely not as definitive as Canada's national game of hockey – three, twenty minute periods, then overtime if necessary. And so it was that I entered the world of cricket. Craig was very good at explaining the rules and after his tutelage I was able to follow the game quite handily which seemed to impress them both.

The next morning Barbara drove me around New Plymouth for a short tour. New Plymouth is a lovely place and I immediately wished that I had a few more days to stay and explore. There is a waterfront scenic walk that is over eight kilometres in length; its focal point is The Wind Wand, a free standing kinetic sculpture by renowned artist Len Lye. This is a red, forty-five meter tall wand that sprouts from a metallic silver base resembling a giant's thimble. It has a sphere attached to its uppermost reaches. As the wind blows, it sways and arcs in direct proportion to the wind. I liked its simplicity a lot.

We headed back to Barbara's where I got ready to leave as she got ready to go to work. At one o'clock, we walked to our cars and said our farewells. They have travelled to fifteen countries so far so it is my hope that they add Canada to their list soon and that I have the opportunity to host them.

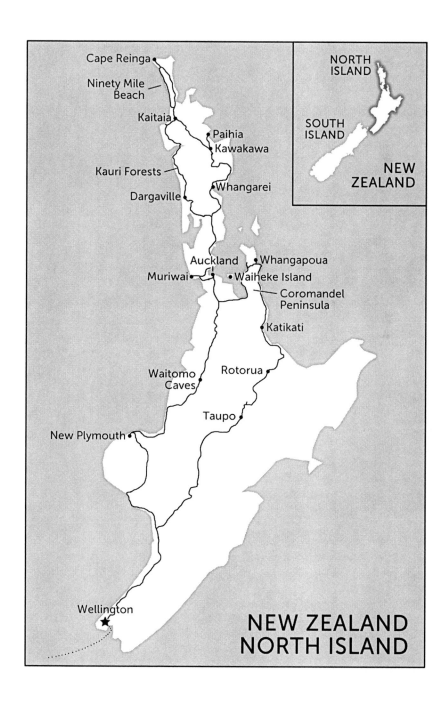

NORTH ISLAND

SOUTH ISLAND

NEW ZEALAND

Cape Reinga
Ninety Mile Beach
Kaitaia
Paihia
Kawakawa
Kauri Forests
Whangarei
Dargaville
Whangapoua
Auckland
Muriwai
Waiheke Island
Coromandel Peninsula
Katikati
Waitomo Caves
Rotorua
Taupo
New Plymouth
Wellington

NEW ZEALAND
NORTH ISLAND

WELLINGTON TO THE SOUTH ISLAND

Rain was the order of the day for the five hour drive south to Wellington so when I stopped en- route for lunch I ate in the car. I pulled in to town at seven and found the Base X hostel downtown. I checked in for the night paying an extra five dollars to stay in the Sanctuary, which is a floor for females only. It was a bit more peaceful than sleeping in co-ed areas. My bottom bunk was adorned with immaculate crisp white linen and topped with a luxurious red blanket, all tucked in with military precision. While there was room for six, I had the room to myself that night. My own personal bathroom was a few steps from my door – this is hostel luxury! I had a great sleep in my private room.

This Friday, the thirteenth of February I would take the ferry from Wellington on the north island to Picton on the south island. At home it's only an eight minute drive from my house to the Swartz Bay ferry terminal. When I want to leave Vancouver Island – which is a rare occasion - I simply decide which of the twelve or more daily sailings I wish to take, leave my house thirty minutes before that time, drive eight minutes to the terminal, pay sixty dollars for my car and myself, park on the car deck and walk up to one of three passenger decks and enjoy the comforts of one of the finest ferries in the world.

Therefore, I was totally unprepared for what transpired when I wanted to catch a ferry from Welly – as the locals call Wellington- to Picton.

I determined that the drive from Base X hostel to the ferry terminal was only twice as long as that at home, being about fifteen minutes - good so far. I had the foresight to inquire about the ferries Thursday night. That evening, I went on the internet to book a passage for the next day. There were only four sailings to Picton: 2:30 AM, 10:30 AM, 2:30PM and the final one at 6:30 PM. I found out that all the ferries were full until the 6:30 PM sailing. I booked my passage on this late sailing. I thought I'd have a laid back day in Wellington the next day, go to the museum and wander about.

Friday morning I was checking out of Base X and talking about the ferry situation with a staff member. She told me it was possible to go to the ferry terminal and get on the standby list, then if there was an opening I would be able to travel earlier. It sounded like an excellent suggestion. I took the ten minute walk to the parkade, retrieved my car, drove back to the hostel and picked up my luggage. Getting out to the ferry was very easy and I was soon parked in the car rental lot and then walked over to the terminal. At the departure desk I was told that I might be able to make the 10:25 if I ran back to the car and got my stuff. I looked at the clock on the wall and saw it was already 10:23 - so this seemed an extremely unlikely goal for me to attain.

To the young male attendant I said, "Well, I don't, I just can't do the running thing anymore. I can walk quickly, but definitely not run."

"I think you can still make it – maybe. The ferry is a bit late today."

So, I limped back to my car as quickly as possible. I had been living in my car for three weeks and wasn't expecting to get on this ferry so I hadn't yet tidied my car or packed up my things. I am an organized person, but I had taken advantage of having all the extra room a car affords, so things were spread out. I quickly began arranging my possessions into my two travel bags, and another large nylon bag. By now it was well past 10:25 and I heard the ferry's whistle blow. "Oh crap!" I thought, "There is no way that I can possibly make it now." I slowed my pace slightly then noticed a young couple running past me.

"Are you trying to catch that ferry?" I asked. They said yes, they thought they could make it, so that spurred me on. I did a last check of the car's glove compartment and storage spaces, locked the doors and headed towards the terminal. So there I was, quite the sight I imagine – blue shirt, khaki shorts, sandals, fanny pack around my waist, toting a stuffed, black, duffle bag, pulling a small, black, wheeled suitcase with a blue nylon bag balancing on its top and leaning against its handle. And so I quickly limped across the parking lot towards the rental car booth. It was a tiny booth, unmanned at the time, so with the ferry whistle once more sounding and failing to see the key drop box, without even slowing I tossed the car keys in an arc through the open window and on to the desk – all the while trying to hold everything together.

Now I pressed on to the ferry terminal some sixty meters away. The tiny wheels on my suitcase whirred and bounced along; the nylon bag fell off twice. "How the heck am I to make this ferry?" From the far left side of the building a fellow beckoned and I took my luggage to him. He took my bags and put them into the luggage truck. Then he directed me in through the back door of the baggage area into the terminal, where I climbed over the baggage shelf and made it to the ticket counter. I was somewhat bemused by the fact that the agent said "The ticket will be an extra ten dollars because we are busy at this time." What could I do – I paid the man, secured my ticket and was ready to go. Then the same agent said "The passenger gate is locked and the gangway is pulled back from the ferry." Mysteree to the rescue. Mysteree was the driver of the ferry's red and white luggage truck. He walked me over to the truck and placed me in the passenger seat, where we waited for a few minutes. I was going to get on the ferry in a way that no other passengers use. He slowly began backing the truck down the loading ramp and onto the ferry's vehicle deck filling the last spot. And that is how I made this early ferry. (Travel Luck). Mysteree gave me his name and number and said to call him if I had a day in Wellington on my return and he would show me around. I thanked him and gave him a huge hug. There are just wonderful, friendly people everywhere in New Zealand.

Soon I found myself up on the outside passenger deck looking at the views of Wellington. It was not for another ten minutes that we pulled away from the dock. The ferry left a half hour late. I used some of this time to call the car rental agency in Picton. I explained that I had managed to catch the earlier ferry and would therefore be in Picton, seven hours earlier than I had originally thought. Upon checking the reservations, she told me "No. You are not in the system. I don't have any car reserved for you." Now, I distinctly remembered the conversation with the young rental agent in Auckland and how she assured me that "It was all set." So while it didn't help at all, I had been right; it really did matter that they had the right dates for my car rental. Go figure! After some time at her computer terminal, the agent in Picton informed me that there would after all, be a car waiting for me. So that was a relief.

I took one of four blue vinyl seats at a wobbly wooden table on an out-side deck. Soon I was talking with a couple who were around my age; Carrie and John who were heading out on a two-week holiday to the South Island. We sailed out of Wellington Harbour and past Pencarrow Head where the houses march up the hillside six layers deep; what a spec-tacular view they must have! The first two hours of the trip were passed traveling across Cook Strait. Then we sailed in to Marlborough Sounds where we made our way between the islands of the area. Grassy slopes abruptly ended in rocky plunges to the ocean below where white surf lines separated land from sea. In the tight passageway of Tory Channel we passed another ferry that was heading to Wellington. As it is in Canada, passengers on both boats took to the decks and waved at each other and took a myriad of pictures. The horizon became filled with the higher hills of the south island as we passed through Queen Charlotte Sound. The vegetation grew more lush and splayed down to the waters' edge. The tiny town of Picton enlarged before us and we were soon at the end of our three hour journey and securely docked.

The good thing about getting on to the ferry last was that my bags were the last ones to be loaded in the luggage truck and therefore the first to be unloaded. This enabled me to get to the car rental office first. At this time, the agent said I would not have had a car but someone had cancelled their reservation only a half hour previously. Say, what had she just said? I had talked to her, just three hours previously, and she said a car was there for me. Now she's saying, that wasn't actually true, but due to the late cancellation I did have a car. (Travel Luck)

The agent was quick to finish off the paperwork, and I soon had my new car keys in hand. The scenic road to Nelson clings tenaciously on the hillsides like shrink wrap on a new product. I was so glad to be here in the daylight instead of the black of night as I would have been had I not caught the earlier ferry. This was a very pleasant and scenic drive as the road runs along the coast for the first thirty kilometres. Lush foliage framed my photos of water, islands, boats, homes nestled in to the greenery and private piers jutting into the salt water. It was reminiscent of the Gulf Islands around my home in Victoria.

The road left the shoreline and coursed through the hills of the south island. Pastures were occupied by black and white Holstein and caramel brown Jersey cows who posed for the camera with curiosity. With bright yellow tags in their ears, they looked like they were dressed up, adorned with gold earrings, ready to go somewhere. But they languished in pastures, either standing or lying down, all chewing away at the grass that was their food.

NELSON

I am constantly grateful that I inherited my father's sense of direction and not my mothers' for without it I would have been lost in an airport somewhere in California or on a beach in Vanuatu and perhaps never even have reached Nelson.   I would definitely not have ventured out of my living room without a GPS as my constant companion let alone halfway around the planet.

I visited the Nelson information center and picked up maps of Nelson and Abel Tasman Park. Finding the house of Eva, with whom I couch surfed for two nights, was relatively easy with map and address in hand. Her long driveway was narrow and parking by the house was limited, so I parked my car out on the street. Eva is near my age and has an interesting profile so I contacted her in January about couch surfing with her. Her current mission: *"To be here now and have fun with it."* Her philosophy: *Life can be pretty bloody hard; we might as well help each other to make it better.* Eva studies homeopathy and sings in several world music choirs. She also practices organic gardening.

I was met by two dogs who escorted me to the side door where Eva soon appeared. It turned out that she had her boyfriend, Ian, staying with her at the time and that her daughter had shown up from Rotorura for the weekend as a surprise. We shared only about twenty minutes together as she showed me my bed, a lower bunk, and the rest of the main floor. Eva would not be around much while I was there, but she said that the WWOOFers would be at home that evening and I could have dinner with them.

WWOOFers? Having never heard the term, I was expecting more canine companions or dog sitters or people who perhaps thought they were canine? It turns out that WWOOFers are Willing Workers On Organic Farms. In exchange for room and board the WWOOFers assist their hosts for about four hours a day. They learn about organic methods of horticulture and agriculture by performing various jobs for the hosts. This is a great way to learn about the country you travel in and is a growing form of ecotourism.

Eric and Goodrin were from Germany and Rachel from the United States. Though Eva didn't live on a farm she had these three staying with her for the past two weeks. They had cleared her overgrown property and learned about pesticide and herbicide free ways to manage insects and weeds. They were very happy and outgoing and I found it ever so easy to connect with them when they arrived home. So it was the four of us for dinner. They were right at home in the kitchen and the three of them worked together to prepare a great dinner of salad, pasta and vegetables. They wouldn't let me help prepare or clean up from dinner. We had a really great evening together talking about our homes, families and travels. Eric moved on to a new farm the next day, having met a farmer at the market the previous Saturday and had made arrangements to work with him for a week. Goodrin and Rachel were leaving Eva`s in three days to travel to the east coast and work at a vineyard where they had been at before.

This Saturday I was going on a day long kayak trip in Abel Tasman Park so I got up at 6:30 and drove to downtown Nelson. I didn't think parking would be a problem, but as I drove around looking for a spot it appeared that there were not a lot of places to park for more than four hours in Nelson. My bus was due soon so I had to find a place; I parked the car in a spot that definitely didn't have eleven hour parking. The area was posted as a tow away zone so I found myself thinking about that a few times during the day. I was hoping that my car would be right where I left it when I returned with perhaps only a ticket under the windshield wiper.

My bus arrived a few minutes after I had walked back to the pickup area. I was the ninth person on board and we made several additional stops, ending up with a total of twenty-eight people onboard heading to Abel Tasman Park. It took almost two hours to reach the park and once we did, everyone headed off to their various activities. Mine was a day of kayaking, a very Abel Tasman Park iconic activity! It's quite a system they have there. We met our guide, Paul, and got geared up with waterproof jackets, spray skirts and life jackets. The next step was to get on the Abel Tasman water taxi, an aluminum boat with a yellow and black chequered pattern running down each side. But this boat was on a trailer hooked to the back of a tractor (a farm tractor). After we jammed into the forward seats, they stacked and lashed six bright yellow kayaks across the stern. Our tightly packed unit was then towed down the road for about two kilometres, then across a half a kilometre of beach, then backed up to the ocean and launched as a unit. So up the coast we went in the spray and the swells for about twenty minutes. At our beach destination, the driver reversed the boat into the beach, the kayaks were un-tethered and offloaded and then we climbed off the boat and onto the beach. This was happening all over the place in this popular park. It turned out that the kayaks we had ferried here weren't for us, so off we trudged after Paul, down a beautiful beach for about five hundred meters to our kayaks. We had six double kayaks in our group. I was paired with an affable fellow, Tim. After packing our gear and getting proper instruction, I lowered myself into the forward seat and we launched ourselves straight out through the surf. We all found ourselves struggling a bit with keeping our kayaks perpendicular to the waves so as to not be rolled over. One of our kayaks was unceremoniously rolled near shore, the twosome tumbled their way out of the kayak, pulled it up on shore, emptied it, re-entered it and gave it a second try which was successful. So just getting onto the water was an adventure in itself, but of course that was just the beginning! The ocean had large wind driven swells - well for me in a kayak they were large - of about five feet. We paddled up one side and slid down the other, settling in to this pattern as we made our way out to a rocky island a half hour away. The rhythmic dipping of our blades was relaxing to me – nothing to think about, just let muscle memory take over – Tim was steering from his position. All I had to do was watch the changing scenery and I immersed myself in the magical surroundings.

The small island had a seal colony so we were able to watch a lot of adults and their pups on the rocky shoreline and in the water; that was cool. There were all sorts of birds too. Soon we left the island and paddled across a long expanse of open water to a new beach where we landed the kayaks. It was on this small but beautiful beach that we had our picnic lunch - this was about two and a half hours after we had set out. Our sandwiches were really big – loaded with all sorts of healthy fillings: meat, cheese, sprouts, seeds - most of us ate every bite. Fruit and beverages rounded out the meal. It takes a lot of energy to paddle a kayak. We had a bit of time for a walk and a stretch after we had eaten. We sardined back into our kayaks and paddled straight out into the waves again. Paul helped steer the last kayak out into the waves then got in his kayak only to be tossed sideways and rolled into the shore. He scrambled out, emptied his kayak then re-entered and soon joined us out in the ocean swells. He said he'd hear about that from his buddies for a long time to come.

My back was starting to tell me that it had been paddling long enough. The thing is that we were about three hours away from the final beach of the day so I just hunkered down and kept at it. We paddled about a hundred meters off shore along the coast. Spectacular granite cliffs and tumbled boulder fields lined the shore; there were several sea arches that had weathered through rocky headlands. It was all very grand and great to see. By this time the sun had come out and the skies were clear which gave us a perfect day. We pulled into a very quiet lagoon - it was so calm and pretty – the water being that perfect turquoise blue that graces thousands of tourist flyers around the globe. My kayak partner, Tim, and I agreed that this is the spot where all the pictures on the Abel Tasman flyers for kayaking were taken! We got out on this beach too and had a welcome break from sitting and paddling. Soon, it was once more into the kayaks; forty minutes later we landed at another beach where we got out of our kayaks and once more boarded the water taxi that was just off shore in shallow water. Then our kayaks were lashed on behind us and our captain turned the boat back along the shore. We had about a ten minute ride to the beach where we had started our trip from. We stayed in the water taxi as it was loaded onto the boat trailer and then the tractor pulled us back to headquarters; first the kayaks were unloaded then we got out of the taxi. All in all, quite a day on the water.

We were all pretty tired and quiet on the ride back to town but we did share our adventures with one another. I started thinking about my car as we approached Nelson – would it still be there? I got off the bus then began the walk up the block and around the corner to where I had left the car. There she was, right where I had left her – I was so relieved – I didn't even have a ticket on the windshield. Thank you, Nelson!

PANCAKES AND ROSS

Today I would head south along the west coast. I thanked Eva, said goodbye to Goodrin and Rachel and was on my way.

The drive was pleasant, first passing through forested hills. There are a lot of tree plantations in this area with broad swaths of clear-cut hill sides and other areas of re-forestation with regimented lines of trees marching up and down the hill sides.

Driving along a short time later, a flash of yellow caught my eye and I pulled over and parked near the Buller River. I walked to a bridge and saw that the bright yellow was a short kayak paddled by a young woman. She was one of a group of eleven people who were wedged into these colourful, small kayaks that from above resembled wooden clogs: short and wide with a bow that tapered upward slightly. These water craft are like sports cars compared to buses. They are very agile and can be 'turned on a dime' - pulled into eddies behind rocks at the single pull of a well placed paddle. The water was crystal clear making it easy to see the thousands of rocks and boulders that lined the river bed. I watched as they paddled beneath me in their yellow, blue and red kayaks and then went down river and disappeared around a bend. It looked like a lot of fun; I would like to try it some day.

The road is fairly windy here and I found myself climbing, descending and making turns through the hills. The Buller River is gorgeous and I was able to steal glimpses of it as I drove (not too safe) so I pulled over where possible for longer looks and picture taking.

A short time later the hills opened and gave way to flatter areas with large areas of fenced pasture land. This is dairy country. Holsteins dotted the fields with their black and white bodies, the occasional butterscotch of a Jersey cow in the mix.

Now I was travelling along the Lower Buller Gorge. It is quite a striking drive, narrow and often windy, that follows the Buller River. Kilkenny Lookout is on a large bend in the river and I pulled over to join a few others at this spot. From here I was able to look back at the road I had just come along and take some pictures. Here at Hawks Crag the road has been cut out of solid rock so that the cliff actually hangs over the road. It is like half a tunnel has been made. There is a right wall and a ceiling, but no wall on the left side; it's just open air to the river a few meters below.

The road now passed through more open country as I got closer to the coast and half an hour later I was at the Tasman Sea again and heading out to a seal colony.

Cape Foulwind Seal Colony Walk – "suitable for people of most abilities and fitness. A short walk – twenty minutes. Good path to platforms overlooking seals." These were words I liked to read. I set out on this short trail that hung on the rocky shore of the Cape, rocks to my right, ocean to my left. It was great to be near the ocean again as I love the water. There were only a few others on this walk which I liked. I rounded a bend in the trail and saw my first seals. Observing the New Zealand fur seals swimming, snoozing, sunning, playing and feeding just meters below my lookout was great fun for me.

The trails in New Zealand are dotted with interpretive panels. Here, they provided information on the seals breeding cycle, colony activities and historical information about the sealing industry that once existed in New Zealand. Female seals live in the same colony all their lives. They give birth to their pups in late November and mate a week or so later. They may leave their pups a few days at a time now as they swim out to sea on feeding trips. Upon their return they may nurse their pups for up to seven days before going back out to feed.

The males arrive in late November and begin to compete for the right to mate; usually a male will gather a harem of less than seven females. During the mating season the males stay on shore and do not eat for up to two months, although most return to the sea by mid January. There is always plenty to see in the colony at any time of the year. I followed the path to its end spending more time watching the seals below. Satisfied, I made my way back to the car then turned back to the main highway.

The Coast Road is one of the most spectacular coastal highways in New Zealand and I loved it. A one hour drive south of Cape Foulwind took me to a 'must see' for west coast visitors. Punakaiki, a small coastal town, is best known for Pancake Rocks and Blowholes. One of the most amazing things I found about New Zealand is that the geography seems similar, and then 'Wham!' out of nowhere there arises suddenly, with no warning, something like the formations that are Pancake Rocks. Where did they come from? Why is it only here, in this one place?

Information at the site told me - "They were formed thirty million years ago from minute fragments of dead marine creatures and plants landed on the seabed about two kilometres below the surface. Immense water pressure caused the fragments to solidify in hard and soft layers. Gradually seismic action lifted the limestone above the seabed. Mildly acidic rain, wind and seawater sculpted the bizarre shapes."

Pancake Rocks are a series of limestone columns rising from the sea like so many stacks of dark grey pancakes. Now these are huge pancakes, there is no pan in existence that could cook up one of these geologic wonders! I walked along the first part of the path and was blown away by these most unique formations! Imagine many huge walls, standing next to, but independent of each other. The walls are elephant grey. They are as tall as ten elephants and as long as a line of elephants in a circus parade. The walls are lined horizontally every half meter or so, just as a stack of humongous pancakes would be lined. Wow! How cool is this?

I was framing a photo and I remarked to the fellow next to me that it looked as if we would have at least one or more similar pictures in our digital diaries. And so I met Tom and Lyn from Sydney, Australia. We enjoyed the rest of Pancake Rocks together, taking more photos and chatting easily about a variety of topics. When they asked where I was staying, I explained couch surfing to them and Lyn said "Well, you'll have to come and stay with us when you're in Sydney." Ten weeks later, that's exactly what I did.

The walk loops out on to the headland and wends its way on top of the rock formations and is what I call an immersion experience. That is, I was up close and personal to this striking geological offering. You know I love trees, well I love rocks too. Maybe this has something to do with genetics as my dad had a master's degree in geology. He would have loved seeing all that is wonderful here in New Zealand. The path is well maintained and easy to walk on. It goes up and down, over bridges, out to viewpoints, alongside deep ocean-filled holes where the water can be heard rushing in to spaces and emitting a deep throated barumpff before receding, only to come in and do it over and over again. There is one section where care has to be taken as the path cuts down through the rocks as a staircase that is rough cut and very narrow. Although the tide was out and I didn't get to see the blowholes in action it was still a fabulous place to experience!

Tom, Lyn and I said our goodbyes and wrote down each other's information. Notice that I said wrote down; if we were younger we would have whipped out our incredibly smart phones and entered the new data there. But I find that pen and paper work well too. I added them to my email list and kept them informed of my travels until I saw them again in Sydney.

I continued down the Coast Road, enjoying the landscapes and seascapes and adding many more photos along the way. I stopped in Hokitika, a coastal town between the ocean and Hokitika River and with the Southern Alps as a backdrop, quite a spectacular setting! Hokitika is home to New Zealand's finest pounamu or jade. Here, you can watch master carvers create treasures or under their expert tutelage, can try your hand at carving this precious stone. There are many opportunities for travellers and it would be very easy to spend several days in the area. I spent some time walking around the town and went in to several jade shops where I admired the creations of talented artisans. I would have loved to have another day here - I would have enrolled in a one day jade carving class and carved a pendant. After I enjoyed a Chinese buffet dinner, I continued south to the small town of Ross where I would surf with Dave. I had first contacted Dave eight weeks earlier and was looking forward to staying with him and his Jack Russell Terrier named Rocky.

Dave's Current Mission: *"To help travelers see our country at the best price"*

In his personal description he states that: "The reason I joined this site was to learn about other countries and people from anywhere in the world. I am an average KIWI guy. My interests are fishing, hunting, boating, sailing, and walking the many tracks here on the west coast. I have an old home which I am trying to fix up in a rustic sorta way at a modest cost. I love showing people around, meeting new friends."

Dave is a few years older than I am and we share some interests in the outdoors and animals. Rocky is a rescued dog, one that was taken in by Dave from a bad situation. He is adored and so very well taken care of by Dave and now is one lucky dog. Rocky has a white body and tan head and tail and at age seventeen he has the white muzzle of his age group. In addition to Rocky, Dave keeps some parrots just outside the back door in an aviary which he built. Dave is a skilled handyman who is relied on by people up and down the coast.

We got in to Dave's red truck, Rocky securing a place on my lap, and set out on a tour. I could tell that Dave took great pride in showing me around. He drove me to the hilltop cemetery which is quite old and has a spectacular three hundred and sixty degree view. Some of the newer headstones marked the graves of children, taken at such a young age from their families. Once again I counted the blessing of having Jason and Jenna in my life.

Our last destination was the beach. Wow, such a beautiful sandy beach! It was now just a few minutes before sunset, so the lighting was just great for pictures. I have a few of Rocky sniffing his way along the sand with his little legs lengthened four-fold in his shadow. He didn't look old in his shadow, just another dog enjoying his evening walk. We watched the sunset over the Tasman Sea, and then waited for Rocky to reappear. Rocky had a routine at the beach, and being deaf, Dave couldn't call for him to come, so we just waited for him to come back to us. Of course he was damp and covered with sand but I still had him on my lap on the drive home. It was a good tour.

We enjoyed a pleasant evening with Dave telling me all about the history of the region and giving travel advice. Ross is small with a population of around three hundred people - a small town with a big heart. There is a history of gold mining here, evidence of which can be seen on the hillside just south of town. There is a very nice museum all about the gold mining in the area.

I took the chance to do a laundry which was very nice to get done. When I said goodbye to Dave and Rocky the next morning, we both wished that I had another day to spend there. Dave has so much to share and he loves doing it. So my advice to you is to allow four or five unscheduled days so that when you come to a place of hidden delights you are able to take the time to enjoy them. I drove around town one more time and made a few photo stops.

What has a crankshaft, shovel, valve handles, an engine block, numerous wheels of large and small dimensions, milk can, circular and long saw forestry blades, heavy vehicle springs, a transmission or two, a car chassis, chains, hinges, a pick head, a tractor rake, weighs several tons and is stationary? Why a fence of course. This fence is a unique creation of a Ross resident. As a fence goes, it does provide a definite boundary of properties. But, if it's privacy you want, certainly this is not the way to achieve it as it has lots of open spaces and it is a much- photographed attraction in the tiny town of Ross. If you Google Ross, New Zealand, metal fence, you can see a picture of it. Privacy is afforded by the heavy foliage that grows just inside the properties' boundary and twines its way around and through the fence itself. After taking pictures of the fence, I drove back to Dave's where I picked up my journal. Yes, even with a routine, I forgot something – but I did remember it in time to retrieve it easily.

I left Dave's around nine and stopped at a place Dave recommended, The Bushman's - it was a really neat store with some unique crafts and a little museum. Outside they had goats and a huge male deer with a large set of antlers! Suspended from the front of the store is a humongous model of a sand fly, some two meters tall.

A GLACIER, PUZZLES
AND TOYS

My next stop was Franz Joseph glacier. Having grown up in the Rocky Mountains I have seen quite a few glaciers. They are all similar yet different so I wanted to walk to the toe of the glacier and see how it compared to the ones back home. The first thing that struck me was that I parked my car in a lot surrounded by a temperate rain forest. It was so lush and green as compared to the sparse, stunted growth and rocky terrain of the high altitude Rockies. The Franz Josef glacier is very close to the Tasman Sea and is at an altitude of less than three hundred meters above sea level. I knew that the walk would be over some uneven terrain so for the first time on my trip I would use my trekking poles. My poles look like ski poles, but are telescopic and shorten to fit easily into my duffel bag. I lengthened and locked them then set out to the trail head. I was standing at the information sign and map when who came along but Tom and Lyn from my walk at Pancake Rocks. Just as we had finished saying hello, I heard another voice, "Hello, Joan". This greeting came from Carrie and John, the couple I sat with on the ferry trip from Wellington to Picton three days earlier. They had just come back from their walk. The five of us exchanged greetings, introductions and information for a few minutes then went on our separate ways. Tom and Lyn walk much faster than I do, so they set off ahead of me.

The trail through the rain forest was flat and easy to walk. The foliage was lush and green with branches sometimes forming tree tunnels over the trail. When I emerged from this part of the trail the landscape opened up to a wide flat bottomed valley that was covered with rocks. There were around fifty people spread out over the length of the trail and in the distance I could see Tom in his jeans and brown and orange plaid shirt and Lyn in her white top and black slacks as they walked ahead. The first picture I took of the glacier seems like someone touched it up using Photoshop - a study in contrasts. In the distance there is a mass of ice and snow, in the foreground is a border of lush ferns and bright green, almost tropical foliage. The glacier is very steep and flows deep in the valley made by the mountains on each side. These mountains are not the stark greys and browns of the alpine Rockies, but are bright green with the foliage of the area. From this point the glacier looked fairly close, perhaps a twenty-five minute walk. Looks can be deceiving – it took about forty minutes to get to the final viewpoint but of course I made quite a few stops along the way to admire the views and take pictures. The glacier and mountains are on such a grand scale that they had seemed much closer.

The path travels over a river bed where glacial streams burble and gurgle their way around, between and under glacial till. The rocks vary greatly in size from a few meters across to grains of sand. They are dark grey and streaked with lines of white. The path is marked from time to time with a dollop of fluorescent orange spray paint. I am so glad I had my trekking poles as the walk is rocky, uneven and unstable in places, and there were several streams that needed crossing by stepping on rocks. With the added stability of my poles I was able to look around more frequently as I walked but I still stopped many times as the view constantly changed. The path keeps to one side of the valley which offered 'nose to nose' experiences with the numerous waterfalls that cascaded freshly over ledges to join streams below.

When I got to the final viewpoint I noticed the bright yellow warning signs: graphics of a person being hit by falling ice, falling rocks and being swept away by rain swollen torrents and by massive waves created by falling ice. Four signs at this one place. There were warnings written in English and German too. Access beyond this point was only recommended if you were with a guide. My daughter, Jenna, was worried that I might go somewhere dangerous, so I had my picture taken at the signs showing me on the safe side of the barrier. Soon, three ladies and one of their daughters joined me at the viewpoint and we got to talking. They were from the United States, touring New Zealand and Australia for a month before leaving the daughter to attend university in Sydney. They loved all of it just as I did.

I stayed there for a half hour and with my binoculars watched some guided groups as they made their way to the toe of the glacier and then up the face. They were mere specs without my binoculars and their progress seemed very slow to me. To some of the climbers, who were doing the huffing and puffing, the pace probably seemed fast enough. Eventually, I turned my back to the glacier and made my way back to my car, with stops to turn and look again at the area. This little trip reminded me of how much I love being in the mountains, there is just something so grand and magnificent about them!

The drive south from Franz Josef glacier to Wanaka winds through hills offering forest and mountain views and at some points, ocean views. At one of the ocean lookouts, I wandered over to the viewpoint and said,

"Hi Lyn, hi Tom." They had arrived a few minutes earlier. This viewpoint was a few hundred meters above the ocean so we could see a long way out to sea and along the coast. There was a gorgeous sandy beach off to our left and I told Tom and Lyn that I saw sea lions on the beach. They didn't believe me but I persisted and dug into my fanny pack for my binoculars. Sure enough, those tiny brown blobs weren't rocks, but sea lions. All those years of eating carrots has sure paid off for me with good eyesight. We took similar pictures and then said our goodbyes once again.

There are a lot of one lane bridges in New Zealand! Most have fairly good lines of view and drivers stop at one end to allow oncoming traffic to pass over before their turn comes. The one I soon found myself travelling over was very long and it was impractical for cars to wait at either end. Cars started from each side then pulled out into passing bays to stop and wait for other cars to pass. These pullouts were placed every hundred meters along the bridge. Drivers really need to pay attention when driving down here!

At that point, the road turned inland and headed east around the south end of the Southern Alps. There were a lot of places where I made short stops, stretched my legs and took pictures of mountains, forests, waterfalls and the Haast River. The river is a series of rapids tumbling down and around a heavily bouldered stream bed. The water is the clearest of clears and pools and eddies are tucked in behind the huge boulders that dominate the river. At one stop I perched on a rock by the river. The accompanying sounds of rushing water drown out the rest of the world and I was just one with nature – a peaceful meditation.

Once over the Haast Pass summit, it wasn't long before valleys opened and I got my first view of Lake Wanaka, lush foliage in the foreground, teal blue water in the middle, and steeply rising, bare, brown hills in the background. I had entered the arid landscape of Central Otago, where hot, dry summers provide the perfect climate for fruit.

If you have seen The Lord of the Rings, you have seen some of the country around the town of Wanaka, located in a spectacular area of mountains and water. Rappelling down waterfalls, rock climbing, swimming, hiking, biking, skiing and snowboarding are just some of the myriad of outdoor activities in this play land region. It was already seven in the evening when I arrived and as I was just staying one night, would not be partaking in any of these activities. I settled in to my room at the hostel then went to stroll along the beach with other like-minded people. A tired little peanut butter and jam sandwich that I had made at Dave's that morning rested in the car and was a dinner possibility. But, I wanted something a little nicer and figured the sandwich would be lunch the next day. I walked up the touristy streets and found a small Turkish restaurant where I ordered a chicken kabob over rice that came with two salads. I dined at a small round table outside in front of the restaurant and enjoyed both my dinner and watching the diverse groups of people walking around town.

After eating, I ventured across the street and in to an All Blacks rugby gear store. My son, Jason, is very particular about the clothes he wears, but I was hoping to find something for him here as he had played on our school rugby team. A plain black toque caught my eye. It had a very small New Zealand fern on the edge of it and All Blacks was stitched inconspicuously beside it. I made the daring purchase and thought that if Jason didn't like it, I'd give it to my brother, Geof, who had played rugby at university.

Another beautiful summer day with clear blue skies greeted me upon rising the next day. While at the *i* center in Wanaka I picked up a flyer about a place called Puzzling World. A lover of weird science, intriguing puzzles and illusions, this would be my first stop of the day. Just a five-minute drive east of town, you really can't miss it. Across the green expanse of lawn rise a group of four, tall, colourful buildings each topped with a triangular shaped roof of red, green, blue, or yellow. None of the four stand vertically, but lean as an array of cards in your hand. A few meters to the left of these is the Leaning Tower of Wanaka. It is connected with the ground at only one of the four corners of its base as if some giant prankster had tried to topple it and met with only limited success leaving it at an angle eight times as severe as the Leaning Tower of Pisa. I turned off the road, parked the car, walked around the grounds taking pictures then went into the building.

The illusion rooms were my favourite part of the complex. Most likely, we've all had the experience of having the eyes in a portrait or photograph seem to follow us as we moved across a room. Now expand that experience one hundred sixty-eight times and you will know how I felt in the Hall of Following Faces. Here on the walls are mounted larger than life sized models of famous faces. Just looking at twenty Lincolns at once, was pretty cool. When I got up really close I realized that the faces were not sticking out of the wall but were concave and pressed into the wall - kind of trippy. Einstein, Mandela, and Mother Teresa were some of the other famous faces.

The Ames Forced Perspectives Room looks normal when viewed through an outside window. But once you enter the room and walk across from one corner to the next, the room seems to shrink or expand depending on your direction. This was really trippy! There is a time delayed video so I was able to go outside the room and watch myself grow first taller, then shorter as I had wandered about. It was a very Alice in Wonderland experience.

The Tilted House looks very normal, but it feels anything but normal, when you step inside and try to move around. The room is tilted, but my mind's eye said it wasn't. There was a pool table, where balls rolled uphill. I sat on a sliding chair mounted on the wall that looked like it was carrying me uphill, but I felt like I was moving downhill. It was very confusing to mind and eye and led me and the other visitors to stumble around as if we were all somewhat inebriated. When I exited the house it took a while to get my 'land legs' back.

The Hologram Hall was very interesting - illusions were painted on walls and puzzling displays were found throughout the building. There is a Puzzle Center and Café where I passed some time working out some of the many puzzles that were on the tables. Over all it was a weird and wonderful experience.

In conversation with a fellow traveller I was advised to visit The Toy and Transport Museum which is a short distance down the road from Puzzling World. He talked so enthusiastically of a huge collection of toys and vehicles from the past one hundred years that I was inspired to visit it. Shortly after leaving Puzzling World I was at the entrance to this most marvellous of places. There are over thirty thousand items housed in four large buildings and on the grounds of the museum. This collection has been gathered by one enthusiastic collector over his lifetime.

The toy collection is beyond imagination. There are display cases filled with thousands of : Barbie items (more than five hundred), Dinky Toys, porcelain dolls, McDonald`s toys, Star War items, Hot Wheels, Transformers, fire engines, cars, trucks, planes, boats, soldiers, trains, LEGO, teddy bears, money banks, prams and many, many more items.

It seemed to go on forever, each turn yielding new surprises, one of my favourites being a large gathering of the Peanuts dog, Snoopy, figurines. I was simply fascinated by all of it! I found myself smiling with fond memories as I saw many toys of my childhood, some which I had owned, some that had been shared by friends.

Then there were the large toys: bicycles - lots and lots of bicycles - tricycles, huge stuffed toys, doll houses, prams, pedal cars and wagons to name only a few.

There are hundreds of cars, some rare such as a 1924 McLaughlin Buick Limousine (there were only four made). There are Datsuns, Cadillacs, Toyotas, Alfa Romeos, Packards, Mustangs, Buicks, Daimlers, Rolls Royces, Austins, BMWs, Jaguars, Minis, Ferraris - too many more to mention here, all dating from the early 1900`s to a 1998 Nissan EXA. They are parked in enormous hangers, side by side in an infinite array of color. There is one small yellow car that has two steering wheels facing in opposite directions – it can be driven from either end.

There are aircraft, construction machinery, farm machines, over thirty fire engines, military vehicles, motorbikes, scooters, mopeds, pick-ups and trucks, horse drawn and marine transportation. It was amazing to walk among this vast gathering of vehicles.

The museum also has household items, scale models, car licence plates, cameras, lawn mowers – even dentist chairs.

In the few hours I was there my mind had been able to process only a small percentage of what was in front of me. I managed to take in the details of many things but overall had just skimmed the surface of recognition. If you ever get the chance to visit a place like this, take it, venture forth, you won't regret it.

The drive from Wanaka to Queenstown was full of beautiful scenery: mountains, lakes, rivers. At one of my frequent stops, I walked to the center of a bridge that spanned a turquoise blue river. The river was fairly narrow and ran quickly through the rocky gorge. This turned out to be the end of a sledge run. I had never heard of river sledging before, but it sure looked like a lot of fun. The water is cold so participants are dressed in full wetsuits, complete with fins and life jackets. They began their journey at some unknown distance upstream where they followed their guides into the water. They held on tightly to their boogie boards, as they navigated the river's calm spots and rapids. There were two Water Jets with the group and I watched as their skilled drivers swung by some of the swimmers and picked them up on a sled that each towed. Then they ferried them to the take out area. At another river stop I watched a group of kayakers playing in the water. It was a great route to follow into Queenstown.

QUEENSTOWN

I knew that the gondola would give me that eagle-eye view that I love to experience when in a new place. The gondola in Queenstown is the steepest lift in the southern hemisphere at an average incline of thirty-seven degrees. I had the four person car to myself and enjoyed the freedom to try all the seats and to stand to get the best views possible. In the cleared area beneath the gondola, sheep were grazing. The ride is seven hundred thirty meters long and at speeds up to three and a half meters per second, takes only a few minutes to reach the top. The Skyline complex has a restaurant, souvenir shop and hosts a variety of functions.

It was not crowded on the different viewing decks which offer a 220 degree view of Lake Wakatipu and mountains. To my right, this lake of The Lord of the Rings fame, faded in to the distance as do the mountains on the far side of it. Across the lake at this point, rose Cecil and Walter Peaks, with elevations of just under two thousand meters. The ice-blue lake lapped at the base of Cecil Peak then disappeared around to the left and then behind the mountain. The shore on the left side of the lake appeared from near the horizon in the middle of the vista. Above the shoreline marched a long chain of similar snow-capped peaks, The Remarkables. The shape of the left shore can best be described as flowing first like a capital S, jumping across Frankton Arm, and then flowing like a backwards capital S at the town of Queenstown. In the S that is furthest away, the lower bulge of that S is home to the Queenstown Golf Course. In Queenstown, the upper bulge of the backwards S is a peninsula upon which lies the Queenstown Gardens. The backwards bulge forms a perfect horseshoe bay where the beach provides a perfect waterfront for the town. To the left of all this magnificence stood the buildings of Queenstown, occupying the flatter land and climbing along the hillside that is below the gondola. Queenstown Hill dominated the view at the left side of the panorama with another chain of snow-topped peaks in the distance. The zoom feature on my camera allowed me to take close ups of the golf course, the gardens, downtown, and mountains.

The view was not the only draw at the top of the gondola. There was a chair lift that carried riders to the top of two, eight hundred metre long luge tracks. One was fairly gentle, a scenic route, where you can pull out to one of the several viewing areas to admire the view and take pictures. The other was the advanced track where there was a 'rush' factor built in with a steeper grade, banked corners, dips and even a tunnel. I really missed Jason and Jenna at that point as we had ridden on luge runs before and had so much fun together. Some things are just meant to be shared. It just wouldn't be the same without someone to share it with, so I elected not to go; a decision I later regretted.

Another activity was bungy jumping. The takeoff platform was cantilevered out through trees. There was a path which allowed for a 'run and jump' style which is not available at most bungy jumping places. Of the eight jumpers I watched, only three elected to run for it. There was even the opportunity to jump at night, four hundred meters above the lights of Queenstown.

New Zealand is a trekker's dream land. From Skyline there were a half dozen walks from easy half hour walks to stamina testing six hour treks that require a good level of fitness.

After I descended the mountain, I drove to the waterfront where I parked the car for the next several hours. Queenstown isn't a large city at just over ten thousand residents but it is a huge city in terms of adrenalin rush outdoor activities: jet boating, fishing, skiing, bungy jumping, trekking, para-gliding, mountain biking and white water rafting and sledging to name a few. Its location is spectacular sitting on the edge of a lightning bolt shaped lake, with a sandy beach that is lapped by crystal clear water. The beach looks down the lake to the west with spectacular mountains rising on both sides of the lake. To the left is the park I had seen from Skyline and this is where I headed next.

The Queenstown Gardens are edged by a waterfront walkway through natural forest, a gentle hill sloping up to my left and the lake a few meters away on my right. It was very peaceful, enough people for company but not too many so it seemed I had to share. I heard a familiar sound, of chain being rattled softly by plastic, so I walked up the hill a bit and found a Frisbee golf course. There were four people playing the game and I watched and followed their progress for a few holes. There is a good eighteen hole course meandering through the gardens and was being utilized by quite a few people while I was there.

I climbed to the top of the slope and entered the formalized area of the gardens. There was a white gazebo, the usual rectangular beds of blossoms, gloriously blooming orange marigolds with purple alyssum borders, red salvia with white alyssum borders and many other flowers inviting me to stop and take notice. There was a long pond with a stone bridge arcing across its middle. The pond, with its lily pads and water grasses was inhabited by mallard ducks; I could have been at any park at home.

No one was hurrying about in the park - its very nature says to slow down, live in the moment and enjoy the sight and smell of the flowers and trees. So I did.

My circular route completed, I was back at the south end of the beach. The beach is separated from the town by a row of mature, graceful willow trees that offer shade. Then there is a short concrete wall and a grassy area where young birch trees grow. It was between two of these trees about ten meters apart, that two young fellows had tied a nylon strap. They had a mechanism to tighten it making it somewhat taut, and so had an outdoor tightrope to practice feats of daring and balance. As there is still a lot of play in the strap and it dips under the weight of the performer it is called slacklining, a new version of tightrope walking. One of the men was dressed in long orange shorts, sunglasses and a Beatles haircut, his friend in beige shorts and a goatee. Both also wore varying expressions of doubt, concentration, disappointment and elation as they put on a show of sorts. Many people stopped to watch the two as they tried running mounts, walking, crouching and other stunts. Applause broke out now and then when a successful try was made. The men loved what they were doing and I noticed an improvement over the time I was there. I was talking to a couple I shared a bench with. One of the young men looked over and asked if any of us would like to try. I graciously declined knowing my knee and my balance weren't that great and secretly afraid that the rope would stretch embarrassing low and perhaps even touch the ground if I dared to get on it. But the man I was talking to was gung ho and at age seventy-one did fairly well at balancing with a little help from his new friend. While he was on the rope, his wife told me that he had recently joined a circus gymnastics group back home! The act of setting up the tightrope on the beach brought strangers together to watch, admire and be entertained for awhile. I just love it when that happens!

Now I wandered to the north end of the beach where there is a dock for jet boats. Two hours previously I had bought a ticket for this, my first jet boat ride. I arrived in plenty of time as I thought it might take a few tries to find a life jacket that would fit me. No need to worry - they have a huge range of sizes to accommodate the diversity of bodies that come their way. As is customary with most attractions, pictures are taken of each group before going on the tour. Posing there by myself I felt a bit alone and wished that Jenna and Jason were with me. But that feeling didn't last for long. I recognized the foursome right away; it was the three ladies and one of their daughters that I had met at Franz Josef glacier two days earlier. We had walked and talked for about a half hour at the glacier so it we just picked up our conversation and traded stories of the last few days. We were seated near each other in the boat and I just morphed into their group. Tanner, our driver stood at the helm, ready to take off when we were all settled into our seats. He looked totally cool: spiked platinum blonde hair, designer sunglasses, tall, tanned and chiseled.

The trip began calmly enough when we departed and came to a stop a hundred meters off shore. There was a brief safety talk then Tanner introduced us to turns. With his left hand held up pointing to the sky, he made a circular motion with his index finger. "This is the signal that we are about to make a turn, a tight turn. You may want to be holding on." He revved the jet engines and we sped over the water a short distance before he made the turn signal. We made a sharp turn to the left turning one hundred eighty degrees, the bow dipped low and the stern rose. Then we bobbed up and backwards while the boat levelled. At the same time, many of us got wet to some degree, especially those of us sitting on the side like I was. We all cheered and raised our hands - "One more time". And we did! The water is very cold so some of us tried evasive manoeuvres in these turns to keep a bit drier. This worked a little bit, but it was still a damp trip. The water is so cold and with high speeds of up to eighty-five kilometres per hour we were all thankful for the ingenuity of the person who thought to heat the rails we clung to with our bare hands.

We roared over the still waters of Lake Wakatipu and in to the Kawarau River. The banks were lined with homes and a lot of willow trees and it looked like a lovely place to have a house. That is if you can live with the noise of jet boats now and again. We whooshed our way up the river, making turns and enjoying the scenery.

We turned left after a time and entered the Shotover River. Tanner stopped the boat and told us that this was a very shallow river in parts, especially now in the middle of summer. We would be travelling through some stretches that would have water only ten centimetres deep. That's just a little deeper than the length of your middle finger. The boat was designed to travel in such areas. We took off again clearing shallow sand and gravel bars, with a tiny scrape three times. Then there were the boulders. The river has some places where the bed has been carved through the rocks resulting in vertical cliffs as the river bank. Of course, Tanner took great delight in heading straight for the imposing rocks and swerving away at the last second. I for one was thankful that he did not sneeze at this critical time or it would have been quite a mess and I can't imagine the paper work that would be involved!

We didn't do any tight turns for fun here, as the river was just too shallow. The rugged scenery was very picture worthy and Tanner stopped the boat several times for us to get our cameras out and take some shots.

Soon we were half way in to our hour long, forty-three kilometre trip, so the boat was turned down river and the entire process reversed. We had three final power turns once we got back to the bay that is Queenstown Harbour then slowly rode in to the dock where we disembarked. Lifejackets were handed back and then we went downstairs to Underwater World viewing room. We looked directly out in to the lake which was three meters deep at this point. There is a feeding time when food is tossed in to the water from the dock above. This always brings large trout to the area so we had an aquarium-type view but it was into their natural world. The water in New Zealand is crystal clear and gave great visibility. In addition to the trout there were also diving ducks, which when seen on the beach or on the water were brown, but streaked to a bright silver color when they dove for food. They would dive deep to get their food, turn, pop back to the surface for air then repeat the process. It was very cool.

This viewing room was also the room in which we looked at the pictures that had been taken of us in the boat. I bought a fabulous picture package! It includes: three five by eights of me on the dock, a close up of group in the boat at rest, a close up at full throttle, five post cards of those shots and a DVD of the trip we had taken. All set in a high gloss professional coil binder – first class as far as I've ever seen.

GORE

All of a sudden my brief stay in Queenstown was over and it was time for the drive south to Gore about two hours away. I made one stop in the mountains where there was another company offering jet boat rides on the Shotover River. I stopped and watched the boats coming and going and could totally relate to the excitement and happiness on the faces of the riders.

After a short time the mountains fell away and the countryside opened up to reveal thousands of acres of pastures where I got my first good pictures of herds of sheep. Sheep are a skittish animal and are as united in their movements as a school of fish. As I slowed the car and pulled well off to the side they instantly went on alert. They held their ground when I got out of the car and as I slowly took my first steps in their direction. Then as a unit they raced away a few meters, stopped and looked back at me in unison sizing up the threat I might pose. I took a few pictures with my telephoto feature, and then moved a few steps closer. That met with the same reaction – race away, stop, and size me up. I did this two more times and realized I was not going to get any tight close ups. For a time I watched them as they watched me, then I turned back to the car and continued to Gore.

Gore is a town of about twelve thousand people. It is a service town for the surrounding area's residents. Gores claim to fame is as the World Capital of Brown Trout Fishing; as such it has a fabulous welcoming sculpture of a leaping fish. He stands almost eight meters above ground level, jumping out of a foundation of large grey boulders. His body arcs to the right, painted in pale tans and greens with hundreds of black dots covering most of his body. The sunlight shone through his tail and fins that were perfectly crafted and folded in a manner that made him look every bit as real as a wall mounted trophy in a mountain lodge. Welcome to Gore.

I was surfing with Kate that night and she was still at work so I oriented myself with a drive around Gore and parked the car at the centrally located park. I quite enjoyed the park with its colourful flower beds, impressive big trees, aviary, tennis courts and lawn bowling facility.

I arrived at Kate's at almost the same time as she did. I had found Kate's couch surfing profile and contacted her in late December. John and Robyn are a couch surfing couple who live near Kate. I had initially contacted both of them and knew I'd be well taken care of at either home. It turns out that they are good friends and they had talked about hosting me. Being high school teachers of similar age and interests it was decided that I would stay with Kate while in the area.

Kate's Current Mission: *"Enjoy family - Grand children Friends old and new"*

"Just starting and would like to offer a place for people to stay and enjoy in a small town. I love to show people around my town and letting them experience the way that life is in Southern New Zealand. I like to hear about their lives as well and would like to continue travelling, hosting and learning. I live by a great trout fishing river (the Mataura). I have family nearby and enjoy meeting people, travel and socialising as this is a small town with great community facilities. I like to host people who just want to chill out and see heartland New Zealand. When it all boils down there seems to be a commonality amongst the desires of so many people world-wide and I feel fortunate to have had the opportunities that I have had to share the lives and experiences of so many great people."

As soon as her car pulled into the driveway I stepped out of mine and walked over to hers. I liked her the moment I saw her, wearing a gen-uine Kiwi smile and looking happy and relaxed. We exchanged greet-ings and introductions then went into her home. Kate lives in a spacious home overlooking the Mataura River. Her family is grown and gone but visit frequently. She has two or three bedrooms that she keeps made up for family, friends and couch surfers. Like me, Kate is easy-going. We slipped into conversations about travelling, families and school realizing that we have shared a lot of common experiences. Teaching high school has the same pros and cons whether it be in Canada or New Zealand: kids are kids, governments are governments, underfunding, large class sizes, cell phone use, fantastic students, coaching teams – all basically the same. Kate has two sociable cats who liked to climb in my lap and soak up the attention I offered. It was nice to spoil them. Kate cooked up a dinner of lamb chops and veggies which we enjoyed together. Later that evening she had two other surfers show up, young German girls who would stay two nights. We all shared tales of family and friends and of course travel before heading off to bed.

The next day was overcast. Kate went off to school. The girls headed out on a full days trip on a scenic loop to the Catlins, a protected area of natural beauty.

I had a day of rest and recuperation. Travelling is a lot of fun, but it is tiring as well. It was so nice to sleep in. Mid-morning I visited Kate's school and had a tour. It is a small school of about three hundred students as compared to my last school of twelve hundred. It was very nicely laid out and very quiet overall. I could tell by the interactions that Kate had with staff and students that she is a popular and caring teacher. She just has that magic 'it' quality. I got to meet Robyn when she walked into the staff room and joined Kate and me at a table. We had about twenty minutes to chat before she had to return to her work. We got along well and I know that I would have had a good time staying with her and John.

I left school after an hour's visit and did some grocery shopping. Having Kate's house to myself for the afternoon was peaceful and relaxing. It was easy to get a laundry done. I made my fail-safe chicken casserole for dinner which Kate and I enjoyed when she got home from school. We put aside two plates for the girls who ate when they arrived home from their day trip. They were very appreciative and I was so happy to have helped them in this small way. But the biggest treat for them was a loaf of bread! To no avail they had asked a number of people where they could buy 'real' bread - heavy, whole grain bread like they were used to back home in Germany. When I was grocery shopping I managed to find two loaves of 'real' bread. They were tucked on the far left end of the bread section, on the bottom shelf – like lonely little outcasts keeping one another company. Bread in New Zealand is generally white and light and the word 'toast' is often on the packaging. The girls squealed with delight and did a little happy dance when I gave them the bread. From small acts of kindness can come much happiness; pass it on.

The girls shared their computer with me so I could send home some emails then I left them to do the same and joined Kate in the living room. We watched the news (the fires in Australia still dominated the headlines) and weather (forecast of light rain for the next few days) and talked about family and travelling until it was time to turn in.

The girls left the next morning. Kate went off to school and I made a sandwich to take on my day trip. It was my turn to drive the scenic loop of the Catlins that the girls had done the previous day. It sounded beautiful and I was quite looking forward to a day alone with nature. From Gore, I would be able to drive on a circular route that would take me through farm land and out to the Catlins and the coast. There are many amazing places to visit and the ocean views are spectacular. Even in the rain. Today was just another of the two hundred or more rainy days that envelop the region each year. I was lucky in that it didn't rain very hard, more of a thorough misting that came off and on during the day.

The forecast was for rain with highs of twelve degrees Celsius. So it was typical of a February winter's day back home in Sidney, rain and all. It didn't start raining until fifteen kilometres out of Gore, and then it wasn't coming down too hard. I was going to go around the loop in a clockwise direction. I had driven about fifty kilometres when I came to the town of Balclutha and turned to the right, now officially on the Catlins loop.

Kate had told me a lot about the area. The Catlins is the isolated south-east corner of the south island that is brilliant in its ruggedness and natural beauty. They are the highlight of the Southern Scenic Route. This area is a combination of dense temperate forests, pastures, rocky coastlines, valleys and cliffs and I got to experience all of them on my outing. Because the land rises sharply from the South Pacific Ocean, there is an abundance of waterfalls in the area. A lot of the land was cleared in the 1800's when the forestry industry was at its busiest. These cleared areas became pastures to the thousands of sheep that followed. There are still a lot of native plants in rugged areas that weren't harvested or cleared by farmers. These plants have adapted to the salt laden air that sweeps in off the Pacific. The area is largely unpopulated with only about twelve hundred people in a handful of small towns and farms; I hardly noticed any signs of civilization, just a few homes on acreages so it was lovely and pristine. Owaka is the largest town with a population of just over four hundred people. Now it relies on fishing and the growing industry of eco-tourism. It is a paradise found.

My first stop was to walk in to see a waterfall. The walk in to Purakaunui Falls is a short bush walk through a dense temperate rain forest of mainly Podocarp and Beech forest. The foliage muffled the sounds of nature and provided some shelter from the rain. Even a wheelchair could have managed this path to the upper observation deck where I could see the water vanishing over the lip of the first drop. Then the hillside path became much steeper and the path meandered down a twenty meter drop to the lower viewing area. And there it was, perfectly framed by native trees and plants, the three-tiered falls, the most photographed falls in New Zealand. Now it was time to be thankful for the rains, as there was an abundance of water cascading over the highest rocky ledge, splashing off semi-submerged rocks, then falling off the wider second stair and finally off the widest of the three ledges to the pool below and passing by me in the stream. The falls formed curtains of water at each level with the symmetry of a pyramid. My pictures are like thousands of others I assume, as there is limited mobility at this site, but if you venture out on to the rocks off the deck, other angles are possible. The famous photographic falls are in many books, have graced countless calendars and have even appeared on a stamp.

My second stop was at Curio Bay, a unique and amazing place. I walked to the large viewing deck at the top of the cliff. From here I could see the beach stretching off to my left. I talked with a ranger who was on duty and he filled me in about the areas unique features – the petrified logs and the penguins. I walked down the long staircase and landed lightly on the sand. I headed out to my left and it wasn't long before I found petrified logs from a forest that stood here when all the land on Earth was one giant mass, Godwana. The fossils I saw are one hundred sixty million years old! Imagine walking on a rocky beach and having your eye caught by a ramrod straight formation that upon a closer look, appears to be a log that has been lying in the forest. Well, that is what I saw here, logs perfectly preserved, the grain of the wood apparent right down to the knotholes that indicate where branches had once grown. Back home there are hundreds of logs tossed up on the beaches, escapees that have broken free from log booms along the coast. These fallen trees had been covered by volcanic mud flows then silica gradually replaced the wood and morphed in to these incredible fossils which the sea later exposed. The fossils are not just on the flat expanse of the beach but can also be discovered in the cliffs. I have a great picture of one of these cliff side tree remnants that bears a striking resemblance to a wolf head. These fossils can be seen only when the tide is low enough. I hadn't checked any tide tables but happened upon the beach at a good time. (Travel Luck)

Having a keen eye (well, two keen eyes actually) trained on the cliff side, I noticed a pair of small, yellow-eyed penguins nestled at the base of the cliff. They had a cosy nest under some foliage and behind some rocks. These are two of the five to six thousand of this, the most endangered penguin species. There are informational signs at the top of the staircase that leads down to Curio Beach. One sign tells about the penguins, and the minimum distance that needs to be kept between them and people. There are several other graphic signs as you walk down the stairs and again at the bottom of the stairs to remind people of this distance. All the signs, but people still walked up the rocks to within a few meters of these nervous little birds. The penguins don't like to be blocked from their way to the safety of the water. Having grown up in a small Rocky Mountain town and having had a summer job as a naturalist at Lake Louise in the Rockies, I have a special affinity for nature. It bothered me to see the penguins being made so uncomfortable. I approached the interlopers and diplomatically mentioned that they should move further away from them. They apologized and said they had simply 'not seen the signs.' I noticed the park ranger doing the same thing when I finally left the beach and climbed up the stairs to my car. Don't even get me started on litterbugs!

Having been to Cape Reinga, the northernmost point on the northern island, I was happy to be visiting Slope Point, the southernmost point of the south island. Access to the headland is restricted from September through October for lambing season - once again I had arrived at the right time. From the car park, I could see a small solar powered lighthouse on the distant headland. Access is along a gently sloping path that follows a pastures' fence line - a twenty minute walk. Other people were braving the drizzle and wind, making their way to and from this special place. It was a little breezy at the car park so I donned my windbreaker before setting out. This was the only piece of cool weather wear that I had packed with me and I was glad to have it at this time. Also, for the first time on my trip, I had put on long pants instead of shorts and wore running shoes instead of sandals. I was happy that I had bought my son, Jason, the All Blacks rugby toque because I was able to borrow it for this walk. The drizzle stopped soon after I got out of the car so I thought this was a good sign.

Then there was the wind. By the time I had trekked half way to the point, the wind had more than doubled in strength. By the time I reached Slope Point it was blowing hard enough that small children were tethered like kites from outstretched parents' arms, and Mary Poppins was grounded due to dangerous gusts that may have flung her and her umbrella in to the ocean. Okay, that may be a bit of an exaggeration, but you get the point - it was very windy! I loved it! My windbreaker filled with air and fluttered noisily in tandem with my pants. My hair was tightly tucked under Jason's' toque and my face was blown taut into a 'wind-lift' and I looked, I'm sure, ten years younger – maybe a bit weird looking, but the wrinkles were gone! Breathing was easier too with the wind forcing all that fresh ocean air through my nostrils and filling my lungs. You get the point - it was very windy! As there had been at Cape Reinga, there was a sign that told me how far I was from the Equator and the South Pole. I had shifted over thirteen hundred kilometres south. I had the point to myself for about ten minutes before a young couple showed up. We took turns taking pictures of each other at the Slope Point sign before being blown apart. I stayed awhile longer, eyes closed, wind ripping all around me – I had such a strong feeling of connection with the Earth. As I walked back up the gentle sloping path to my car, I could feel the force of the wind lessen as I got further away from the ocean. Slope Point was the last stop I made on my visit to the Catlins. It is beautiful on an overcast and misty day. It must be mind-blowing on a full on sunny day!

Across the road from the parking area there is a brick red, wooden building that is protected from the wind by a line of trees. They had been planted in a straight line on the windward side of the building. They are unrelenting sentinels, standing steadfast against the wind, protecting the building and its occupants. Their solid trunks are bare and silver, their canopies non-existent on the windward side but blown sideways to the right, from the uppermost branches. They have been windswept from the vertical to an alarming degree and form a quarter circle of branches that protect the building like a hen's wings protect her chicks. You know by now that I love trees - I took eighteen pictures of this special line of defence.

I continued around the loop and soon the last kilometre of my trip arrived and closed my travel circle. I was back in Gore after a seven hour trip. It was raining fairly hard as I pulled in to the exhibition grounds where I would find Kate. Kate is the coach of her schools netball team and was at a sheep shearing and wool handling contest. The players and their parents were manning the concession stand as a fundraising project to help cover travel expenses to a tournament. I had seen sheep shearing only on TV so was quite excited to see the up close and personal version. I plunked myself down in a front row seat and started a new learning experience.

The process begins with the opening of the gate of the holding pen behind the sheep shearer. The front legs of the sheep are grabbed and the beast is up-ended onto its lower back and dragged a few feet out on to the stage, its head firmly grasped between the legs of the shearer, its belly exposed.

Now, fully secured, the sheep (victim) is subjected to a specific order of operations that is carried out with speed and precision. The process begins with short straight strokes down the belly pushing the wool off to one side. The sheep shearer (the perpetrator) uses the right hand for cutting while the left hand and legs control the sheep. The strokes become longer on the next pass and the wool is pushed off to the left in several strokes. Then the inside of the back legs are sheared working from the hoof to the rump. The sheep is rolled slightly and the outside of the back legs are next. Short strokes are used working up the rump towards the back. The sheep is now sitting on its rump, leaning against the shearer legs. The wool around the upper neck, head and around the ears is the next to be cut. The wool does not fall away, but is kept together as one piece – sort of like trying to strip an orange and having the peel in one piece. The sheep is laid on its back and the left flank is cleared using long strokes along the back from head to rump. The sheep is now rolled to expose the rest of the back and long strokes are taken up the back to the head. Then strokes slide from the head down to the shoulder. Now the task is almost complete and the clean white sheep emerges as the dirty wool gradually falls away from its host. The sheep is now turned exposing the final right side. Just a few well placed strokes down the side to the hip and the whole wool suit falls off as a unit. With a grab of the front legs the shearer turns the sheep on to all four legs and directs it away with a pat on the rump. Next!

Now it's your turn – imagine you are the sheep. Put yourself on the inside of a ten centimetre thick wool suit - a suit that covers everything but your face, hands and feet. The suit has five long zippers: one down your torso, the other four running the length of each of your arms and legs. The suit is Velcroed to your body. Another person has the job of getting the suit off you while you squirm around a bit. He sits you down on his feet and leans your back against his legs while clasping your head between his knees. He starts by unzipping the torso, then sliding one hand along under the suit to release the grip of the Velcro, first on one side, then the other. Now on to your right leg where he repeats the action. Moving to your head, he releases it around your upper neck, face and ears. Then the unzipping and release process is copied twice more for each of your arms. He turns you on one side and begins to separate the suit from your ribs and around the side to your back. One more roll to your other side where he releases your head from the suit and the suit hangs from only your back. A few more sliding motions of the hand, the last of the tiny Velcro hooks are released and the suit falls off. He grabs your arms, helps turn you over to a crawling position and with a pat on the butt and you're done.

I was very excited by it all and thought the men were working very quickly. I introduced myself to Tamara, the teenage girl sitting next to me and started asking questions. It turns out that this wasn't a sheep shearing contest at all but a wool handling contest. Who knew? I'm guessing everyone else in the whole region around Gore knew. Being so focused on the activity of shearing, I hadn't really paid that much attention to the people who were handling the wool right in front of me. It turns out that wool handling competitions are a growing concern and are very popular and exciting contests.

The judges table was on my left, so after saying thanks to Tamara, I went over and had a conversation with a few of them. It was from them that I learned about some of the proper procedures and rules.

Once the wool had been parted from the sheep, it had to be taken from the stage, hand processed and bundled into huge blue storage bags. The handlers stood at the edge of the stage and began to process the wool as soon as they could reach it. The fleece should be of similar length throughout, so some shorter or stray bits were pulled aside as the shearing happened. After the sheep had been shorn, the handlers gathered the wool in to a huge armful, turned, and took a few steps to a slatted table.

Approaching the table, the bundled fleece was tossed in an arching motion, expanded in the air as if one was tossing a quilt on a bed, and landed on the table. What was once on a compact sheep now spread over an area the size of a ping pong table. It looked like there should have been enough wool to keep several sheep cozy. There is a rule that governs the toss. 'Where 10-12 month fleeces are handled, the slatted table must be used, and the wool must land with the neck at the top end and the back legs at the bottom end of the table. The fleece must be even, flat and not hanging over the edges of the table.' www.shearingworld.

The handlers sped around the table pulling off shorter or loose pieces, or pieces that may have been clumped by dirt or doo-doo. The fleece was folded with precision like lumpy origami and bundled into huge, blue bags. A pivot-headed plastic broom was used to sweep up any stray bits and pieces, first from the stage and then from the floor around the handling table. There are penalty points if all the wool is not cleaned up. The odd and ends are placed in bins set aside for that purpose.

Just when I thought the nimble-fingered handlers would take a break, they quickly turned back to the stage where the shearer would be finishing the next sheep. The handlers sorted the wool from three sheep in this competition, judged on speed as well as the quality of the fleeces.

I watched several heats over the next hour and then the finals, won by a slender girl with the nimble fingers of a ragtime piano player. We cheered the victor and the efforts of all the contestants.

The contest had been everything I thought it would be and so much more. Kate and I headed back to her house, had a cup of tea, and then went out for dinner, my treat (or so I thought). Kate is a member of the Liquor Control Board for the region around Gore. One of the perks she receives is dinners at licensed restaurants, so we went to one of these. Kate knew most everyone who worked or came into the place. From teens to older folk, they greeted each other like long lost friends. We stopped at two groups to chat before we secured a table and had our dinner. After dinner, we stopped at another group of eight people and talked for another hour. Kate has such a sense of community and is loved and respected by everyone she knows.

My reference for Kate – "It was fabulous to be able to stay with Kate! We have many things in common including our careers, our sense of humour, our housekeeping styles, and love of animals and travel. I loved spoiling the cats as they allowed me to. I got to see Kate's school which was interesting too. Shearing and wool handling competition was on, so got to see that. Kate has a keen energy for her family, her school family and her community! It was truly a great time! Thanks again!"

Kate's reference for me; "I feel like I have known Joan for a long time and it has only been three days. It was great to have her to stay and to see her travelling around enjoying herself. She fitted in so well with my way of life and just made herself at home. You really did spoil those cats and I think that they miss you. I am sure we will meet up again."

I also got a reference from Robyn, the other couch surfing friend of Kate's who offered me a place to stay. "I met Joan through Kate (fellow CS'er and close friend). In the brief time I spent with Joan I found her to be very easy to talk to and could tell she would be very easy to host. Hope we can meet her again sometime somewhere."

BAGPIPES AND BOULDERS

I left the comfort of Kate's home and headed out to the east coast of the island. My goal was to drive up the coast to Timaru where I would spend the night.

'You don't know what you don't know', so my driving plan for downtown Dunedin was tossed out the window when I hit the first barricade across a major street. The center of Dunedin is bordered by Moray Place, an octagonal road that encompasses many of the sites I wanted to see. But, what I didn't know was that there was a Scottish band competition that day, and that the bands would be parading around the octagon. I found a parking place a few blocks away and walked to the octagon of activity. Unfortunately, it was raining lightly, but this didn't seem to dampen the enthusiasm of pipers and drummers. The band members ranged from young children to older adults, all putting on a show as each marched along playing for all they were worth. I really liked that I had stumbled across this competition as Dunedin is a town of Scottish heritage and I was wondering how this would present itself. What's more Scottish than skirling bagpipes and people in kilts? I joined the sidewalk crowds in their applause as first one, then another and yet another encircled the downtown core.

St. Paul's Cathedral dominates the skyline on one side of The Octagon. Built in grey stone, its massive staircase climbs up to the multi-arched main entrance then the building stretches tall to a group of three rose windows bracketed by two towering spires. A stone retaining wall is on the right side of the grounds, while a green wrought iron fence is on the left. The sidewalk has been created by the laying of thousands of bricks that are bordered with grass and foliage creating a welcoming visage.

The building that had the most interest for me was several blocks from The Octagon, the Dunedin train station. Imagine a long black basalt rock building with white limestone highlighting all the corners, windows and doors, a building so intricate and delightful, that it gave the nickname 'Gingerbread George', to architect, George Troup. Access to the covered walkway on the front of the building is through a series of arches topped with limestone. On the right end of the station rises a clock tower twice as high as the main building, topped with a copper cupola, that has turned green with oxidation. The roof is covered with red tiles. Anzac Square is at the front of the train station. The gardens are gorgeous with beds of flowers in blue, purple, reds, white, gold and yellow. There are grassy areas and a more formal box hedge design.

The floor in the entranceway and ticketing area is a complex arrangement of about seven hundred and fifty thousand Royal Doulton porcelain tiles that are laid out mosaic style in a variety of patterns. The center tiles form an area of repeating squares, seventy in all, sport NZR and a lone, eight-spoked train wheel. Around these is an intricate border in green, yellow, black and white. In the center is a design of four small corner circles with a much larger circle in the center in which a locomotive is pictured. It must have taken craftsmen a long time to design and then lay these thousands of small tiles.

I walked up the stairs to the gallery around this foyer. I was able to get some great pictures of the tiled floor from up there and appreciate the fine craftsmanship of the whole area. At one end of the gallery is a most magnificent stained glass window, comprised of three sections. The middle part has a beautiful train engine, full on front view, cow catcher coming right at you and steam billowing from its stack. It has been created using blues, greens, browns, purple and white surrounded by textured, clear glass. I smiled as I took several pictures and thought of my nephew, Christopher. He had recently got a job working as an animator for Thomas the Tank Engine and the stained glass reminded me of Thomas.

The only trains that use the station now, are sightseeing trains, going fifty kilometres north to Palmerston, eighty kilometres west to Middlemarch or west to Pukerangi through the Taieri Gorge.

Cadbury World was to be my last stop in Dunedin. OMG – I do love chocolate! Cadbury World calls itself 'Dunedin's tastiest tourist attraction'. I think that is probably true. I entered the factory foyer in the hopes of entering their store and experiencing the same delight as when my daughter, Jenna and I had visited M&M World in Florida. No such luck! As it turns out there is a guided tour offered which carries a fairly hefty price tag - one that proved to be a bit much for my limited budget. Unless you take the tour, you cannot get in to the store. I didn't want to spend the time or the money for the tour. Consequently, I had a short look around the displays at the front area then left. I know it was probably for the best, but I was disappointed in not having some absolutely fresh, delectable, chocolate to melt in my mouth and take me to that place that only chocolate can – sigh!

So now I slogged back to the car (in the rain and with no chocolate to comfort me) and headed out of Dunedin to the north. The next stop, a few kilometres away was at a Guinness Book of World Records holder. Baldwin Street is the steepest residential street in the world. I trudged up the street for about a third of its length, when my knee and the rain indicated that was probably about as far as I should go. From my vantage point, I could see that the steepest part of the street was the top third. The information sign at the bottom of the street indicates that for every 2.86 meters you walk horizontally, you climb one meter vertically – that's really steep! The street has concrete paving as asphalt paving tends to run downhill in hot weather and simply would not stay put. I watched a young fellow pass me and walk to the top, leaning forward as if encountering a strong headwind and on the return, leaning back just as much. His girl friend made it about two thirds of the way up then waited for him to come back down. With my pictures taken and safely back in the security of my car, I found my way back to the highway and headed north to Moeraki.

The pictures I had seen of the Moeraki Boulders looked like a semi-submerged model of a massive solar system sitting in the sand. As I love all things geological, they were a 'must-see' for me. I pulled in to the parking lot, got out of my car and was met by some people who were making their way back from the beach. There had been so much rain over the past few days that the creek that cuts across the beach south of the boulders was a raging torrent and fording it was only for intrepid souls who were willing to get very wet and perhaps lose their footing and take a fall. Fortunately there was an alternative. I drove a half kilometre north and pulled in to the Moeraki Boulders Restaurant which is on the other side of the creek. From the restaurant there is a gravel pathway down to the beach which provides safe and reliable access.

The boulders are a gathering of large, dark greeny grey-coloured spheres varying in size from a meter to almost three in diameter. I didn't count them, but I'd guesstimate there were about a hundred we could see at this time. The tide was about half way in (or out) and some of the semi-submerged stones had water and kelp sloshing around their bases. People had their pictures taken around and on top of the boulders. My favourite is of two people on two rocks. They are facing each other, each balancing on one foot and holding hands for support. Everyone was smiling.

The boulders, called septarian concretions, were formed millions of years ago on the seabed. Minerals cemented particles around an organic object, much like a pearl is formed in an oyster, and the boulders grew into spheres. Skeletal remains have been found in some concretions on the north island. The seabed rose over time carrying the boulders above sea level. When I walked along the shore, I looked to my left at the cliff. I could see that this was the place that the boulders originated. As the cliff is eroded by wind and water, more erosion-resistant rocks become exposed until finally, gravity pulls them from the cliff face and they tumble down to the beach. There were boulders in various stages of being 'born' from the cliff, some barely visible while others seemed as though they must succumb to gravity at any moment and come tumbling down upon me. The boulders are marked with cracks similar in pattern to the stitching of a soccer ball or the shell of a turtle. The cracks are the off-white and light yellow colours of calcite and quartz. There are many fragmented boulders which give a unique look into the structure of these curious wonders.

The Maori have a legend about the origin of the boulders. A canoe, the Araiteuru, was returning to the area after travelling north to get sweet potatoes and other supplies. Off the coast, it became waterlogged and sank, spilling her cargo. The boulders are the sweet potatoes, gourds and eel baskets from the sinking.

It was lunch time and I made my way back along the beach and up to the restaurant where I purchased a bowl of hot potato-leek soup and a sandwich. There were two couples sitting together, so I approached them and asked if I could join them.

"Yes, of course". One couple was from New Zealand on the north island, the other pair were friends visiting from England. None of them had been to see the boulders before and as I had, they had enjoyed their time on the beach. That is how it came to pass that I had a good conversation with 'Kiwis' and 'Poms', as New Zealanders call the British, over lunch that day.

I had loved my visit to these amazing rocks on the beach and sharing a table with strangers. Now it was time to head up to Timaru. An hour north of the boulders, I stopped to take a picture of a yellow warning sign – it was a silhouette of a little penguin with the words 'Penguin Crossing - Slow' scribed beneath it. One to add to my picture collection of 'Signs I don't see at home in Canada'.

The drive along the coast is very scenic with lots of opportunities to get off the road and get down to beaches but the rest of the drive was in a downpour so I stayed in the car and just drove. There were about ten spots on the road where the traffic was reduced to one lane. The water was up to the bottom of the car door. I saw one abandoned car in about two feet of water. They had driven too close to the side of the road and the car had stalled – flooded engine.

When I got to Timaru, the hostel recommended in my Lonely Planet book was full. There was a hostel next door but the manager recommended that I not stay there as it was a bit 'rough'. He said to try the motel across the street as I would be happier there. I took his advice and ended up in a lovely little one bedroom suite. It was so luxurious compared to staying in hostels - a living room with my own couch and TV, a little kitchen with no one else to share it, my own bathroom and a nice queen sized bed!

CHRISTCHURCH

It was a short drive to Christchurch so I took my time in the morning, had a sleep in of sorts and a leisurely breakfast. The part of the coastline I had already covered was fairly rugged with mountains coming down near the water. At Timaru the land opens up dramatically and there is a fifty kilometre wide plain that is sandwiched between the Southern Alps and the South Pacific Ocean. I was now immersed in the region of Canterbury, an area of thousands of farms and dairy cattle. The views across the plains to the snow-capped mountains are most definitely post card worthy! The weather had cleared and it was back to sunshine and twenty degrees, very nice indeed.

I would be couch surfing with John and Robyn who live twenty kilometres south of Christchurch. Their Current mission: *"available for surfers"*. They were inspired to join couch surfing by their daughters who had successfully surfed their way around Europe a year earlier. They had been members for ten months when I arrived.

I loved their interesting profile and when I read it, I already felt welcome. "John and Robyn are a married couple. John has been a Policeman for the past 30 odd years and is currently working at the International Airport at Christchurch. He is very sporty enjoying water polo, rugby, swimming and tramping. Enjoys meeting new people and seeing new places. Robyn is a trained nurse but is currently working for the police on contract. Working mostly in the evenings now enjoys her days in the garden and catching up with friends. Enjoys tramping, swimming, traveling and gardening. We are outgoing, fun loving and friendly people. Looking forwarding to meeting like minded of different cultures. "

We have similar personalities in that we are easy-going, non-judgemental people. We also share similar philosophies: *"To be positive and have fun. To help people. To care for people. To treat others as we would like to be treated."*

Robyn had given me excellent directions with the final instruction to look for a very bright yellow mailbox out front. Bingo – I saw it from quite a distance and knew I was almost there. I wasn't expected for another three hours, but since their house was on the way in to Christchurch I thought I'd stop by and drop off a note or perhaps say an early hello. I was met by the canine greeting committee, all five of them, three small, one medium and one large. John and Robyn were not home so I left a note telling them I was off to Christchurch and would be back around six.

Loving aerial views, I first made my way to the Christchurch Gondola. The building at the summit, four hundred and fifty meters above sea level, sits atop the rim of an extinct volcano and offers 360 degree views of the Southern Alps, The Canterbury Plains, Lake Ellesmere, Lyttleton Harbour, Christchurch and Pegasus Bay. There is a cafe, a gift shop and a restaurant at the summit. There is also an attraction called the Time Tunnel Ride Experience. This is a six minute ride that covers twelve million years of history from the volcanoes that formed the region, through the lives and hardships of Maori and European settlers to modern inhabitants of the area. There are models and audio visual displays that go along with a young person's narration. I found this to be a great way to learn a lot in a little time.

Outside there are various trail options. I followed one trail for about twenty minutes then decided that was enough going downhill for my knee and would be enough of a climb on the return. It was a nice bit of exercise and offered different vantage points and spectacular views.

Being a bit of an adventurer I decided to drive back to John and Robyn's along back roads. A few minutes from the base of the gondola is the Lyttelton Road Tunnel, the longest tunnel in New Zealand. Cut through 1.9 kilometres under the hill, it joins Christchurch with the seaport of Lyttelton. As my dad had done for us when we were kids, I honked the horn a few times to hear its echo, a smile on my face. It was the longest tunnel I had been in that I could remember.

When I came out the other end of the tunnel I was near Lyttleton. The harbour is very deep as it is on the edge of a volcanic crater and the drive offers spectacular coastal scenery along an often narrow and winding road. I pulled over when it was safe to do so for picture taking and just to get a chance to have a good look at everything. The road headed west and inland after twenty minutes. Many hilly areas were covered in knee deep grass that shone like golden wheat in the late afternoon sun. Sheep grazed contentedly amidst sudden outcroppings of volcanic rocks that looked like the magma had instantly solidified upon belching out on to the surface.

I got back to John and Robyn's house and once again was met by the dogs. Robyn and John came to the door and the note I had left for them slipped out of the door jam and floated to the ground. Quick introductions and then I read the note to them. It turns out that Robyn's mom lives in a house on the property and they were at her place when I had stopped by earlier. At the time they had wondered what the dogs had been barking about. They use the back door most of the time so didn't see my note. It all worked out fine and I was in time for dinner, a lovely barbeque of sausage, lamb chops, salad and veggies. It was very easy to talk to Robyn and John and we shared a lot of interesting conversations about school, work, children and the good things and the not so good things that life tosses our way.

John and Robyn live on a gorgeous twenty-five acre property and have a lawn big enough for simultaneous rugby, cricket and soccer matches! With four children and their many friends, the area has been highly utilised. Their children are grown and gone (most of the time) so the lawn is primarily the playing field for the family dogs. John keeps it manicured using a large, sit down lawn mower.

When I was visiting, there were five dogs. They have two large outside dogs and a smaller blonde Cockapoo of their own. Robyn's mom also has a dog, another Cockapoo, which often joins the pack for part of the day. A third Cockapoo was at the house while her owners were on vacation to bring the number of dogs to five. With the three small dogs (who happen to be mom, daughter and granddaughter) in the house, I always seemed to be able to have some 'lap time' which was great! I really missed my Fox Terrier, Emma while I was travelling and a couch surfer with pets was an added bonus. When the couple came to pick up the granddaughter, she was really hard to catch – she was having such a great time there with the other dogs and running around in the country side that she didn't want to go home. In addition to the dogs, they also have a very sociable Siamese cat by the name of Calico. She is a sweetie and loves her cuddles too.

After a restoring sleep and breakfast I drove north to Christchurch to see the city. Parking was plentiful and I managed to find a shady spot to leave the car for the day. I wandered down Worcester Street to Cathedral Square, the site of Christchurch Cathedral. The church is constructed in dark grey stones with off white blocks used for decorative edging and the framing of doors and windows. The grey and white blocks used at the corners of the church make it look as though giant zippers hold everything in place. The tower rises over sixty meters above the square and has a green upper section that goes nicely with a few burgundy window features and a burgundy front door. It is a striking building and the focal point of the plaza.

This seemed to me a place where tourists and locals gather. I joined the small crowds and watched the buskers juggling, doing magic shows and playing different instruments.

I watched several moves of a chess game being played with black and fire engine red pieces on a permanent game board three meters square. One player in jeans and a blue shirt, hand over mouth, contemplated his next move, while his elder opponent in grey slacks and cream-colored windbreaker looked on.

There is an interesting sculpture, the Metal Chalice, near one side of the plaza. It looks like an ice cream cone or a tornado, with the base being about two diameters across and the top, eighteen meters high, measuring eight and a half meters across. The design is of the leaves of several types of native trees. The leaves allow for increasing open space moving up the sculpture giving a view to its interior. The aluminum sculpture is silver on the outside and a bright blue on the inside. I don't know why blue was used – if it was my sculpture, I would have used shades of green as it is the natural color of the leaves depicted.

There is a tram that makes a loop around downtown Christchurch so I stayed on for the complete loop to get oriented. On my second time around, I first got off at the Christchurch Art Gallery. The building is a stunning mass of convex and concave glass walls with the light from each of the hundreds of panels casting off a unique hue and reflection. On seven poles in front of the gallery are sculptures of seven boats, 'Reasons For Voyaging'. Each boat is made of two pieces of metal tubing that resemble the narrow outline of a waka, a Maori canoe. Inside this frame are other pieces of metal crisscrossing the hollow space. They are made in elegant simplicity. The clean lines of the steel structures sail along high above the spectators and picture takers. They are as tall as a four story building.

Beyond the main doors the foyer gallery and the front of the stairs to the first floor are 'rain-bowed' with thousands of tiles and insets in the brightest of colors, a piece of contemporary art in itself.

As I climbed the stairs a black statue of a seal came in to view. He sat on a round white pedestal, was glossy black with brown eyes and balanced a four legged, white stool on his nose with a black, front bicycle wheel on top of the stool. Very talented if you ask me!

The gallery was a delight from traditional landscapes and portraits to vivid contemporary works. One of my favourite works was an interactive piece. Imagine a square, off-white piece of material that looks like a shaggy carpet hanging on the wall. It's half the size of a ping pong table, lush and inviting to be caressed. Now see a smaller square in the center, this one having fibres as long as your baby finger. The fun part is that you are invited to don a glove and swirl and twirl the 'rug' into your own pattern. While others stood back, I jumped right in and played with numerous patterns. Then I clutched a comb and a brush that were beside the 'rug' and continued in arcing patterns, large and small. When I had reworked it for a few minutes, I stood back, admired it and took a picture. My creation was to last only a minute as another 'artist' donned the glove and let her imagination run free.

Across from the gallery is the Arts Center which is described in my brochure as "a vibrant and exciting venue for a huge range of New Zealand made art and crafts, shopping, education and entertainment. There truly is something for everyone, with highlights including over forty specialty shops, fine art galleries, world-class theatre, art house cinemas, bars, restaurants and cafes, a bustling weekend art, craft and produce market and an array of festivals and special events throughout the year. Once the sites of the University of Canterbury, these distinctive Gothic Revival buildings are today a maze of fun, wonder and delight, and form part of our award-winning tourism attraction."

Having an interest in arts and crafts and a background in teaching woodwork, I love exploring places like this. The craftsmanship is of the highest quality and covers a diverse range such as fibre arts, stained glass, wood turning, wood, jade and bone carvings, jewellery and pottery. The Maori designs are fabulous and I loved comparing their style to that of the First Nations people of Canada.

Walking a few more blocks brought me to the Botanic Gardens, a place of refuge as all parks are. The Avon River winds its way in a large pinched U around the edge of the gardens. There is the opportunity to go punting on a relaxed ride or to take control and rent one of the many colourful plastic kayaks and paddle along the river. I watched a bunch of youngsters having a blast as they splashed each other and tried to steer kayaks away from and into each other.

The garden has areas of themed collections. I got on an open tram to take the tour and later walked to specific areas I wanted to spend more time in. The rose garden is magnificent with sweet smelling, flower-laden arbours arching over the paths with a box hedge border alongside. There are gardens of herbs, New Zealand plants, azalea and magnolias and a rock garden and a water garden. The trees are what started it all with an English Oak being planted in 1863 to commemorate a wedding. There are towering pines, and linden trees whose branches canopy walkways and lawns.

After a pleasant and refreshing time in the park, I re-boarded the tram and rode back to Cathedral Square where I spent a bit more time before walking back to the car and heading home. I made two stops on the way: the first at a hardware store to buy a toilet paper holder and the second at a grocery store to buy chicken breasts and a few other things for dinner.

Staying with people like John and Robyn make me appreciate just what a treasure couch surfing is. I always like to help out somehow when I'm a guest. Something as small as helping prepare a meal, setting or clearing the table, doing the dishes, sweeping the stairs is a way I like to give back to my hosts. Whenever I stayed for more than one night, as was the case here, I like to make a meal for my host family. I left Canada with a few sure fire recipes. Mushroom chicken casserole is a simple and tasty dish, doesn't require a lot of ingredients and is great over a bed of rice with accompanying veggies. John and Robyn were not home when I returned so I made my casserole, just as I had done at Kate's, and had it in the oven when they arrived. They appreciated my efforts and we enjoyed our dinner; I left the recipe with them. At home, I'm quite independent, and very capable around the house and yard. When I noticed the toilet paper holder needed replacing in the bathroom I was using, I stopped at a hardware store, bought a new one and quietly installed it. I got an email from

John a few days later, thanking me for doing it which brought a smile to my face – it still does. That's just a part of my character, random acts of kindness that may or may not be noticed.

We had another lovely evening together playing with the dogs and chatting until bed time. They are just excellent people and hosts! With hugs, and pictures taken the next morning I left my new friends in Christ-church. It's the people that make a country great!

This is the reference I left for John and Robyn: 'My stay with Robyn and John was an absolute gem! They are such a warm and caring couple and I immediately felt right at home. It was great to have the dogs and cat around too. Their hospitality, conversations, BBQ and meal skills (joint task force), home, pets, and family members shall always be remembered fondly. I hope I am able to host them back in Canada'.

Their reference: 'We enjoyed having Joan to stay very much. We had some very interesting conversations. A lot of sharing which we feel very privileged to be a part of. Thank you, Joan for your talents of fixing things also. All the best for your future, you will always be welcome back here.'

KAIKOURA AND BAD JELLY

Three weeks in to my time in New Zealand found me driving north from Christchurch to Kaikoura. The name Kaikoura comes from the words kai-food and koura-crayfish. The Canterbury plain narrows here; it is a visually stunning place with the ocean, beaches and rocky limestone cliffs on one side and the magnificent Seaward Kaikoura Range on the other. "Few places on earth possessed the magic of Kaikoura. It is a special place of powerful natural energy. Many who visit leave transformed. It is also meeting place. Tectonic plates collide. Towering peaks fall into the sea. Sea currents converge. Such rare combinations lure an abundance of sea life, the most famous being the sperm whale. It was a whale that led the Maori ancestor Paikea, to New Zealand many centuries ago. His descendents live in Kaikoura today. Fittingly, the whale continues to guide the people of Kaikoura and the visitors they host. It is both a talisman of prosperity and a symbol of passage between two worlds of experience." (with permission from the book – Kaikoura New Zealand, Whale Rider publishing)

As usual, my first stop was the *i* - center. As soon as I saw the brochure for swimming with New Zealand fur seals I was intrigued. I saw the potential for this being a highlight of my trip so made my way to the counter and booked a spot on a tour the next morning. The girl at the desk was most helpful in the transaction, but did have a warning for me that the trip might not go ahead as planned. It had been quite windy over the last few days which had stirred up sediments, making the visibility in the water very poor. The companies that take people out to swim with the seals hadn't been out for the past two days.

I got a few names of local hostels and a map of the area. While walking back to my car an interesting sight caught my eye. There in the parking lot, on a trailer towed by a truck, sat a large sphere, about three meters in diameter, made of twigs and foliage. Very interesting. The people attending the area looked very friendly and made eye contact as I walked over to them. "Would you like to make a video and send it back to your family and friends?" Well, I thought that was a great idea and I asked them what was going on and how things would work. It turns out that these people were shooting videos of tourists and offering to send the video and some still photos over the internet to friends and family. I signed a release saying that they were allowed to use any part of my video in an upcoming promotional video for New Zealand. I walked up a few stairs and into the trailer where the techies were waiting for me. They directed me to the back of the trailer and into the hollow core of the sphere. I was now encased in a large replica of a kiwi nest. What to say? What to say? Starting off with, "Hi everyone!" I launched into a summary of how beautiful New Zealand is and what a great time I was having seeing the sights and meeting and staying with so many wonderful people. Of course, I said how much better it would be if one of more of them were with me and that it missed them all, but I was having a blast. I talked for about a minute and a half and then left the security of the nest. I was pleased when I viewed my video, and very happy to know that everyone back home would receive this, along with ten pictures that had been downloaded from my camera. So now with a huge smile my face and 'thank yous' all around, I said goodbye to the crew and got back to my car. I found one of the hostels that had been recommended to me, Bad Jelly Hostel, and secured a bed for the night. I had a room to myself so I considered it very posh.

Now, I drove from the sheltered town site along the northern shore of the slender Kaikoura Peninsula. I had seen aerial photos of the peninsula in the *i* center and thought it looked like some wonderful golf course magnificently perched on limestone cliffs above beautiful seascapes. Parking the car at the end of the road, I continued on foot at sea level, around the headland and along the shore. Grass topped white limestone cliffs were on my right, while flat, rocky areas with the occasional white sandy beach were on my left. When I stopped to look seaward, I noticed fur seals lounging on the rocks a short distance out in the water. The existence of this seal colony in this nurturing habitat was no surprise to me. I shared the experience with other people in the area for the next hour. There were rock formations that looked like the Pancake Rocks that been laid on their side so that the rocks were rising from the water looking like so many abused toothbrush heads.

After a half hour or so I walked back past my car and headed up the beach in the other direction. I noticed a few people looking into the bush. My curiosity aroused, I joined them to see a fur seal sleeping on the grass. Like the others I kept a respectful distance and took my pictures then left him in peace. I was a little bit surprised that the next animal I saw was a Canada goose sitting on a grassy area not far from the seal! What the heck was this Canada goose doing all the way down in New Zealand? I knew how I had arrived, but what flight plan had this goose followed? I was saddened by the fact that this goose was alone as Canada geese mate for life. When geese fly overhead at home I always try to count them to make sure each one has a partner. I just like to see that they are doing all right; it just makes me feel better. Not that I can do anything for them if they don't have a mate. When I passed by again I was very happy and relieved to see that another goose had joined the first one.

It was getting dark when I arrived back at the hostel to find five other ladies to share the hostel with that night. Bad Jelly is a very small hostel set up in the basement of a home - I had one of the four bedrooms to myself. There was a nice kitchen, dining room table and small living room in which we gathered as we prepared our meals. We spent the evening sipping tea, journaling and exchanging travel stories.

As I left the hostel the next morning I was hopeful but not too optimistic about the seal swim, as it was still windy and the ocean unsettled. I checked in at the *i* - center and was told that there would be no tours that day, so I was issued a refund. The only good thing about it all is that I wouldn't have to get the help of someone else to squidge in and out of another wetsuit.

The peninsula had been so beautiful the day before, that, once again, I drove out and took a short walk along the beach before heading back and leaving Kaikoura. My destination for today wasn't far to drive to - Blenheim, just over one hundred fifty kilometres away. With the short distance to cover and the cancellation of the seal swim, I had a lot of time to make stops along the way.

SEALS, A BUDGIE AND A CAT

My favourite seaside stop was at a seal colony. What can I say? I just love watching them play. The older seals were lying on the rocks sunning themselves and drying to a beautiful, light, chocolate brown. The pups, twelve of them, on the other hand, were frolicking in a perfect tidal pool and had the wet color of dark cocoa. They would inch worm along the rocks then plunge in to the water and streak along to the other side of the pool, looking around to see where playmates were. Then in mid-motion, they'd stop while they took a time out to scratch behind an ear before continuing. I am so glad that I had my binoculars with me! Young animals love to play and socialize, and I love to watch them do it. As a child, my friends and I would often go to the outdoor swimming pool and do the same things that seal pups do. We played tag: walked along the edge of the pool, jumped and dove into the water and chased each other as we honed our swimming skills. I'm sure there were times that we had to scratch our ears too. It was fun to reminisce and compare my childhood game to the seals'.

At another stop I accidentally came within a meter of a seal that was concealed from me behind a large rock. He made a low grunt, but hardly even moved. I took a picture then quietly moved along.

Back on the road I noticed a small sign that said Ohau Waterfall, a waterfall that is not on the map, but is sign-posted. What a great way to stretch the legs and add to the number of pictures on a memory card! The walk started with a stroll along a well marked trail that led me first under the highway then up a small flight of wooden stairs. It was nice to be in the lush and hush of the forest, a sharp contrast to the openness and crashing of waves at the sea. Fifteen minutes of meandering through the vegetation brought me to the pool that the waterfall had made and to the only other people I encountered on the walk. There I met a young couple and we took turns taking each other's pictures before they left the pool. I sat on a large rock at the edge of the pool and watched and listened as the water left the ledge some ten meters above me and splashed down, sending a fine, cooling mist over me. Who needs air conditioning?

The afternoon passed in this fashion: slow driving with lots of little excursions. I arrived in Blenheim in the late afternoon where I couch surfed with Angie and Grahame and their three children, Matt 18, Christina 16 and Brie 11. Their current mission: *"to meet wonderful people and share different lives different cultures"*

When I read their profile, it was immediately apparent that Angie and Grahame are very passionate about everything in their lives: their family, camping, fishing, horses, travel, music, cooking and motor sports to name just a few pastimes. They are both busy working parents, "Ang works in distribution for our paper company. Grahame Earthmoving industry."

Having grown up in Blenheim they have an intimate knowledge of the area and are keen to pass along local knowledge. I'm sure they could have directed me in ways to keep active for weeks in the area and I wish that I had more time to share with them.

They had been couch surfers for three years when I stayed with them and have surfed while on holiday in the United States. They have hosted a good number of 'couchies' as they call their guests (don't you just love the name?) and enjoy both aspects of the system. They went out of their way to make me feel welcome.

Their philosophy is great in its simplicity: "We love our life and are very happy within- and we want to live to be 100+". They consume and market gogi juice to help them live to a ripe old age.

Angie and Grahame enjoy people who are "positive funny people, love to do things with one another, have a good sense of humour." I think of myself as meeting those criteria, so I knew we would get along just fine.

We share some common travel experiences and sense of wonder in the size of both the Kennedy Space Center and the Grand Canyon. They had also been entranced by the beauty of Bryce Canyon. I had been to Bryce Canyon when I was fifteen, but still vividly remember walking to the viewpoint and been blown away by the sight before me. The unique upright spires of orange rock marched along in easy going formations, along the canyon walls and down its middle. I just stood there and soon realized that I wasn't breathing, couldn't breathe – this sight had literally taken my breath away. I had never experienced that before and it wouldn't be until I was twenty-one and stood before Michelangelo's statue of David that it would happen again. It was nice to share this experience while talking with Angie.

The home is also shared with a beautiful grey Manx cat and a blue budgie that live in harmony. I felt honoured when the cat came to me for some pampering as Angie said he doesn't usually take to strangers that way. The budgie, Polly Polly, was just too cute! His prize possession is a small, round, metal bell that is attached to a short piece of fishing line. He plays with it endlessly while in his cage and takes it with him when he goes out of the cage. It becomes his soccer ball as he pushes it around with his beak, his instrument as he shakes it back and forth and his treasure when he plays hide and seek. Polly Polly and I amused each other as I would hide his bell in my hand and he would gently peck away at each finger until I made a tiny opening. Then he would work his head inside to my palm where he would find the bell and we'd start again. If I dared move away, he would chase me until I played again.

I got to spend the night in their twenty-five foot, six berth caravan which was parked next to the house. I used my sleeping bag to save Angie from some extra laundry and spent a comfortable night in the caravan. By the time I got up and showered, Grahame and the kids had left for work and school so Angie and I had breakfast together after she got back from a morning run. She shared her tasty home-made yogurt – very delicious! With a hug, we said goodbye and I headed north to catch the ferry at Picton.

Here is the reference I left for them. 'Thanks Angie and Grahame for hosting me for the night. You have a nice family, and it was nice to meet them over the brief time I had. I love your cat, he is very social. And that budgie is just too cute with his bell - such a strong attachment and so funny.'

Their reference; 'Joan is a lovely lady and we shared many interesting chats. She loved our pets. I think my cat took a liking to her, which he doesn't to people he doesn't know right away. As for Polly, he's so lovable. Thanks for coming to stay, we recommend her to others.'

TE PAPA

It only takes a half hour to drive to Picton from Blenheim so I spent several hours in a waterfront park in Picton wandering around, tidying the car and reading about the north island. Now familiar with the car exchange ritual in Picton, I felt perfectly at ease turning my car in and verifying that there would be a car for me on the Wellington end of the ferry trip. It went smoothly and I got on board without a hitch. I split my time between being on deck for the first, more scenic part of the trip and then moved inside for the next part of the ride where I did more reading about the north island.

On the Wellington side I breezed through the car rental procedure and was soon parked in downtown Wellington in the same parkade as two weeks previously. Now I walked to my destination for the evening - Te Papa, the Museum of New Zealand. "The Place of Treasures of This Land" is the broad translation of Te Papa Tongarewa. Located in Wellington, this renowned museum tells of New Zealand's history, art and natural environment. Over a million visitors pass through its exhibitions each year. Te Papa is free and open every day of the year. I had arrived back in Wellington on Thursday, at five in the afternoon. I was very happy to discover that the Museum stayed open until nine o'clock on Thursdays, closing at six on the other days of the week. (Travel Luck)

This asymmetrical museum 'had me at hello'. Six stories tall, Te Papa rises like a sculpture of assorted geometric shapes, each section different but united by their individuality and I absolutely love the architectural result. From the lazy W shaped turquoise canopy over the main entrance, the rounded façade of the building to the left, the massive gray wall of the building on the right, the suspended structure that resembles a large airplane wing flying at the buildings apex, to the large charcoal colored wall that runs into, through and out of Te Papa. The massive wall represents and parallels an actual fault line that runs nearby on Wellington's west side.

One of the greatest things about this museum is that it's free! Many exhibits are interactive and this is especially true in the Discovery Centers.

I have no inner child, but an active and curious outer child. I became as engaged in each of the four individual centers as the many children who were there. I seemed to be the only adult in attendance without a child. I have never seen such a large array of specimen drawers as in Te Papa; pulling on the cool, metal handle of one drawer revealed a treasure trove of insect specimens; the next drawer gave me the same, and the next and the next. From beetles, ants, and spiders to the muted colors of moths and the bright colors of butterflies - a true sense of wonder enveloped my senses as I realized that all of these creatures were from this small island nation. I wished my children were five and nine again and that they were there with me to share the excitement of discovery.

I observed a father and son as they stood before the Colossal Squid, the only preserved specimen of its kind in the world. They were both wide-eyed, standing in front of this display. The Colossal Squid is believed to be the largest squid species in the world and this one weighs in at more than five hundred kilograms and is ten meters long. It was caught by an accident of sorts in that it was consuming a hooked Antarctic tooth fish that was on a long line. Just clinging to life, the crew thought it would surely die if they released it. They managed to get the creature on board during an arduous two hour process and in to the onboard freezer using a cargo net. This squid was caught in 2007 and meticulously preserved for all to wonder at who pass by. Its limbs are covered with hooks and teeth which glom onto prey and manoeuvre it towards it large, black, razor sharp beak where the victim would have had no chance of escape. Its sea monster appearance is enhanced by the largest eyes in the world, larger than a dinner plate. The calamari rings it would offer up would be the size of tractor tires! Now, that's big! But how to deep fry them?

The museum has incredible permanent exhibitions covering such things as Maori culture, geology of New Zealand, history of the land and its peoples, and flora and fauna of both land and ocean. Like most museums, Te Papa has hundreds of thousands of items and has much more in storage than it can display at any one time. There are temporary exhibitions in some rooms where individual entry fees are levied to pay for the cost of bringing these to Te Papa.

Loving Earth science, I spent a long time on level two, where 'Awesome Forces' and 'Mountains to Sea' are displayed. Their multi-media presentations are fabulous. I entered a small house where soon, the floor began to shake and household items rattled and moved. This was accompanied by a video giving the sights and sounds of an earthquake. Being a teacher, I really appreciated this type of interactive education where the learner is actively engaged.

Te Papa is only a short distance from a major fault line so the museum was constructed with earthquakes in mind. The whole building sits on earthquake resistant supports that will slow down the effects of any quake. But, I think if a large enough quake occurs, New Zealand will lose a treasure trove.

The displays of rocks and minerals kept a smile on my face for quite some time. There were samples that shone in every imaginable color; the endless patterns had me enthralled. I hadn't seen rocks that glow in the dark before! Excellent videos of volcanoes and earthquakes rounded out the experience in this area.

Level four is all about Maori life and history. Te Papa has a large collection of Maori items: everything from a re-created life-sized house to clothing to small pieces of jewellery. We have similar displays of First Nations people artefacts in The Royal Victoria Museum back home, so I found myself comparing items. Both groups have rich and vibrant cultures and have created unique styles of art based on the same theme of being one with the land. It's impossible to put in to words, the visual and spiritual impact these artefacts had on me.

Another excellent collection was of non-native species, both plants and animals. Along with the specimens there were explanations as to how the introductions of these species have affected life in New Zealand. The King Fern is in decline now as a result of introduced animal species adding it to their diet. It is now rare to find this plant in the wild. This made me appreciate the opportunity that I had with Barb in Pukekura Park in New Plymouth where she took me to King Fern Gully. The introduction of rats, stoats, ferrets and cats caused the extinction of the Laughing Owl almost one hundred years ago. The little owl didn't have any defences against these predators who ate their prey, their eggs, owlets and adults. Their demise was sealed with the clearing of their habitat for farms.

At the entrance to Mountains to Sea, a large green parrot flies overhead with a bright blue banner trailing in his talons to show the way. This area is geared for kids, so I loved it. A winding boardwalk with bright green railings, took me gently uphill, wound around several cleverly crafted trees and in to the center of the largest. There were a few trees that could be used for hide and seek and it was fun to walk around them. It was a bit like being at the Swiss Family Robinson tree house.

The final stop was at 'The Map': a large satellite image map of New Zealand that is laid out on the floor in one room. The tiles all around the island are as blue as the ocean. The country looks so perfect, all green with beaches everywhere surrounded by the blue ocean. It is large; my recollection has it approximately four meters by ten meters. The map is made up of eighteen-inch squares and as I stepped on the first square it lit up so I could see the map with more detail. As I stepped on square after square, I finally tuned in to the fact that there were thirty monitors on the walls. As I stepped on a square, pictures and information would appear on the monitors for the appropriate section. Again, being an interactive display, I found it to be an engaging learning experience. Fun!

When I got outside I had a few minutes to walk around an outdoor area where I saw wetlands, native bushes and caves. I think that is a great addition to the museum!

The logo for Te Papa is a thumbprint. When I first saw it on the front of the museum, I didn't really 'get it'. But when I had finished my four hours in this very loveable building I knew that it was perfect. The collections in Te Papa are the fingerprint clues that led me to identify the characteristics of New Zealand, old and new. I learned so very much about New Zealand while there. I know my brain couldn't process all the things that my eyes had seen, but what I do remember with brain and camera tell me that it is a fabulous place.

Satisfied with my evening I collected my gear from the car and made my way to the now familiar hostel. Here I was, two weeks to the day that I had first checked in to Base X hostel in downtown Wellington. I had the same bed as before but this time shared the room with five young girls. (You do realize by now that to me 'young girls' refers to anyone under the age of thirty-five.)

TAUPO

The next morning I went down to the lobby area where the free break-fast was spread out on the counter. With the choice of fruit, cereals and toast I put together a good meal. I trundled off to the parkade, re-trieved the car and then set out north from Wellington to Taupo. It was a pleasant five hour drive along Highway One. Just south of Lake Taupo the highway is called the Desert Road. The harsh habitat is covered with plant life that was at once hardy and also soft with purple blooms. I trav-elled alongside the Tongariro River on my right and flat desert on my left. Across the desert rose the magnificent volcanic mountains in Tongariro National Park. The elevations of these peaks are two to three thousand meters so it was no surprise that half way through the summer, they still had a frosting of snow on them.

In Taupo my first stop was at the i center where I went through the vast array of pamphlets and selected the things I wanted to do in the area. I booked a ride on a boat for later in the day on Lake Taupo. The Base X Hostel was across the street, so I checked in there, the last of six females in a dorm, and found my room and bunk assignment - a top bunk. Not my favourite as the climb up and down was a bit of a struggle, but I didn't mind too much. I had a clean, comfortable place to stay.

Getting in my car, I headed north to the Aratiatia Rapids for the four o'clock 'show'. The Aratiatia Dam is a hydro dam, water being diverted through a tunnel to a small power station downstream. When I arrived and joined others on the nearby bridge the Waikato River was quite calm. Water flowed down over rocks from pool to pool, beautiful turquoise blue marking the deeper parts. The gorge was quite deep and parts of the river were hidden behind massive boulders. Three or four times each day, water is released into the river bed to show people what the river looked like before the dam's existence; four o'clock is one of the sched-uled release times. The double control gates opened and what was a calm, low-flowing river was quickly transformed. The river rose in the first pool then spilled to the next in line. Over the next few minutes, surging water buried rocks under froth and foam with the power of millions of gallons of water rushing through the gap. The whole river was now mostly white; one huge series of rapids that an experienced kayaker would love to play in. This process continues down river for a kilometre where the river widens and water runs more slowly. After a half hour, the gates closed and calm returned to the river. I was only one of about sixty thousand visitors who come here each year. I left the area as soon as the show was over and drove back in to Taupo and found a parking spot near the dock in preparation for my boat tour.

The gorgeous Lake Taupo fills a huge volcanic caldera on the north island. It is sixty-three kilometres long and thirty-three kilometres wide and as such is the largest fresh water lake in Australasia. The caldera is shaped like a jagged edged outline of Africa and the high mountains of Tongariro Park form striking backgrounds to the blue water vistas. I went down to the pier to take a two hour cruise on a replica steamship, the Ernest Kemp. I loved the boat as soon as I saw it! The hull was dark green with bright yellow lettering 'Ernest Kemp' popping off the background. The wheel house and enclosed deck area were white with beige highlights. There were a lot of benches under cover, but I chose to go out on deck at the bow. I nestled in to the perfect seat just below the wheelhouse, which I had to myself for most of the trip. We began our tour by travelling a short distance down the Waikato River and into Lake Taupo. I really liked the pockety pockety sound and rhythm of the steam boat, much more relaxing than the roar of most power boats. We travelled along the north shore where expensive homes, varied in architecture, grew from the hillsides and sat atop rocky outcrops. The common theme was lots of windows and expansive decks. They have spectacular views of the lake and mountains in the distance.

An hour in to the trip brought us to the Maori Rock carvings, the highlight of the trip. They are accessible only by boat. A master carver, Matahi, and several friends released figures from the rock face over four summers around 1980. They did not get paid for this undertaking, but did accept donations which helped pay for the scaffolding that was used. The main feature is a ten metre high face in the likeness of Ngatotoirangi, a famous Maori navigator who led tribes to the Taupo area over a thousand years ago. He stands watch with his large, clear, eyes over the lake, his face carved in a series of arcing lines that reminded me of waves, like tattoos on his face. I think he would have been very proud to know that his image is looked upon by thousands of people each year; people like me, who come and learn of the ways and stories of the Maori people. He is not alone, but accompanied by other, smaller sculptures: many faces, lizards, a mermaid and a Celtic design depicting the south wind. We sidled up mere meters away from the carvings and admired the detailed work, the precision of the lines and the grey granite that was riddled with flecks of black and white. Being there had a spiritual feel for me. It was a stunning cultural highlight.

In the wheelhouse, our captain turned the boat back the way we had come; we rounded the headland and crossed the lake to cruise along the waterfront of Taupo. On that leg, we learned that Lake Taupo is known for its trout fishing with seven hundred tons being taken each year. While you can't buy trout in Taupo, you can take your catch to a local restaurant and they will cook it for you. Our skipper also showed us where Hot Water Beach is. Water is heated by geothermal activity and there are places that you can dig a hole and have it fill with hot water – your own free hot tub! He also mentioned that it was recently discovered that lava still flows into the bottom of the lake. Quite a place! I loved being out on the crystal clear waters of Lake Taupo and I found it a bit sad that my tour had ended so soon.

Saturday was a bit of an overcast day. I departed Taupo just after nine and drove the five kilometres north to Huka Falls. The Waikato River has a bed of about two and a half football fields wide for the first part of its journey from Lake Taupo. Then it comes to a canyon where the same amount of water has to pass through an area only one eighth as wide. The Huka Falls is quite a display of huge amounts of plunging water, sometimes over 220,000 litres per second! In the Maori language huka means 'foam' – very aptly named. This results in a gorgeous cascade of multiple falls which culminates in a precipitous plunge over a twenty meter ledge to form a large green-blue pool in the river. It became one of my favourite waterfalls.

Twenty minutes from Huka Falls is Orakei Korako thermal area. The Lonely Planet guide states "it is arguably the best thermal area left in NZ. Although three quarters of it now lies beneath the dam waters of Lake Ohakuri, the remaining quarter is pretty amazing." I left the car and walked to the shop and restaurant. After purchasing my ticket and getting a map I joined a few others who were waiting on the dock a few meters below the restaurant. There were umbrellas for us to borrow so I took one from the barrel as it was raining lightly. The tour starts with a short boat ride across the lake to a dock near the base of the Emerald Terrace. The two and a half kilometre path is made almost entirely of boardwalk and many, many stairs. The owner transported all the wood across the lake in a boat then manually hauled the individual pieces, thousands of them, to their places and assembled them to form a safe walkway. Having recently rebuilt my fence and the stairs on my deck at home I could appreciate his Olympian feat of carpentry.

The Emerald Terrace is a silica terrace, but looks like a volcano has erupted over the area and is oozing multi-colour lava down its slopes. Some of the algae were hot dog mustard yellow. Other parts of the flow were green, black and off-white. Rainbow Lookout offered a great view of the terrace where hot water trickled its way over the terrace and down in to Lake Ohakuri. The area was misty in spots with steam rising from boiling water. On a positive note, because I had my umbrella with me, it stopped raining after just a few minutes so I had both hands free for picture taking.

The unbelievable variety of colourful algae at the Rainbow and Cascade Terrace was very impressive. More impressive was the knowledge that something is able to grow in the water here, which is about 60C. It seemed as though the more I was learning about geothermal areas, the less I knew. ('You don't know what you don't know.')

The next signed point of interest was 'Te Kapua' – The Cloud – so named by the Maori. The sign indicated it is The Golden Fleece. It really does look like a giant fleece that has been laid down on the spot in the middle of the park. It would have been a giant sheep as it is five meters high and some forty meters long. I have no idea how much wool that would have produced, but I think a kilt could have been spun for each and every Scotsman. Being from a colder climate, I liken it to a waterfall, frozen for the season and would name it January Niagara. But this is New Zealand.

The next lookout was over The Artist's Palette, a name that predicted a variety of colors. The information on the back of my map said "Activity varies so much, that at times, the springs discharge masses of hot water which cover the silica flat creating ideal conditions for algae growth. The myriad of browns, greens, yellow, oranges and pinks, pock marked by over 120 crystal clear blue pools, transform this awesome area into an unimaginable beauty aptly named The Artist's Palette." I found it to be very picture worthy.

The walkway now turned away from the geothermal marvels and for a time I walked alone in the bush through native plants. The sulphur smell receded and was replaced by that of damp, green foliage and earth. The next sign pointed to the hundred plus stairs that led down to Ruatapu Cave, a mystical place, "one of only two geothermally situated caves in the world" according to my guide map. It was well worth the multitude of stairs as I found myself alone beside a crystal clear pool of tropical blue warm water. I followed the directions on my guide map, immersed my left hand in the pool and made a wish. I can't tell you what that wish was or it won't come true. All I can tell you is that what I wished for seems to be happening. I believe. Do you? The bottom of the pool is covered with rocks and recedes back under the rock overhang that forms the cave roof. I found it to be a place of true solitude and quiet and I spent some time there, just being in the moment, not worrying about the upcoming climb or where I would travel to next. The world was just a gentle place. It was fabulous! Turning to go back up the stairs a perfect picture was formed with a rock arch; under the U shape grew a group of fern trees high above my location. Pictures taken, I pulled on the handrail with each stair to climb back up and then I was back on the boardwalk.

Next I saw mud pools which I watched and listened to for awhile before making the final turn and heading back towards the lake. I arrived safely at the dock and waited a few minutes while the boat was loaded with new visitors on the far side, then made its way over to drop them off and to pick me up. This is a very natural setting, not 'touristy' and wasn't too busy when I was there. I loved the relative isolation and the chance to be alone with nature. It started raining once I got back in the car. (Travel Luck)

My next stop was at Wai-o-Tapu Thermal Wonderland, an extensive geothermal area near Rotorua in the central region of the north island. When I got out of the car I could see columns of vapour rising from the area behind the visitor center. After purchasing my ticket and picking up a map of the area, I made my way to the entrance of the walking tracks and read the informational signs. 'This is an active volcanic area. Sandals are not recommended footwear. Stay on the track.' As I read the names of the twenty-five main attractions I realized the diverse nature of the park: Bridal Veil Falls, Devil's Ink Pots, Rainbow Crater, Artist's Palette, Devil's Bath, Champagne Pool. There were pots, craters, caves, cliffs, geysers and pools on the list. Again, I was so glad that I have a digital camera!

The map gave me all the information I needed to chart a course. There are three paths that vary in terrain. Imagine a snowman with a large lower section, a somewhat smaller torso and a yet a smaller, oddly shaped head. All three routes start at the base of the snowman. The easiest, red path covers a loop of one and a half kilometres and is accessible to all visitors. The next section, orange path, combines with the red path to form a two kilometre loop. This path has six sets of stairs at the far end and covers more varied terrain. The final loop, the yellow path includes all three parts of the 'snowman', covers a distance of three kilometres and has an additional ten sets of stairs. The stairs might be a set of only ten or as many as fifty, but even with a bad knee I wasn't going to leave the park without taking it all in. I knew I wasn't 'in Kansas anymore' when I crossed over a creek on the way in to the park. The water was boiling!

The next three hours were spent in a foreign landscape. I took my time as I utilized the viewing areas and benches to sit or stand quietly and let the sights, sounds and smells of the area soak in. Such a unique place to be! I crossed a boardwalk about as long as a football field that passed over a huge silica terrace, mainly off-white, that lay under a few centimetres of mineral rich water. I stopped at the turquoise blue Champagne Pool that is bordered by a shallow, two meter wide, orange ledge that then drops off in to the main pool. So the color scheme is white silica terrace, antimony orange ledge then turquoise blue pool. Quite striking! The pool is over sixty meters deep. The water in the pool bubbles from carbon dioxide adding to the champagne likeness.

The Primrose Terrace has been formed by mineral rich water that overflows from the Champagne Pool. It stretches as long as a football field and gently cascades down to a waterfall, stream and into a lake at the far end of the park. Looking at the details of this formation, it looks like an off white conglomeration of thousands of rice paddies all falling down the hill, one below another. The steps are tiny, averaging five or six millimetres tall in most places. This is a place where I stayed a long while, took pictures, and closely examined the minute details of tiny areas. Then I tried to imagine these terraces on a grand scale, say with steps as tall as several meters. It was mind blowing then, to realize what a massive and stunning wonder this would be. I liken it to Pamukale in Turkey – you should Google both of these places for pictures as they are just too amazing to adequately describe.

The Artist's Palette, is a large, flat area of mud and steam that lies between the Champagne Pool and the Primrose Terrace. It is a water-covered area of yellows, greens, oranges, and the turquoise blue of the occasional small, deep pool. It does indeed look like a palette, where in one small area, there can be found dollops of many different colors. The difference here is that the palette itself is the completed work, nature's art. The colors are carried to the surface by ground water that has been super-heated by magma. This hot water dissolves minerals underground. When the water rises then evaporates, the colourful minerals are left on the surface.

The Devil's Bath is a yellow pool of hot water that comes with the unique smell of sulphur. The Devil's ink pots are dark grey and black areas that get their color from crude oil and graphite. The Frying Pan Flats are at the most distant end of the park; the first viewing platform which is on the hillside above the flats gives an overview of the larger area. The most striking feature here is the Oyster Pool, a circular pool that is the color of a green-blue glacial lake. Walking down into then along the edge of the flats, I was able to see many places where boiling water came to the surface and stained the surrounding area with a variety of colors. In places where mud bubbled, I stood and listened to the bloop, blooping and watched the different muddy shapes that are popped up by this activity. Wai-o-Tapu is truly a wonderland, a great activity for everyone.

Even though it was a bit smelly, cool and wet, I'm so glad I went. Both areas were loaded with stairs, up and down and around then repeat, for about five and a half kilometres all together so I got a good work out. It was a great experience.

The drive to Rotorua was now only a half hour. I would be couch surfing with Lorraine who lives on an acreage just north of town. I wandered around Rotorua for a time, visited the i center, and did some grocery shopping. I had been in contact with Lorraine so knew when she would be home. I found her place and read my Lonely Planet guide book while waiting outside her gate.

Lorraine's Current Mission: "I just feel that it's a shame not to have our spare beds used by needy travellers....." As soon as I looked at her profile I knew we had at least one common interest – horses. The picture on her profile is of her, glass of wine in hand, standing beside her horse, Zak, both looking off in the same direction with smiles on their faces. I saw her car slowing as it approached the property, right turn signal blinking. Lorraine pulled in front of the gate and got out of her car. She greeted me with a warm smile, unlocked the gate to the property and drove her car through the gate and in my car I followed her to the house. I would have my own separate bedroom and bathroom which occupied a small building a short distance from the house; posh quarters after hostels. Lorraine was at home with the animals: horses, hens, sheep and cats, while her husband, John and son were tramping on the south island.

Lorraine has some very good guidelines on her profile about how to be a good guest in her home. Meals aren't included in the stay: they have hosted an average of ten surfers a month since becoming couch surfers, so that was easy to understand. Smokers aren't welcome and if you are allergic to cats, this is not a good place for you as the cats are indoor cats. Clean up after yourself. These are typical of the important bits of information that can be found on profiles so I was careful to re-read profiles just before my stay.

A few hours after my arrival, another surfer arrived, a young girl from Germany. I gave her the rest of the supper I had made earlier, a chicken noodle stir fry for which she was grateful. We talked about our families and our travels before turning in for the night. Lorraine is a kind a lovely host and it would have been nice to spend another night with her.

MURALS AND HOT WATER

Today would be an easy Sunday drive up the coast to the Coromandel Peninsula. There was not a lot of traffic on the road and after a pleasant hour's driving I stopped in the small town of Katikati. Katikati has been the recipient of New Zealand's "Most Beautiful Small Town" award several times. It was a town of special interest for me as it has a similar story to that of Chemainus, a small town on Vancouver Island about an hour and a half drive from where I live. Twenty years ago the forest industry was leaving town and Chemainus put on a fight for survival as jobs disappeared. Today, over 300,000 tourists per year come to Chemainus to view the giant murals that line the streets, decorate buildings and tell the story of Chemainus.

Much like Chemainus half a world away, the project in Katikati was begun in the 1990's to regenerate tourist interest in the area and town itself. The murals are similar to those of Chemainus in that they tell the story of the town, so have many similar themes: pioneer stories, special events, farm life, agriculture and industry. One of my favourites was a gathering of pukero birds. Pukeros became my favourite New Zealand bird, mostly I think, because of their bright blue plumage and colourful red beaks. Other murals included a cutaway view of a homestead house: grandma sitting on a chair, mom giving a baby a bath in a small tub on the kitchen table, a little girl playing with a bowl, her brother sitting at the table watching mom, a black and white cat washing itself, large brick fireplace, big black pot hanging over the fire with steam rising from it, hens walking on the porch, a visitor arriving at the front door. Kauri trees had been logged in the area and one mural showed three bullock teams hauling a massive log uphill through the forest. The mural with a man standing between two of his horses looks as though he had stopped and posed for the picture, taking a break from a day's work. There are other works of art in town other than murals. In my home town of Sidney we have half a dozen bronze sculptures of everyday towns' people sitting on benches. Now I have a picture of me sitting with a bronze fellow on a bench in Katikati. He's reading the paper while his dog sits impatiently at his feet, ball in his mouth – "C'mon, let's play catch." This is just what my Fox Terrier, Emma does back at home with me; she is always up for a game of catch. I also found a line of brightly colored 'story poles'. These were about three meters tall and stood in a long row of ten. They were created by the children of Katikati Primary school and are decorated to show many different cultural symbols. They reminded me of the totem poles of the First Nations people of British Columbia. After immersing myself in the outdoor art I visited a few stores. Soon I found myself chatting with a lady in a store who asked if I was camping. I told her I was couch surfing and staying in hostels on my trip. She owns a campground on the Coromandel Peninsula where I was travelling to that day. So no camping client for her, but she told me about a great beach front hostel in the tiny town of Whangapoua in the area I was heading to. I didn't have any particular place in mind to spend the night so I thanked her for the information and set out to my new destination.

The coastal drive to, then along the Coromandel Peninsula is one of wondrously beautiful coastal forests and sweeping beaches. On my left rose the hills of the Coromandel Range, jagged peaks - remnants of volcanic activity thousands of years ago. The hills are covered with native vegetation, much of which lies unspoiled in protected areas. There were a lot of pohutukawa trees which are an extremely hardy plant that live in the harsh conditions of salt spray and few nutrients. Unfortunately I had missed the crimson red blooms that envelop the trees in December through January but they were still nice trees and I saw them along many of the beaches.

My first stop in this most marvellous region was at Hot Water Beach. It was a beautiful sunny day with a temperature of 26C. Hot Water Beach is located along New Zealand's Pacific coast at the northeast tip of the Coromandel Peninsula and is known around the world. When I was little it seems as though every summer involved packing a brightly coloured plastic shovel and bucket to some beach at our summer cabin or on Vancouver Island or the Oregon Coast. Simple castles were a central theme, all having appropriate cold water moats. The moats at Hot Water Beach in New Zealand's Coromandel Peninsula often carry warm if not hot water. The reminders that New Zealand has an exciting geothermal past pop up all over this island nation. I had no tools with me but many people came to Hot Water Beach with various types of shovels, prepared to dig their personal spas in the sand. The rest of us dug with hands, feet, flip flops, sticks and whatever else we could fashion a tool from. Digging a hot water pool can only happen a few hours on either side of low tide and I arrived at an ideal time. (Travel Luck) You can excavate a personal pool which fills with water from a heated underground river from a volcanic reservoir that comes to the surface at this beautiful beach. This fresh water can be as hot as 65C and that's when a bucket can be very handy to get colder ocean water to put in your pool to cool it off. A very regal place to be sitting: relaxing in your own soaker tub on the beach, watching the waves crash endlessly into the white, sandy shore and a myriad of others seeking their own Nirvana by doing the same. Abandoned pools that dimple the beach are reclaimed by new guests or flattened by the surf only to be re-dug by the next influx of visitors. Everyone has a smile on their face, a sense of wonder – how can it be possible to squidge your feet down just a few inches into the sand and have to withdraw them seconds later because it is simply too hot to stand there? Even though we were from varying countries and backgrounds we were sharing a common human experience which brought us immediately close to one another. You might expect this natural wonder to come with a price tag, but that's just one more beautiful thing about it, it's free! Both locals and tourists to the tune of one hundred thirty thousand people come to Hot Water Beach annually.

COROMANDEL

It was a short drive from Hot Water Beach to Hahei which is home to a spectacular white sandy beach. There were not a lot of people around, but that was fine with me. I love to be in a natural setting with the place more or less to myself. After beach time I drove up the hill just a few minutes north of Hahei and was rewarded with a spectacular view back over Hahei and the beach, brilliant white in the sunshine. I pulled in to the car park which is high on the white hillside. This is the starting point to a walk to Cathedral Cove and blow holes. I had seen pictures of Cathedral Cove, a natural arch cut through the white headland, white sand beach at its base and turquoise blue waters off to the sea side. It was to me, a pot of gold at the end of the rainbow. I changed out of my sandals and in to my walking shoes and set out along the hillside path. The views were spectacular and many pictures were taken by me and the other hikers. About fifty meters along the way, the path began its descent, a descent that never let up as I continued with my knee asking, 'What are you doing to me?' All of the people who were on their way up looked tired, even the young ones. I went on for a half hour and sea level still seemed impossibly far below. I took a short side trail down to an ocean lookout and surveyed the situation. I was only about half way down and my knee was half way 'gone' so I made the decision to let go of this pot of gold and turned and started my way back up to my car. I was a bit disappointed in myself because I hate to quit anything - once I have the mindset that I'm going to do something it's hard to stop. But I knew it was the wise choice and when I got back to the car, I was glad I had turned back.

I now enjoyed a leisurely drive north towards my new destination, Whangapoua where I arrived a half hour later. I drove through the town and along the waterfront in search of my hostel, which took me all of five minutes because the town is very tiny with a population of about three hundred people. This is the town that the lady I had talked to in the store at Katikati had told me about. The only problem was that the hostel didn't seem to exist; at least I couldn't find it. I stopped and talked to a few locals and no one had ever heard of it. I noticed a large white tent nearby and the locals told me that there had been a wedding the day before – yes, I briefly thought that I could always camp out in the tent. I saw some other people walking off the beach who turned out to be tourists. They had seen a sign on the side of the road a little way back that said 'Place for Rent' so I found the house and knocked on the door. It turns out that this family had an apartment that they rented out by the month and it was already occupied. So there I was at the end of a road on the Coromandel Peninsula, with no place to stay. It was late in the day so I didn't want to head out of town. As I was slowly backing down the yard I was watching an approaching couple walking their dog who was not on a leash. Just then the lady of the house called out to me from the balcony, "Wait, we just thought of a friend who has started a place for tourists to stay at her house. She doesn't live far from here. My husband will show you where it is."

I was still backing down the yard at this time, keeping a close eye on the couple with the dog so as not to hit them. Okay, so perhaps I was paying a little too close attention to them, because I failed to notice the mailbox near the street and made crunching contact with it. The mailbox was none the worse for wear, but the plastic cover over my taillight had a golf ball sized hole in it. This small hole would add over $200 to my car rental bill - oh well, a small price to pay for not having hit people or the dog.

After surveying the damage, the husband led me to the home of Jo and Russ. They have two children, James age eight, and Emma age five. James and Emma were very happy to show me the small building on the lot that would be my home for the night. There was a set of bunk beds, a desk and a chair. Jo showed me the 'long drop' (outhouse) just around the corner from the building, that I could use if I wanted to for convenience – I chose to make the short walk to the main house in the middle of the night. I had a picnic supper with them and a family friend, out in the yard. We had a nice evening in the house playing with the kids and watching a bit of TV. Then under a blanket of southern stars, I walked to my 'dorm'. It was much better than sleeping in a large impersonal wedding tent or the car. (Travel Luck).

After a nice breakfast with the family in the morning I headed west out of town. Travelling across the Coromandel Peninsula is a windy and scenic drive. The land is at once forested then opens to pastures that have cows and sheep grazing. The grasses are as bright as the finest putting greens and then as dull as an un-watered fairway. (Did I tell you that I like to golf?) Cattle paths or land slumps cross hillsides like rice paddies in Japan. But the views as I approached the western coast were the most spectacular features on the drive. I was hundreds of meters above sea level. The road was a series of twists and turns that snake along the hillside and requires driving slowly with full attention so I pulled out at each opportunity and took pictures and just relaxed and enjoyed the view. I made myself take my time at these stops as it was easy to get distracted when driving - then I could tell myself that I had already seen the view and had pictures as well. When I got down to the ocean I turned right and drove up the coast to the tiny town of Colville. The sealed road ends just north of Colville, so I turned around at this point. With the ocean now on my right, I enjoyed the enchanting ocean views as I made my way to the base of the peninsula. The Coromandel Peninsula is an area of great beauty and peacefulness. I would love to return and spend a week there.

From the peninsula it was an hours' drive to Heather and Mike's place in Auckland. I stopped on the way, at a roadside fruit stand and bought a selection of treats including passion fruit which I had never tried before. The fruit seller sliced one open and shared it with me and I was hooked – so yummy! By three o'clock I was back in Auckland at my home away from home. We had another nice supper: lamb chops and sausage that Mike cooked on the barbeque, accompanied by a salad that I made and some veggies. We sat out on the patio in the back yard and ate and talked about my travels around New Zealand. I had been gone twenty-four days so I had a lot to share.

The next day was a day to sleep in, relax and reorganize as I had an early flight to Australia the next morning. Mike and Heather were at work so I had their house to myself until their return. We spent another nice evening together sipping wine in front of the TV before turning in for the night. There had been a bit of relief with the forest fires in the southeast corner of Australia and many fires were now under control; others still ravaged the countryside. It was interesting watching the weather news – it had been in the mid to high thirties in Cairns for most of the summer. After enjoying the cooler New Zealand temperatures in the mid twenties I was resolved that I was going to be wet in Cairns – either sweating from the high heat and humidity or from the frequent showers they had been experiencing. There had been so much rain that sections of major roads had been closed over several days. I hadn't realized that Cairns is in a tropical rainforest.

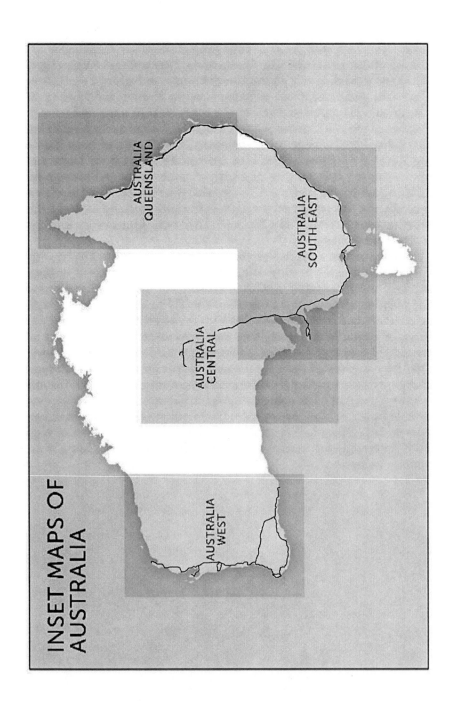

INSET MAPS OF
AUSTRALIA

AUSTRALIA
QUEENSLAND

AUSTRALIA
SOUTH EAST

AUSTRALIA
CENTRAL

AUSTRALIA
WEST

AUSTRALIA

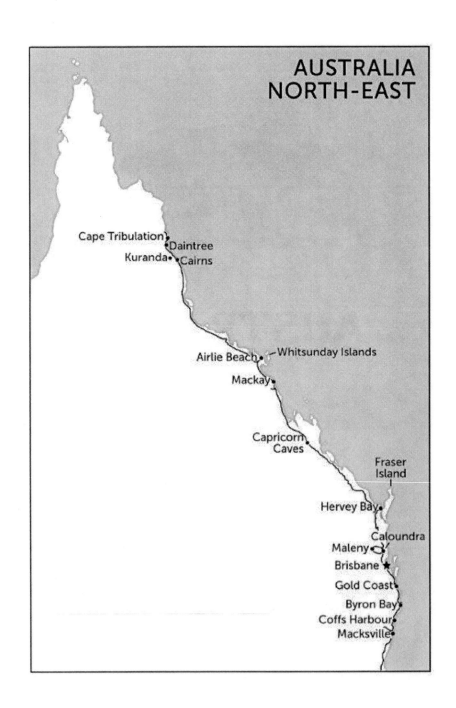

AUSTRALIA
NORTH-EAST

Cape Tribulation
Daintree
Kuranda • Cairns

Airlie Beach • Whitsunday Islands
Mackay

Capricorn
Caves

Fraser
Island

Hervey Bay
Caloundra
Maleny
Brisbane ★
Gold Coast
Byron Bay
Coffs Harbour
Macksville

FROM KIWIS TO KOALAS

We were up early on that Wednesday - six o'clock. One last breakfast on the front deck and it was soon time for me to go. It was sad to be leaving the comfort of Heather and Mikes', but I knew that I was going to fly to Australia and that was very exciting. As it is a bit complicated to drive from their home to the main road, Mike drove his car and I followed him out of North Shore. We parked on the side of the road and said goodbye with a hug - then I was off to the airport, over an hour away. It was relatively easy to follow the signs. I like to be sure of my directions so erring on the side of caution I got out of my car at a red light, walked to the airport shuttle van in front of me and asked if he was on his way to the airport. When he replied, yes, I asked him if it was okay to follow him – well, really, what choice did he have? So I felt at ease and didn't have to worry about missing a sign or a turnoff as I had my personal guide ahead of me. When I got to the car rental parking lot, I unloaded my gear, double checked the car and gave it a pat on the trunk before turning in the keys and heading into the terminal. I checked my baggage and passed through security. I was quite happy to be reading my new Lonely Planet guide about Australia over next two hours while waiting for my flight.

It turns out that there is a lot of water that separates New Zealand from Australia – four hours of it as a plane flies from Auckland to Cairns in Queensland which is in the north east (top right corner) of Australia. After retrieving my luggage and making it through customs I found the car rental desk and checked in. Guess what? "No, I can't find you anywhere in the system." So I decided to forgo getting a car at the airport and took a shuttle into town which dropped me off at the door of the Northern Greenhouse Hostel. This would be my base for the next five days. After I claimed a lower bunk in a female dorm for six I went to the front desk and met Joanna. She did an outstanding job of helping me plan my stay in Cairns. We knew that the weather should be good the next day so I booked a tour out to the Great Barrier Reef. Powerful cyclone Hamish was forming off the Queensland coast and we knew that the ocean would be very rough in two days time and there was a good chance that the tours would be cancelled for an indeterminate period. With winds of nearly two hundred forty kilometres per hour the storm intensified as it moved south along the east coast of Australia.

Joanna and I spent a half hour together as we filled in the skeleton of my plans for the next four days. I discovered that I didn't really need a car yet. Cairns is a nice town with all that I could have asked for and more. I walked around downtown for the afternoon and yes, I got wet. It was hot and muggy but I handled it all right as I had told myself I would most always be wet in Cairns.

Cairns has created a most beautiful oceanfront lagoon along the esplanade. Locals told me that Cairns used to have lovely sandy beaches but the dredging of a nearby channel caused the removed mud to wash over the beaches and bury them. With no nice beaches near the city something had to be done and the Cairns Esplanade Swimming Lagoon was made. It is both a family friendly place to relax and play and a work of art. Approaching from the town side I could see where the lagoon started but not where it ended. It blends with the horizon – an infinity pool where water and horizon come together in subtle hues of blue. The lagoon itself is huge and can easily host one thousand people at a time. I kicked off my sandals and waded into the experience. What really struck me as cool was the sandy beach that runs along one side of the lagoon. Little children were building sand castles while parents watched. Many people were just sitting or lying in the sun enjoying this pristine beach protected from the mudflats nearby. Opposite the beach were a few wooden docks where people sat and dangled their legs in the water and were just hanging out; there are also benches just under the surface of the water. The lagoon is deepest (one and a half meters) at the end nearest the ocean and was occupied by a few people swimming laps.

The sand is cleaned regularly and any foreign objects are removed. A filtration system scours the ocean water every few hours so it is always clean. I didn't see anyone leave any litter lying around anywhere. I liked that a lot!

There are several multi-level flat roofed areas that provide shelter from the sun or rain. Barbeques can be found in these areas and several families were cooking an early dinner when I first visited. It is just such a great community resource! It draws locals and tourists and there is no charge for enjoying the facility. At night, there are underwater lights as well as those above giving the whole area a totally different look than in the day.

I loved the four large art boulders at the shallow end of the pool. They had wrinkled backs and if they were an animal they would be Sharpei dogs. The largest and most magnificent art works at the Lagoon are the fish. Elevated on metal poles, the five stainless steel, larger than life Angel fish swim in the air and keep watch over the lagoons deep end. It's truly a wonderful recreation area and it drew me back for two more visits during my stay.

At the lagoon I asked someone where I could buy groceries and was directed to Cairns Central, the largest shopping center in town. There were two huge food stores – I shopped at each one on separate trips. I was putting drinks in my cart when around the corner of aisle six came a shopping cart with a good looking, blonde man riding on the front end of it and an equally cute teen aged boy pushing him. My daughter, Jenna, twenty-five, always loves to ride in the huge shopping carts and have her brother, Jason, twenty-nine, push her when we shop in the big box stores at home. I introduced myself to the twosome and explained our common ground then with their permission took a picture to show my children. Dad had pushed his son already, so now it was his turn to ride. It's great to see these two having fun and not worrying about what other people were thinking. I would be walking back to the hostel and carrying my groceries so I was very conscious of how heavy my purchases should be and shopped wisely. When I got back to the hostel I was very happy with my first day in Australia.

Northern Greenhouse Hostel is a great one! The previous year it had won the best backpacker award from Tourism Queensland with her sister hostel in Melbourne also having won a similar award. The rooms each have their own bathroom which is not the norm in the hostel world. There is a lovely outdoor pool that was frequently in use during my time there. Had I been less self conscious about my size, I would have gone swimming. There are poolside barbeques and lounging chairs to enjoy. Tropical trees grow around the pool and their branches invade the second floor deck here and there.

The deck that is under cover is huge and serves a variety of functions. The kitchen occupies a corner of the expansive deck that is furnished with a dozen or so long tables for eating and the same number of blue couches for relaxing on. The kitchen is fairly large and well equipped, but line-ups for the use of certain cooking items were the norm at busy times. A daily half hour of free computer time is included in the cost of staying here. All I had to do was to sign up for a time slot and I had a place at one of the three computers on the deck. Huge white canopies offered protection from the sun and rain; they were supported with an array of wooden poles and spread like circus tents over the whole deck. Large, ten-bladed ceiling fans spun overhead acting as air conditioning.

The evening passed with the preparing of dinner, sending off an email to family and friends, chatting with new friends and then going to bed at a reasonable hour.

THE REEF

This Thursday would be one of the most memorable days in my life! I was on the east coast of Australia and would travel out to and then snorkel at The Great Barrier Reef. I was at the dock at 7:30, ready for our 8:00 departure. I immediately liked the staff - they were very 'user friendly'- upbeat and full of life, had great people skills and were enthusiastic about their jobs. Each of us took off our footwear before boarding, which was placed in a large mesh bag and kept back on shore.

Passions of Paradise is a motor-sailing catamaran that makes daily trips out to the reef. The twenty-five meter boat easily accommodated our group of about thirty people. We gathered inside shortly after we left the dock and headed out to sea. There was ample seating inside with tables and benches for everyone where morning tea was served with fruit, pastries and beverages available. Rob and Dickie went over the day's itinerary and safety regulations. I became really excited when told that there was an opportunity to SCUBA dive – yes, even if you have never tried it before! Wow, I could hear myself back home, talking to people, "Well yes, I have tried SCUBA diving." "Where did I try it?" they would ask. "The Great Barrier Reef," I would casually reply. Oh, the name dropping that would happen!

But of course, I was just so ecstatic to be getting a chance to try it out. Jenna and I had gone snorkelling in Hawaii the previous year so I knew how good that would be. To add another dimension of being able to dive and swim at depth was just - well, it just made me really happy. I had no apprehension about trying it. Rob and Dickie seemed so caring and knowledgeable that I had a ton of confidence about the dive.

"You know, it doesn't even matter if you don't know how to swim" said Dickie. "I will hold your hand and drag you around in the water. All you have to do is stay calm and remember to breathe."

Those of us who were going to SCUBA dive for the first time stayed inside and Dickie gave us an introduction to the gear we would be using: air tank, regulator, inflation valve, mouth piece, mask, weight belt, ankle knife (no, just kidding on that one). There were new safety rules and hand signals to be learned as well. Apparently if you give a 'thumbs up' signal underwater, it does not mean 'I'm okey-dokey', but indicates that you need to surface. We all practiced giving the thumb and index finger 'OK' sign for 'okey-dokey'.

After our introduction I spent the next hour and a half on deck lying in one of the two nets at the bow, leaning against a railing and sitting on a seat elsewhere on deck. It took two hours for us to motor to our first destination. With a half hour to go until we got to the first dive site the first SCUBA group was called to get ready. I was in the second group, but went to the rear of the boat to watch and learn. We were at Michaelmas Cay, a pristine little white sand island that is an important bird sanctuary and home to as many as 20,000 seabirds.

It was only a few minutes after the first group entered the water that my group was called to the stern. The first thing we had to do was put on a Lycra stinger suit which protected us from the sun and from jelly fish. There is a tiny box jelly fish that inhabits the Great Barrier Reef that is the most venomous creature in the ocean. It leaves marks that can look like a lightning strike or an interweaving of tiny streams crisscrossing the afflicted flesh. The pain is excruciating, and people have died from the stings. Being translucent and blue it is virtually invisible in the water thus impossible to avoid. Getting into this full body suit was a much easier task than getting into the wetsuit back at Waitomo Caves. Now we were all one people – not separated by nationality, age or occupation – we were the People of Lycra – united in the safety of our black and blue suits.

Next, Rob helped each of us find a pair of fins and a mask. Then he sized up the first person, got a weight belt, and from behind, reached around her waist and buckled the belt in place. He repeated this procedure for each of us. I was watching and wondering just how many weights would be on my belt, and if he was going to be able to reach around my waist to buckle it in front - he managed to complete the task. Next we all moved to a long bench and sat down. Behind each of us was an air tank, which we now harnessed onto our bodies with Rob and Dickie coming to each of us and making sure everything had been properly clipped in place. They explained to us how the regulator worked and we all tried breathing from our air tanks. On the very likely chance that some water would leak in to our face masks we were told how to clear our masks under water. Rob told us that the more we smiled, the more water would leak into our mask because a smile caused wrinkling around the mask. He told us to smile inwardly or be ready to clear our masks frequently. We were also shown how to clear our noses if our sinuses became blocked. We practiced hand signals, one more time, and then it was time for us to move to the stern of the boat, walk down the staircase and put on our fins.

With one giant stride off the bottom stair I was submerged into a new world. I turned to my right and swam over to the yellow nylon rope that was strung between the catamaran's two hulls at the stern. The three other people in my group soon joined me and we hung onto the rope with both hands in front of us at the surface. The first thing Rob asked us to do was to simply put our heads in the water and breathe. Having passed this first step the next thing to do was to let go of this top rope and go down to the second rope, which was a meter below the first. The four of us descended and hung onto this lower rope with Rob directly in front of us. We practiced some hand signals, and then Rob had us clear our masks, and our noses. We were all good to go. We let go of the rope and swam away from the boat. Rob turned and waited for us to link arms with him and the person beside us with Rob in the middle. We swam in this way for a minute or so then he stopped us and we unlinked elbows. In sign language, he asked each of us if we were okay to swim on our own - we all said yes. So just as simple as that I found myself diving at the Great Barrier Reef!

The coral formations were very close to our anchorage so we didn't have far to swim until we were over them. The turquoise blue waters and the white sandy bottom provided spectacular backdrops for the colourful coral formations and wildlife. SCUBA diving is fantastic! It opens up a whole new world. Moving underwater in three dimensions is just amazing. It's flying under water and being able to swoop down to look in nooks and crannies, under coral ledges and to follow a fish highway. So very cool! My favourite encounter was feeding sea lettuce to a turtle that seemed to know the routine - Rob picked some lettuce then gave each of us a bit to feed the turtle. We were even allowed to touch him - he was quite happy in his routine of following us and having his food given to him. The half hour dive went quickly and before I knew it Rob was leading us back to the boat. I took my fins off, climbed up the stairs and sat down on the bench where Rob helped me get the gear off. Then the four of us just babbled away about the experience, huge smiles on our faces!

Next, a group of us got on the glass-bottomed boat and were taken to the cay. There is a short stretch of roped off beach that that people are allowed on, making easy access for swimming and snorkelling in the warm, shallow water. The rest of the island, the bird sanctuary, is out of bounds to humans and was populated by thousands of sea birds that were noisy and interesting to watch. After an hour we all made our way back to our boat, some swimming and others riding in the smaller boat on the return.

All of us were happy to hear that it was lunch time. The buffet offered a variety of cold cuts, veggies, fruit, buns, hot dishes and the biggest bowl of prawns I had ever seen. There was lots of food and I, like many others went back for seconds. Being outdoors and exercising sure does build an appetite! During this time, our captain, Popeye, piloted the boat to the outer reef which is where the hard coral gardens exist.

There is an established private mooring site called Paradise Reef. Due to an extra cost for a second dive I elected to try snorkelling at this new site. 'You usually don't regret the things you do, but regret the things you don't do.' I regret not spending the extra money to dive again! The water at the outer reef was a bit choppy and had significant ocean swells to deal with, which made swimming on the surface a bit difficult. I also had to blow water out of my snorkel quite a few times and empty water from my face mask.

It was still an incredibly beautiful experience with much more to see here than at our first stop. It was more colourful, and there were more fish! Thousands of kinds of sea life inhabit the Great Barrier Reef and it didn't matter that I didn't know the names, for they were jaw-droppingly beautiful! I saw every possible color I could imagine and some I have never imagined in the tropical marine life and corals. The reef is fantabulous! Just so many corals, wildlife and action! I saw sea cucumbers moving their way along the sandy ocean floor. I saw giant clams almost a meter across - a beautiful blue edge to them - and lots of smaller ones. Some schools of fish were like colourful snowstorms swirling in unison all over the place. The walls of the reef teemed with fish as they stay close to good hiding spots and to their prey. There were little orange and white clown fish (like Nemo) snuggling in the swaying arms of anemones. I even saw a tiny fish in the open mouth of a very large fish – he was cleaning the big fish's mouth and getting a meal in this symbiotic relationship. I just didn't know that happened! The little guy, just about two centimetres long, is a type of wrasse. I also saw a huge Maori wrasse that was about a meter in length. When I looked down the mini-canyons in the reef I was always delighted by all the sea life that was cruising around. It was just mind boggling. I was totally happy with all that I saw. The only thing I wanted to see but didn't, were sharks - there are sometimes smaller ones (about one meter long) in the area, but none today.

The corals were incredibly varied in color and composition. Everywhere I looked there was a myriad of colors and unfamiliar shapes to behold. There were huge plate corals that began from a central core, then rose and grew sideways to resemble, well, plates. But these were plates for giants; some that I saw were several meters across. The fan coral was a delicate inter-lacing of millions of tiny coral polyps, all growing independently but uniting to form some of the most spectacular features on the reef. Some coral looked as though hundreds of deer had crashed together and interlocked antlers. Others resembled the heather that grows in my garden. It is absolutely amazing that this reef has been formed over thousands of years from tiny coral polyps about the size of tapioca ball. The coral forms a skeleton of calcium carbonate which is left behind when the polyp dies. New polyps grow on top of these old skeletons and layers are built up. The Great Barrier Reef is the largest reef in the world and supports tens of thousands of species. It is over 2600 kilometres long, composed of a few thousand small reefs and about nine hundred islands.

After we were all safely out of the water and a head count had been taken three times, Popeye turned the catamaran to the west and we headed back to the coast of Australia. A kind of satisfied peacefulness took over as we enjoyed afternoon tea and lounged about on the return. Half way back to the coast the engine was turned off and the bright red spinnaker was raised - it filled with wind and carried us towards Cairns.

I talked to quite a few different people - we all looked similar in our blue stinger suits, but everyone had an interesting story that was unique to them.

As we departed the boat the entire crew lined up and personally thanked everyone for coming out to the reef. The last task was to find my sandals which were in a neat line along the edge of the dock. Wow – what a day!

CAIRNS

When flying into Cairns two days previously, I was somewhat surprised to see mountains covered with tropical jungles, marching right down to the water's edge. The chance to spend some time traveling through and over this jungle canopy was something I was really looking forward to. At my hostel, Joanna had recommended a day long trip to Kuranda, 'The Village in the Rainforest.' I purchased a ticket for the excursion which consisted of a shuttle bus to the Skyline terminus, (which is a gondola to the town of Kuranda), entry into the Wildlife Experience: Australian Butterfly World, Bird World and the Koala Garden and then the return trip on Kuranda Scenic Railway back to Cairns.

Showers dampened the streets on the morning of this trip so on the advice of Joanna I made my way to a nearby convenience store and purchased an inexpensive umbrella. The shuttle bus picked me up at my hostel in downtown Cairns and took me on the fifteen minute ride to the Skyline terminus at Caravonica. The Skyline treetop gondola ride is the most popular tourist attraction in Cairns. It was raining lightly when I entered my gondola which I had to myself. I was at the beginning of the world's longest gondola ride, totalling 7.4 kilometres in length. My trip would take approximately an hour and a half to the small tourist town of Kuranda. The Skyline has three sections and there are two stations at which passengers disembark and get onto the next section. As I ascended the mountain, the flat agricultural lands of Queensland quickly gave way to the vast green expanse of tropical rain forests beneath me. Even with the rainy weather I could make out Cairns in the distance and enjoy the landscapes of the rain forest and agricultural lands at the base of the mountains.

The first stop was Red Peak Station which is at the top of Red Peak Mountain. There is a lovely, short, boardwalk which is just less than two hundred meters in length. It is user friendly with little elevation change. I walked happily through the forest in the pouring rain under my umbrella. For those who had come unprepared for rain there were umbrellas at each station that could be borrowed while enjoying the walk. Some people didn't seem too happy about having the rain, but I thought it was absolutely perfect, because it is, after all, what makes this a rain forest and I was literally immersed in a tropical rainforest experience. The rain had washed the air clear of any imperfections and what was left was the smell of wet leaves and freshly cleansed dirt. A cacophony of raindrops pattered my umbrella as I walked along in the damp, reading the information about the forest on signs posted along the way. It took me about twenty minutes to meander back to the gondola station.

I boarded the second stage of my ride and found myself skimming just meters away from the emerald canopy of the many types of trees in the rainforest below. My gondola now descended slightly through the canopy to Barron Falls Station. The station has a fairly short walk, which takes you to the falls viewpoint where there were two other damp souls; we smiled and took turns taking each others' pictures with the falls in the background, keeping the cameras as dry as possible in the tropical downpour. On my return I spent a few minutes in the interesting Rain Forest Interpretive Center at the gondola station learning about the flora and fauna in the area.

Back on the gondola, I entered the third and final stage of my trip up to Kuranda. The magnificent tropical rainforest I was skimming over is a World Heritage protected site. As we descended the last few meters into Kuranda station the rain stopped and the sun actually came out (Travel Luck). The long gondola ride had been absolutely magnificent, but it would be nice to go back on a sunny day and see the view uninhibited by the clouds.

I had been told by several people that there are only two places in Australia where you are allowed to actually hold koala bears; one of them is in Kuranda. And so it was with the intention of having my picture taken with a koala that I went first to Koala Garden. The Garden is not physically large, but for me the emotional aspect was huge. It was very easy to find the place to have my picture taken and I was happy to see no one else in line. I walked up to the counter and told the two ladies,

"I just have to have my picture taken with a koala bear here in Australia". It was a few steps to the photo area where there was a painting of gum trees for the background. One of the ladies came around the corner with a very sleepy little female Koala bear.

"Now hold your left arm straight across your waist like this and make a seat for her. I'll place her bum on your left arm, and she will lean over your right shoulder. Then you take your right hand around her back and give her a very gentle hug. Just like holding a child."

"What's her name?"

"Anna".

She was sound asleep on my shoulder and I cuddled her as I had my children and began the natural maternal swaying of reassurance. Her gray hair was thick and short and much coarser than I had imagined - much like touching a thick crew cut. Touching her was way better than holding a stuffed toy because I could feel her breathing and the warmth of her body on mine.

One of the ladies took our photograph with her camera. She then took pictures of me embracing Anna using my own camera. I stood in that comfortable, warm position for about five minutes until a family came and entered the line. They too wanted their pictures taken with Anna. It was with reluctance that I turned Anna back over to the lady in charge and watched her give my Anna to be held by total strangers. The picture of me with Anna is my favourite one out of over four thousand that I have from my trip.

Anna's caretakers love their jobs. There are quite a few koalas at the Garden and each takes a turn having their photos taken with visitors. Anna is only expected to pose for photos for one half hour a day for three consecutive days. Then she is given a day off. Koala bears sleep, on average, twenty hours a day, while the other four hours are dedicated to eating eucalyptus leaves. Eucalyptus leaves have very little nutritional value so Koalas must eat a lot in order to maintain their low energy lifestyle.

While Koala Garden was small, close encounters with the animals are encouraged and it provided a great opportunity to interact with kangaroos and wallabies in a large open area. People are free to sit on the grass beside the animals, pet them, feed them and take pictures. It's almost like being on the lawn with the family dog back home. It's a very up close and personal experience.

There is also a walk-through reptile house where snakes and lizards roam freely in their mini-habitats. Other animals on display include wombats and a freshwater crocodiles.

Bird World houses over five hundred free flying birds from the endangered rainforests of the world. I entered the huge aviary that is the Rainforest Freedom Exhibit and joined others already interacting with birds on a large wooden deck. The first birds to catch my eye were brightly coloured Lorikeets. Although I've seen these birds before I'm still amazed every time I see their impossibly bright greens, blues, yellows, reds and oranges. There were blue and yellow Macaws, Cockatoos and many other birds who sported their own techni-colored dream coats. I just love to get up close and personal with birds and have the chance to examine the precision of their feathers and how they combine with one another to form distinctive areas of color and function.

I soon had a bright green parrot perched on my right shoulder. His claws gently grasped my shoulder as he sidestepped to my head and approached my ear. His feathers felt soft against my cheek. He leaned forward and his bright orange beak began pulling at what I thought were loose threads on my shirt. Well, I was right, but soon found that the threads he was cutting were holding my blue buttons to my blue shirt, and in quick time he had flown off with the first of his prizes. The other people watching were as amused as I and one person tried unsuccessfully to retrieve the button. This beautiful bird was soon back on my shoulder, vying for his second button, which I let him have. The buttons were a very small price to pay for this intimate encounter.

The birds have beautifully re-created habitats in this, their rain forest home. I left the deck and began my clockwise journey down and along the path that took me through native plants, past lakes, and beside waterfalls. The smell of wet greenery, water and dirt hung in the air. The sounds of birds were ever changing and enchanting. There was a great variety of birds roosting in trees and others wading in the small ponds at the bottom of the aviary. I watched the Cassowary birds for a time and found myself saddened at the prospect of their demise. Habitat destruction has left only about fifteen hundred Cassowaries in the wild. I spent a long time watching the Mandarin ducks with their beautiful and distinctive markings as they strutted about fluffing their feathers and elongating their necks to try to impress one another. All through this journey I stopped frequently to enjoy the beautiful birds in their home. There were few other people, so in many places I could just stand alone and be at peace with the birds and the rainforest. There is no evidence in my photos that they are in a man-made enclosure, but seem to be in their natural world.

My next stop in Kuranda was at the Australian Butterfly Sanctuary which is the largest butterfly enclosure in Australia. My tour group was made up of eight people: two children and six adults. As soon as I entered the aviary I was immersed in the warm, humid climate of Queensland's tropical rainforest. Our knowledgeable guide, Kate shared a lot of interesting information about the butterflies and the Butterfly Sanctuary: their Birdwing butterflies eat about five kilometres of a certain vine each year, around twenty-four thousand pupae are released in the aviary each year, the aviary opened in 1987 and has had over a million visitors at the time of my visit, all of the fifteen hundred or so butterflies found here belong to species from the local rainforest. This was truly amazing to me as I don't get to see many butterflies back home in Canada. Kate pointed to hundreds that I would not have noticed on my own. Butterflies are highly visible when in flight, but once they land and fold up their wings, they became well disguised to my untrained eyes. Their colors are just what I expected from a tropical rainforest - not that I had any previous experience – but I had seen pictures. From the fluorescent blue of the Ulysses, the yellow and green of the Cairns Birdwing, the oranges, reds and greens of other species, it was a flying rainbow of delicate winged insects which brought smiles to all of us. The butterflies are attracted to bright colors and our group was lucky to have four of us with brightly colored shirts who served as landing pads for our camera prey.

The paths in the aviary wound through tropical plants and flowers of the rain forest, along a stream and past waterfalls. We stopped at a feeding station and got a chance to take close ups of the many bright yellow and orange butterflies that were at the station. Before long, our half hour tour was over and I exited to the museum which has hundreds of butterflies from around the world on display.

Walking along the plant laden streets of Kuranda was very pleasant – it was now sunny in this small tourist town and shop windows invited me to look at the myriad of items available inside. After a late lunch I made my way to the Kuranda Railway station for the last part of my trip. I loved the station as it is a tourist attraction itself. It has a back drop of tropical trees whose branches dip and sway over parts of the station. Then there are the potted plants – hundreds of them. They hang from the station walls and from the edges of the roof. They march along the walls of the platform three or four deep, a meter or two tall, varying shades of green, variegated leaves, solid leaves, leaves with reddish veins. They give a cool and relaxed atmosphere for the hundreds of daily passengers.

This tourist railway winds its way through the Macalister Mountain Range from Kuranda which is at an altitude of three hundred twenty-eight meters, down to Cairns at sea level. The train cars are painted red on the bottom half with metallic grey tops. I took a seat in the third car back from the engine and settled in for the two hour ride. The views of the rainforest, waterfalls and ravines were spectacular all along the route; unless you happened to be in one of the fifteen hand carved tunnels, then 'not so much'. There were even places where I could look out and see the Coral Sea. With the never ending view and the comforting clickety-clack of wheels on steel, I found it to be a very interesting and relaxing mode of transportation. Each car is equipped with three monitors that provide a running commentary about the construction of the railway and about the features of the surrounding area. The mountainside is very steep making it a dangerous work site. There was no modern equipment used for the removal of thousands of tons of rock, soil and plants; it was all done by hand making it an incredible marvel of engineering as the track passes through tunnels, slices along mountainside cuts and is elevated along thirty-seven bridges. All this was done over a nine year period between 1882 and 1891 with many lives lost during its construction, the first happening when a man was standing on the wrong side of a log and it rolled over him.

Our first stop was at Barron Falls. I had been on the other side of the gorge when I took a walk at the second Skyline station that morning. Now I got a chance to see the falls from the other side. The rocky face is about three hundred meters wide and eighty meters tall, so covers quite a large area. The falls were spilling down only a small portion of this face, but were still very picture worthy. Much of the water is diverted for hydroelectricity production but in the rainy season or if a cyclone happens by, the volume can be huge. We had a fifteen minute stop here, and then it was time to re-board. One of our guides told a few of us that the last car was empty, so three of us high-tailed it in that direction and had the car to ourselves – weren't we feeling so special? (Travel Luck)

We continued in this glorious fashion, enjoying the view and experiencing the pitch black of the tunnels and an aerial sensation when going over the bridges, just a 'suspended in space' feel. There is a special place on the journey where the train crosses the face of Stony Creek Falls and routinely gets wet. The three of us in our private car moved to the right hand side of the car, stuck our heads out the window and were misted by the fresh water. How cool was that? Pretty cool!

Finally, the descent eased and we were on the flatter section of the trip. The train now travelled through large tracts of sugar cane which reminded me of my trip to Maui. Our second stop was at Freshwater Station where some passengers departed. There was more sugar cane to look at before we reached the outskirts of Cairns and crops gave way to buildings. Soon after, we pulled in to the Cairns train station – I had a whole new perspective of Queensland! What a great third day in Australia.

The rain began in earnest in the early evening, a result of the system that was cyclone Hamish. It was still lovely and warm; people were swimming in the hostel pool and socializing on the covered deck. I joined two ladies my age who were in Cairns for a long weekend. They had come up from the Gold Coast to visit a friend and to have a 'girl's weekend' – a little get away from their usual routines.

This Saturday, my fourth day in Australia was a day of rest. I found it important to take some down time and catch up on the required chores of buying groceries and doing a laundry. I was looking forward to taking time to walk around and talk to locals. My home town of Sidney is a sister city of Cairns and I had visited my town hall and now had with me a dozen Sidney pins to hand out. Joanne received the first one.

A few blocks from the hostel, I found a great open air market. Approaching this market, I noticed a man sitting on a bench who had a small white dog at his feet. Never one to pass up an opportunity to get a dog fix, I sat down beside Bill and introduced myself. We struck up a light conversation about travels and Cairns while I got a chance to hold his dog, Rex for awhile. Bill told me all about the market and which vendors had the freshest produce and which merchants at the back of the market had the best souvenirs. I gave Bill a Sidney pin, thanked him for the local insight and went off to shop.

I went to the back of the market first where I looked for a jewellery seller, Terry. I told him that Bill had told me to come to him for an honest deal and he smiled at the compliment. He had a good selection of things to choose from. The pearls were absolutely gorgeous, but out of my price range. I'm not really a fancy jewellery wearer so that didn't really bother me. What caught my eye was a string of button pearls; my necklace has thirty pearls – each one flat and slightly smaller than a dime – that shimmer with changing colors of green, copper and pink. It is one of my more interesting pieces of jewellery. Bill made an appearance after a few minutes and the three of us chatted for awhile before I gave a Sidney pin to Terry, turned and headed off to get my groceries.

I love shopping at markets and do so at home when I have the chance. The selection was great and the produce fresh. I made several purchases and handed out the rest of my pins to various vendors. They were all delighted to receive the pins and hear about a sister city half the world away. It was a wonderful interaction and I felt really good about it. Just one little idea back home of getting some Sidney pins to give to people in Cairns opened up a huge opportunity to talk to locals.

After I had taken my groceries back to the hostel I took time to send an email to my group back home to tell them about my first few Australian days. Then in a comfy blue couch on the deck, I snuggled in and read for awhile.

Later in the afternoon I was strolling along the street, back towards the lagoon, when I noticed a tan colored dog lying at the door of a pub. He was lying flat out on his stomach with rear legs straight back in 'frog fashion' so his entire stomach was in contact with the cool tiles of the sidewalk. His front paws were straight ahead resting on the door sill to the pub. Head raised and panting lightly, his attention was on his owner who was enjoying a cold one or two inside. I continued to the waterfront lagoon and esplanade where I spent an hour or so people watching. On my return, the dog was still patiently waiting at the door to the pub. I asked about the dog and was told that he is there quite a lot – another local with a story.

After making dinner for two nights and enjoying one, I crossed the street in the pouring rain and went to a movie – Last Chance Harvey. It's a light romantic comedy starring Dustin Hoffman and Emma Thompson - a movie that celebrates 'new beginnings at any age.' I felt a certain timely kinship with the theme as here I was, travelling far from home – who knows what new beginnings waited?

BILLY TEA AND
CAPE TRIBULATION

The Daintree Rainforest is part of The Wet Tropics, a World Heritage area designated for the unique flora and fauna found in the region. It is a living museum whose plants and animals can be traced back over millions of years of evolution. This was where my tour would take me on this, my first Sunday in Australia.

Waiting at the curb at 7:00, I saw the mini bus turn the corner, come down the street and stop in front of me. Bright orange letters spelled out the company`s name, Billy Tea Bush Tours. The vehicle was sturdy, ten feet tall, (it was a four stair climb up to the seating level) windowed like a bus, had a ladder to the roof rack, and was fronted with a substantial crash bar. The lowest half meter was clad in a heavy-duty metal skin. Our naturalist and driver, Robbie stepped out and came around to meet me. His blonde hair was tied back in a pony tail and he had large mutton chops on the sides of his handsome face – a flashback to the seventies. He wore a blue company polo shirt, khaki shorts and sturdy hiking boots. With a huge Aussie smile and 'g'day', Robbie checked off my name and I climbed aboard. I was the fifth person on board and being on my own was able to call 'shotgun', taking the front passenger seat beside Robbie.

It was nice sitting up front – almost like being on my own private tour as everyone else was behind me! Others got on board at various stops until we had twelve on the bus. With the last of his passengers accounted for, Robbie headed out of town onto the Captain Cook Highway. It is a most beautiful coastal drive, one of the prettiest in Australia, with the rainforest covered mountains on the left and the Coral Sea on the right.

Our first stop was at a small store to stretch our legs and purchase a drink. I wandered down a little side road as it was lined with most wonderful shade trees. I asked Robbie about them and they actually have an interesting story. They were planted over a hundred years ago to give shade to workers at the site. The only problem with the idea was that by the time they were of any size to offer shade, the workers were long gone from the area. Their branches now serve as a home to thousands of ferns that grow in the nooks and crannies offered by the rough bark. There was a large grassed area next to the trees that had playing fields as well as a canvas covered children's playground and a skateboard park.

Our next stop was beside the tidal Daintree River. George Dalrymple came upon the river in 1873 and wrote: "no river in North Australia possesses surroundings combining so much of distant mountain grandeur with local beauty and wealth of vegetation. The river valley is here surrounded by a panorama of great beauty . . . a perfect picture of rich tropical country. . ."

It is most definitely a stunningly beautiful area, and I`m glad that it is a protected sanctuary.

We had morning tea here beside the river – beverages and snacks. Next we boarded The Crocodile Express for a one hour informative trip down river. The canopy-covered boat was wide with rows of seats on each side and a meter wide path down the middle; set up like the interior of a bus; each seat could comfortably seat three adults. Others had joined us for this part of the trip so we had twenty-four people on the boat that could accommodate fifty people in a pinch. While we were on our trip, Robbie drove our vehicle down river and took the ferry across the Daintree.

Our captain and guide, Chas, was very knowledgeable and taught us about Saltwater Crocodiles, mangrove forests and other flora and fauna of the area. Daintree National Park offers a unique ecosystem with a large array of wildlife. This area is home to a whopping fifty-eight percent of Australia's butterflies, forty-eight percent of its birds and thirty percent of its marsupial species. There are over seventy animals and seven hundred plants that can be found nowhere else in the world. I didn't know that there are two types of kangaroos that live in trees! Of course they are much smaller than most other kangaroos, but I found it so interesting to learn that these kangaroos have abandoned life at ground level and eat and sleep in trees. They do come to ground on occasion to look for food or to move to another tree. (You don't know what you don't know)

The Daintree is what I imagined a tropical river to be: slow flowing with lush foliage growing right down and into the water. A huge variety of trees and shorter plants compete for prime real estate along the foreshore where there is more sunlight available to them. Grasses and shorter plants take hold where they can. The river bank was impenetrable except for an occasional small space that looked like a path had been made where animals come to drink. The air was humid and hung over us, the shade of the boat canopy kept us just out of reach of the suns rays. The silence of the river was punctuated only by the birds and the low drumming of our motor which was turned off a few times as we drifted with the current.

The Daintree was fairly high due to recent rains which meant there were very few beaches for crocodiles to sun themselves on. We saw only one crocodile - he was just over a meter long – and was sunning himself on a low lying log that was sticking out of the river. But, that's what happens in the wild - it is an uncontrolled setting so you see what is before you and enjoy what you are privileged to see.

Watching from the bow, I saw the ferry landing on the north shore slowly materialize and grow larger. There on the dock to greet us was Robbie. We were soon reunited with our bus and continued north, climbing now, up the Alexandra Range. We pulled off to the right into a lookout and disembarked. We were looking across lush tropical rainforest which stepped down the mountain to the estuary of the Daintree River. Fresh waters now mingled with the salty azure waters of the Coral Sea. It was a beautiful contrast of blue and green – nature's two most dominant colors. Off to our distant right we could see the sweeping curve of Cedar Bay that is fringed with more mountains. What a spectacular view!

It wasn't too long before we made our next stop; we were at a boardwalk which was slightly elevated where necessary and very easy to walk on. We were right in the 'thick of things' - literally. To observe the forest from a distance is one thing, to actually be immersed in it is another. It would be very difficult to have to slog along on this forest floor with no path. Robbie was very knowledgeable about the plants and animals that we experienced along the walk and he made it interesting to learn about them. He pointed out large spiders, lizards, ants and plants and gave us lots of time for photos. I have some good close-ups of insects I had never seen before, and that I would not have seen without Robbie pointing them out to me. Their camouflage is incredibly perfect!

We were all happy when we pulled up in front of the building at our next stop as it was lunch time. Robbie had a friend, Jess, join him now as steaks were thrown on the 'barbie' and Jess began cooking. While waiting for lunch we strolled about the property and hand fed and petted the resident kangaroos. There was even a small crocodile to watch; Sal had been injured and would not survive in the wild. She lives in a large grassy pen that has a good sized pool in it. After time with the animals we headed back to the main building where we had a tasty buffet of salads and veggies, some topped with large pink blooms from the forest. My steak was very tasty and a welcome change from the chicken I usually cooked in the hostels.

Now it was off along the four wheel drive track to Emmagen Creek, the furthest point on our tour. Where the road entered the creek we pulled off and parked on a bit of a wide spot on the side of the road. There were quite a few things to carry and the load was shared by all of us: stove, fuel canister, billy can, fruit, beverages and assorted items. A short walk through the bush alongside the creek brought us to a regularly used picnic spot. Here the creek slowed and widened and formed a large pool of crystal clear water. I took off my sandals and enjoyed wading in the shallows while others took the plunge and went in for a swim. We noticed several four-wheel drive vehicles drive through the creek a bit downstream from us to continue on this world famous tropical rainforest track. I`d love to go back and see where the road goes!

After time in the water we gathered around Robbie and Jess who had joined us for this part of the trip. They had boiled a large amount of water in the billy can and it was time to make bush tea. Loose tea leaves were placed in the hot water and let steep for awhile. Then Jess took the can by its handle, moved in to a clear space and began to swing it back and forth. The arc increased on each swing until finally Jess had the billy can doing full circles over his head. Round and round it went, until he was satisfied the tea leaves should all be clustered at the bottom of the can. He slowed things to a halt and then we shared bush tea. It tasted like regular tea to me, but of course the taste was not the point here, it was how the tea was made. I was, after all, on a Billy Tea Bush Tour. There were other beverages too: water, juice and wine to enjoy.

While all this had been going on, Robbie had been busy preparing tropical fruit that can be found in the Daintree area. I recognized pineapple, star fruit, a type of banana and papaya, but was totally lost as to a foul looking species. Just imagine the most warty of toads - a toad whose skin was made of large black bumps. Or think of your dog that has ingested tiny black rocks and then thrown them up in a mound on your floor. Yes, the outer peel looked anything but edible! I`m curious to think of who the heck was brave (stupid) enough to have tried it in the first place. Once sliced and offered by Robbie, most of us tried it. It had only a mild flavour and was not at all unpleasant. After our tea and tasting session was over we gathered up everything and returned to the bus.

We now rode back the way we had come and soon stopped at Cape Tribulation. The headland was named by James Cook after his ship, Endeavour, hit a reef in the area in 1770. Cook wrote: "I named... the north point Cape Tribulation because here began all our troubles."

We climbed down out of the bus and headed out on the trail to the beach. Thirty meters along the path I came to the first point of interest for me; warning signs and these were the subject of my first pictures here.

WARNING Achtung (also in two Asian languages)

Crocodiles inhabit this area- attacks may cause injury or death.

Keep away from the water`s edge and do not enter the water.

Take extreme care when launching and retrieving boats.

Do not clean fish or leave fish waste near the water`s edge.

Camp well away from the water.

This sign also had graphics of a crocodile and of a swimmer in a red circle with the diagonal line slashing through it – the universal 'no- no' sign. And that was just the first sign!

The second, two-part sign was about the dangers of the box jellyfish. The graphic sign (in warning yellow) had a man in the water with a tentacled creature wrapping around his legs. Yikes! 'Marine stingers are in these waters during the summer months'. There was also a large bottle of vinegar for pouring on any unlucky person who ran in to one of these dangerous animals. The vinegar stops the stinging cells from releasing more toxin and stops things from getting worse – but it doesn't lessen the pain.

So it was with quite a heightened sense of surroundings that I ventured out on to this beautiful beach. With the chance of crocodiles and stingers being in the water or lying on the sand, I left my sandals on and did no wading. I walked to the south end of the beach where the tropical rainforest meets the ocean and for the second time on my journey, was in a mangrove forest. It had been wonderful to paddle my kayak through the mangrove trees in New Zealand – this time I could walk amongst them. Being low tide, the intricate root systems were high and dry and the many roots looked as though they outnumbered higher branches three to one. A mom had her small son stand in amongst the trees and from my viewpoint it looked as though he had been caged in some huge time-out complex. I wondered just how deep the roots penetrated to be able to stay firmly planted with the relentless pounding of waves. These are a most amazing tree to be able to survive in this inhospitable habitat of erosion and high salinity.

Left by unseen worms as they burrow just beneath the sandy surface there were thousands of tiny, sandy orbs on the beach, that formed abstract patterns on the sand. My favourite pattern looked remarkably like a Maple Leaf – how Canadian of them – thank you very much for the welcome.

Soon, our time on the beach was over – no one lost or injured and we returned to the bus, drove back to where we had our lunch and dropped Jess off. It had been great to have him along for this part of the trip, but I was happy to be back in the front seat again.

'Who wants ice cream?"

Well, Robbie, who doesn't want ice cream? We had been back on the road for an hour when we pulled off to the right and parked at The Daintree Ice Cream Company. All the ice cream is made on site from produce that is grown in their own orchard – just the freshest of everything. They have a lot of flavours overall, but there were only four when we visited. The ice cream is made from those things that are in season, so flavours vary as the crops vary. For five dollars, I was given a cup with a scoop of each of the flavours of the day. I had never had passion fruit ice cream before – mmmmmm – it was sooooo good! I also loved the delicious cold swirls of wattle seed, coconut and mango.

Next stop was the ferry landing. The ferry runs on a cable so it was a very quiet ride; it is a small ferry, carrying only sixteen cars when full. There were only six other cars on our short, five minute trip. This is the only way to get your vehicle across the river and for years there has been some talk of building a bridge, but that would only increase the number of tourists and the unique ecosystem of the area might be threatened. So there is no plan for bridge over the Daintree River in the immediate future. We have a similar situation back home. I live on Vancouver Island on the west coast of Canada which is serviced by a ferry system. For decades there has been talk of building a bridge to the mainland, but we islanders feel that too many people would live here and spoil the island.

Before long we were once again passing through lush farm lands on the way back to Cairns. Robbie and I talked about our families - he has two young sons. Back at the hostel I had over a hundred small Canada flag pins and fifty paper flags on white sticks. I told him that I would leave four pins and flags at the front desk of the hostel so he could pick them up the next day. Next I asked him where the children go to school up on the other side of the Daintree River. There is a one room school house for grades one to six which has twenty-two students. I asked Robbie if he would like a set of pins and flags for the students too and he was delighted. I really like the idea of being able to do this for the tiny, isolated school. As a teacher I could imagine all the possibilities, the teachable moments that might arise, and just the surprise for the students of getting something unusual at school. 'What did you do at school today?' They would have a 'show and tell' to do at home.

An hour later, we passed through the suburbs of Cairns, now familiar territory. We dropped off the first of our passengers, and then it was my turn. With great thanks for an extraordinary day, I said goodbye to Robbie. This had been a most wondrous day of adventure and education. Nature – I love it!

The evening was a relaxing one. I had made two suppers the previous night and was so glad that I had the foresight to do that. After a long day, all I had to do was to re-heat my meal and enjoy it. This also made for a very minor clean up.

THE BRUCE AND
SQUEAKY SAND

Today would be a driving day to Airlie Beach which is just over seven hundred kilometres south of Cairns. I had reserved a car on line a few days earlier. It turns out that by going on line, I saved over thirty percent! Just how much do they pay the rental agents? I called the rental office first, then walked five blocks and retrieved my compact, red, Toyota Corolla. Then it was back to the hostel where I grabbed my things, loaded the car and said goodbye to Joanne. I gave her the Canadian pins and flags for Robbie to pick up. If the first five days in Australia were any indication of the rest of my trip, I knew I'd have an astounding time!

The Bruce Highway travelled inland for most of the trip that day, passing through pleasant looking countryside. I didn't make a lot of stops other than to get gas for the car, stretch my legs and eat the lunch I had prepared. I didn't realize it at the time, but it was an unusual day in that I didn't take a single picture!

I was going to Airlie Beach to tour the Whitsundays, a splendid group of seventy-four islands. Airlie Beach is the gateway to the Whitsundays and the Great Barrier Reef. Airlie Waterfront Backpackers was right across the street from the beach and swimming lagoon. The views are stupendous, looking out over the ocean to the islands on the horizon; I was really looking forward to heading out to them the next day. The hostel was clean, well maintained and offered dorms, private rooms with shared bathroom facilities, and en-suite doubles. I put my gear in my six bed dorm where I met four roommates. We decided to have supper together so went out the hostel door, turned right and walked fifty meters to a restaurant. We went inside and placed our orders, then found a table to share outside. So here I was sitting with new friends when only minutes before I was on my own. Two others were travelling alone; Carmen, age forty from the United States and Bridgette, seventeen from Germany. The other two girls were in their early twenties and travelling together.

Of course the main topic of conversation was travel: where are you from, what do you do, where have you been, where are you going, and how long are you staying? Carmen and I became instant moms to Bridgette after she told us of some times where she had been put in awkward situations but hadn't wanted to say anything. She had been put in a dorm with guys at one hostel and one of them tried to get in bed with her. She was able to push him away, but . . . . Carmen and I gave her some advice about her rights and expectations and gave her some options to consider if she ever found herself in certain situations. Our biggest piece of advice was to consider finding a friend on the way and travel with someone else. She just had so little life experience compared to us. We talked for hours and finished the evening with a walk along the beach before turning in.

Many people had told me that the Whitsundays are a must-see multi-island experience. Most of the islands are protected by National Park status, but there is some development evident. I selected a day tour that would take me out to three popular locations: Whitehaven Beach, Hook Island and Daydream Island. After a five minute drive, I arrived at the marina and found my boat for the day, Voyager, 'a comfortable, spacious, air conditioned twenty-three meter, high-speed catamaran.' Twenty-one of us would be together for the day plus the crew of four. At eight-thirty we slowly motored out of the marina to open water where the powerful engines were let loose. It was another gloriously warm and sunny day, perfect weather for an outing. The water is pristine and tropical blue. Islands dot the horizon. The islands are not low lying cays, but rise in small hills, rocky outcrops lining the shore. They are the remains of a coastal mountain range that was submerged after the last ice age. Then there are the beaches; every island has one or more sparkling white sand beaches. Any of them would make a great place to stop and spend some time, but we passed by as we were heading for the most spectacular one, Whitehaven Beach. We were pampered with a lovely morning tea of beverages, fruits and sweets while on this leg of the trip.

Whitsunday Island is the largest island in the area. Surrounded by crystal clear, tropical blue water, it is highlighted by the seven kilometre long Whitehaven Beach, "Queensland's Most Beautiful Beach." Our boat was put in reverse and backed gently in to shore where a ramp was lowered. One by one, we stepped barefoot off the ramp into the warm water and waded to the beach. The silica sand here is incredibly white - so white it reflects the heat and it remains cool to walk on. And it squeaks with each step taken. As soon as I heard the first squeak I was taken back to my childhood. Growing up in the Rocky Mountains I had experienced the same sound when walking, but under far different circumstances. When it is very cold the snow makes the same squeaking noise when walked on; the colder it is, the higher the pitch. So here I was many years later and half a world away in a tropical paradise being reminded of winter in Canada.

I waded north along the shore leaving most of our group behind. The simple colors were amazing: dark greens of lush vegetation on my left, brilliant white sand underfoot, bright blue sky above and turquoise blue water on my right. It was a total nature immersion for me and I found it a very peaceful experience. After an hour at the beach, we climbed back on board and headed north along the shoreline of Whitsunday Island.

Hook Island is just north of Whitsunday and was our second stop. There were two activities here: snorkelling and taking a trip on a glass bottomed boat so we were divided in to two groups. My group headed for the boat ride which took place right off the beach in front of Hook Island Resort. The tide was flowing in the area which stirred up bits and pieces of matter. The visibility was not very good, so the view was somewhat disappointing with only a few fish and some ordinary coral formations to look at. But, I had been spoiled by my trip to the Great Barrier Reef, so how could any spot live up to that expectation that had been planted in me. I would find out weeks later, that there is another spot that lives up to the Great Barrier Reef.

The second venture was snorkelling off the beach in front of the resort. We got our gear, no stinger suits necessary, had our safety instructions and headed off to the water's edge. My partners and I put on our swim fins in the water then swam towards the best viewing area. Because of the running tide through the channel there is U-shaped area which is roped off near one side of the channel. It is an easy swim out to this area and once you are there it is possible to hold your position by hanging on to the anchored rope. Again, the visibility wasn't very good, but it was still rewarding to be in the water and see what marine life was there.

A small safety boat accompanied us at all times. The operator, Mark, attracted fish to the boat by feeding them. I had swum over to the boat to get a closer look at hundreds of feeding fish. Mark asked if I had seen the two large Maori Wrasse fish. No, I hadn't seen them. The Maori Wrasse is the largest of the wrasse fish and can grow up to two meters in length. I had seen a tiny, four centimetre long wrasse cleaning the mouth of a large fish while at the Great Barrier Reef. Mark said that the wrasse were hanging out around the bottom but would come up for food. I placed my mask in the water and looked down seeing thirty or so fish but not any large fish. What Mark didn't tell me was that he was going to toss the food almost on top of me! I was watching but didn't see them coming, just a massive blur of motion from the depths coming right at me – whoa, quite a rush. They brushed against me as they cleaned up the food around me and I had a good look at them. They were both over a meter in length, had a large bump on the top of their faces and very well defined large lips. These two Maori Wrasse are very gentle and have become used to human interaction. They love the food of course, but also seem to like the company and the scratches and rubs that come their way. If you Google Maori Wrasse, you will get a lot of references to world famous Wally, who inhabits the Great Barrier Reef off Cairns. This was a fabulous way to end the snorkelling session; we swam back to the beach where we joined the others and took off our gear.

The beachfront of the resort is cliché tropical. Lush foliage provides a backdrop for it all. The sandy beach slopes into clear, turquoise water. There is a volleyball net suspended above the sand. A hammock beckons from its location between two palm trees. A breeze stirs the branches. It is warm.

We spent some time on the covered deck before it was time to get back on board Voyager. It was lunch time. We were treated to a delicious buffet of hot and cold items and beverages. I'm always up for a meal and the ones offered on Voyager were sumptuous. Now we headed southwest to Daydream Island, our third and final island on the tour.

Daydream Island is the closest island to Airlie Beach, just five kilometres off shore. It is a resort island and offers a variety of activities typical of a tropical resort, many of which are water related. Cyclone Hamish had been through the area and had beaten up the island a bit, closing the pool on the south side which is the one usually used by Voyager tourists. The resort had opened up the whole island to us because of this.

A walkway led me from the pier where we docked through a day use area where several businesses and a pool with tropical fish are located. I followed the path north through a dense jungle which is home to tiny sunbirds, parrots and lizards. Once through the forest the path follows the shoreline and offered wonderful ocean views. The main part of the resort lies at this end of the one kilometre long island. The buildings house the usual selection of rooms and suites, also conference rooms and those suitable for weddings and other special occasions. The path took me alongside a man-made lagoon that was populated by rays, sharks, sea stars, coral and a variety of colourful fish; I spent several minutes leaning on the railing looking at them. Of course there were beautiful swimming pools that offer ocean views. Perhaps my favourite animals were the rock wallabies who roamed the grounds. I always find it somehow magical to share space with any wild creature and these small marsupials were delightful. These animals have shorter claws than other wallabies, an adaptation enabling them to climb on rocky terrain using skin friction.

From this end of the island I walked down to the beach and south along it for a hundred meters to Mermaid Point. There were quite a few people gathered round, having their pictures taken with one of the three larger than life mermaids who sit on three large rocks at water's edge.

It was time to head back to the boat which meant another enjoyable walk through the jungle with those gorgeous birds once again.

Back on board they fed us again! This time we had an array of mouth watering appetizers and beverages during the short ride back to the marina. We docked at five and I headed out of Airlie Beach for the two hour drive to my new couch surfing hosts.

JACK AND THE GECKOS

You may recall that one of the questions I asked myself about couch surfing was, "What if I end up in a very isolated house at the end of a country road?" Well, this is precisely where I found myself on my first Tuesday night in Australia. I had driven south from Airlie Beach, passed Mackay and following directions from a recent email, found the turn off to Don and Annette's. As I headed west, the sealed road became narrower as the light began fading. I knew I had become temporarily misplaced when I came to an intersection that pointed back to Mackay. I phoned and talked to Annette and got the name of the road I missed and needed to turn on to, an unsealed road, more of a country driveway, to their house. I turned the car around, retraced my steps, found the sign, made the turn and headed into the bush. After a kilometre or so I could see a light which gave me a sense of relief. I don't like to be driving at night searching for places and it was twilight by this time. By the time I had pulled up to the house, Annette was standing on the porch with the family dog, a German Sheppard cross. I liked Annette from the moment I saw her. She was standing out on the porch and greeted me with a welcoming wave and warm and friendly smile that lit up her face - sense of relief. I got out of my car and we gave each other a hug and introduced ourselves. The dog, Jack, wagged his tail and with a sniff from him and a pat from me, he accepted me as a friend.

I had arrived safely at the home of my hosts, Don and Annette. Current Mission: "To downsize and travel outside our comfort zone and share with others."

Don was eighteen kilometres away, playing tennis in Sarina. Annette also plays tennis – it is a family sport. Annette fed me a most tasty supper which I greatly appreciated. We chatted about our families and travels until Don came home. Don has a welcoming manner and wonderful smile too – what a great couple! We talked about family and travels some more. Having grown up in the area they were able to tell me all about the area: the coal industry, markets, attractions and growing city of Mackay. They have been couch surfers for about a year and have had only good experiences with their surfers. They live on a beautiful acreage – I had driven past some of their cattle while travelling along their 'driveway'. Their home is open and airy with sets of French doors left wide open to allow the breeze to flow through to keep things cool. I was sitting on the couch when my peripheral vision caught a glimmer of motion on the wall. I turned in its direction but didn't see anything. Then out from behind a picture emerged a gecko! I was both surprised and delighted.

"Is that a pet?"

"No, it's one of many that frequent the house. Don has actually got the numbers down significantly from a few months earlier. They had become too numerous, even for us."

Fascinated, I watched them clamber, suction-cupped with their specialized toe pads, to the walls and ceiling. The geckos vocalized, made little chirping sounds in social interactions that shall remain a mystery to me. They loved to hide behind the artwork on the walls – it gave them a safe place to stop and decide on their next move. I am so easily entertained.

We passed the evening talking and headed to bed around eleven. I had a lovely room with a double bed which was draped round with a mosquito net. There is a second bedroom with two single beds so Don and Annette are prepared to accommodate up to four surfers at a time. I used my sleeping bag to reduce laundry for Annette. I always told my host families that I was quite happy to use my sleeping bag. Some had told me that laundry had become overwhelming sometimes. I suggested that they could change their profile to indicate sleeping bags are requested. Several hosts specifically asked me not to use my sleeping bag. So this is something to be discussed at each home.

Don and Annette's three married children enjoy close family ties and they love spending time with their grand children. Don, a few years older than me, is a retired teacher so we have that in common. Annette is retired from office work. They have a wide variety of interests as outlined in their profile. "Don enjoys gardening, home maintenance, handyman, baking bread, fishing, camping, tennis, travelling. Annette enjoys gardening, quilting, embroidery, sewing, tennis, baking, camping, and having visitors". Don lists his education as being The School of Hard Knocks and the University of Old. Like I do, they try to live their lives 'doing unto others what you would have them do unto you.' There is a reason that this rule is golden, for it is a treasure to live by and makes us all richer.

Breakfast was a continuation of the previous evenings' chats. The three of us share a good sense of humour. After breakfast, they showed me around the property near the house. Jack was by my side quite a bit and I enjoyed his canine company. The outside of their home is beautiful. Tropical plants surround the house and gardens. A large vegetable garden is well tended and Don and Annette harvest a lot of their own food. I have a much smaller garden at home, but do enjoy the fresh produce I get from my plot. There is a tennis court, built by the family which has been well used over the years.

When it was finally time to leave, I didn't really want to go, but knew I had to get going. They are a wonderfully warm and hospitable couple and I knew it would have been easy to stay with them longer. Annette handed me a snack pack she had created of cookies, nuts, berries and fruit – all from their land and her kitchen. I mean, how sweet and thoughtful is that? Just a great couple; I would miss them.

This is the reference I left for them. 'I immediately felt at home at Annette and Don's place in the country. They live in a beautiful, peaceful setting and grow a lot of their own food. I loved spending some time with Jack (the dog) too. Altogether a warm and friendly couple who I would highly recommend to anyone looking for a special place to stay. I hope they may come to Canada some day and will stay with me'

This is their reference for me. 'Joan visited at a very busy time for us, but she adapted well and we enjoyed her company. We only wish that we had more time to share with her. She is a positive, outgoing person - one we felt very comfortable with. We would like to renew a meeting some day, and have more time to chat. Thanks for your friendly addition to our couch surfing experiences.'

IN THE DARK AGAIN

Today would be another driving day with just over seven hundred kilometres to cover. The Bruce Highway runs well inland for this section of the trip so I wouldn't stop at a beach until reaching my destination, Hervey Bay. My map of Australia showed Capricorn Caves a few hours south of Mackay so I had planned to stop there for a break. The caves are the number one natural attraction in central Queensland and have won many tourism awards. The timing worked out almost perfectly for the one hour tour; the group had actually left five minutes before I arrived, but a guide took me down the trail to join the five other tourists before they had reached the entrance (Travel Luck). Part of the cave roof had collapsed here, leaving a large canyon as the beginning of the tour with Stephanie, our knowledgeable guide. The canyon walls are partly covered with vines and with the roots of fig trees on its rim. As most guides, Stephanie was a source of all that is interesting about the caves. They had been formed hundreds of millions of years ago under water as part of a massive coral reef. The caves lie within a huge ridge of limestone which rises from the surrounding land and are called above ground caves for this reason. Their name comes from the Tropic of Capricorn which is close by. At midday, when the sun is over the Tropic of Capricorn, during December and into January, a sunbeam pours in to the cave through a fourteen meter high hole. I would like to come back some day to see this happen.

Stephanie led us through a series of small caves with gatherings of stalactites and stalagmites. There is one small formation that is lit from its interior – it looks just like the open jaws of a T-Rex dinosaur. Images of ferns could be seen on some walls. There were a lot of stairs taking us down and around parts of the cave. Some passages were very large while others required me to duck and at times turn sideways to pass through. In one spot we glimpsed small bats hanging from the ceiling. I like bats; they are just so very cute with their little puppy-like faces and I find it cool that they hang upside down and wrap themselves round with their wings.

The largest hall is Cathedral Cave where Kate ushered us to sit in any of the twelve pews that have been arranged in the chamber. The six of us sat and listened as Stephanie told us about the events that happen here: weddings, concerts and a yearly 'Carols in the Cave'. The acoustics are of a magnificent quality. Stephanie asked if any one of us would like to sing. I'd have loved to sing, but have been told by my children that I shouldn't. No one came forward so we had to take Stephanie's word about the sound.

Off to one side there was a ceiling to floor - twenty meters perhaps - brown column that caught my eye. I thought it was a very strange cave formation as it was dark brown and of uniform thickness (about fifteen centimetres) from top to bottom. I had a closer look and found out that it was a root! A fig tree high above us had sent down this very long explorer in search of water and it now is a curiosity for thousands of visitors each year.

Stephanie gave us a warning before absolute darkness enveloped us as she turned out the lights and began telling us how the caves were discovered and explored. A Norwegian explorer, John Olsen found the caves in 1882 an opened them to the public two years later. They are still privately owned. Stephanie lit a single candle, her face emerging from the darkness. John Olsen did not have lanterns or flashlights. He did not want to share his discovery until he had an idea of the cave's size and location in order to lay claim to the land so he explored the cave alone, with a single candle as his source of light. He tied one end of a rope to a tree outside the cave and the other end to his waist. Stephanie told us of the guano – bat poop – that lay over a meter thick on the cave floor that Olsen would have tramped through. Later, it would be removed and sold as prime fertilizer. Imagine being underground with the smell of the guano, alone with the guano, walking in the guano, with only a single candle to light your way. Imagine doing this over a period of two years while trying to map out the cave system. Such was the undoubting courage of John Olsen. Stephanie handed each of us a candle, supported in a light weight holder and lit each one for us. It was near the end of the tour and we had two options: we could follow Stephanie out on a wide and friendly path or we could follow John Olsen's zigzag path through the dark with only our single candle to light the way. The three young men in our group immediately opted for the zigzag path and were soon out of sight. The wife of the couple on the tour was a bit fearful of the zigzag so she was going to go with Stephanie, her husband would do the zigzag after me. I waited for a few minutes until the threesome ahead of me had a good lead as I wanted to be alone, to really feel like John Olsen had felt like, down here so many years ago. I set out and soon discovered that not only did the path zig then zag, but it did so in a very confining manner; the walls are so close together that I had to turn sideways many times and adjust my plus size body to squidge through the passage. Did I tell you that caves have breezes? Streaming winds that come from the darkness and can extinguish a candle at any moment. My candle was a valiant one – it wavered and flickered in the wind and came incredibly close to being snuffed out three times; yes, I was counting. If it had blown out, I could always feel my way along the walls and call Stephanie and she would come to my rescue. John Olsen didn't have that backup system when he was down here all alone. He didn't know where he was or how close an exit might be. I had a small sense of what he might have been thinking when watching his tiny flame dance in the breeze. The candle stayed lit and I made it through the zig zag passage and saw Stephanie waiting for us. The couple followed a few minutes behind me - the wife had changed her mind and braved the darkness with her husband. She was quite happy that she had stepped out of her comfort zone and conquered a fear.

We were at the cave's exit now and we gently blew out our candles as natural light took over. I followed the others over a suspension bridge and on to the path that looped back to the entrance area. Sitting framed in the gateway a female rock wallaby watched us as we passed, her joeys' feet protruding from her pouch. It was a perfect ending to this cave experience.

Happy that I had toured the caves, I travelled non-stop to Hervey Bay, arriving at eight o'clock. It was raining as the effects of Cyclone Hamish were still being felt along the eastern coast of Australia.

My hostel was fairly large and had a variety of amenities: laundry, nice kitchen, TV room, internet access and common room. I grabbed some takeout from a local eatery and settled in to my new dorm. Several people I had talked to on my trip had told me I should visit Fraser Island. A few days before I arrived at Hervey Bay I had surfed the internet at australia.com where this invitation jumped off the screen –"Four wheel drive next to the coloured sand cliffs of The Cathedrals or planes making joy flights on Seventy-Five Mile Beach. Bushwalk through rainforest growing from the sand and heath lands full of wild flowers and swim in mirrored lakes ringed with gold. Visit Lake McKenzie, picnic next to turtles at Lake Allom and spot whales from Indian Head. Discover the historic Maheno shipwreck in Happy Valley and see kangaroos, wallabies and possums on a bushwalk into the interior. Learn how the island was formed, and about its fascinating Aboriginal and pioneering history. It's easy to see why the Aboriginal owners called Fraser Island 'K'gari' or paradise." How could I pass up an invitation like that? I couldn't.

Fraser Island is the largest sand island in the world – one hundred ninety-seven kilometres long and up to twenty-two kilometres wide. It is a world heritage site with tropical rainforests, over one hundred fresh water lakes and sand dunes that shift with wind and waves. The photographs showed white sand beaches around tea-colored or blue inland lakes, ancient rainforests, stretches of sand and surf along Seventy-five Mile Beach, four wheel drive vehicles filled with happy campers, tall sand dunes and colored sands. I went to the front desk of the hostel, looked at the available options and signed up for an overnight camping trip that would leave in two days. Fraser Island had been closed for some time due to the pummelling it had been taking from Cyclone Hamish and would not be open the next day. Hopefully the weather would turn for the best and it would re-open in two days.

After sleeping in the next day I took a drive around Hervey Bay in the intermittent rain. There are a lot of nice beaches and I managed to get a walk along one and then out to the end of a very long pier and most of the way back before it started to rain. It was a day of laundry, rest and relaxing. The four previous days had been long ones so it was nice just to kick back and wait to see what the weather would do.

Well, it was still rainy the next day and Fraser Island was still closed. I didn't want to wait around indefinitely so decided to continue south. Perhaps this was a good thing because there was something about the tour that I wasn't totally at ease with. The island is all four- wheel drive territory. My group of campers would all be strangers to me which in and of itself didn't bother me, but the great unknown was how good were these people at driving in sandy conditions, over shifting sand in dunes and on beaches; how much experience would they have if any? Personally, I had no experience. There would be twelve of us in two vehicles. When I signed the papers for the trip I read a section that states that all people on the tour are responsible for all vehicles and equipment on the tour. So if a vehicle driven by a novice got in to trouble, I would be partially responsible even though I wasn't driving or perhaps not even a passenger in the vehicle. The information from the tour company said that no experience was necessary to drive the vehicles. Five weeks later on April 20 it was in the news that a twenty-two year old British man and a twenty-six year old Italian woman died in a four-wheel-drive roll-over at Seventy-Five Mile beach. Nine others were injured. It was also reported that the number one cause of accidents on the island is inexperienced drivers. So I missed out on a trip around Fraser Island. (Travel Luck?)

CRIKEY! CALOUNDRA

The drive south to Caloundra took only three and a half hours so I arrived there in the early afternoon. I checked my couch surfing email to see if there was a message from Lisa, my next couch surfing host, giving me directions to her place. There was no message so I checked in to a hostel. Caloundra is a beautiful town set near a headland and after a short drive around town I drove to the waterfront. The northern tip of Bribie Island lies just a few hundred meters off Caloundra with Pumicestone Passage between them, creating a sheltered area that is perfect for swimming, boating, fishing and sail boarding. There are also good surfing beaches at hand. Caloundra has an absolutely brilliant oceanfront walkway along this stretch of waterfront. The water is a gorgeous array of turquoise and darker blues and is the background for the sandy beaches of Caloundra and the island. I headed north along the walkway which is elevated several meters above sea level, some of it resting on huge boulders dumped on the shore line for that purpose. The rest of it stands on wooden supports which rest on pumice stone. The vast expanses of pumice stone are a delicious blend of caramels and butterscotches, mixed here and there with chocolate browns. They are a reminder of the volcanic activity that once occurred here.

I watched as a young boy, surfboard under his arm, said goodbye to his mom and headed out to the breakers with his dad. Just like millions of moms everywhere, I could see that she was concerned for their safety.

"You boys, be careful!"

I watched as father and son paddled out to the breakers then rode in, the boy managing to get to his feet several times under the watchful eye of his father. Many people were in the area walking, wading, surfing, resting, chatting, playing in the sand and fishing. This is a place where you can catch your meal and then cook it on one of the many barbeques that dot the foreshore.

As I retraced my steps back to my car I noticed a nice beachfront park where a large group of people were enjoying a barbequed supper. A number of them played a game of cricket on the field next to the shelter. It was just a wonderful place to be. I wanted to walk over and join them, but somehow just couldn't work up the muster to do so but sat to the side and watched them for a time – another decision I regret.

My second Saturday in Australia would be spent at Australia Zoo near Caloundra. I checked my email in the morning to find a message from Lisa with directions to her house so I sent her a reply and signed out of the hostel. A short drive later I arrived at the zoo for the opening time of nine. The death of Steve Irwin, the Crocodile Hunter, had a great impact on me and even though it had been three years, I was a little choked up when confronted with the many pictures of him at the zoo. Near the entrance a huge welcoming mural has a montage of family pictures along its length with Steve, his wife Terri and children Bindi and Bob interacting with animals. "Crikey, Welcome to Australia Zoo" are the words beside Steve's larger than life sized picture, a look of surprise on his face, mouth open, hazel eyes wide with excitement, as he holds up a meter long baby crocodile. The Irwins eat, sleep and live for wildlife. "Our love, passion, and devotion is to educate and share with the world our magnificent - often threatened or sometimes threatening - wildlife. Our job in this world is to bring misunderstood and feared animals (as well as the cute and cuddlies) right into your house, so that we can share and learn about the world's wildlife." Steve's legacy lives on at this place and in many other rescue and conservation projects around the world.

I'm not really a person who likes zoos. It seems to me that the animals should all be out enjoying life in the wild, in their natural habitats. I have seen animals in small cages and their endless pacing can bring me to tears. I was hoping to find a different kind of zoo here; one where each and every animal is not only cared for but loved by the people who work with them. A place where they are comfortable and happy. The Australia Zoo's motto is "Conservation Through Exciting Education". As a teacher, I know that people learn best if they are actively engaged in the learning process. I would discover many opportunities for close interaction during my day at the zoo.

The zoo's website is an education in itself and it would be easy to spend hours there learning about the zoo, the animals and all the projects that Australia Zoo is involved with. Already I had used the site to learn about the zoo itself. Among the recommended items to bring to the zoo are water, snacks, camera, watch and comfortable shoes and clothes. I don't wear a watch; I don't even own a watch. If I am outside I can usually tell what time it is within fifteen minutes or so by looking at the sun. The watch is recommended because there are many wildlife shows and hand-feeding opportunities throughout the day: 11:00 Wildlife Warriors Crocoseum Show, 12:00 Slinky Snake photo session, 1:00 Otters Live, 1:15 Totally Tortoise Encounter and many more! With a schedule to pay attention to I admit that I did take a glance or two at other peoples' watches and even asked for the time on several occasions.

The zoo offers a lot of services: everything from playgrounds or renting a wagon to a full service travel agency. There is a one hour photo service and a place to print your digital photos. There are four retail outlets, food kiosks and an open air, fifteen hundred seat food court called Feeding Frenzy.

A very large grassy area was the site of my first stop. It was tortoise feeding time. The Aldabran Tortoises at the zoo are the largest species of tortoise in the world! There were three keepers in khaki colored shorts and short sleeved shirts and a volunteer in her bright yellow tee shirt looking after the tortoises. When they entered the enclosure with buckets of fruit and vegetables Goliath came running out to meet them - well, he was going fast if you consider the usual lumbering of a tortoise. Soon he was followed by Igloo, another Aldabran tortoise. They were interested in the food of course, but I soon noticed that they also wanted the attention that was showered upon them; they wanted to be close to the keepers, to be scratched and stroked and petted. They seemed to love the human contact, following the keepers as they moved. Piece by piece Goliath and Igloo took the food offered to them. Soon there were several water lizards enjoying feeding time too, streaking in to nab bits of food that the tortoises had dropped. These lizards run freely throughout the zoo and I loved watching for them on the paths and taking their pictures.

At my next stop I stationed myself on a seat beside a small natural pool, waiting for feeding time with two Asian otters, Bonnie and Marie. I have always loved watching otters. If they were a dog they would surely be Fox Terriers because they are almost always on the move, love to play and like treats! They live in a fantastic enclosure with a creek, waterfall and pool. Lush foliage provides the background as they swim under water then scamper up on logs to pause briefly to see what is going on - if keepers are coming with food. They are conditioned, just as we are, to scheduled feeding times and recognized the keepers with great anticipation. The girls were fed their favourite crayfish which they crunched with sharp little teeth. Then around the pond they would swim, scramble back up on the log and get another morsel. They were definitely the cutest and liveliest animals to watch. A picture is of these two posing on a log, focused attention on the keeper's approach, is one of my top ten pictures taken in Australia. I spent a half hour here in the morning and also the final half hour before closing.

I had seen elephants a few times when they came to my home town when I was very young and once when I had taken my young children to the circus in Victoria. But I had never fed one. Along with many other visitors I would get the chance today. Three Asian elephants showed up from their enclosure at the appointed time and stopped a few yards from us behind a rope fence. Every day of the year, the three resident Asian Elephants; Siam, Sabu and Bimbo are taken on a number of walks around the zoo grounds.

An informative keeper told us about the three: they were born in Thailand, they came to the zoo in 2003 from a circus; Siam is fifty-two, Sabu fifty-one and Bimbo fifty. Those of us who had chosen to feed an elephant formed three lines, one for each elephant. The keepers had buckets full of cut fruit and vegetable pieces ready to go. One by one I watched as others went before me, holding the morsel, hand flat and arm outstretched as the elephants nimble trunks snaked forward, deftly grabbed the food and transferred it to their mouths. As soon as one person had their turn, they were replaced by another forming a continuous feeding for the elephants. My line moved quickly along and soon I was standing in front of Sabu with half an apple on my hand. She reached out with her trunk and with precision, scooped up the tasty tidbit. All that was left on my hand was a bit of trunk snot and a great impression of a huge but ever so gentle beast. It is only when I stood so very close to such a large animal that I could really appreciate its size. Elephants are big!

Next, I checked my map and headed for the Crocoseum, an arena that seats five thousand people and is the 'heartbeat of entertainment at Australia Zoo'. I found a seat about five rows above the stadium floor. Birds swooped in from behind me, streaks of color that glided down to the keepers who stood in the center of the arena.

"Who wants to have a bird come land on their arm?"

My hand shot up along with many others and I gave a double armed wave of Canadian enthusiasm. It worked.

"Yes, you, the lady in yellow-striped shirt." Cool! Four of us were selected and now stood, one on each side of the Crocoseum. "Okay, now wave your arms up and down. Now flap your arms like wings – you are really flying now. Now make a bird sound and bend your knees...... Great!" Oh the things we do sometimes! But I really wanted to have a bird come land on my arm, to be part of the action. It would be worth acting a little weird in front of a few thousand people. "Okay, thanks – that's all. We're not really going to have birds land on you!" What had he just said? I tell you, I was quite disappointed but I didn't feel embarrassed (well, maybe a little). The four of us had been hoodwinked into becoming part of the show as animal impersonators. Did I mention that our images were displayed on the forty foot jumbo screen for all to see us just a little bit better? For our efforts each of us was given an eight by twelve color glossy of Steve Irwin feeding a crocodile at the Crocoseum. Okay, it was worth it. It was fun watching the cockatoos, parrots, falcons and lorikeets flying overhead and learning about them.

In Florida my daughter and I had visited an alligator attraction. While some of the animals we saw were amazing, many habitats were just so very small which saddened me. Jenna and I went to the alligator show where this poor alligator was lured from the water, then pounced upon and eventually manoeuvred so a man put his head in to the gator's mouth. I didn't find this entertaining because I couldn't imagine the animal got any reward from it at all. I was hoping this crocodile show would be different – and it was.

The Crocoseum has a large, C-shaped pool with grass in the open side of the C. The pool is about a meter deep and is filled with perfectly clear water to allow an unparalleled view of how the crocs move underwater. This allowed the keepers to 'highlight for you the dangers that can be lurking just below the surface of a seemingly serene billabong.' The Crocoseum was one of Steve's dreams that most people said could not be done. But of course, he knew it could be done and made it so. There are several male crocs which are kept in individual enclosures behind the main arena; they enter the Crocoseum through a system of cleverly designed channels and gates.

In their wild territories crocodiles live in murky waters that provide camouflage as they lie in wait for their unsuspecting prey. We had three enthusiastic keepers, Bruce, Matty and Tom who would be working with Murray, the thirty-five year old crocodile. Richie was the commentator for the demonstration. Our attention was directed to the jumbo screen where we watched Murray swimming his way along the channels behind the Crocoseum to the main pool. Then he cleared the last control gate and was right in front of me. Murray is just over three and a half meters long and looks gorgeous and very well fed. Saltwater crocs are at the top of the food chain; they are the largest of the crocodiles and also the most aggressive. Bruce moved to the edge of the pool, lightly stamped his foot a few times and cued by those vibrations Murray swam over to him. Bruce stepped back a few meters as Murray climbed up on to the grass and raised his head looking for the food he knew Bruce had for him. With Murray moving forward and Bruce moving backward the long strip of red meat was swung back then forward and let go in a gentle arc into the jaws of doom. Murray had his first snack and now he retreated into the water. The next ten minutes were fascinating as we all watched Murray swim about the pool and come out five more times to get food. The final part of the show had Bruce climb a platform that hangs out over the pool, meat in hand.

"Crocodiles will hunt animals that hang from branches over the water – so if you are out in the bush, it is not a good idea to climb trees and swing from branches over the water." Murray swam beneath Bruce and raised his head out of the water, and then in a sudden skyward effort he raised two-thirds of his three hundred kilogram body straight out of the water and got his reward. Very cool! And I had a picture of Steve doing that same thing. While the show was going on, Richie told us about endangered habitats and ongoing conservation efforts as well as safety rules for human-croc relations. I left my seat with a new love and respect for crocodiles. The human-croc encounters were educational and did not cause any stress to Murray, rather he enjoyed a nice series of appetizers. I loved it all!

This was a great zoo experience so far and I knew that I would be staying until closing time at five o'clock. For the next two hours I roamed the zoo, stopping often and staying with each animal for more than just a minute or two. I took time to find as many different birds as I could in the expansive aviary, walking back and forth and looking high in tree tops then down to ground level. There were several different birds taking baths and getting a drink at a series of waterfalls and pools that make up a creek in the aviary. Then of course, there was the picture taking, trying to capture some of the magic that was before me at every turn.

Minibus, Dozer and Chisel are the three resident wombats. They are closely related to koalas and look similar in many ways. They are the world's largest burrowing animal and their lovely enclosure has a building with sleeping quarters for them, a large grassy area and an equally large burrowing area because they love to dig. Tanya was the keeper in the pen when I stopped by. She is very knowledgeable and loves her job, and a perpetual smile lit up her face. Tanya told me that the wombats are very gentle and love human contact. She got down to Minibus level and petted her as she gave her some food; I could tell that they have a great relationship. It is this loving relationship that I saw repeated all over the zoo, a genuine affection for each other.

Lunch time was spent at Feeding Frenzy. I took my tray to a table on the outside edge of the huge deck which overlooks several crocodile enclosures. Each of the three crocodiles had its own pool surrounding by coarse green grass. These crocs have all been rescued from situations of cruelty or imminent death because they had become nuisance crocs. As I ate my lunch I got to see keepers enter each enclosure and feed the crocs. Quite a lunch time viewing experience!

After lunch it was back to visit the many animals: dingoes, Kirra, Mia and Cooya; Koalas including Berry and her mother Matilda; camels, Teela and her friend Dajarra who had been rescued as an orphan by Steve and Terri in the outback. There were lots of amphibians and reptiles to see: lizards, snakes, frogs and turtles. At the furthest reaches from the entrance are enclosures for the elephants and the tigers. No, not native to Australia, but two of Steve's favourites and are at the zoo to promote conservation and education. Sabu was standing in the large elephant enclosure with her friends: ankle deep in grass, trees in the background, flowering plants in the foreground her eyes were half closed as if ready for a nap. Across the path the one visible tiger was having a rest, lying fully stretched out on his left side on a large platform as two keepers petted and stroked him. They didn't try to get him to move just because people were there. Things are done at the animals choosing – I love it like that! The cheetah enclosure is under construction beyond these last two displays and I managed a glimpse of a keeper taking a cheetah on a walk through his new territory.

After my visit at the furthest end of the zoo I turned back in the direction of the entrance and stopped in the one enclosure I hadn't yet visited – The Roo Den. This is a huge walk- through close-encounter area with a great number of kangaroos and wallabies. The animals were for the most part lying down and resting and were very approachable. I walked up to several and was able to pet them at will. Lots of people were feeding them special food that can be purchased at the gate and many pictures were being taken. Just an iconic Australian experience!

I had seen every animal in the place and had timed my arrival back to the otters for their last feeding of the day. Once again I delighted in their playfulness and alertness. I waited through the scheduled feeding time then realized it was not going to happen. Five o'clock had come around and it was time to leave. I walked past the Komodo dragons' pen and then through the souvenir shop where I bought some postcards. Out at five; what a wonderful day at the zoo! Australia Zoo is a place where the animals always come first and are truly loved and well cared for. I felt very satisfied and had a sense of peace for this special place. Good on ya, Steve and family!

GLASS HOUSE MOUNTAINS

It was under a half hour drive through pleasant countryside to the town of Maleny where I would couch surf with Lisa. Current Mission: "Meeting people from different cultures and making friends". Both being retired teachers who love to travel, we already had a lot in common. Lisa is very well travelled having visited almost thirty countries. During my visit she pulled out various Spanish books as she was leaving for a trip to South America soon and wanted to improve her language skills. That`s what I call a dedicated traveller. I felt immediately at ease in Lisa`s company and found that she is a gracious host.

In her personal description she says that she has "no intention of growing old soon or gracefully at any time. I have lived and worked in four countries and visited many others. I enjoy learning from other cultures. More I see, more I want to see. I am a very down to earth, no nonsense person. What you see is what you get. Independent traveller, well organised, practical, lateral thinker. I enjoy meeting like minded people." Lisa likes "ancient cultures, visual arts, photography, computers, tennis, sailing, outdoors." Her philosophy is like mine and is repeated in many couch surfers profiles - treat people as you like to be treated. I think I fit the bill in her type of people she likes – "Positive, straight forward, honest, interesting and worldly."

Lisa has a lovely, secluded and peaceful home tucked around by a beautiful lush garden made up of many types of plants. She shares her house with a gorgeous Tokenise cat by the name of Lady Suriana who spent a lot of quality time with me cuddled up in a living room chair.

Lisa does a very good job in her profile of describing her couch surfing arrangement and her requirements. You don`t have to share the bed with a Great Dane or other pet or person. I had a nice separate bedroom with a single bed and a door that opened right on to the deck. Lisa supplies linens and towels, so that was wonderful. She didn`t want my sleeping bag in the house which is a precaution from strange and perhaps not so wonderful things that can hitch a ride from place to place. As in my home, there are no drugs or smoking allowed in the house.

The next morning it was time for a Sunday drive with Lisa as my personal guide. The area around Maleny is one of gently rolling, heavily forested hills, a landscape of winding roads and scenic views. We pulled over at a lookout that offers a spectacular view of Glasshouse Mountain National Park. The Glasshouse Mountains are volcanic remnants from twenty-five million years ago; some have worn to leave dome shapes while others thrust up out of the native forest in jagged scraggly-tooth fashion. Captain James Cook named the mountains as they reminded him of the stacks of the glass making factories back home in England. The group of thirteen volcanic plugs are steep-sided and offer many opportunities for challenging bushwalking and rock climbs in the region. They vary in height from the one hundred twenty-three meter Wild Horse Mountain to the five hundred fifty-five meter Mount Beerwah. Aboriginals have a legend that says the mountains are a family with Mount Beerwah being the mother, Mount Tibrogargan the father and all of the other mountains their sons and daughters. The park is surrounded by the Beerburrum State Forests so that the view is one of endless forests with occasional homestead clearings and cultivated fields. The mountains support quite a diverse range of habitats that include shrub land, some small sections of rainforest and montane heath, a rare vegetation type which occurs where the soil is too thin to support large shrubs and trees. There are a number of threatened species in the heath, many of which are found nowhere else on Earth.

Our next stop was at Mary Cairncross Scenic Reserve. Mary Cairncross was an early conservationist who fought against the logging of the area's majestic native forests in the early 1900's. This unique rainforest remnant was donated to the local Maleny council by her three daughters in 1941. The land was given in memory of their mother. The council set aside the reserve for "the preservation, conservation and exhibition of the natural flora and fauna."

We entered the education center which has displays of the flora and fauna typical of the rainforest. It amazed me to find out that in this fifty-two hectare reserve there are forty-two different birds that can be seen. Lisa and I were lucky enough to come across a Brush Turkey on one section of the path. He had hold of a worm that was at least thirty centimetres long! It's the biggest worm I have ever seen; it looked more like a small snake! The forest is home to owls, goshawks, eagles, kookaburras and parrots. Wallabies, possums, gliders, snakes, lizards, bats, rats, mice and echidnas also call this forest their home but we didn't manage to see these during our walk.

The reserve has over two kilometres of well maintained paths and boardwalks that are suitable for wheelchair travel. There are quite a few viewing platforms where we stopped and stood still, enjoying the tranquility of nature. It was a great way to experience this special parcel of original rainforest.

Our longest walk of the day came alongside a small river. There were a lot of families enjoying the sunny afternoon along the banks; many had picnic lunches with them. Smaller children played in pools formed between rocks and little waterfalls. When we reached the end of the path we found the older children playing in the biggest pool at the base of a five meter waterfall. There were a dozen or so brave souls who climbed to a high point on the far side of the river, grabbed on to a rope and swung out over the water, letting go at the right time. Each leap was watched by everyone and accompanied with yells of fear and delight. Some of the boys managed back flips during their semi-controlled fall from a height of ten meters. Lots of fun to watch, I lived vicariously through them, recalling the huge arcing tree swings of my youth.

When we had completed our circular drive of the area I parked the car in Maleny and Lisa walked back to her house. I spent the next hour or so walking around the village which was full of arts and crafts stores. Maleny is a very lovely town. When supper time came I treated Lisa to dinner at a local Indian restaurant which turned out to have so-so food and not the best of service. Lisa decided it would not be a place to take other visitors.

We spent another pleasant evening together talking of travel and watching some TV. I had two lovely nights with Lisa and Lady Suriana. This is the reference I left for her: "It was very nice to be able to spend time at Lisa`s lovely home. Lisa and I spent a nice Sunday together driving in the area around her place where we did several area walks to some interesting places. It would have been easy to spend more time with her. There are a lot of places to go in the area. Australia Zoo was very good too. So thank you Lisa for sharing your home, Lady Suriana and your local knowledge!" For me she wrote: "It was a real pleasure to meet Joan. As soon as we met I felt an immediate connection. Joan is very easy going and a perfect guest. I hope we`ll meet again one day."

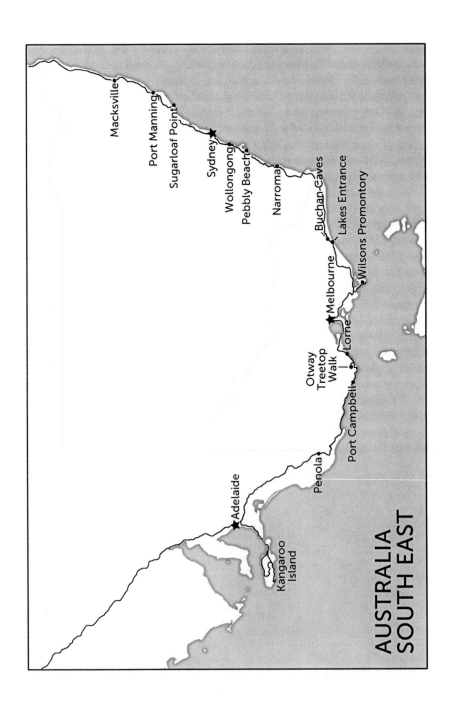

AUSTRALIA
SOUTH EAST

Macksville
Port Manning
Sugarloaf Point
Sydney
Wollongong
Pebbly Beach
Narroma
Buchan Caves
Lakes Entrance
Wilsons Promontory
Melbourne
Lorne
Otway Treetop Walk
Port Campbell
Penola
Adelaide
Kangaroo Island

BYRON BAY AND COFF'S HARBOUR

On this, my second Monday in Australia, Roland and I were scheduled to meet. But, as there had been a lot of rain over the past month, including a lot in the past week, Roland was trapped behind a few raging creeks in the bush land. We would try to connect the next day. Oh yes, Roland. There are so many ways to travel nowadays. Three months before my trip I had discovered a website called catch a ride Australia. This site connects people who have transportation with those who need transportation. I thought it might be a good idea to share my car and company with someone after six weeks of travelling alone. We began corresponding, exchanging emails and pictures and seemed to be a good match. Now with an extra day to get down to his location, I was able to spend more time visiting places along the coast.

Roland had mentioned the beauty of Byron Bay, a lovely small town with a friendly atmosphere. It borders on the protected areas of Cape Byron Headland Reserve, Cape Byron Marine Park and Arakwal National Park. Cape Byron is the most easterly point of Australia and is capped by its most easterly lighthouse which is where I now headed. Car in the parking lot, I began the gentle climb to the lighthouse. The lighthouse looks like a tower rising from a castle and is not tall by lighthouse standards. It is perched on the edge of a dramatic cliff over one hundred meters high. This natural elevation meant the lighthouse did not have to be very tall and it is only eighteen meters in height. Its elevated location and the fact that this is Australia's most powerful lighthouse allow it to be seen from forty kilometres away.

The lighthouse's white pre-fabricated concrete bricks contrasted beautifully with the brilliant blue of the sky. It has been here since 1901, flashing white light every fifteen seconds to signal mariners that they were coming to the east coast of the continent. I walked around the lighthouse twice and took close-up pictures. Then I continued on the cliff-top trail past the lighthouse walking down thirty steps before cutting off to the first viewing platform on my right. The area is absolutely spectacular with sea cliffs, beaches, and lush coastal vegetation. Absolute blue – the ocean undulated with all shades of blue and frothed to white when it hit the shore line. The water was absolutely clear and I was delighted to see a few sharks and other fish passing by a hundred meters below me. A huge smile lit up my face and I was enveloped once again in a sense of wonder. A little further up the path I looked down and saw a lone seal swimming along and leaping out of the water as he swam to join others of his kind. What an amazing place to be!

I followed along the cliff top to the next stop and sat on the bench by the sign that declared this to be "the most easterly point of the Australian mainland." Some strangers and I took pictures of each other at this unique geographical spot. Totally cool! The elevated ocean views were mind-blowing and ever changing as I continued walking north. My last stop on the trail looked out over a low lying peninsula of land far below. It looked like a profile of the Disney dog, Pluto, lying on the ground, mouth open, floppy ears listening to the waves. I started talking to a couple and their daughter who was in her twenties. She was a person who liked to get involved in her surroundings and headed off to climb down the trail to the water. Her parents felt they were not up to it – neither was I - and so the three of us stood at the top and waited for her to pop out of the bush near the bottom of the trail and appear on the open land below us. It wasn't long before she showed up, turned and waved to us and jogged along the path to the water. Oh to have the energy (and knees) to do that again!

On the return trip to my car, I made just as many stops as before, standing still and listening to the waves below, looking for marine life and bird life, smelling the ocean, feeling the wind on my face and tangling my hair, just being on the cliff and enjoying every moment.

Tallows Beach provided the last picture of my visit to the lighthouse. Australia is just a mass of drop-dead beautiful beaches and this is another one. It strikes out south from Cape Byron and stretches in a gentle, sandy 'C' for kilometres.

Back in Byron Bay I wandered around and found a quaint place for lunch. No sooner had my order arrived than it started to pour. This is the rain that comes down hard and heavy, there is no chance to avoid getting wet, even with an umbrella. The day darkened, the mega-drops splattered and joined to form torrents of water raging along the streets and created ankle deep moats in minutes. The sound was fantastic and the smell was that of absolute freshness. Amazing that it had been such a beautiful day just a short time ago when I was out at the lighthouse! (Travel Luck)

Two and a half hours south of Byron Bay is Coffs Harbour, another place recommended by Roland. The Pacific Highway turns inland just south of Byron Bay and comes back to the ocean at Coffs Harbour. Nearing town I saw a much bigger-than-life model of a banana which let me know that the local economy is based on banana farming. Tourism is also a big industry here. Coffs Harbour lies between high mountains with pristine rainforests and gorgeous beaches with kilometres of sand and sea providing surfing opportunities. It was a lovely place to spend the night.

ROLAND

The next morning I received an email from Roland saying that he was able to get across the creeks and out to civilization, so that was good to hear. We would meet at 10:30 in the town of Macksville. I left Coffs Harbour after breakfast and in under an hour turned off the highway to Nambucca Heads. This is yet another lovely little coastal town and lies at the mouth of the Nambucca River. The waterfront is a gorgeous combination of wonderful beaches and the island-dotted river. It is easy to see why this area is such a popular tourist spot and why Roland had told me to stop and have a look around.

The most interesting man-made thing in Nambucca Heads is the Mosaic Sculpture. Imagine taking every mug you have ever seen and then a hundred times that amount and now drop them and break them and combine these pieces with a huge assortment of odds and ends of china flatware and figurines. Then add a jillion tiny pieces of tile. Now that you have a thousand jillion of these pieces, create a three dimensional mosaic which covers a thirty meter stretch of sidewalk and place it in front of the local police station. The sculpture has a marine theme and is complete with cresting waves, too many brilliant fish to mention, dolphins, whales, people, shells, a huge octopus protecting a corner and even a tiny pair of black porcelain high heels. Oh, yes, it even has some bananas! Needless to say, it is a very picture-worthy piece of art – still loving my digital camera! New images of nature and art on my memory card, I headed south to Macksville to meet Roland.

I crossed the bridge over the Nambucca River and made the first left-hand turn on to River Road. Roland was exactly where he said he'd be - standing across from the Star Hotel. Tall and lanky, wearing glasses, a green T-shirt, tan shorts and sandals, he looked like he had just stepped out of a recent picture he had e-mailed me. I pulled over to the side of the road and stepped out of the car. We greeted each other with the comfortable A-frame hug of new friends. Roland traveled very light with just a small backpack and duffle bag so it took little time to store his gear in the trunk.

Roland, from Germany, had been house-sitting up the Nambucca River Valley for six months. In our three months of corresponding he had told me a lot about the valley and its inhabitants and had sent me pictures. He was very enthusiastic about showing me the valley and visiting some friends. He called Hans and Sue, but they weren't going to be home for a while so we elected to drive past their place and go all the way up the valley to where Roland had been staying.

Okay, so this was going against any personal safety rules that I had learned over the years: don't talk to strangers - Roland wasn't really a stranger, but he was only a virtual friend. Don't get in a car with a stranger - well at least I was driving so I had some control. Don't go to a remote location – well here I was driving fifty-two kilometres up an isolated valley to the end of the road.

I think I have the ability to assess people quickly and fairly accurately. Having met Roland weeks earlier and corresponded with him and exchanged pictures I felt comfortable traipsing off into the Australian wilderness with him.

Fifty-two kilometres is a long way on a dirt road. Roland gave a running commentary of the valley residents. This couple has been here for twenty-eight years. They came from Slovakia to get some land to farm. This family has only a father, and four children. He lost his wife to cancer three years ago, and it has been very difficult for him. Roland knew everyone's story - he is a very sociable and well-liked newcomer to the valley. He had lived here only six months so is still considered a stranger. He had been told that only after thirty years or so of residence would someone be considered a valley resident.

We drove through continuously changing green scenery: forests and fields, cows and sheep, houses and outbuildings marking the acreages. An hour passed in this fashion with me driving and Roland giving the detailed analysis. He directed me to pull off to the right, down and around a narrow hairpin corner that I successfully manoeuvred with my small red car. I parked in the large front yard near the house on the property. Roland actually owns this house, but rents it out to a friend. Roland led the way into the house for the tour. It was a nice two bedroom house with a cozy kitchen and living room area. The expansive deck off the back of the house looked out over a nearby creek and the valley beyond. It was absolutely peaceful on the deck, with only the birds and frogs making any noise. It would be a wonderful place to sit and let my mind go still.

After touring the house we walked over to an open garage that had a Jeep parked in it. Roland said that we needed to take the jeep from here as my car simply would not be able to make it the rest of the way. Hmmm . . . so here I am alone with a stranger, fifty-two kilometres up a dirt road in a heavily forested side valley and being taken to yet another location. Now he has the keys and is driving . . . sure, why not?

We drove back onto the dirt road, hung a hard left and stopped thirty meters farther on where Roland got out and opened a gate. He drove through, got out and closed the gate, got back in the Jeep and then we continued another fifty meters to the creek. This was the second forge. The first one we had made in my car through a temporary creek that had earlier crossed the road. This creek was a permanent creek. It was this very creek, one of two actually, that had trapped Roland in his place for six days the previous week. We had hoped to meet on Monday but had to delay a day and wait for the creek to subside enough to allow access. The jeep easily bobbled through the calf-deep water. Now, as a passenger, I got to sit back, relax and enjoy the countryside. What once had been a full dirt road was now reduced to two dirt tracks with tall swaths of grass growing on each side and down the middle of them. Another two kilometres brought us to a second gate which marked the entrance to the property Roland had been looking after. This gate gave me pause as it was locked and kept that way at all times; Al, the owner, liked it that way. Once we passed through, Roland wrapped the heavy chain back around the gate and post and secured the lock. There was a gargoyle perched on the gate post - a figure to scare off any evil or bad spirits. Okay, so here I am with a stranger in the isolation of the Australian bush, locked behind one gate, no control of the Jeep, creeks to cross. Although I still felt pretty comfortable with Roland I couldn't help have different scenarios flash through my mind. Had I watched too many television crime shows?

What to do? Really only one option - I smiled at the scenarios I had created, dismissed them all and put my trust in Roland. We drove through Al's property and came to a third creek crossing. Roland showed me the high watermark of the previous day. The creek had been in flood, more than a meter deeper and I could easily see the line made against the grasses and shrubs that grew along the sides. We made it across quite handily in the Jeep (not a place for a rental car) and climbed the small hill to Al's house. Roland had sent me a picture of the house that had been taken at quite a distance from an elevated vantage point. At first glance at the picture all I saw was bush – forested hills everywhere. When I looked closely, I saw a small clearing with a light yellow house nestled into its surroundings. This is a very quiet, isolated place, a place to reflect and to find out who you are.

The house sits on a level area that has been created by heavy machinery cutting into the hillside. There is also a large area for a long driveway, garage and garden. The main floor of the house has the living room, kitchen and bathroom. The two bedrooms are upstairs. We had a lunch of cheese, bread and fruit then headed outside for a look around. Al had constructed a vegetable garden on a flat piece of land near the house. It was rectangular, about four meters by six meters and had a variety of vegetables growing, all thanks to Roland. To keep animals out the whole thing was covered with fine netting, which rose in the middle to about three meters.

There was a compost barrel that sat in one corner of the garden. As I glanced in the compost, I saw the biggest black snake I had ever seen!

"Joan get away, get back, he is very dangerous." Okay it wasn't a snake after all but the tail of the huge guano, a lizard species common in Australia. This one was over a meter long. He had been dining on melon scraps in the compost. Roland didn't have to tell me a second time as I stepped away and he approached hoe in hand - my white knight. Roland gently herded the lizard out of the barrel, and along the side of the netting. The guano clambered up and along the net until he wriggled and slipped sideways through an opening where two pieces of netting met – or almost met. Drama over, Roland picked a few beans and tomatoes to take to his friends, Hans and Sue.

Roland locked up the house. We got back into the jeep then reversed the whole process of creek crossing and passing through gates. Once back at Roland's property, we traded the Jeep for my car, and Roland called his friends, Hans and Sue. Now we headed to their place. I was just glad to have made it out of the bush safe and sound - definitely too much TV.

Hans and Sue live eleven kilometres down the road from Roland. Hans is a bear of a man, tall and rotund - Sue is a deer by comparison, petite with long brown hair. Hans offered to show me his greenhouses.

"What do you grow?" It turns out that Hans is one of the world's top orchid experts. If botanical garden needs a rare species they call Hans. He ships plants worldwide and regularly attends shows, sharing his knowledge and winning many awards along the way.

The great variety of orchids in the greenhouses was far beyond my expectations (you don't know what you don't know). Orchids grew in pots on the floor, in containers on waist high shelves and hung from every overhead and upright pole in the place – thousands of them! Hans gave me an overview of some of the species he had been growing. There was a show he was would be attending in a month's time, and he explained how he was nurturing certain orchids to be in bloom for that show. He had orchids so small that six flowers could fit on a dime! While not a lot were in bloom I could still appreciate the overwhelming array that I saw.

Tour over, we joined Roland and Sue back up at the house and had afternoon tea. Roland works for Hans in the greenhouses a day or two a week and the two of them love each other's company and the chance to speak German.

By the time we left Hans and Sue's and got back to Macksville it was three o'clock. Most definitely we weren't going to be as far south as I thought we'd be by day's end. But that turned out all right. We headed south along the Pacific Highway talking to each other and enjoying the scenery. When it came to dinner time we stopped and got a meal in a quaint restaurant in Port Manning. We didn't have a couch to surf and there are no hostels in the area, so we ended up staying in a low-cost cabin for the night.

MUESLI AND SATCHMO

The day began with a simple breakfast of Muesli cereal with yogurt and fruit. This would be our staple start to the days ahead. I had learned that I could buy milk in single serving cartons that did not require refrigeration so I usually had three or four of these on hand. We found a place for Roland to get his morning coffee and then drove around the Port Manning - Cape Hawke area which is quite lovely.

Heading south, our first stop was at Sugarloaf Lighthouse near the tiny community of Seal Rocks. The local cafe is situated on an elevated view-point at the north end of one of the beautiful beaches in the area. Roland had been to the lighthouse so elected to stay at the cafe and enjoy his coffee while chatting with the locals and tourists. I drove four kilometres along Kinka Road and found the car park. From there it was a very pleasant fifteen minute walk along a road that was overhung with branches of gum trees which offered welcome relief from the sun. The road took a hair-pin turn left out of the forest and opened up on my right to ocean views. Another two hundred meters of gentle climbing brought me around the final turn and gave me my first look at the lighthouse and support build-ings. The cottages are white, as is the lighthouse. The path brought me to a somewhat flat area between the two cottages. Then I looked up - up the last bit of the path that would take me to the lighthouse. I do mean up, as this last bit climbed steeply another thirty or so meters vertically over a short distance, another good leg workout. The lighthouse itself is relatively short at fifteen meters, but as it sits almost eighty meters above the sea, its location gives it all the height it needs. This is one of only two lighthouses in Australia that have a staircase wrapping around the outside of the building rather than on the inside. I circled the tower just once on the way up and stepped on to the observation balcony. Another view of gorgeous blue waters and crashing white surf landing on a sweep-ing sandy beach was laid out before me and was captured by my camera. The beaches and dramatic scenes like this one are the norm for Australia – incredible beauty everywhere. I circled the balcony once, twice and a third time, stopping for long periods to become one with the sea, rocks, beaches, all under a brilliant blue sky – how wonderful life is! I am easily amused. Finally I descended the spiral staircase and using the handrail made my way back down to the cottages. A few more pictures and then I walked back to the car. Roland was sitting out on the covered porch of the cafe talking with an old acquaintance when I got back to Seal Rocks. After introductions and a brief stay it was time to move on.

Now it was time to drive, heading south on the Pacific Highway. We drove right through Sydney as I would finish my trip here with Tom and Lyn seven weeks later. An hour south of Sydney is the city of Wollongong where we would couch surf with Susan and her daughter Frankie. Her current mission: "Share our house with some nice people and try the system out to see if it could work when my kids travel". I loved Susan's philosophy when I read her couch surfing profile. "I think that being positive and happy is a choice and that it makes life more fun for you and for everyone around you if you make this choice. I believe in being as honest as I can (while protecting other people's feelings) and trying to do your best in everything - why bother otherwise."

I emailed Susan in late December and was happy to hear back from her the next day! "You're the first person I've heard from so I'm excited that you'd like to stay." By the time I actually got to Susan's she had already had one other surfer and it had been a positive experience. He had been a lone male, so she was a little apprehensive, but that soon passed.

With Roland navigating and following a good set of directions it was easy to find Susan's lovely home in the suburbs. She greeted us at the front door. As soon as our eyes met, we had a connection, something that goes beyond mere friendship to a deeper level of love and understanding. Susan just has the aura of a warm and caring person and I knew we would be friends after my trip was over – and we are.

Susan is a single mom of two daughters, Frankie and Daisy. Daisy lives an hour away in Sydney while Frankie has one more year to finish high school so still lives at home. The third member of the house is Satchmo, a large, black Hungarian Sheepdog, called a Puli. Satchmo and I enjoyed each other's company.

Susan works in the health industry and had arrived home from work just before we got there. We offered to take them out for dinner or order in but she made a wonderful, tasty meal for us. Frankie excused herself to finish some homework and spend time on her computer leaving the three of us adults to talk about families and travels. Roland headed off to bed fairly early, sleeping on a long single bed in a small bedroom.

Susan and I now had some time to ourselves and it wasn't long before we were talking about being single moms. It is a difficult job, but a rewarding one. I felt as though I could talk to Susan about anything and I found myself sharing the dramas and incredible lows that Jenna's illness had brought on. Susan was a soft place to fall and I just let caution fall away and trusted her completely. At home I am able to talk to my friend and psychologist, Tina every week and I know how valuable that time is for my mental health. I hadn't been able to talk to anyone in depth about Jenna for weeks now and it must have seemed to Susan that I would never stop. We were now very close for two people who had met only hours before - I had found a friend for life. When I was in Sydney at the end of my stay, Susan travelled up the coast and we were able to spend a few hours together. It was so very nice to have been able to do that. Finally it was time for us to go to bed. I slept on a comfortable futon in the second living room.

Susan is able to accommodate several surfers a night. Susan finds most people interesting, "there's always a story to be told. Having couch surfers visit brings a bit of the big wide world into my home and makes me feel like I'm travelling even when I'm not."

Susan has lived in the area all her life and as such has a lot of great information and advice to share. She lists a number of area attractions in her profile and offered us some great suggestions when we told her our travel plans. Roland and I never would have heard of Pebbly Beach if not for Susan. Susan has a wonderfully complete profile, one all couch surfers should use as a guideline.

Her interests include a passion for reading, "I'm a reader - can't imagine life without a book. Read a variety of things, but crime fiction is an old favourite. Also like going for walks, swimming, seeing films - nothing too extraordinary. I love the big screen - it makes almost anything look good. I have only ever walked out of two movies and that was because I was bored (Dead Man) and really tired (Pirates of the Caribbean II). Travel, of course, is a buzz."

For Susan: I felt immediately at home with Susan and her daughter Frankie. Susan has a kind and gentle spirit and is a pleasure to spend time with. She and her family would be most welcome in my home any time. I would have been nice to have had more time to share. I highly recommend the family.

From Susan: I think Joan is terrific. I really enjoyed having her at my place and only wish it could have been longer. I will really try to get over to visit her in Canada sometime.

When Roland and I left the next morning, Frankie and Susan were already gone. This meant getting out of the house and seeing that Satchmo was outside where he belonged. It turns out that he does not like to be outside for the day. Susan bribes him by giving him food in his dish on the deck. When it was time for us to leave I tried to encourage him out the back door but he was having none of it and went as far as to growl at me. I'm not used to being growled at and didn't want to grab his collar to pull him outside – who knows what that might have led to. So taking a lesson from Susan, I got some food and placed it in his dish outside and closed the door on him. Ah hah – that will show him! Well perhaps 'not so much' for when I got to the front door and picked up my gear who was there but a speeding Satchmo. He had gobbled up the morsel I had given him and had raced around the side of the house and shot past my legs, a black blur, into the house. Sigh!

So, take two. This time I made sure my gear was outside and by the front gate for Roland to put in the car before I tried the food bribe again. By the time Satchmo cleared the corner of the house I was at the gate and managed to slip out of the yard and shut him in the yard for the day. Sorry boy, but those are the house rules.

PEBBLY BEACH

We travelled south for a few hours before I turned the car on to a side road and headed east, out to the area around Jervis Bay. This was a perfect morning stop where we found a nice restaurant on the waterfront for Roland to get his morning coffee while I had a cold drink. This was to become our morning routine for the next nine days. Roland loves his coffee but I have never really acquired a taste for it. When I was teaching I used to drink coffee at school in the morning, but it was more of a social thing and I had to spike my coffee with copious amounts of sugar and milk to get it to my liking. We sat on the deck with its bright blue railings and watched as gulls competed for food bits dropped or tossed by customers of the restaurant. We looked out over Irish green grass, across dark turquoise-blue water, along a stretch of brilliant sand and to the gently rolling partially-forested hills in the distance - quite a lovely place to be. We walked along a beach for awhile then drove to a rocky headland where we were rewarded with more spectacular views. It was a good pit stop.

The day's scenery consisted of rolling hills with a cattle, horse or llama station at every turn. It is a very peaceful and beautiful area and it would be very easy to take a month travelling just seven hundred kilometres to have time to see all the parks, beaches and take in activities on the water.

Susan had highly recommended we stop at Pebbly Beach which is about an hour south of Jervis Bay. We turned off the highway and followed the paved road until we entered Murramarang Park where the road became gravelled. The well-maintained road wound its way through the gum forests of the park for eight kilometres before turning down a long and winding section to the beach. We parked the car and walked a short distance down the path where it opened onto a huge grassy area. The grass is cropped short and fertilized by the resident kangaroo population. We didn't see any kangaroos at this point so continued down the path and down a short set of stairs to the sand. Pebbly Beach is a spectacular, protected cove with a beautiful sandy beach and water that is a gorgeous tropical turquoise. We walked north towards the sea cliffs enjoying this most special and quiet place. During our two hour stay here we saw only a dozen others. We turned and walked back to the middle of the beach where Roland, who loves swimming, walked into the water and was soon swimming and body surfing in the blue and white of the ocean.

I love to explore my surroundings so set off south towards an area where the rocks come right down to the sea and lie flat against the sand like a giant patio. It was here that I came across a most wonderful collection of small tidal pools. Many were circular, small habitats for the individual plants and animals inside their circumferences. A few were shaped like whales. There was one shaped like a comma, a hot air balloon, a duck in flight, a swaddled baby and my favourite, an almost perfect heart with the number two etched in to the rock immediately above it. Inside each pool was a collection of rocks, animals and plant life. While the huge rock patios were of a more or less uniform grey the smaller rocks in these pools were a collection of greens, whites, mustard yellows, oranges and greys. They shimmered with rippling lines of light, reflected down upon them from the surface of the water. There was a delicate, pea-soup green seaweed that looked like strings of pearls fringing each pool – a never resting parade of fuzzy sea caterpillars around the edges. I was totally entranced by each and every little pool and I love the unique set of photos I have of them.

I walked back to the middle of the beach and up to the grassy area where Roland was showering off salt water and sand. He had enjoyed his swim. When I looked out over the grass to the north I saw the first of the kangaroos, then another and then some more as they moved out of the shade of the forest and down to the beach. Pebbly Beach is known as home of the "surfing kangaroos" as there is a well known photo of a kangaroo in the surf, but this is not their usual habit. I started taking pictures from a distance as I didn't know how close I'd be able to get to these animals in their natural habitat. As it turns out I didn't need to rush things as they are very used to humans and are receptive to being petted and scratched. They made their way across the beach and up the rise to the grassy area where they grazed and lazed and then sometime later bounded their way past us and into the forest on the other side of the grass. Too cool! I had added a second set of photos to my Pebbly Beach collection.

There were wild birds walking on the ground near the bushes. They were looking for insects and scratched at the ground and turned over 'roo poo' in their quest for the perfect appetizer. There were lots of crimson rosellas, a type of parrot, that have the most incredibly crimson torso and head with bright blue wings and tails. Another parrot present had a delicate pink torso with white head and grey back and tail feathers. Then there were the Australian rainbow lorikeets, an incredibly colored bird with Aegean blue heads, orange chests and beaks, yellow 'collars' and brilliant green back, wing and tail feathers. Wow, what a show! And so I added another set of photos to my collection. Still loving my digital camera!

Rejuvenated, Roland and I reluctantly left the beach, agreeing that it would be a wonderful place to rent a cabin for a week or so. It was late in the afternoon so we stopped about one hundred kilometres south of Pebbly Beach at Narooma for the night.

I was getting used to the unique Australian place names along the way and loved to say them until I got the right pronunciation. Today we had started at Wollongong and travelled through Klama, Nowra, Minnamura, Kiama, Conjola, Yatteyattah, Ulladulla, Moruya, Bodalla, Kianga and stopped in Narooma.

BUCHAN CAVES AND LAKES ENTRANCE

From Narooma, the Princes Highway travels inland as it gradually bends from its southern heading and heads west around the lower right corner of Australia. At mid-afternoon I turned right and headed up a secondary road to the small timber town of Buchan – population four hundred. Buchan is at the center of a cattle, dairy, sheep and timber region on the Buchan River. The countryside is made up of gently rolling hills that in late summer were for the most part a golden brown. A few fields were green with irrigated crops and trees often lined the borders between properties. There were cattle and sheep here and there, grazing on the already short grass – a very pastoral and peaceful scenic place.

The beautiful countryside is not the main attraction here - the Buchan Caves are. Like the other caves I had visited, they were formed a 'bajillion' years ago by underground rivers cutting through limestone rock. Once the open areas were formed, thousands of limestone formations were created by the drip, drip, dripping of water – tiny drops that each left miniscule amounts of calcium carbonate. These tiny amounts added up over another 'bajillion' years to create the stalactites and stalagmites that are the mainstay of any decent cave.

Roland did not want to tour the caves so he stayed behind at the information and camping area which has a swimming pool. While I was underground he was enjoying himself with a walk around the area and a swim. It is nice that we could travel together and each pursue our own interests.

I walked the half kilometre or so down the road then up a hillside to the entrance of the cave system. It was another sunny summer day with the temperature in the mid twenties so I was very aware of the pleasantly cool air coming out of the entrance to the cave. The cave stays at a stable seventeen degrees year round. I joined two people who were already seated on the green slatted bench by the door. Two others showed up and shortly after, our guide Amanda. Discovered in 1907, the caves have been open to the public for a hundred years.

Amanda would lead us over four hundred meters during the next hour, in a land of imaginative enchantment. We would walk upright, sometimes duck and bend our way along cramped paths, traipse up and down stairs – stairs – always lots of stairs in caves! The path was paved and smooth and a handrail seemed ever present. The handrail was useful in helping me keep my balance and also served to protect the cave from incidental contact. Amanda led us through the King's Chamber, the Queen Victoria Chamber, the Hall, the Jewel Chamber and the Grotto. In the Bridal Chamber we 'oohed' and 'awed' over the Wedding Cake whose translucent formation looks like icing sugar. I took pictures of reddish and bluish colored stalactites that hung from bulbous calcite formations. I took pictures of brown streaked 'bacon strips' that were set perfectly in front of white formations. I have pictures of white helictites; imagine that there are a thousand greyish-white straws and a hundred children have bent and twisted them, then stuck them in to the ceiling above you. Yes, crazy straws – that's what helictites are like.

To create the next scene, imagine that you have hundreds of thin pancakes around dinner plate size or slightly larger. Now take these and overlapping them slightly, lay them out end to end in two, three or four layers deep. Curve the path they take. On top of your pancake creation add several hundred people - some alone, some in twos or threes and one tightly knit bundle of a dozen. Each of them is dressed in a yellow, orange or golden robe and are tall and towards the thin side. The high hat each one is wearing is triangular like a wizard's hat. They are all standing still and quiet. The night sky is awash in shooting stars that hang frozen in time, falling straight down towards them. Now double this vision by turning it upside down in mirror image; the whole scene is reflected in absolutely-still pools of water. The soft, indirect lighting gently washes over the image before you. You are gazing upon a most magical place of wonder in Buchan Caves. I have pictures of that place - they are but reminders of the shapes and colors that I saw there. They are amateur photos. If I look at my post cards of the cave, and sit very quietly, I can put myself back into the cave, into the quiet stillness, and somehow feel that sense of awe that struck me that day.

There were many places where stalactites and stalagmites hung like reptilian teeth. There were some stalagmites that looked as if several huge champagne glasses had been raised in a single column then very thick butterscotch pudding had been poured from the highest one and had deliciously, ever so slowly, fallen and filled and overflowed the glasses below it. Mmmmmm – pudding! One collection of formations and pools ended in a massive bulge – looked like a two meter high, ten meter wide lava flow - except it was a light off-white color and much smoother than lava. Now think microscope and put a caterpillar under the lens and magnify it ten times. Change the color to off-white, and that's what the leading edge of this bulge looked like. On and on the cave went, and offered up an ever-changing parade of cool stuff to look at! Finally we had walked the four hundred meters underground and the tour was at an end.

When Amanda opened the exit door the heat of the day enveloped me and the harsh reality of sunlight caused me to pause. We had come out on the far side of the hill and now had only a short downhill walk to the information center below. I found Roland walking about the campground. We had both had a good time with our respective activities.

We headed back down Buchan Road stopping a few times to take pictures of the hilly countryside. Three quarters of an hour later we came in to Lakes Entrance which is a tourist destination and home to Australia's largest fishing fleet. This town of about six thousand people is at one end of the largest inland waterway in Australia, the Gippsland Lake system. Four large salt-water lakes and their connecting inland waterways are part of a four hundred square kilometre network that includes coastal lagoons, lakes and swamps. This huge area is a critically important habitat for many species of water birds that feed, rest and breed in this place of refuge. Roland and I would take refuge for a night at a local hostel.

After dinner I dropped Roland off at a coffee shop then parked the car on the esplanade. Lakes Entrance is buffered from the ocean by a narrow strip of land which runs unbroken for about four kilometres before a man-made channel allows access for the many boats in the area. In this protected channel there are commercial docks where I stopped and watched the days catch being unloaded from a boat. A full net would be hauled from the storage hold, swing over the side to the dock and then with a slick swoosh emptied of its cargo. The fish would then slide down into one of many plastic bags and then placed into large, white, plastic trays where they would be mixed with crushed ice and then loaded into a waiting truck destined for a packing plant. I spent about twenty minutes here watching the process and talking to the locals. It was very interesting.

The channel also has marinas, grassy areas, attractive gardens and pleasant walkways. Along the walkway there are a number of wooden sculptures carved from the trunks of trees that had died in the 1990's. Rather than totally getting rid of trees, the town commissioned a local artist, John Brady to complete a series of sculptures using the large trunks. The carvings commemorate Australian forces at war.

I meandered along the walkway for a few kilometres. Loving nature, I was happy to see and get pictures of several black swans. Then I saw the pelicans. I had seen brown pelicans before, but this was my first glimpse of Australian pelicans and I was immediately taken by their appearance. Sitting in the water they look mostly white with black taking over for the upper back as the folded black-tipped wings and black tail feathers nestle in place. Adult pelicans have a bright yellow ring around each eye. The upper back of their neck is an area of grey feathers that stick out like an army buzz cut. Their bill and saggy throat pouch are pastel pink. They have the longest bill in the avian world. When I saw them walk out of the water I noticed that their legs and feet are blue-grey in colour. I watched overhead as a few pelicans drew closer and decreased their altitude, coming in for a landing. When they near the water they have their landing gear beneath them and it is their feet that make first contact with the water marking a frothy white trail in their wake. Their wings spread wide and act like air brakes, bringing them to a gliding stop as legs sink and their weight takes them into the water. Landing takes little energy – just glide down, come into contact with the water, keep your balance, apply your brakes. Taking off on the other hand requires a bit more effort. Australia's largest flying bird begins by opening his wings to stretch out fully and wing tips almost touch over his back and then he powers them down to produce lift. This raises him high enough that his feet are now touching the surface. As he goes into his second giant wing flap he runs along the water, all the time gaining speed and altitude. After just four or five flaps and a final kick with his feet, he is air born. Once flying I could see him catching thermals and soaring to great heights above the area. Truly magnificent birds.

As I walked along the shoreline I noticed an older couple up ahead. They were sitting in low beach chairs and had fishing lines cast out into the waterway. I stopped and struck up a conversation about Lakes Entrance and fishing. Bob and Mary had caught four fish for a late dinner and would head home soon to enjoy their catch.

I turned and enjoyed the walk back to the car where I met up with Roland. We headed back to the hostel where we talked with other travellers until it was time to turn in for the night. Roland is from Germany and at every place we stayed there were other Germans for him to chat with. I don't know who was left over there to run the country, but thousands of Germans must have been in Australia at any one time.

While loading the car in the morning I noticed that we had a low tire, not flat yet, but definitely on the way. I asked the hostel staff about a place to get it repaired and after we checked out drove to the tire store. The amiable fellow said he could fix it if we came back in an hour. As it was a slow leak we drove in to town where Roland had his morning coffee and I went across the street to walk along the waterfront walkway again. Once we got back to the tire shop the fellows had us back on our way in quick time.

FIRE'S AFTERMATH

Today we would drive to Melbourne, about four hours from Lakes Entrance. Heading west out of Lakes Entrance we travelled uphill for a kilometre or so and pulled out in to a lookout that gave fabulous views. From here we saw an incredibly beautiful vista of lakes, beaches and ocean. The viewpoint looks out over the man-made channel that joins the lake system to the ocean and it was busy with morning marine traffic coming and going from the many docks in the area. There were low-lying, foliage-covered islands with deep turquoise blue waters running around them. Roland and I both added a few pictures to our memory cards.

A few hours later it was time to stop and stretch our legs at the town of Sale. I parked the car at a large park and Roland headed off in search of a good cup of coffee. Wanting a bit of a walk I headed out on the walking trails in the park which is centered on Lake Guthridge. The park is an environmental playground with opportunities to exercise and play on land and on the lake itself. I came across several areas where picnic tables have been added and people were enjoying a late lunch. It wasn't crowded so I found myself alone in many beautiful places where I could just put the world on hold and enjoy nature. There is an indigenous art path where I viewed wonderful paintings and carvings of animals. I also saw an historic powder magazine which was built in 1865; a brick building that was used to safely store explosives for use in the nearby gold fields. I loved walking around this special place and spent about ten minutes on a wooden deck built over the edge of the lake before I turned and headed back to the car.

We continued along Princes Highway to Foster where we turned south on to the road that leads to the southernmost point of the Australian mainland, Wilsons Promontory, a huge granite peninsula. The Prom, as it is known by locals, has one hundred thirty miles of spectacular coastline that is framed by massive granite headlands, forests and mountains. It was here that I would see the evidence of the fires that I had first heard about while watching the news with Heather and Mike in Auckland. With temperatures approaching fifty degrees Celsius and no rain in the area, fires killed several hundred people, destroyed millions of dollars of properties and laid waste to millions of acres of countryside. The Prom suffered fires over a quarter of its area. It had been closed for weeks and was just re-opened the Saturday we visited as the fires were finally brought under control. (Travel Luck) There would be no entry fee into the park for the next week as an incentive to get people to come back and have a look. The main visitor areas of Tidal River and Squeaky Beach were not affected by the fire and these were the only two beaches open to us. Some of the walks in the park were also open but most of the park would remain closed until repairs could be done to paths and toilet facilities and dead animals could be removed. It saddened me to know that in times of danger koala bears climb higher in the eucalyptus trees for safety; that is the worst thing to do in a fire.

As we drove through the park we could see huge swaths where the fires had raged and had left nothing but ashes and the charred remains of trees. Many of the deciduous trees leaves were still on the trees, not burned but totally dried out which left them a most delicate shade of orangey-brown. Where I got out to take some pictures, the grey ash came half way up my shoes and puffed into the air at each step. What truly amazed me was a most hardy plant that had already grown over thirty centimetres in the few weeks since the flames had decimated them. Imagine a short blackened stump, about ten to twenty centimetres tall and fifteen across. Remember Troll dolls? Well, it looked like a convention of new-growth green and orange headed Troll dolls (without the bodies), just hundreds of disembodied heads each one hoping to grow the best head of hair. These are the first plants to grow back after a fire here. At home, it is the purple fireweed.

We drove to Tidal River first where there are a general store and camp-sites. We walked alongside the river which is tea-colored due to tannin from the tea trees in the area. Ten minutes the path opened up onto the beach, another beauty. At the east end rose a high granite hill dominated by huge bare areas of rock that were streaked with black and orange. Bushes grew on flatter areas and in the creases of the hill. I could see a hiking path that was cut into the hillside about thirty meters above the sea.

Roland set off to have a swim while I walked around the west end of the beach and took pictures of it all. I approached a couple and asked if they would like me to take their picture together – but of course. Then I asked for my picture to be taken in return and the wife volunteered. Tired of being alone in most of my pictures I asked her husband to join me so now I have a picture of me on a beach, arm around a total stranger and his arm around me. I have several such pictures actually and became quite adept at 'borrowing' people. While not crowded, there were quite a few people enjoying the thirty degree weather, surfing, swimming, wading, tanning and playing in the sand.

We had enjoyed the beach for about an hour so decided to head out and drive the short distance to Squeaky Beach. Again, such a beautiful beach – massive granite rocks serving as bookends to the bright sandy arc of sand and water. The sand is composed of rounded grains of quartz that squeak when walked on. The sand remains cool to walk on as most of the sunlight is reflected off its surface. After half an hour of wading it was time to head out of the park. Day visitors were being asked to leave by seven o'clock and it was approaching that time. So we left The Prom and just from our brief two hour visit I could see why it is Victoria's best loved park.

Another two hours of road time got us to our pit stop for the next two nights, Melbourne. We stayed with a nice young couple, Amber and Adrian; Amber is the daughter of one of Roland's friends. Adrian is a huge fan of the Hawthorn Hawks footie team. This is Australian football, a fast-paced contact sport with high scoring and lots of physical interference among the players. There is no padding for the players and possession of the ball is in dispute most of the time. The object is to get the ball by any means and kick it between posts at either end of the field. I have seen it played on television a few times and watched a live game back home. It is a great spectator sport and I can see why it has such a huge following in Australia. We spent the evening talking and watching sports on TV.

MELBOURNE

After a simple breakfast we set out on a neighbourhood walk. Amber and Adrian live in St. Kilda, a fashionable suburb about five kilometres south of Melbourne's city center. This area is a very special place: it is close to the city, has gorgeous beaches, music venues, restaurants, and is located on a very beautiful part of Hobson's Bay. St. Kilda has a famous fun fair, Luna Park. The beckoning entrance is a huge smiling moon face – white with an orange and yellow spiked hairstyle, prominent nose, dark lines showing smile wrinkles, bright blue eyes and a top row of brilliant white teeth which you walk under as you enter this popular tourist destination.

There was a lot of activity in St. Kilda on this beautiful, warm, summer Sunday. We shared the streets with hundreds of other like-minded people and after a short time crossed the last busy street before the beach and walked onto the esplanade. This is another wonderful waterfront area with the walkway paved in earth-tone bricks, a six foot wide board walk running along one side of it, and then the beach meeting the white surf and blue water of the bay. As at home, there were a lot of people walking and running along the paths.

One of Melbourne's popular Sunday attractions is St. Kilda's Esplanade Market. Almost two hundred artists come here to sell their work every Sunday of the year. It was a perfect Sunday morning at the market. The smell of the ocean and of sweet treats intermingled with that of sausages from food vendors in the area. I could hear screams of delight and fear from people enjoying the rides at neighbouring Luna Park.

The work of the artisans was of high quality. I found the usual fare of items for sale: leather work, scarves, jewellery, clothing, hats, beauty products, kids' toys and paintings. Individual stalls sold: an array of Australian body scrubs, boomerangs, juggling supplies, wooden dice, puppets, marionettes, metal animals. No two items were the same – all hand-crafted and unique. It was a lot of fun to see unique items at the market and had I the space back home, more dispensable income and a free shipping offer I could have dropped hundreds of dollars here. As it was, I turned off impulse shopping and took a number of pictures instead – always asking permission first of course.

Amber and Adrian were heading out to a barbeque for the rest of the day. Roland and I decided to go in to Melbourne instead of going with them. We had different itineraries so while Roland was able to hitch a ride with them and be dropped off near the famous cricket stadium I was going to take the tram downtown.

The tram stop was only half a block from their house so I was there in short time. I was confident that I was at the right stop but in order to strike up a conversation I asked the only other person waiting if this was the tram in to Federation Square.

"Yes, you are at the right place." Craig was in his twenties, a slim fellow with dark eyes, close cropped black hair and wore a blue striped rugby shirt and jeans. We fell into an easy flowing conversation and continued once on the tram. Craig changed his plans and said he would come to the square with me and show me around the downtown area. How sweet is that? I was very taken with this gesture; I realized that I have often done the same thing back home in Victoria. What goes around comes around. Karma! We got off the tram and immediately noticed several older people dressed in bright red jackets. We walked over to Fran, one of a dozen or more tourist information volunteers in the area. Fran was in her sixties, had short, curly white hair tucked under a straw hat and wore glasses and a welcoming smile. In addition to her red jacket she had on a matching red shirt, a lanyard identification tag, a fanny pack that was overflowing with maps and pamphlets and carried a clipboard. We chatted for a few minutes and when we left her we had a map of downtown, a few pamphlets and a warm feeling. What a great ambassador for Melbourne!

Craig showed me around the downtown core pointing out various landmarks. One of the most endearing buildings is the Flinders Street Station, one of Melbourne's most recognized landmark buildings. It is the best known railway station in Australia. It is a very long three to four story building that dominates the view when you are anywhere near it. It is a deep golden yellow and is topped with three interesting domes at one end and by a clock tower at the other. Craig and I climbed up the steps to the main entrance and stood under the nine clocks that indicate the departure times of the trains. More than ten thousand suburban trains come and go from the station each week – that's about one every minute! Platform one is an unbelievable seven hundred eight meters long – the fourth longest in the world!

Next, Craig took me across the street to Federation Square, a cultural precinct on the edge of downtown Melbourne. Well, knock my socks off and get out the camera! This collection of buildings has some of the most unique architecture that I have ever witnessed. How on Earth to describe it? The main geometric shape is the triangle. Thousands upon thousands of triangles – cleverly put together to form walls that rise in non-square shapes, walls that hang off inner skeletons, walls that are made of glass and Earth-tone ceramic tiles that are framed by silver metal. The buildings contain cinemas, exhibition area, bars, shops, restaurants, art galleries and a museum. The huge areas of open space around and between the buildings are paved with four hundred seventy thousand ochre colored tiles which are an undulating work of art. I absolutely loved all of it! Apparently the square was very controversial with the citizens of Melbourne because of its architecture, cost and delay in completion. It was finished in 2002, originally scheduled for January 1, 2001, the centenary of Australian federation. People got used to it quickly however and soon, the majority of them reported liking it. (In 2009 it was voted fifth ugliest building in the world by members of the website Virtual Tourist). It is Victoria's second most popular tourist attraction and a very popular place for performances, celebrations, protests, cultural gatherings and as a place to meet and just hang out.

Craig and I were here to take in the sixth annual Thai Culture and Food Festival which is a celebration of Thailand's culture. Hundreds of people were here to visit the many stalls with Thai arts and crafts, tourism and food, and to watch kick boxing, amazing cultural shows, and a beauty contest. We slowly made our way through the square enjoying all the festivities. We passed through the crowds and made our way down a flight of stairs to the food stalls. The aroma of Thai food: sizzling chicken, vegetables and noodles, permeated our senses and we realized how hungry we were. We stopped at a vendor and ordered chicken satays and beverages.

We walked over to the grassy slope that borders the Yarra River, sat down and enjoyed our meal. The Yarra River passes through Melbourne and is very beautiful lined with trees, restaurants, galleries, museums and grassy parks. We saw the frequent passing of water taxis and river boats. It is a pleasant river, full of life and activity.

While we were having lunch Craig got a call from his partner who had been having some troubling pain with gall stones. He was in distress and needed to be taken to the emergency room at the hospital so regrettably, Craig had to leave. We parted friends and unfortunately didn't exchange contact information. But what a wonderful time we had together – and it all started with a simple question, "Am I at the right tram stop?"

I crossed the Yarra River on a pedestrian bridge and roamed through a few shops and walked along the waterfront before crossing back over the river on another bridge. I returned to Federation Square and watched a dozen young Thai performers on the main stage. Then it was time for the final parade of beautiful young ladies who were in the beauty contest. They were dressed in shimmering, glimmering traditional Thai costumes of blue, green, hot pink, pastels and white. Each was adorned with gold earrings, necklaces, arm bands and headpieces. The teary-eyed winner was crowned Miss Songkran and a huge cheer and round of applause rose from the appreciative audience. With that finale, I left Federation Square and headed the few blocks up the street to the tram station. It had been a wonderful afternoon. I got off the tram at St. Kilda and stopped for a simple supper in one of the many restaurants. It was dark when I got back home to an empty house. Roland, Amber and Adrian returned about a half hour later. We talked about our separate ventures of the day, watched some sports on TV then went to bed.

MELBOURNE TO THE GREAT OCEAN ROAD

O n this, my third Monday in Australia, I would leave Melbourne with
Roland. We thanked Amber and Adrian for a lovely stay. I presented them with a baby jumper and a scarf with the Hawks logo on them,
both in the gold and brown of the team. Adrian was beyond thrilled and
said the baby would wear them all the time if he had his way. It had taken
shopping in eight stores before I found any Hawks wear so I was very
happy that the gift was a hit. We finished packing up the car then headed
south on the east side of Melbourne's huge harbour. We drove a third
of the way around the circle that is formed by Hobson's Bay to Sorrento
where we got on the ferry that carried us across the entrance to the bay
and deposited us on the west side of the channel. We drove to Anglesea
which is a lovely resort town near the eastern end of the Great Ocean
Road. I walked along the beach to stretch my legs and take a few pictures,
while Roland went off in search of a good cup of coffee.

From Anglesea to Lorne the road is very scenic: fantastic beaches,
quaint towns and mountains marching down from the continent right
into the sea. There are a lot of great surfing beaches along this stretch of
coast and we stopped at world famous Bell's Beach where the Rip Curl
Pro competition is held every Easter. Roland was really happy to be here
and we walked around the trails together, took pictures and admired the
few surfers who were out playing in the waves. The warning sign told of:
strong currents, high surf, submerged objects and unstable cliffs – an area
for experienced swimmers only.

Our next stop was at the small town of Aireys Inlet. We parked the
car near Split Rock lighthouse, a thirty-four meter white tower with a red
roof. It was closed for the day but we enjoyed the expansive beach views
along the coastline. There is a huge limestone formation just off the coast,
a piece that has split away from the shore. It is shaped like a huge three-
tiered birthday cake with a thick layer of icing enveloping impossibly

thick candles. The late afternoon light made the golden color richer and it rose in beautiful contrast to the blues of the ocean and sky in the background. This was our first of many outstanding rock formations that we were going to see along The Great Ocean Road.

Just a few minutes further along the road we came to The Great Ocean Road Gateway, the fourth one constructed at this site. The other gates were lost to a fire, a truck crash and the first one had been taken down once the road toll was removed. Rising from rock foundations, the side pillars are each made of four large logs that support longer logs that span the road some seven meters above the road surface.

Roland and I parked the car and walked to the memorial gate. One plaque reads "This road was built to commemorate the services of sailors and soldiers in the Great War 1914-1918." There is a monument of two diggers complete with shovel, pick and wheelbarrow full of rocks on site. This is a reminder that this road was not built using machinery, but was hacked out of sometimes vertical rock faces by hand. The road was constructed by over three thousand returned soldiers spanning a fourteen year period. The road is serpentine and twists and turns for two hundred forty-three kilometres, one of the world's most scenic drives.

Roland had been telling me for months that he was very excited about getting the chance to come here again and to show me this spectacular coastline. After seeing split rock, I was really looking forward to it too. My dad always loved the Oregon coast and we spent many holidays camping along its rugged shoreline. This coast was already bringing back memories of Haystack Rock and my childhood trips.

While the distance can be covered in a single day, I can't imagine anyone who would ever want to do that. Roland and I planned to spend three nights along the coast. We continued to the town of Lorne where we checked in to a gem of a hostel that was nestled in trees on a hillside. Roland shared his dorm with two others while I had my room to myself for the first night here. The cockatoos were the highlight of the hostel. These are a very common bird in Australia and many consider them to be pests. But to me, someone who sees seagulls, robins, ducks and crows a lot at home, they were an absolute delight! Of course I started snapping pictures from quite a distance and again found out that they would come right up to people and take any offered food right out of a person's hand. Feeding of the birds or any wildlife is discouraged, and I can understand how having fifty of these large white 'poopers' on the deck and picnic tables could leave quite an awful mess. But I was enthralled and spent a long time just watching them as they perched on the railing just a meter away from me. I have some really great close up pictures of these almost all white birds. These were the sulphur topped cockatoos, so named for the yellow upward curve of feathers that rise from the back of their heads. I found them rather regal in white 'formal' wear, each with a little puff of white feathers that came forward from their cheeks and ruffled against each side of their black beaks. On some unknown signal to me, they took off in unison, gathered in a white blur of motion and set off for the tree tops not far away. There they carried on loud conversations until once more they took flight and set off on a new adventure or came back a few hours later to the hostel hoping for new 'untrained' tourists who would offer them a bite to eat.

We drove into town and past it for a few kilometres before turning around and then stopping at the Lorne Pier. We were hoping to find a restaurant at the north end of Lorne but had no luck with our search. What we did find was a lovely pier which we walked on and were rewarded with a grand view of Louttit Bay as well as a nice view looking back along the curved and sandy waterfront of Lorne. We drove back to town where we found a small restaurant and had our evening meal. We talked about plans for the next day. I wanted to drive out to the Otway Fly Treetop Walk and also take a walk in to Triplett Falls while Roland, who doesn't really like heights, elected to stay back in Lorne for the day. So with plans in place we headed back to the hostel where we talked with some fellow travellers until it was time to turn in.

TREETOP ADVENTURE AND WATERFALL WALK

After a refreshing sleep I walked down the stairs, across the large deck and into the communal kitchen. I enjoyed the usual breakfast of lemon yogurt and museli and a perfectly ripened banana. Today, I would be on my own as Roland had decided to stay in Lorne. I looked for him in his room, the kitchen and the grounds of the hostel but had no success, so without saying goodbye for the day I set out alone and drove west along the winding, cliff-hanging road. The coastal views are spectacular and I was tempted to take glances more often than I should. I pulled into lookouts where possible to take pictures. After forty minutes I arrived at Skenes Creek and turned the car right, now heading inland. I was going to experience the Otway Fly Treetop Walk and take a hike in to Triplett Falls. This is a very pretty drive up into the forested hills. The next hour of driving was with hands at ten and two and paying very close attention to every dip and curve. The road engineers had spared every tree possible which is fantastic. However, this meant that the road was very tight and narrow and often single lane width with dirt pullouts for passing oncoming traffic. There was no shoulder; the blacktop was laid down as close as possible to the base of the trees without doing them any harm. Of course it turned and twisted its way around preserved trees and that meant my speed averaged fifteen kilometres an hour and never got greater than thirty kilometres an hour over the total distance of twenty kilometres. It was an up close and personal tour, an absolutely beautiful drive through the ancient trees of a rain forest; I loved it!

Then there were the logging trucks. Having lived in British Columbia my whole life, and having travelled to some out-of-the-way places, I am somewhat familiar with logging trucks and logging roads. The road I now found myself on was posted with warning signs that logging trucks use the road. Logging trucks? Surely they were kidding! The massive trucks of British Columbia would never fit on this little road; even the cabs would find it a tight squeeze on this narrow track. I imagined the trucks here would be substantially smaller. Still they were bound to be a whole lot bigger than my little red Toyota. As it turns out I never came face to face with one but found myself driving a little more cautiously because of the potential hazard.

After that amazing forest drive I came to the treetop walk, pulled into the parking lot and found a shady spot for the car. At the information center I bought my ticket and picked up a map. The Otway Treetop walk is the longest and tallest of its kind in the world. Imagine yourself half a football field high at the highest point, and walking on a metal pathway that is six football fields long. To get to this remarkable structure I would walk a kilometre downhill along a wide path. The path started its gentle descent almost immediately, something that my knees could easily handle. A few hundred meters along the path I turned left on to an optional Prehistoric Loop. This path was narrower and wound its way snugly through the trees of the rainforest. I rounded a corner and came face to face with the first of the dinosaur replicas nestled around the trees, a Tyrannosaurus Rex, staring right at me. This walk could be frightening for some people! The dinosaur models were not large averaging two or three meters long, but had been crafted with attention to detail in shape and coloring. A few more meters along the path and I came across a Triceratops protecting her large eggs. The replicas were a reminder that dinosaurs had lived here, had walked in this very area. I enjoyed this short diversion and I'm sure it must be a hit with the kids.

As I continued down the path, the people coming up my way were trudging along, breathing heavily as they paid the price for having been able to walk downhill at the beginning of their journey. Uh oh - again, "What have I gotten my knee into?" Well, I was going to do this walk and knew I'd make it back up to the visitor center somehow, sometime.

Another ten minutes of walking down through the forest and I was at the end of the path. A small sign - Entrance to Otway Fly Treetop Walk - directed me on to a five foot wide boardwalk. I walked a few meters around a gentle corner to the left where there was a large covered deck for groups to gather. Just off the far side of this deck I stepped on to the metal grating of the walk and began walking slightly uphill. It was a welcome change to be walking uphill after the long walk downhill. The Otway Fly is a marvel of engineering; it is a steel structure, six hundred meters long, averaging twenty-five meters above the forest floor. The sides are made of shoulder-high wired fence which allows a great view at all times while providing safety. The floor is made of open mesh so you can see the forest floor beneath your feet if you choose to and it flexes slightly as you walk along. This makes some people uneasy and I noticed a few people who would not look down as they made their way along the walkway.

Where sufficient light gets through the trees, the forest floor is covered with ferns growing in spherical shapes, clusters of beautiful green on an otherwise brown landscape. By tower one which is nine meters above the forest floor, I was already feeling a part of the Myrtle Beech and gum forest. The gum trees have ramrod straight trunks, devoid of branches until their canopies spread out, high above the forest floor. Massively long strips of rust-colored, thin, bark hung from their trunks as if some giant had come along with a carrot peeler and carefully stripped the bark away but left it still attached.

By tower two I was six meters higher and I stopped at a large observation area and listened to the few birds that were around and tried to spot them in the trees. There was an information sign about the birds in the area; scrubwrens, treecreepers, rosellas, yellow robins, kookaburras, but I didn't see more than a hint of motion here and there. I don't imagine that the birds like all the people and noise on the walkway.

By Tower five, I was at the path's highest point. Tower five is also the location of the Spiral Tower, a structure that rises forty-seven meters above the forest floor and brings you level with the forest canopy. The spiral staircase wraps four times around a central pole which is a meter in diameter. Up the one hundred or so stairs I climbed, carefully passing people on their way down. The staircase was reminiscent of the staircases I had taken up lighthouses, the difference being that these stairs were wrapped around the outside of the metal core while those in the lighthouses are usually hung from the inside wall of the enclosed towers. But the result is the same - I was taken to a place with spectacular views. Forty-seven meters is pretty high. I live in a modest two-story house and have ventured on to the roof on several occasions for maintenance purposes. This was as if I was standing on the roof of six of my houses, stacked in apartment style. Now in line with the forest canopy I got a different view of the magnificent dense forest dominated by Eucalyptus, Mountain Ash, Blackwood and Myrtle Beech trees. From here I imagined what it must be like to be a bird and have the power of flight - to be able to rise and then swoop down among the trees twisting and turning with a slight wing adjustment. I often have dreams in which I am flying and I really love it. Yes, to be a bird would be very interesting, but I really wouldn't want to give up my opposable thumb anatomy. I walked around the large circular observation deck several times and made lengthy stops along the way. With its protective fence and umbrella-like roof, it looks as though someone has stuck a gazebo high on a pole in the middle of the forest – well, I guess that someone has done precisely that!

From the lookout I could see three metal paths. One was the route I had taken to get here, one was the way to continue on the clockwise route and the third was the path to a springboard cantilever. I was satisfied with my time up in the tower so made my way back down to the base of the tower and turned to my left and out on to the cantilevered path. A cantilever has no direct supports under it. This path is similar to a diving board in that it is well anchored at one end, but the rest of it just hangs in the air. It was marvellous to bounce along this steel structure as it dangles out over Young's Creek, twenty-five meters below. I spent some time at the end of it, standing still and feeling the motion that others created as they came then left this remarkable place. After a few minutes out there, I headed back to the tower, turned left and continued my walk. The path now started its gradual descent and I walked through the various levels of the forest until my foot left the steel and I felt earth underfoot. A sense of wonder and gratitude filled me for where I had just been. What a unique experience. I felt closer to the forest and nature than when I had started my walk. Now there were two choices, to return back over the walkway or to continue on the forest floor back to the entrance. I chose to take the forest floor path. I had spent a lot of time on high and now wanted to be close to what I had seen from the walkway. The path wound along Young's Creek and through the forest. I got a new perspective of the walkway as I looked up at it. Again I was struck by the great engineering and the minimal impact of the supporting structures on the forest it showcases. I liked the forested walk that took me back to the bottom of the main path. Now it would be all uphill for the next kilometre but I knew that I could do it if I took my time and locked my knees in place at every step to reduce the stress on them.

On my trip down to the walkway an open-sided vehicle carrying passengers had passed me a few times. Then I knew that I could make it back to the top for sure, even if I had to ride. Now I was struggling with this decision – to ride or 'grind' it out at the expense of my knees. I felt a bit embarrassed at the idea of taking a ride – 'it's my own fault for having bad knees. I'm too big and I should be walking to get more exercise!' So I came up with a plan. There is a pickup spot a hundred meters or so from the walkway where people waited for the 'bus'. If there weren't too many people waiting for a ride and I wouldn't take someone else's place, then I would 'cave' and get a ride. As it turns out there were only enough people to fill half the seats, so with only a little bit of guilt I got on board and was whisked away up the kilometre long hill. At the top, my knees felt great – so that's how I rationalized the easy way up.

It was lunch time and I stepped into the restaurant where I ordered a sandwich and diet Coke. I carried my tray to an outside table and asked an older couple if I could join them – of course. David and Lily were travelling from Melbourne to Adelaide to visit their daughter and grandchildren. They had never been to the walkway as it's a bit of a drive off the main road. They had decided to take the time to come here on this trip and had really enjoyed themselves. Now armed with some new toys for the grand kids from the gift shop they were ready to continue their trip. We talked about families and holidays and of course travelling. Dropping in on strangers for a meal like that gave me some delightful times that I would have missed out on if I hadn't learned to say "Hi, I'm on holiday alone. May I join you?" Everyone really seemed happy to share their time and stories with me. You really should try it sometime, even if you're in your home town.

Spiritually and physically satisfied I left the treetop walk and continued along the road I had arrived on. A short three kilometre drive took me to the parking area for the Triplett Falls walk. These spectacular falls are an iconic site for visitors to Otway National Park. This was a walk that I would take my trekking poles on, as my research had indicated there were some steep sections along the way. I retrieved them from the trunk and telescoped them out to the purple lines I had marked on their shafts – just the right length for me. Next I put my green and black fanny pack around my waist, clipped on my camera, deposited my water bottle in its holder and started off.

During the next hour and a half I would encounter only three others on the trail. It was wonderfully amazing to be walking through this rainforest alone - it swallowed me and the rest of the world faded away. There was only this time and this place. I was at peace.

Soon into the walk I was so very thankful I had my poles. There are a lot of steep places and they gave me balance and stability as I walked down the trail with its many, many steps. "Here I go again. Descending means I'll be puffing uphill later on. I'll be okay - I'm not in any hurry. I can do this." Walking through the dense forest was quiet and mystical. I didn't see many birds or other wildlife but there was a varied selection of magnificent trees, plants and fungi everywhere.

The path had gone through a recent re-construction due to some vandalism a few years back. Many trees had been severely cut and damaged with chainsaws. It is thought that some people who are pro logging and anti parks may have done it but they have not caught the guilty persons. I didn't notice any evidence of the destruction as I didn't know about it before the walk. The two million dollars worth of work that had been done and the rapid re-growth of the forest made the path and its surrounds pristine. The path itself had many places that were slightly raised on steel mesh sections. There were also a lot of places with the mesh flush with the ground to keep the path less muddy and to stabilize it when it rained; it rains a lot in a rainforest. With all this in place, the path was in superb condition and it was easy and safe to walk on. Where side rails are needed instead of using bulky wood, they have used curving metal uprights that look a bit like the ribs of a giant whale lying upside down. Between the uprights are strung pencil-thin wires so that the whole effect does not detract greatly from the setting and the views. It has an open, airy quality.

After half an hour I could hear the faint sound of water rushing along. Very soon I would be at the falls. The path widens at the falls and has several areas to stop at and view the falls from different angles. I stopped at the first one and was able to look down to Young's Creek cascading along through the forest. This is the same creek that I saw on the treetop walk. The sound of water was getting louder and at the next elevated viewing platform I got my first view of the falls. The water runs down the face of a very wide rock face that splits the falls in to three broad cascades of water that seem to appear from nowhere out of the rainforest. Framed by bright green ferns it all seemed very tropical. A slow shutter speed on the camera softens the falling water and the place seems even more serene and magical. I love standing still, closing my eyes and just listening to waterfalls, trying to figure out where the different sounds are coming from. "Which boulder makes that splash? And how about that softer sound I hear now? Where is the most water falling? The least?" During this time I also inhale - huge gulps of air - so I can smell, almost taste the forest that envelops me. Wet foliage and earth have a special smell. We have all experienced the freshness that follows a spring rain. It is that freshness that enveloped my senses as I stood near the base of Triplett Falls.

I moved on to the other viewing platforms and repeated my routine at each stop. Pictures successfully stored on my memory card I reluctantly left the falls and began the long uphill climb back to the car park. Two thirds remained of the path so this meant that this part was less steep than the trip coming down to the falls. This was a continuation of a beautifully spent time in the ancient rain forest and I really enjoyed my surroundings. One of the interpretive signs along the way explained that there used to be a timber mill in this forest. Logging peaked around 1960 and has declined ever since so the trees have had fifty unhindered years to grow and are now protected in Otway National Park. With my poles I was able to easily make it back to the car where I sat for a moment and replayed the walk in my mind as I looked at the photos I had taken.

Satisfied with my two stops I now turned and headed back the way I had come along Phillips Track and then along the windy and stupefying Beech Forest Mount Sabine Road. After a time the road wound its way down and around the hills back to sea level and the town of Skenes Creek. I had only driven about a hundred kilometres but I had been a whole world away from the captivating ocean seascapes that are all that most people see along here. Roland is good company, but I had been on my own for the first six weeks of my trip. Roland talks a lot, and he is interesting to listen to but to be in the close confines of a car with him was a bit overwhelming for me and my somewhat addled brain. I was so very glad that I had a day to myself and that I had made the effort to visit these two inland Otway attractions.

In Kennett River, a small coastal town, I pulled off the highway to my left on to Grey River Road. I had read somewhere that the area around town was a koala sanctuary so I pulled into the local store's parking lot and was going to go inside to ask about them. I didn't get into the store as my attention was caught by several kookaburras sitting on the railing just in front. This was my first sighting of these birds in the wild and they looked much healthier than the ones I had seen at Australia Zoo. I moved slowly so as not to disturb them and soon found out that it was impossible to deter them from staying around the store. They had learned that this was a place of people and food and a few of them would come right up and take food from your hand. There were half a dozen or so that stayed close by while I asked about the koalas.

"I hear that I might be able to see koalas around here. Do you know where I might find them?"

"Turn around." Pointing to first one tree then another and another, the lady told me to walk over to any of them and look up.

"Look in the branches where several come together and make a fork. The koalas will be sitting and sleeping at this time of day."

True to her words I saw two of these cute bears in the first two trees I looked at. There was just a big burst of happy in my heart and I was smiling broadly as I watched with binoculars and took some pictures. Then I walked up the road for a few hundred meters and saw some more. I had loved holding Anna in Kuranda but it was special to see koalas in the wild. That's just the way it is with animal sightings as I know they should be in the wild, in their natural habitats.

When I got back to the hostel I found Roland sitting out on the deck talking to a few young travellers. I said hi to them and to Roland. The girls said hello, but nothing from Roland. Not a hi, hello, how was your day – nothing, he didn't even make eye contact with me. He continued talking with the others and I didn't push him on talking to me. He never did tell me why I got the cold shoulder but I was to learn this was his way of acting sometimes if things weren't to his liking. Perhaps he was angry because I hadn't found him in the morning to say goodbye. We had talked about our plans the day before – several times - and had agreed that I would go to Otway on my own and he wanted to stay in Lorne. I let it slide and after a few hours he talked to me again. I have a world of patience and would find myself waiting him out on several other occasions.

With darkness settling in I was looking for something to do other than more reading so I looked at the movie offering of the local theatre and went to see 'He's Just Not That Into You'. It was light fare, easy to follow and a nice way to end the day.

GREAT OCEAN ROAD

Roland and I met in the kitchen the next morning with everything back to normal between us. After breakfast we checked out of this pleasant hostel, packed up the car and headed out along the picturesque coastal drive. The highway between Lorne and Apollo Bay is absolutely awesome. I know that is a tired word, but in all fairness the scenery inspired awe at every glimpse. The Great Ocean Road winds its way along the cliffs, climbs out onto headlands, and passes through rainforests offering a huge range of visually stunning beauty.

In places this road has been cut into sheer cliffs - on the right side of the road they shot upward and on the left they dropped off dramatically into the ocean. Just a reminder - I was driving on the left side of the road so often had nothing but a short guard rail between us and a gravity-induced plunge. Sometimes there was no rail at all. Hands at ten and two, eyes on the road, Joan. When we got to Kennett River I pulled in so Roland could have a look at the kookaburras and koalas by the store. We drove up Grey River Road for a few kilometres and managed to see more koalas in the eucalyptus trees.

Our next destination was Cape Otway, a fourteen kilometre drive south off the main road. Much of the land around the cape is part of the Otway National Forest. A short distance in to this 'detour' I noticed a few people and cars stopped up on the road ahead. Back in Canada this means only one thing – an unexpected wildlife opportunity. I slowed the car and pulled off to the side behind some other vehicles. There he was, a lone koala on the side of the road. A lone koala that was drinking water off the road. A girl was pouring water from a bottle for him and his little pink tongue was lapping up what he could. This is not usual koala behaviour. They usually stay in trees and get whatever moisture they need from the eucalyptus leaves they eat. He appeared quite thin and was obviously dehydrated. It was so hard for me not to pick him up and give him water directly from a bottle – but I knew he was wild and shouldn't be handled. The group of us thought he needed some special care; someone called animal rescue as Roland and I were about to leave. We later learned that he had been taken to a shelter where he would be cared for, then returned to the wild when ready. So a good end to the story.

In the mid 1800's there was great concern over shipwrecks in the area of Cape Otway so a lighthouse was built. It is made of sandstone, was completed in 1848 and is the oldest surviving, officially built lighthouse on mainland Australia. Roland did not want to pay the entry fee into this heritage site as he had visited it before, so he stayed back with the car and bought a coffee and did some reading.

The complex is a large one and has not only the lighthouse, but a telegraph station, keeper's residence, assistant keeper's cottage and lighthouse station along with several other buildings. I wandered through several of the historic buildings before making my way out to the lighthouse which is perched on the edge of towering sea cliffs. The white conical structure is only twenty meters tall, but its location makes it visible from over twenty-five nautical miles away. I walked down the sealed path between the short white fences that form a corridor for visitors - an effective way to keep people on the path. Soon I was at the lighthouse. I stepped through the doorway and glanced up at the red, spiral staircase that wound its way upward. When I reached the top I stopped and talked to Bruce, a guide who was sitting inside at his station. I have a great picture of the two of us sharing smiles and information. I left Bruce and stepped out on to the observation deck that circles around just below the lens. The railing matched the red of the stairs and is the only part of the building outside that is not white. I 'borrowed' another husband and asked him to please take a picture of his wife and me together on the deck. Another 'perfect stranger' picture for my collection. Of course, I took a picture of them together first.

The view from the lighthouse is stupendous – 'so great in size or force or extent as to elicit awe'; vast stretches of ocean and sky, plunging cliffs, sandy beaches and patio expanses of wave-washed black rocky areas. I stood on the deck for quite some time, taking in the sheer magnitude of it all and gulping in huge amounts of sea air. I finally tore myself away, entered the tower and descended the red stairs back to the reality of being a tourist. I stopped at the little shop and bought some picture- perfect post cards before finding Roland and driving away from this wonderful place.

The road took an occasional turn inland and we would find ourselves passing through gently rolling hills and small flat-bottomed valleys where we saw crops and livestock. Then back to the ocean, always back to the ocean. This next stretch of road offered up the most amazing limestone rock formations. They are formed by the relentless forces of nature. Pounding waves and blasting winds erode the cliff face, leaving harder rock as headlands that jut out into the ocean. On each side of these headlands, waves continue to crash upon and eat away at the rock, forming a cave on each side. The water eventually eats through the last bit of rock between the caves and an arch is formed. This is how Island Archway and London Bridge were formed, along with many other arches in the area.

The most famous of these rock stacks (or I like to call them rock stars) are The Twelve Apostles. There aren't twelve of them - apparently the name was changed from Sow and Piglets to The Twelve Apostles to entice more tourists to the area. Erosion eventually causes the stacks to collapse into the ocean - in 2005 another Apostle was lost into the sea. These are stacks of varying heights and widths that are isolated from land. They stand out in the ocean as testament to the solid landforms that were here millions of years ago. Imagine a humongous lasagne with all its beautiful layers cast in shades of soft gold and brown. This is the cliff that runs along the shore. Now take a huge slice of that forty-five meter tall pasta dish and carefully transport it a hundred meters off shore. Steady your hand as you place it on the ocean floor to keep it upright. Now repeat this process so there are many of these off-shore pieces. That's where my artist's imagination took my brain while viewing this most intriguing place on The Great Ocean Road. Maybe I was hungry? Each and every stack is similar yet unique. They seemed to glow in the late afternoon light. They were surrounded by a multitude of turquoise blues in the ocean that frothed white around them and onto the sandy beaches. More blue in the sky completed the background for this remarkable creation of nature. Well done! Roland and I took lots of pictures here as did the other visitors. With an erosion rate of two centimetres per year these stacks will have all tumbled by the year 4050. Not to alarm you, but if you want to see them, better sooner than later.

We continued across the breadth of Port Campbell National Park, making frequent stops to walk to the ocean and experience The Blowhole, Thunder Cave and secluded bays. We talked all the way to Port Campbell about the marvellous features that we had seen that day. We found two beds in an adequate hostel and had dinner in a small hole-in-the-wall restaurant. Good food at a good price.

Port Campbell is situated on the waterfront at the end of a deep U-shaped cove that is bound on both sides by tall headlands. I went out for a drive after supper and went west of the city to the taller of the two headlands. The sun was low in the sky and provided great lighting for my pictures of the town. There is a wonderful system of paths along this scenic headland and I meandered around on them for about a half hour before returning to the car. Now I turned the car back east and drove through the town and out onto the headland on the opposite side of the cove. Again, I set out along a path and wound my way to the cliff's edge. I watched five surfers who were catching a lot of waves just out of the cove. As any mom, I thought it was time for them to be heading in as the light was fading. They kept on catching wave after wave until I had trouble finding them in the increasing darkness. Then with the knowledge they had picked up over many hours surfing here, they rode their last wave the final hundred meters safely back into the cove. I made my way back to the car and settled in at the hostel talking to my two roommates before turning in.

Today would be our last on The Great Ocean Road. We set out from Port Campbell shortly after breakfast, found a coffee for Roland and drove west up the hill that took us away from town. I stopped at the headland I had visited the previous evening so Roland could look at the view and take some pictures.

Not far from Port Campbell we stopped at London Arch. For many years it had stood as a double arch masterpiece of nature and was called London Bridge as it looked like its namesake. Everything changed on January 15, 1990 when the land-side arch unexpectedly collapsed, leaving its mate alone, isolated from the mainland, as a single arch with a new name. Two tourists were out on the sea side end of the bridge when it happened and were rescued by helicopter – what a story they would have! There were no injuries in the incident. I actually got a bit jealous when I heard about their adventure. I would have loved to have been able to walk out to the far end of London Bridge – imagine the picture possibilities!

With a dozen pictures taken we hopped back into the car for a very short drive to the last of the erosion-created features on our tour here. The Grotto is a hidden gem. Access to it requires a walk from the car park of a few hundred meters to the cliff edge. Still no sign of The Grotto, but now I could see the top of the stair system. Roland stayed at the top as he had seen The Grotto before and didn't want to go down again. That is a difference with him and me – I would walk down those stairs at each and every opportunity just to be able to spend time in that special place. I joined a few others as we wound down and around the stair cases that had been so cleverly attached to the cliff side. Still no sign of any grotto or cave. Upwards climbing people encouraged me to keep going down – it would be worth it. And it was. I finally rounded a corner in the rock and walked out on to a viewing platform where I could see The Grotto. It is a serene place – a hole in the rock face frames a view of a calm tidal pool with the more active ocean beyond it. I stayed until there were no others to share this place with and then enjoyed every second I had it to myself. When I heard others coming down, I turned and began my climb. Now it was my turn to tell the new comers to keep going – it would be worth it.

We had our lunch break at Portland where we got our last view of the ocean. Portland has a protected marina along a river-like body of water. Tied to the dock that ran along one side of the harbour were fishing boats, sailboats, pleasure boats – eight foot dinghies to eighty foot commercial vessels. White was the dominant color but splashes of green, red and blue dotted the line up of boats. Roland and I walked along the marina's wooden dock and talked with a few people tending to their boats. One fellow was a third generation fisherman and was busy cleaning his boat and getting his gear ready for an up-coming trip. We wished him good luck, then turned and made our way back to the car.

I pulled the car over in town to take a picture of a bottle shop, what we call liquor stores back home. This was one of many drive-through shops that I saw on my trip. My drive-through shopping has been limited to fast food places and I have never noticed a drive-through liquor store back home. But then again, I hardly ever drink alcohol so my shopping experience is very limited. Motorists simply drive right into the store, entering through one wall, making their purchase while staying in their vehicle, then exit through an adjacent wall.

We had called ahead and reserved two spots at a hostel in the small town of Penola. We found the place without too much difficulty but when we pulled closer to park the general upkeep of the building's exterior wasn't at all encouraging. The interior was even less impressive. Many hostels are used as temporary accommodation by seasonal workers and this one was being used by a group of hard working young people. They were busy in the fields harvesting onions and potatoes, hundreds of pounds of onions and potatoes - every day. They would come back to the hostel very tired and very dirty from a hard day's work. The kitchen hadn't had a good cleaning in quite some time - dirty dishes in the sink, on the grimy counters, on the food-streaked stove. I ventured down the hall to use the toilet and was taken aback by the condition of the showers, sinks and toilets. Roland and I walked through the commons room where a long haired fellow was eating his supper - a huge plate full of - you guessed it - onions and potatoes. I asked him if this was his usual fare and he said yes, it's free and there's lots of it. He was sitting on one of several dirty blue couches that looked as though they were harbouring any number of bacteria, germs and perhaps a mischief of mice. The linoleum floor throughout the hostel cried out for a vacuuming and mopping. Roland and I looked at each other, walked out the door, got into the car and left.

"Oh, that's a very bad place to stay. If I was there with these kids, I would be quick to tell them how they should keep a place clean. I'd show them how to clean the kitchen and be on them to keep everything clean and tidy every day!" offered Roland. I agreed that they weren't following hostel etiquette, but if the manager of the place lets it slide there was little we could do for a one night stay. We drove back to the center of town, found the hotel with a pub and restaurant and checked in there. This was like a hostel in some ways in that the floor shared a men's and ladies bathrooms and toilets. My room was spartan and provide me with a twin bed, small desk and a closet. Roland and I went down to the dining room and ate a nice supper. After supper we walked around town and went in to the few stores that were still open. One was a winery store so we got to sample several local wines all of which we liked. After our evening walk I spent some time in the lobby reading before turning in for the night.

The hotel, as most buildings of the town, sat on the main road. This meant that there was an almost constant rumbling of big trucks passing through during the night. I got used to it pretty quickly and had a fairly good sleep. It was another story for Roland who is noise sensitive. Roland had been living in the bush for the past six months in a place of serenity - no traffic, few people - just nature's symphony of sounds. Being here and trying to sleep was very difficult for him.

The hotel provided a breakfast of toast, fruit and cereal which we had on an expansive covered balcony overlooking Main Street. Roland told me of his many awakenings and tossing and turning in his bed, wishing for the quiet of the bush. We finished our meal and were walking down the hall to our rooms when he told me of a noisy machine that rattled away during the night. "Off and on. Off and on. It just kept on making such a noise!" He was on a search for this source of noise, travelling the length of the hall, walking and talking loudly, not realizing that there still might be people who were trying to sleep and he would be a source of noise to them. He finally found the source by looking out a window and spying a generator humming away down near the kitchen. Satisfied, he turned and went back to his room and collected his gear.

TO ADELAIDE

On this Friday in Australia Roland and I would drive northwest through a lovely area between Gambier and Adelaide which is home to many fine vineyards. Roland loves wine so we found a well known place to visit, Wynns Coonawarra Estate which is the oldest operating winery in the region. This winery is far from any substantial market but is located here for two very important reasons. The first is the red earth, terra rossa, which runs in a narrow fifteen kilometre long, one kilometre wide, stretch of soil. The second is the cool climate that gives the grapes a long, cool, ripening period that lets flavours build in intensity and gives a balanced acidity. The wines that are produced here are famous for their richness, intensity, longevity and depth of flavour.

The vineyard is fronted by an impressive entrance and signage with a driveway leading to a large stone building. The building, a magnificent triple gabled winery, serves as the logo for the wines produced here. We parked the car and strolled over to the vineyards where we took each other's picture cupping huge bunches of succulent dark purple grapes in our hands. We entered a large room where staff were lined up behind a bar serving portions of various wines to visitors. Roland and I joined the others and began tasting too – mmmmm, it all tasted wonderful to me but I limited my samples to three as I was driving. Roland tasted six different wines and bought a bottle to take with him for friends in Perth.

We continued to Naracoorte where I dropped Roland off and headed back along the road a short distance then turned off to visit Naracoorte Caves National Park. There are about four kilometres of caves in this system, four hundred meters of which have been developed for tourists. I had timed my arrival (accidentally) well for the guided tour of the Alexandra Cave. (Travel Luck) I started in the Wonambi Visitor Center where I picked up some information pamphlets and viewed bats through a live feed web cam from a nearby cave. There were only nine of us in Becky's group this time which is a nice number to travel with. Becky would show us enormous domed chambers, straw clusters, stalactites, stalagmites and other delicate cave formations. We would walk along paths that turned and twisted; required walking bent over, to protect our heads, and of course went up and down narrow stairs – stairs, always lots of stairs in caves. This cave has a most spectacular straw cluster – a gathering of delicate, hollow formations that hang from the ceiling – the best one I had seen so far. Some hung down for several meters.

The most beautiful feature of this cave is the Mirror Pool. Here, there is another, smaller cluster of straws that hang from the ceiling like some magical upside-down city that has slender, towering, cylindrical buildings of different heights and widths, all in glowing shades of golden browns. Below is a perfect replication of this cluster. At first glance I wondered how this was possible. How can stalactites have a group of identical stalagmites rising from the floor beneath them? But this was only for the shortest of times because the name, Mirror Pool, told me that this was a reflection of the beauty above. The water is absolutely clear and still in this cave and the resulting effect is truly awesome. This was definitely a 'buy a professionally shot post card of this feature' formation.

The most famous part of the cave is the fossil chamber where many remains of animals were found in 1969. Animals often fell through holes in the ceiling of the caves and having no means of escape, perished and left extensive fossil records of ancient Australian mega fauna (big animals). In some places the fossils can be found in layers to a depth of twenty meters. The fossil records in the caves were the main reason that the Naracoorte Caves were added to the World Heritage List in 1994. We walked into a fairly large chamber where Becky invited us to sit down while she showed us the two reconstructed fossil skeletons on display here. Just beyond the skeletons the cave ceiling dropped to only a meter off the floor. Scientists have been hunched over their work here for a number of years, digging out a large number of fossil remains. David Attenborough has filmed a segment for Life on Earth at this spot. As I sat and listened to Becky I tried to imagine the immense time frame over which all this had happened – the formation of the caves had begun over two hundred million years ago when this area was under water – nope, couldn't do it – way too many years to think about. But I did understand that the process took a very, very long time, and now here I was, sitting underground trying to wrap my brain around it. Next Becky led us to an active dig where she hoped we could watch an archaeologist at work, but she was not there at the time. It was still interesting to look at the site, criss-crossed with strings that laid out a specific search grid. That was the end of new features to look at in the cave and we followed Becky to the exit. The Alexandra Cave tour was a great one!

I headed to the self-guided Wet Cave a hundred meters or so from the visitor center. It has two large entrances where the cave ceiling has collapsed. These windows allow enough light in so that ferns grow in a few places in the cave. I walked down the trail, through the first chamber, then into a large dome chamber. This cave does not have spectacular formations like Alexandra Cave but has some stalagmites and some cylindrical holes in the ceiling that were interesting. I spent about ten minutes walking through the cave before looping around back to the staircase that took me back up to ground level. I had finished my visit so made my way back to the car where I turned on the air conditioning and enjoyed some time to myself.

I drove back to Naracoorte, to the swimming lake where I found Roland just drying off from his swim. He had found a place to get a coffee and had passed the time talking with people, walking on local trails and then gone for a swim. To me, a swimming lake was simply a natural lake in which you could swim. Naracoorte has made a large artificial lake that is almost as big as two football fields. It holds eleven million litres of water that is kept clean and safe by chlorination and filtration systems. One side has a concrete wall along it while the opposite shore is a sandy beach. There are large canopies in several areas so that children can play with protection from the sun. The whole thing is surrounded by well-maintained lawns and features Red River Gum trees which offer more shade for users. There was only one other man swimming in the lake but I imagined that on the weekend many locals would be enjoying the water. I talked to three young girls who had come to wade in the lake on their way home from school. They told me that the pool was due to be drained and closed for the winter next week so I was very glad to have had the opportunity to see it full of water. (Travel Luck) This is a fabulous recreational facility for this town of under five thousand people – and it's free!

Now it was time for some serious driving as we decided to drive all the way through to Adelaide. We thought we could make it before it got dark and as it turned out we only had to drive about a half hour after the sun went down. We had called ahead to the Adelaide YHA and booked our spots for the night. It had been a long day, but a good day and with Roland navigating we got into the hostel and had the car secured in the parking lot for the night. Then we walked two blocks over to North Terrace Street, the busiest for nightlife, where many clubs and restaurants are found. Roland took me into a small, dark, somewhat seedy Turkish restaurant. We walked up to the tiny service window at the back and placed our orders with a dark skinned woman in a white blouse. Roland and I talked about our trip together: the scenery, the places we visited, our accommodations, the flat tire, the animals, the people, as we waited for our meal. He was due to fly out the next day to Perth on the west coast where he was going to visit friends for a few weeks. It had been an interesting ten days together, but I was looking forward to being on my own again, to have some solitude after travelling in close quarters with him. Back at the hostel we said good night and goodbye. We would keep in touch by email a few times.

The YHA hostel has a wonderful central location in downtown Adelaide and is very close to city markets, museums, art galleries and all major city attractions. It is considered one of the top YHAs in Australia. As at most hostels there is a booking service for travel, tours and hostel stays. The hostel is fairly large and is well-maintained. It has many amenities; internet, laundry, dining room, several TV rooms, linen, tea and coffee, storage and daily activities. A lot of hostels have special activities and this one offered table tennis competitions, bingo, drumming classes and free pancake days. I had learned to check the notice boards in the lobby whenever I checked in to a new place to see what they offered.

I was in a dorm with five other girls, but managed to score a bottom bunk. The showers and toilet were just a few steps down the hall which was especially convenient in the wee hours of the morn.

The next day, while I still had the car, I drove out to Glenelg which is an ocean-front suburb of Adelaide. Only eleven kilometres away it didn't take long to get there and I quite enjoyed the quiet of the drive by myself. I nosed the car to the curb snagging the only available parking space for blocks. How lucky was I? No meters in sight, I thought it was wonderful of Glenelg to offer free parking. A short walk over lush grass, then I passed between two buildings where I felt the ocean breeze. Walking out on to the esplanade I caught my first view of the long, white, sandy beach that is lined with picnic areas, restaurants, cafes and bars. There were quite a few people enjoying the beach on this summer Saturday: singles, couples, families, old and young, slim and not so slim. Everyone was just having a good time in the sun; it was twenty-nine degrees. I walked to the far end of the beach on the hard-packed sand then turned and started wading back in ankle-deep water along the shore. The water was warm and inviting and soon I found myself out a little deeper in calf-deep water, then the hem of my shorts were wet, and soon after the water was splashing half way up my thighs. You know how it goes – if a little can be so good then a lot must be that much better!

Looking onto the beach I noticed a bright yellow, triangular tarpaulin, which had about fifteen people gathered around and under it. They wore red swim shorts, brilliant yellow shirts and each was topped with a red and yellow beanie style hat, tied under the chin with a white lace. These were people of the Surf Life Saving Club, a group that had been put together in 1931. They were here in large numbers to keep an eye on all the people at the beach that day. Their equipment included yellow surfboards and a small red zodiac boat. I wandered over and started talking to a few of them. Sara has been a surf life guard for four years and loves her job. Today she had Shelly with her, a large golden-colored dog. She and Shelly were just heading out into the water so I followed them as Sara carried her surf board and Shelly pranced and danced around her with excitement. Sara launched the board on to the water and Shelly scrambled aboard. Sara pushed her off. This was repeated once more on the way out to larger waves. Sara now allowed Shelly to get on the board and she sat on the front as Sara lay flat behind her and started paddling. They caught a wave that carried them back to where I waited. They repeated this several times as I went into the water again and got some great pictures. They both looked absolutely happy on every trip. I asked Sara why she pushed Shelly off while heading out to sea. "Well, it's good exercise for her and it makes the board lighter for me to push and paddle out." Makes sense to me. The other life savers and Sara loved the pictures I had taken and later I emailed them to Sara. It is this type of interaction that makes a trip even more special – such an opportunity to find out what is going on with people who live and work in an area. I loved it! I left the group and continued to the jetty where I walked under it then along on top of it thus getting pictures from all angles. Many people were doing the same thing. I left the beach, put on my sandals and turned towards the shops. It was another great visit to one of Australia's more than seven thousand beaches.

Before I had lost sight of the beach I noticed a tall, self-supporting structure made up of metal pipes. These formed four stations, each with a bright blue and yellow, inflated landing area and each with a child harnessed and jumping up and down. If you remember your babies bouncing away in Jolly Jumpers then just expand on that idea. These kids were about eight to ten years old and bounced, suspended by bungy cords, up and down, two to six meters high. Gravity – what's gravity? The amazing fun they were having was splashed across their faces, euphoric smiles and laughing ongoing. One girl was good at doing back flips and was attempting to do some front flips. This is not a ride, but an activity that can train and tune the body and help with coordination. Oh, to be a kid again!

I walked along the pedestrian-only street and looked into some of the shops and had lunch in a cafe. It had been a very pleasant day out at Glenelg but now it was time to go back to the city and I headed back to the car.

It's never good to see a piece of paper stuck under the wiper blade of your car. Especially when it's a piece of paper that says you have overstayed your welcome and we're going to give you a fine for doing so. Yes, I had acquired a parking ticket. I hadn't seen any 'Pay Here' signs or meters when I had parked the car. Now I looked more carefully and sure enough, about twenty cars down the road I saw a large meter. Walked down to it. Read the directions. Seems as though I had to note my parking space number, enter it into the meter, pay for a certain amount of time, get a receipt, return to my car, place the receipt on the dash, then I was free to roam at will. I hadn't seen this system before on a street, only in large lots back home, but was now an educated parker and would not make this same mistake again. I walked to a nearby bank where I paid my ten dollar fine and was on my way. I suppose I could have ignored the ticket – I mean what recourse would they have? But, I'm pretty honest. I got into the car for the last time and drove to the nearby airport where I handed it in to the rental company. From Cairns three weeks ago, I had travelled five thousand nine hundred fifty-two kilometres, a good distance overall. I hopped a bus for the ten minute ride back into Adelaide.

For supper, I got together with a few others and we ordered pizza. It was delivered to the hostel where we took it to the dining room and gorged on triangular bits of heavenly fare. We had leftovers so I walked around and offered them to other people in the lounge area. I was offered a beer in exchange and sat down with new friends. At eight o'clock the lights were turned off and candles lit. What was going on? Earth Hour was going on.

Earth Hour was conceived by the World Wildlife Fund and the Sydney Morning Herald in 2007. Over two million Sydney residents participated by turning off all non-essential lights for an hour that first year. What began as a Sydney event became a global event and in 2009 over four thousand cities in eighty eight countries took part. Earth Hour occurs on the third Saturday of March each year. Candle light was used in our hostel and remained the only light source in the common room for the rest of the night. It was such a cool thing to be doing with people of all ages from all over the planet – just a really nice pause from our technological hustle and bustle lives of today.

Later that evening I went on the internet and sent out a group email. Although I had been having a great time, I missed hearing from family and friends. I had sent emails to Jason and Jenna quite often and out to my group every week or so. In hopes of generating more responses this time, I added a list of questions to this mail out. "I'd love to hear from you; makes home seem a little less distant . . .

How are you?
How's the family?
How's your pet?
How's your game?
How's grade 12?
How's work?
How's retirement?
How is the math class doing?
How's the new place?
How's the old place?
Have you mowed the grass yet?
What's the weather like?
What have you been up to?
What was the best thing about your week?
What's for supper??????????
Just anything you care to share . . .
All for now,
Mom, Joan, AJ

And it worked. Over the next week I got a lot more mail even though several people thought it was just boring information that they sent.

I went to my room and packed up my gear as I would be leaving for the next two days. I put most of my gear in storage before I went to bed.

KANGAROO ISLAND

This Sunday and Monday I would turn myself over to Surf and Sand Adventures for an overnight trip to Kangaroo Island. The all-inclusive package included: transport by van, ferry, farm stay, meals, entry fees and activities. Steve arrived with the van at 6:15 am, right on time. I got in and scored the front seat beside the driver. We drove down the peninsula enjoying the countryside and the kangaroos that were out and about in the cool of the morning. We walked on to the ferry and at nine o'clock we set out on the forty-five minute ride across Backstairs Passage. We walked off the ferry at Penneshaw on Kangaroo Island where we boarded our new van after tossing our gear in the small trailer it towed. There were thirteen of us on the tour, three males, nine females and Steve. Everyone else was in their early twenties, so I just told myself to go back to the seventies and pretend I was off on some summer adventure with a bunch of kids from university. I fit right in and we all had a good time together.

We stopped briefly at our accommodation, a dry little farmstead, to drop off gear and claim beds. We were welcomed by Stella, a black lab who was the official 'meeter and greeter' – she'd be great at the door of any Wal-Mart.

The bedrooms were tiny and mine had three sets of bunk beds in it and not even a meter of floor space between them. Again I got a bottom bunk. Yay! Small pleasures. Perhaps the most 'interesting' thing about the place were the thousands upon thousands of small black worms that littered the ground outside and the floors inside the buildings. We even found a few in the fridge. They were totally harmless but just the idea was a little off-putting to some of us. They would send out little popping noises as we stepped on them. We tried to avoid this mass murder but it was impossible so the first tiptoeing steps were soon replaced with steady, full-foot walking – pop, pop, popping.

Soon we were back in the van and heading down the road to Vivonne Bay to visit Raptor Domain. Dave has a small but dynamic collection of birds. His face took on a special look of wonder and pride when showing each of his special birds. I could tell he loves doing this and cares for his animals greatly. He first brought out the smallest falcon species which I got to have on my arm for a time. Then he brought out Casper, a white barn owl. Not a large bird he was nevertheless quite striking with little grey flecks on his body and a light brown line of feathers that highlighted the top of his eye area. He took time to hop from lap to lap and when he landed on me allowed me to pet him. He was so very soft! Then Dave brought out laughing kookaburras, Banjo and Clancy who are free fliers. They would land in nearby trees then come back and land on Dave's arm. He asked if anyone wanted them on their arm, so of course my hand went up. I got the chance to put on a protective glove and had both of them perch on my arm. They are a stocky bird, with white and brown feathers, but weighed little. It was so cool. For the grand finale, he brought out a Wedge Tailed Eagle that flew into a tree. Dave started swinging a piece of meat around that was attached to the end of a string. With all eyes on it he soon had it going in full circles just above the height of his head; the eagle swooped in and snatched his prize out of the sky and flew away to eat it. We saw this demonstration a few times and were all amazed with the eagles' speed and precision. Finally, Dave held a wallaby bone in his gloved hand and we watched and listened as the eagle's powerful beak ripped through flesh and cracked the bone.

After the bird encounter we headed west, driving along the undulating sealed road through mallee wilderness - bush country that has a covering of evergreen shrubs and trees. It was not, however, green as a fire had ripped through the area and the vegetation was still trying to recover. At the southern tip of Flinders Chase National Park is Cape du Couedic. The scenery here rivals any seascape that I've seen. We walked from our van to the lighthouse that was on the headland and around it, taking pictures of the twenty-five meter tall, beige, red and white building.

We crossed to the beginning of the boardwalk and began a gentle descent towards the base of the headland. If viewed from the air, the boardwalk looks like two backwards, giant, lazy, letter zeds. As we neared the cliff tops we could see more and more of the ocean's relentless waves crashing into the rocky coastline below. We zigged and zagged our way across the terrain and came to a stop by Steve. He told us to look closely at the rocks below to see if we noticed anything. In moments the movement of the seals caught my eye and I saw first one then another then another, all sorts of New Zealand fur seals on the rocks below. They were a long way from the water at the top of an almost vertical cliff and I wondered for a time how they had reached their precarious perches before figuring out that they had come up the far side of the rocks which has a gentle incline. This colony of about four thousand seals was almost decimated by the fur trade a hundred years ago. Steve hadn't told us what to expect here, so this was an amazing and delightful surprise. We stopped many times to watch the seals as we continued our descent along the boardwalk.

With the spectacular scenery and the frolicking seals I didn't expect any more from this walk. But then it just got better. Around another corner I could see that stairs curved and went down even more - to what I didn't know, but I surely wasn't going to miss out on any chance to see anything. Even if I had to hop back up on my one good leg, I was going down each and every step. Once I had tramped down and around the corner to my left I looked into the headland. This headland that I had walked over, that I thought was solid, had been eroded by the wind and sea over thousands of years resulting in a massive arch. A huge smile lit up my face as I walked down the final steps and landed on a large viewing deck in front of Admirals Arch. The arch is about as tall as a three story building and half a football field wide. The slanting rocks of the headland make up the floor on the landward side while on the left, huge stair-like rocky terraces are found. The ceiling was extremely rugged with pieces of rock hanging like so many deranged stalactites. Below all this magnificence of nature, seals were resting and playing. It is one of the most wonderful scenes of nature that I have ever seen! We spent about twenty minutes there before it was time to climb back up along the boardwalk to the van.

We got our first view of Remarkable Rocks from a distance, Steve having pulled the van off to the side of the road. The massive granite headland looked like the right forearm of a giant. The elbow emerged at the ocean's edge and the arm stretched up and on to the green scrubland. High above the water a huge right hand lay flat upon the land and upon this hand was a gathering of rocks that looked like an outbreak of giant warts.

About ten minutes later we arrived at the parking lot and disembarked to begin our exploration. Remarkable Rocks sit up on a granite dome (the arm). They form a cluster of individual pieces of nature's art, each standing alone like a magnificent impressionistic sculpture and at the same time standing together as a unit. The closer I got to them, the more interesting they became. When first sighted, they were a unit, seen from only one vantage point. As I approached they stood out as individuals with different personalities. Walking around each rock yielded new and wondrous views of these massive granite boulders. The rocks are, well, remarkable, and awesome, inspiring, huge and amazing. Everyone at the site wore a smile as they let their hands glide over the smooth granite surfaces and posed for photos from every possible angle. The rocks are not square or rectangular, but have been water and wind shaped into curvaceous forms and each rests on just three contact points. One had a massive overhang shaped like an eagle's beak and I had my picture taken standing beneath it and 'holding' it up with just one hand – strong Canadian woman that I am. Most everyone else ended up with like photos – who can resist? A sad pig's face projected from the base of another rock. A profile of Elvis, with collar raised and hair flipped up and back was found in another. Darth Vader lives there too. They were eroded and pocked with recessions. I could see a Dali painting in one, a lion's den in another. There was a narrow passage formed by two boulders, one leaning against the other that I squeezed through.

The stark greys of the rocks were contrasted with bright orange lichen that grew on the un-trod upon areas of the dome. A most interesting feature are the rain-formed runoff channels. Some of these channels are over thirty centimeters wide and fifteen deep. The waters have been running here for millions of years carving these canals into the granite. As I approached the sea side of the rocks, the ground steepened and a few small signs warned of the slippery slopes that lead directly down to the foaming water below. I was thinking that if I was at a site like this in the United States or Canada, there would be many more signs and a chain link fence and perhaps a guard or two to keep people safe. But here on Kangaroo Island, there were simply a few warning signs and they didn't really intrude on this natural phenomenon. It's as if Australians think that common sense is alive and well. What a concept! I liked it like that.

We were motoring along the unpaved road of the island when all of a sudden Steve slammed on the brakes and brought us to a skidding halt. He jumped out in a flash and took off running back down the road. I bailed out too as did the others, and we all began to follow him.

"Steve, what's up?"

"Echidna!" Steve had now scrambled up the red earth bank at the side of the road and was bending low, looking for the elusive echidna, one of Australia's interesting marsupials. And there he was, curled into a ball, as still as a ball of clay. He had nestled himself in between two fallen branches and was using his best protection, keeping still and presenting the intruders with a bristling ball of spines to contend with. We stayed as still as possible for a few minutes in the hopes he might feel safe and stick his head out and perhaps move. But, he just stayed curled up so we left him in peace. Pretty cool to have seen an echidna in the wild.

We arrived back at our farm in the late afternoon. Ours was a pretty basic building and not very large. It was a simple one level three-bedroom house with one washroom for the men and one for the women. I know I've told you that Australians love their barbecue, and it was no different here. For dinner we had spaghetti and meat sauce, the spaghetti was boiled inside on the stove while the meat sauce was of course made on the barbecue. The barbecue had a griddle surface upon which the meat, tomato sauce, onions and other ingredients were cooked and continuously tossed to the center only to work their way out to the edges where once again they would be sent flying back to center. And that's how barbecued spaghetti is made in Australia. With accompanying salads and garlic bread it was a fine dinner, indeed. We dined outside under the eucalyptus trees. After dinner, everyone pitched in with cleanup and we soon had the kitchen in tip top shape once again.

I took a short looping walk around the buildings and came to a grove of eucalyptus trees where I spotted a koala bear wedged into a tree sleeping soundly. Soon others quietly made their way over the tree and were able to observe this iconic Australian symbol for themselves. For about half of them it was their first contact with a koala in the wild.

Next on the menu was a campfire in the fire circle in front of the building. We gathered around and sat on the logs provided, had a beverage of choice, roasted marshmallows and told stories. It was just a perfect Australian evening, sharing this experience with kids thirty to forty years, younger, but all of us equalized in the dancing glow of the flames.

At nine o'clock we climbed into the van and headed out in to the night. You are probably wondering what would have prompted us to leave our campfire at this time. Well, it was nothing anywhere near the size of Remarkable Rocks or Admiral's Arch. What we were seeking was small in comparison, averaging just thirty centimetres in height and weighing about a kilogram. Our night time foray was to see the tiny blue penguins of Kangaroo Island. After we got out of the van we had only small flashlights to guide us down the rocky road to the colony. So as to observe the penguins with minimal interference, the flashlights were covered with red plastic. The road cut down through a steep ocean-side hill. Steve had us gather half way down the road. We were to be very quiet and stay back at least four meters from the penguins. Hushed, we stepped lightly and then stopped as Steve shone his light into some bushes to where two penguins stood next to each other. So very cute - once again I was grinning, just a burst of well being and happiness. I am so easily amused. And so we made our way down to sea level, Steve pointing out penguins as we went.

Most of us have seen the waddle walk of penguins on television or perhaps in a zoo. These little guys have very short legs and are amazing in that they actually make their way out of the sea and climb up in to the rocky hillside to make their nests. Liken it to climbing a set of stairs with both of your legs encased in only one leg of your pants! The penguins feel safe in their rocky island habitat.

Location, location, location. One male had prime real estate. He had been working on this nest for several years and had an advantage with the ladies to whom a good nest is very important when choosing a mate. Sounds like a theme that runs through the animal kingdom. And so we saw him standing in this most magnificent of nests, little flippers stretched out to the sides and beak pointing upward. "Look at me ladies. What more could you ask for?" The march of the penguins happens every evening when after a perilous day at sea, they come ashore to rest in an equally dangerous environment. They are preyed upon by sharks and seals in the sea, and by feral animals on land. Some colonies are disappearing due to habitat encroachment while others are still being found. I'm glad to know that there is a place for them here on Kangaroo Island.

Happy with our penguin encounters we walked back up the road admiring the stars as we did so. A short time later we turned off the road into the farm where we were staying. We had just passed through the gate when suddenly Steve yarded the steering wheel hard left and we found ourselves witness to hundreds of kangaroos! It seemed they were all looking at the van, eyes lit up by the headlights. Some remained where they were while others bounded away to a safer distance. Steve drove around the field so we had excellent views of these iconic animals. The kangaroos remain hidden in the brush during the day and come out at night to forage and to play. While we had been travelling around the island during the day it was apparent that many kangaroos did live on the island, the evidence being carcasses and bones that littered the road sides. So it was with great satisfaction and delight that we got to witness all these bouncing kangaroos at such close range.

Back inside we spent time in the living room listening to Beatles tunes and reliving the day's adventures before turning in for the night.

The screen door lopped softly behind me as I stepped out onto the red brick patio in the morning. Stella approached me and was rewarded with an ear rub. The eucalyptus were lit by the early-morning rays of the sun. I could see several koalas sleeping in branches high above. I grey shorts and sandals I fit into the style of the others in the group, extreme casual for hot weather. A loose fitting blue short sleeved top and Tilley hat completed my outfit. I was welcomed by morning hellos and I joined the others at the breakfast table. Breakfast was of course barbequed. Yes, circles of bread were torn from the middle of slices, the slices put on the griddle then an egg deposited in to the hole to cook. The griddle also cooked ham, bacon and pancakes. Along with fruit and a selection of juices we were well powered up for our day. We tidied the kitchen, packed our gear and got back into the van.

Our first stop was at Seal Bay, for one of Kangaroo Island's amazing experiences. The park was established to protect the seals and their habitat. We were here in time for a guided walk. Don would take us on a personal forty-five minute tour of the colony during which we would learn about the biology, breeding and behaviour of the seals. He was dressed in a short-sleeved khaki shirt with matching shorts, had on sturdy boots and wore an Indiana Jones style hat. Don's face was ruggedly handsome, tanned and windswept – he looked right at home in this habitat he obviously loved. This seal colony is on a sandy beach which means great interaction opportunities. We set out on the boardwalk which gently declines along its eight hundred meter length. This took us through and sometimes above the seals terrestrial habitat. When we got closer to the beach we passed through an area of beautiful sand dunes held in place somewhat by the rugged plants of the region. I heard a muffled kind of noise so looked over the edge of the boardwalk. Two meters below me a gorgeous baby seal looked up at me with his huge brown eyes - the kind that say "Don't you just want to pick me up and spoil me?" Little plots of sand marked his nose and bits of wet below his eyes. We stopped here while Don told us that the seals here in the dunes were young males, teenagers as it were. They were trying to figure out how life works and how to approach females – sound familiar?

We continued to the lookout over the beach and saw a long sweep of sand with seals lined up like bar codes of nature. They were lying on the sand, a dry, light brown color, resting after their long feeding trips at sea. They often lie around for up to three days before setting off again in search of food. Some moms were nursing calves; most were lying stretched out, eyes closed. This is their beach – unless you are a seal, swimming and fishing are not allowed here. We walked down into the soft sand on the beach and approached to within six meters of the seals. They didn't seem to even notice us – no reason to be alarmed – more important to rest. This allowed for some wonderfully close observations in which I could see whiskers twitch, and eyeballs move under lids. There were seals in the water too, some swimming out beyond the waves, others surfing towards the beach. They are dark brown when they come out onto the sand and become lighter brown as they dry off; the shade of brown let me know which seals had recently come out of the water and which had been lying around sunning themselves for some time. Glancing to my left, I noticed a male making his way quite quickly in our direction. He 'flippered' along for a bit then stopped and stretched his nose high into the air and let out a barking seal noise, paused for a moment, then continued. Don told us to remain still and we did so as this seal passed only three meters from us. We all 'oohed' and 'awed' and snapped more pictures as this was unfolding. It was just spectacular! Don left us now and we spent another fifteen minutes before we had to head back up the path to the van. It was truly one of the best wild animal encounters I have ever had. We popped in at the visitor center to buy a few souvenirs – post cards for me - and use the facilities before heading out to Little Sahara.

Little Sahara is only twenty minutes from Seal Bay. This is an area of some of the largest sand dunes on Kangaroo Island. Steve had us there in short time and it was like Ninety Mile Beach in New Zealand all over again. Everyone else grabbed sand sleds and trudged their way up the side of the dune while I trudged part way up and took pictures. There were similar levels of success as in New Zealand and a lot of tumbles as gravity took over and gave each rider a bit of fun and a generous serving of sand.

We stopped back at the farm and picked up lunch supplies then headed off across to the northern coast of the island. The rolling hills of the island gave us a beautiful drive into the Western River valley and after an hour we stopped for lunch at a picnic shelter. There was a tour group of only six people there and when they left, they gave us the rest of their food. They were going to throw out what they couldn't eat. We ate some of it and took the rest back to our various Adelaide hostels to put in the free food shelves. The shelter had one closed wall and a roof overhead. The wind blew fairly briskly over the tables and flipped over more than one tortilla wrap. There was of course, a barbeque which was fired up to cook our chicken, ham and veggies which were the ingredients for the wraps we enjoyed for lunch.

For dessert, Steve opened up a box of Tim Tams, a most delicious chocolate coated biscuit cookie. A chocolate cream filling is trapped between two layers of chocolate biscuit then the whole thing is coated with a layer of rippling chocolate. Steve showed us what a Tim Tam Slam is. You bite off part of each end, then use it as a straw to drink your coffee or hot chocolate. As the hot liquid passes through the cookie the biscuit softens and the chocolate coating begins to melt. We all decided we needed a hot beverage so water was boiled and hot chocolate was made. In a few short minutes I was happily slurping through my new straw – yummy, yummy, and yummy! Tim Tams are an institution in Australia and I became very familiar with them for the rest of my stay and passed on the knowledge of the Tim Tam Slam in hostels everywhere. I thought I should acquire the import rights of Tim Tams to North America – wow, the money I'd make! When I got back home it was with delight and the realisation I wouldn't be making any money on Tim Tam imports, that I saw the cookies on the shelf of my local grocery store. I wonder how many times I had walked by them in ignorance.

Lunch over, we set out over a footbridge, and followed the river to the sea. The cove is quite beautiful: spectacular ocean blues and white breakers with cliffs and rocky outcrops protecting it. Several people went in for a swim. I headed for the unique rock formations with their bright orange algae covering. Hmmm . . . how to describe them to you? Imagine a range of extremely rugged mountains that thrust up in huge slabs running parallel to one another. They are all leaning at a forty-five degree angle. The long rows and valleys look as if some legendary cat of gigantic proportions has scratched along the earth leaving the rocks and carving out valleys that lie deep with snow. Now take that image and shrink it so the mountains are 'jaggedy' rocks that rise only a few meters from a white sand beach. There you have it, a fascinating place to visit.

We left the beach, walked along the river, over the bridge and climbed the small hill back to the van. Over the next hour we drove along the unsealed road enjoying the hill country and ocean views. Our final destination on Kangaroo Island was Stokes Beach. When I got out of the van all I could see was an uninviting rocky shore. Steve pointed in the direction of the beach and told us that we would have to walk between some rocks to get to the beach. I was first out on the trail as others were still getting things out of the van. I walked towards the rocky headland in front of me and couldn't see any path slicing between the towering rocks. When I got closer to the rocks I noticed that they were huge individual pieces that were tightly packed. The path that cuts through these guardians of Stokes Beach only materialized once I got right up to the rocks. The path was a meter wide in places and narrowed at one point to half that. It required some ducking and 'squidging' here and there. Emerging from this interesting trail a new world opened up – Stokes Beach. This is a fabulous beach and it immediately seemed to be worthy of its seventh place finish in the best beach category by Tourism Australia. The near end of the beach is a perfect play area for kids. In addition to the sandy beach there is a gorgeous, calm pool that has a sandy bottom and a protective rock wall forty meters off shore. Of course the water was a collection of striking blues with some small waves off shore. After taking some pictures here, I headed off to the far end of the beach wading in the warm water and taking pictures as I went. It was a wonderful bit of time to commune with nature and have some time to myself. I returned to sit on the sand with two other girls where we talked and watched others who were swimming and trying to do a bit of body surfing. It was with some reluctance that we left Stokes Beach after an hour and a half, wove through the rock trail and re-boarded the van.

The last part of our time on the island was spent driving east towards Penneshaw where we would catch the return ferry. The highlight of that short drive was coming upon a herd of sheep in the road. I had hoped that might happen to me, to be in the midst of these woolly animals, in New Zealand, but it hadn't. Now I was getting to fulfill that wish here in Australia. Their shepherd told Steve to simply continue slowly and the sheep would get out of the way. We spent the next few minutes idling along at about a kilometre and hour until each sheep had bounded out of the way on to the sides of the road.

At the ferry terminal we said farewell to our van and got back on the boat for the short ride back to the mainland. We gathered around another van on the far side and had our group photo taken. As I look at it now, I can see that physically I am much older than my companions, but when I look at the smiles generated by our two days together we are all the same. The trip back to Adelaide was fairly quiet as we were tired and contented. It was dusk and the kangaroos were coming out for the evening. My last memory of the road trip is of a group of bounders bouncing along a nearby hillside in the fading light of day. Dropped off at my hostel at eight-thirty, the adventure was over. Kangaroo Island was an amazing experience that has often been in my thoughts. I loved it!

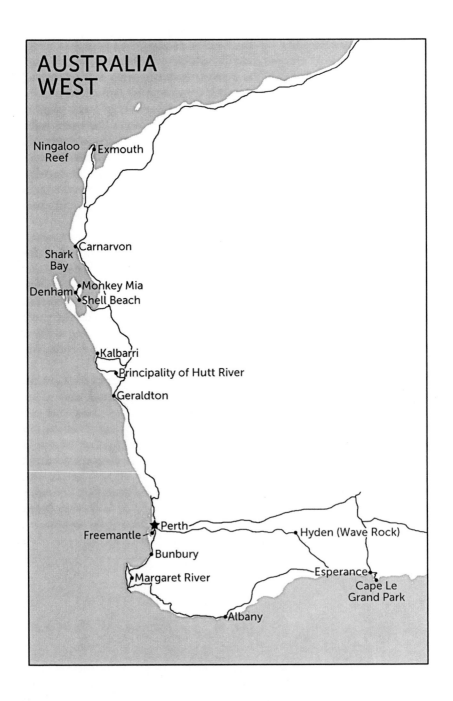

AUSTRALIA
WEST

Ningaloo
Reef
Exmouth

Carnarvon
Shark
Bay
Denham Monkey Mia
Shell Beach

Kalbarri
Principality of Hutt River
Geraldton

Perth
Freemantle
Hyden (Wave Rock)
Bunbury
Esperance
Margaret River
Cape Le
Grand Park

Albany

PERTH

On this last day of March I was up at five to catch a flight from Adelaide to Perth on the west coast of Australia. Being up this early and flying west meant that I arrived in Perth at eight in the morning and had a full day ahead of me. At the airport information desk I talked with a very helpful lady. She gave me some pamphlets and several maps of the area but most importantly, she advised me where to stay. I had made note of a few hostels in my guidebook but she made a recommendation to stay at The Emperor's Crown for which I shall ever be grateful. She called them for me and reserved a spot for the next four nights. Thanking her very much I proceeded to the bus stop and hopped on an airport shuttle. The driver took me to the front door of my hostel so I had very little walking to do; very good service. The Crown is a small hostel. It seemed more like a hotel than a hostel as I walked through the front door. The brilliant smile on Nick's face added to his already too-cute face. Nick could be a twin of Nate Berkus, Oprah's 'cutie pie' designer guy. I paid for my stay then followed Nick up one flight of stairs to my female dorm.

My room had only one other person in it, Katie, who was staying there long-term while working three jobs. Katie was a bubbly young girl who worked as a waitress in two restaurants and worked at the hostel in various capacities. She had been there for three months and was hoping to move into an apartment with her boyfriend before long. Katie had a vast store of knowledge that she shared with me and was always willing to step in and lend a hand. The room itself had three sets of bunk beds, was carpeted and had a large locker for each person. Each dorm had an en-suite which is a feature that I hold in high regard.

After settling in I took a look around the hostel and was impressed with what I saw. It is the cleanest hostel I stayed at – it seemed every time I walked around, I saw people vacuuming, dusting, disinfecting and tidying the place. The Emperor's Crown offered the best amenities of any lodging on my trip. The communal kitchen is all stainless steel and has a great supply of pots, pans, dishes and cutlery as well as two large fridges and a freezer. There is a marked cubby hole for each person staying in the hostel so that food storage is easy and efficient. Just outside the kitchen are garden courtyards and a barbeque area. There was a cosy TV lounge a few feet from my dorm and I spent some time each evening lounging on the couches watching TV with other guests. There is a lounge in the large foyer where could sit at a computer and send e-mails and do research for a third of the usual cost. Above the computers was a row of international clocks and I would always glance at them to see what time it was back home. What would Jason and Jenna be doing now? Would Phyllis be golfing? Was it Emma's supper time? A bit goofy maybe, but it brought home a little bit closer.

There was a laundry room, DVD and video game rental, a pool table, free parking, vending machines, and security with the building backing onto the police station. Thanks again to the lady at the airport who set me up here!

I still had most of the day ahead of me so set out to explore Perth, Australia's fourth largest city and capital of Western Australia. There is a wonderful free bus service that operates around the central business district. The buses are called CATS (central area transport service) and each has a bus-long silhouette of a panther painted on its sides. Red, blue and yellow color-coding made it easy to find the correct bus stops. There are three main routes that service different areas of the CBD with continuous looping of the buses. The buses arrive every five to ten minutes depending on the route, time of day and day of the week. I found that travelling on the buses was fast, friendly and convenient. There is also a free transit zone in the core of Perth where I could hop on any bus and travel for free. It was really nice not having to drive in a city - to find and pay for parking would have been an unnecessary hassle. This bus service must cut down on a lot of congestion and pollution.

I left the hostel and walked around the block to arrive across from the police station. I was at stop number seven, the Museum, on the blue CAT loop. The three bus routes pass near most of the main attractions in Perth. I pressed the information button on the kiosk and was told that the next bus was due in four minutes. I looked down Beaufort Street a few minutes later and could see the bus approaching. I hopped onboard and stayed on the bus for the entire first loop and got oriented to the city. The blue CAT travels north to south with twenty-two stops on its route. I really liked the Horseshoe Bridge as I had never seen a bridge curved like a capital U before. The unique shape was used to allow a gentle climb to the required elevation over the train station.

We had driven through the towering buildings of the downtown, when with a single turn we left the buildings and the view opened up to reveal the foreshore. My eyes were immediately drawn to the fifty meter high Perth Wheel and the Perth Bell Tower that dominated the skyline. I got off at the Barrack Street Jetty which put me on the shore of the Swan River. The Wheel is an observation wheel that has enclosed gondolas that offer panoramic views of the city and river. I really liked the architecture of the Swan Bell Tower which was opened December 2000. Huge copper 'sails' rise from the ground and a gorgeous green-glass spire rises still further looking like a massive mast for a ship that travels nowhere. The sound of the bells toned music throughout the area. Its eighteen bells make this the largest change-ringing instrument in the world. The wheel sits a short distance from the bell tower and a few tourist shops. There wasn't a lot else to see down there on the waterfront, but for a short visit I liked it very much. There is also a passenger ferry terminal at this location, which is used to service boats destined for the short trip across the Swan River to south Perth. There is so much potential at this beautiful under-developed waterfront property – I hope something special is planned for the area.

I wanted to go to Kings Park and Botanical Gardens so I got back on a blue CAT then transferred to the red CAT and rode out to Havelock Street. Larger than New York's Central Park, Kings Park receives over five million visitors each year. Two thirds of the park is conserved as native bushland. The park is about a four block walk from the bus stop so it wasn't long before I was in this magnificent park. I entered by walking along Fraser Street which is lined with towering lemon-scented gum trees standing in columns like soldiers. Each tree has a brass plaque beside it, honouring the members of Perth's centenary committee. They were planted in 1938 and now, seventy-one years later, cast long shadows across the road. I saw several of these 'honour avenues' on my visits to the park. There are over eleven hundred plaques honouring service men that died in the wars. As I walked around the park I would notice a high number of statues and memorials, many in tribute to those who fought in the two world wars. The Cenotaph and Court of Contemplation lists over ten thousand people who died in the wars. In a circular pool an eternal flame burns and there is an atmosphere of quiet and respect. A mom and dad were passing through when one of their boys put his skateboard down and began to glide along. The dad got his attention immediately "Son, this is a memorial. There is no skateboarding here. Show respect." Just as simple as that, the boy had learned something valuable as had his siblings and anyone else within ear shot. I really liked that the dad gave that lesson to his family.

Across from the visitor center is ANZAC Lookout. The memorial here is for the twenty-five hundred men of the Australia and New Zealand Army Corp who died at Gallipoli in 1915. The view from here is magnificent as the park is poised on Mt. Eliza overlooking Perth and the foreshore: skyscrapers on the left, a huge expanse of green grass and the Swan River in the middle and South Perth on the right. It was gorgeous under the blue skies of another sunny summer's day. I walked along the scenic path that follows the edge of the cliff, stopping at several places to sit and enjoy the views. It had a calming effect on me as nature always does.

It was getting late in the day so I turned and walked back along Fraser Street. The side lighting on the trees was fabulous, just right for picture taking. It was very peaceful and beautiful and I enjoyed the walk back to the bus stop.

I got off the CAT at Hay Street Mall. I'm not much of a shopper so after an hour of browsing, I had had enough of it. I had supper at a small restaurant in the mall then bought a few groceries. I carried these in my green reusable shopping bag, back on to the bus then to the hostel. All in all it was a good first outing in Perth.

The Emperor's Crown has a movie room that is set up with six rows, each three couches wide and fronted with a huge plasma screen. This was Tuesday, movie night. About fifteen of us gathered at seven-thirty and watched the Simpsons movie. We were generations apart, but all laughed at the same places in this animated entertainment. It was also chocolate cake night! (Travel Luck). I do love chocolate! I was still tired after the busy trip to Kangaroo Island and having been up early to catch my flight to Perth. My bed was very comfortable and I slept for ten hours.

After a healthy breakfast I walked back to the bus stop and caught a ride on the blue CAT downtown. I switched over to the red CAT and headed west until I came to The Mint. I hadn't been to a mint before so thought I'd take advantage of the opportunity. I walked through the majestic wrought iron gates and guard house and into the circular courtyard. The mint still operates from its original premises, a gorgeous three story Victorian building with arches and columns. Red tiles underfoot, I walked over to a bronze statue of two gold miners, Arthur Bayley and William Ford. One story says that when Bayley and Ford stopped at a gnamma, a deep rock water hole, they found nuggets lying right on the surface at a place called Fly Flat. Later, my guide would tell the tale of them almost dying during their search due to lack of water and provisions. They had decided to quit the search and head back to civilization. As they slept, a bit of rain fell. When they woke the next day they were dazzled by sparkling nuggets of gold lying on the surface of the earth. They simply had to bend over and pick up the gold! They stuck pegs in the ground and laid claim to one of the richest pieces of land on Earth. If they had not stopped right there and if it hadn't rained the gold would have been found by others. With their discovery of gold at Coolgardie in 1892 there was a huge gold rush and the mint was established to process the gold that the miners brought in from the outback.

I walked up the six stairs to the solid green doors, pulled open the door on my left and entered the foyer. The interior is splendid in grand Victorian era style. At the information desk I picked up a guide to the mint and found out that the next tour began in fifteen minutes. With a bit of time to kill I walked off to view the world's largest exhibit of gold bars. The room had subdued lighting with the bars highlighted in splashes of light. There was an amazing array of unique bars from around the planet that came in a variety of unusual shapes, designs and sizes. One case had a fanned out 'hand' of five bars that ranged from five grams up to two hundred eighty grams (ten ounces). At a value of about ten thousand dollars, I'll take the big one please. Well, maybe several of the large ones!

On my forty minute tour I learned a lot about the gold rush, refining gold and processing it. In a small courtyard there is a mock up of a prospector's camp. Life was very difficult for the miners. Simple canvas tents were their shelter and rudimentary tools their means of work. The temperature would have climbed into the forties on some summer days and have dipped below zero on some winter days. Water was a valuable commodity and was often sold at grossly inflated prices; as you need water to live, it wasn't really an optional purchase. There was a foam replica of a gigantic gold nugget that was the size of an extra large pizza box and twice as thick. Now that would be the real nugget to get hold of!

We passed the 1899 vault where we each got a chance to glimpse into the interior. In the subdued lighting I saw millions of dollars worth of gold bars from countries all over the world. The gold is sent here to be minted into an array of coins and bars and then these finished products are sent back overseas to the owners. Some of the gold is made into coin blanks and upon their return, individual countries put their unique stamp on them.

The mint houses Australia's largest collection of natural gold nuggets. They have been gathered over the years as a result of years of intense work in the outback by prospectors. The second largest gold nugget in existence is on display here. Newmont's Normandy Nugget weighs three times as much as my Fox Terrier, Emma. It weighs a little more than a fifty pound sack of flour. It weighs a whopping twenty-five and a half kilograms. At the time I saw it, it had an approximate value of seven hundred eighty six thousand US dollars. A year later it would be worth just over a million dollars. Sigh – another opportunity missed . . . .

Next we were back inside and following our guide to the next stop on the tour. Place yourself on a wooden bench in a century-old building. The brick walls here have a special glow to them – they have been embedded with gold dust from the continuous refining of gold here over more than a century. There is an area like a stage across from you and soon a young man appears from the left. He is dressed in a leather apron and heavy boots. Kent is going to pour liquid gold for us. The lights were dimmed to give a more dramatic effect. He placed some gold into a crucible and then placed it over a source of intense heat. After a few minutes he told us that the gold had melted. Grabbing the crucible with sturdy metal tongs he carefully positioned it over a metal mould and slowly but steadily poured the treasure. We 'ooohed' and 'awed' as the gold fell downward, its molten color mesmerizing us. In a matter of seconds the gold was in the mould and had solidified. Kent put down his tongs and popped the fresh gold bar out of its place and into his heavily gloved hand.

"This is worth about two hundred thousand dollars. No, there is no way I can steal this, although I must confess, I have given it some thought. There are cameras in the area and you see that big uniformed guy over there on your left? Well, he's a guard. I'm always watched by a guard when I pour the gold. This bar is the same gold I use every time. It just gets melted, poured, hardened, over and over again. It is weighed at regular intervals to make sure that none of it has gone missing. As I said, I have thought about taking it – but what chance do I have?" I was thinking that maybe Kent and I could work out a plan . . . .

Lights were turned back on and we filed out of our seats to continue the tour. We entered a room full of coins. The coins on display here went way beyond my imagination. (You don't know what you don't know) The coins are made from silver, gold or platinum and are each a work of art. I loved the Lunar Series. There are twelve coins in this group, each one featuring an animal from the Chinese Lunar Calendar. They were minted, a new one each year, from the Year of the Rat in 1996 through the Year of the Pig in 2007. They proved to be a very popular series for two reasons: their absolutely exquisite quality and the fact that they are limited production coins.

My favourite coins were a new series called The Dreaming. Daryl Bellotti is the artist who was commissioned to create three designs of each of fifteen Australian animals. What a fabulous job he has done! His coins "tell a story with traditional life styles with a contemporary edge." Through his art, Daryl hopes that people will be inspired to learn more about the animals on the coins and more about the land and traditional people who inhabit it. This is a three year series with five new animals being introduced each year from 2009-2011. The 2009 coins illustrated the kangaroo, dolphin, echidna, brown snake and brolga, a type of heron. The gold coins were plain gold, beautiful and lustrous. I liked the silver and platinum coins better because Daryl used other colors in these coins. The silver coin has an outline of a kangaroo in which Daryl has used simple lines and dots which are prevalent in Aboriginal art. This is an active kangaroo, bounding along in the outback. The most striking part of the coin is the colourful earth that is displaced by the impact of the landing kangaroo; orange, gold and rusty earth-tones spray up and out from the impact zone. The gold coin kangaroo is sitting low, in a restful pose. The platinum coin kangaroo has stopped, but is alert, looking back over his left shoulder, and standing on a colourful Australian landscape. When I taught art in high school, I gave the students a coin design project, so I was quite entranced by the coins and spent time looking at the finest details of Daryl`s art. Ravens, pack rats, babies and me – we like the shiny things – it was difficult to leave the coins in the gift shop. I just wanted to give them a home, to have them close by so I could get pleasure by looking at them any time I wanted. "No VISA card, you must stay in my wallet. You really cannot come out to play!"

I was on my own now and spent a bit more time looking at beautiful coins, gold bars and jewellery in the gift shop. There was a great variety of coins: space travel, a great white shark with teeth bared ready to strike, lots of cars in red, blue and yellow and the one that surprised me the most – Dame Edna, bespectacled with her trademark, purple hair. There is a ten kilogram pure silver coin that has a Kookaburra on it – it is one of the world's largest legal tender coins. I can't really imagine carrying it around or finding a slot it would ever fit in, but it might be fun to have it for a day. One of the most endearing silver coins has a gilded koala bear sitting on a eucalyptus branch. I also sidled over to a special scale, 'Worth Your Weight in Gold?' With no one watching I got on the scale and really pounded out a vast fortune on the dial!

I left the building and walked around the front yard for a few minutes before stepping back out through the gates. Now I wanted some quiet time with nature so I turned left and walked several blocks to Queens Gardens. This is a lovely small park with ponds, grass, trees, plants and bird life. I found a bench in the shade and sat for about fifteen minutes enjoying watching the ducks in the pond next to me. Then I continued around the edge of the park, stopping at several benches and going through the same routine. It was a nice time of respite from people and things. Rejuvenated, I headed back past the mint and entered the grounds of Government House. This is an impressive building and well known Perth landmark. There were a lot of cockatoos about so they gave me a little burst of happy as I watched their antics and took some pictures. The building was not open to the public, but I was able to walk around it and that was okay by me. I saw a window washing crew of three men who happened to be on the ground by their van. I walked over to them and started chatting about their job. How long it took to wash the windows here – four days. How long they had been working for the company – two months, two years and six years. Did they like it - they loved it. They were all wearing the standard colors of workmen throughout the country. Their short-sleeved shirts were fluorescent lime green on top with navy on the bottom half and on the collars. The two older fellows had shorts on while the youngest wore long black pants. They all had baseball style hats on with sunglasses perched on top of them. I asked if I could take their picture – "Ya, sure!" So to my collection I added a great shot of three mates, arms over their friends shoulder's sporting huge grins. I love that shot!

I rode back into town on the red CAT and found the Travel Medicine Center. With all the walking I had been doing, my right knee had been getting more painful during the past week. I decided that I would try to get a cortisone shot as I would be doing a lot more walking over the next five weeks of my trip. After making several calls that morning, I had an appointment at a health travel clinic. The clinic's focus is to get you ready for a trip with such things as vaccinations, but I was able to get in and see a doctor to tell him what I wanted. The doctor was a nice man and said that I could get an injection at this office. However, he hadn't done this type of shot in a long time and was not comfortable doing it. The only doctor who could do it was not working that day. So I set up an appointment to see the second doctor two days later. I had a prescription for the cortisone, so filled it in a nearby pharmacy.

I spent a quiet evening back at the hostel and laid out plans for the next several days. Tomorrow I would spend the day in Freemantle.

Located at the mouth of the Swan River, Freemantle is the main port for Western Australia. Paying four dollars for a ticket, I caught a morning train that took me nineteen kilometres through a mixture of housing on the way to Freemantle. The train station in Freemantle is just over a hundred years old and is a designated Heritage Place. It was a very important transportation hub for the gold prospectors who arrived by ship and then travelled east by train to the goldfields. I found the architecture of the station picture-worthy. It is not a very large station but the front entrance is striking with its beige, Donnybrook stone, arched door and windows, gilded lettering and detailed work on the side of the building and rising from the roof.

I walked the short distance from the train station to my first stop, the Maritime Museum. The museum is on the Swan River at the entrance to the harbour. When I first saw the building I thought of the hull of a monstrous ship turned upside down. Most of the museum is white while the tinted windows are blue – true maritime colors. I walked up the few stairs and into the large structure. The main gallery, which celebrates Western Australia's maritime connection, is just amazing. The ceiling towered over me, rising thirty meters above. The walls taper in from the bottom to the top and reminded me of the Sydney Opera House design. The gallery ceiling is high enough so that the 1983 America's Cup winner, Australia II fits easily. It was really great to see this yacht out of the water, to see the unique winged keel that helped take the Cup from the American team. From high tech yachts down to outrigger canoes, there were a great number of boats on display. While looking at the Parry Endeavour, I tried to visualize the challenges of Jon Sanders as he sailed this small boat around the world three times. Of course I couldn't imagine what he had faced as my boating experience is primarily of canoes on lakes and rivers. I could however, imagine that it must be one of the greatest challenges of nature that any one person has ever undertaken.

The Gallery of the Indian Ocean displayed the story of people linked by trade over thousands of years. Not only were boats showcased but there was an excellent display of gold, grains, pearls, spices, ivory and fabrics. Hung on racks were oriental rugs, rich in tones of red and gold. A great variety of trunks, woven baskets and sacks showed how things were packed for transportation hundreds of years ago. The packed exhibition was brought alive by the sounds of a fifteenth century Middle Eastern

Market which I found to be a wonderful immersion experience – one that I hadn't expected at a maritime museum.

The Fishing Gallery showcases Aboriginal fishing methods, the pearl industry, how fishing operations have changed over the years and the problems now pressuring the industry. The evolution of the industry is well represented using lots of original items, interpretive photos and informational signs. Boats are suspended several meters above the displays, and looking up, I realized how large even a small boat can seem. There is an upper level where I viewed the same boats from deck level, so was able to get an appreciation for the whole boat, not just the part that shows above the water.

Next to the main building sits a decommissioned submarine, HMAS Ovens. I signed up for the 10:30 tour and was happy to find out that I was the only one on the tour at that time. (Travel Luck) Keith, my guide, was a handsome fellow with wavy red hair that followed a Conan O'Brien style. He had green eyes that crinkled with his Aussie smile. Keith had served in the Australian Navy for twenty years and had actually been stationed on that very submarine. We walked over to the black submarine and climbed the stairway that took us to the top deck where, from that perspective it becomes apparent just how long and narrow these ocean craft are. I looked down the deck to the tall coning tower, a black monolith rising alone from the deck.

We began our descent down the first set of steep stairs, Keith going forwards but I elected to go down backwards as it seemed safer for me. As we made our first stop I was really glad that I didn't have to share the space with ten or more people as I had an unobstructed view of everything in the area. And there were a lot of things to see. We were in a torpedo bay. There were six tubes: one had a torpedo inserted two thirds of the way, an empty one was open with a spot light shining into it, one was open and dark and the others were shut. Wires and cables snaked everywhere against the painted white background. There was a fluorescent orange full body suit hanging in wait for a submariner to don while working here. The most surprising thing to find there was a bunk – yes a mattress lined up with one of the tubes as if waiting its turn to be launched into the sea. Keith said it was actually one of the best places to sleep because you had a bit more room and it was a more comfortable environment.

Marine engineering is a precise science and never was this more apparent than in the confines of the submarine. Virtually every square inch had something in place. Keith explained the major features at each of our stops and I got to carry on a normal conversation asking all the questions I wanted to. This was interesting for both of us because apparently I asked questions never before posed and noticed things previously unnoticed. This was so great to have Keith all to myself, just two people walking and sharing information.

There is one narrow walkway down the center of the submarine. I managed this path quite handily but had to slow down to negotiate the bulk head doors where the passageway becomes a raised oval and there was a high lip to step over. These could be closed and sealed with a water tight door. Keith said it was very spacious right now because there were no supplies on the pathway. When all supplies, especially food, are loaded at the beginning of a mission, a lot of it is stacked along the side of this already narrow path making it even tighter. The passable space may be reduced to just over twelve inches wide with boxes stacked three high to one side. As the trip progressed and supplies were consumed more space would become available.

Keith showed me his small bunk. The mattress was a piece of foam, four inches thick, very narrow at about eighteen inches wide and six and a half feet long. It was covered in vinyl, then simple bedding put on top of it. To keep you in place while you slept, each bunk has a belt, like a car seat belt, that you buckle across your waist when you go to bed. The bunk beds are three high, the lowest mere inches off the floor. The vertical spacing is only about twenty four inches, so this is not a bed that you can sit up on. The top bunk has a concave wall as it follows the shape of the boat. There are tiny storage spaces along the back wall and head or foot of each bunk. Personal gear is kept to a minimum.

The toilets are tucked in on the outside walls; thus requiring a person to shuffle out of their overalls and back in, leaning forward so as not to bump their head, then lowering onto the throne. It's a very snug fit.

Boy, the kitchen is small! It is about two meters deep and perhaps three meters wide. And from this compact area, two cooks turned out meals and snacks each and every day for up to sixty crew members. The cooks had to be good as meals were about the only thing to look forward to each day.

Keith told a food story: The crew was going to be able to go ashore unexpectedly and talk soon turned to the possibility of having pizza for a meal. They were very excited at having something that wasn't usually on the menu. The cooks, who had already prepared the evening meal, heard of their plan and issued this warning, "Any crew member who has pizza and doesn't eat the meal I have for them, will be unable to get any food from the galley for a week!" And that is how the pizza dinner plan failed to materialize. Everyone ate the meal prepared onboard.

Keith showed me where they stowed a barbeque. A barbeque? On a submarine? Yes. Aussies love their barbeque and every now and then when the submarine would come to the surface, the crew had the chance to set it up on deck and have a swim and a barbeque. I never did see Sean Connery do that in The Hunt for Red October! And of course, they had a special place where they stored the beer too - an empty torpedo tube at the bow. Our time together went well over that of the usual one hour tour. I found it especially interesting and wouldn't hesitate to do it again.

By this time I was ready for lunch. A short walk from the museum is a beautiful harbour filled with boats tied up at numerous finger slips. It is a beautiful backdrop for a number of restaurants and shops and it is where Keith had recommended I go for lunch. I had fish and chips, a dish I like to try at waterfront places. It passed the test and I rated it as four out of five stars.

Replenished and rehydrated I walked to the nearby Shipwreck Museum, a world renowned maritime archaeology museum. The main entrance gallery has a collection of paintings, full display cases and artefacts. Arched brickwork beams support the ceiling. A huge anchor pitted and lined with age and erosion is supported at eye level. I was already impressed by the place and I hadn't even been there five minutes.

The museum has a huge collection of artefacts from Dutch shipwrecks and items from Australia's first mariners. They are displayed in many cabinets in different galleries in the museum. The items are a mixed lot, anything you might find on ship of the time: glassware, shoes, coins, chains, games, dishes, pottery, charts, books, cannons and various pieces of metal.

My favorite gallery is about a famous shipwreck - that of the Dutch ship, Batavia. In 1629, on its route to secure priceless spices, the Batavia had managed thousands of nautical miles around the Cape of Good Hope, then east to the coast of New Holland (Australia). Sixty kilometers west of the coast, at the Abrolhos Islands, ships would change course and steer north to Djakarta. This was a mostly uncharted area and was an extremely treacherous place for ships. In the middle of the night, with raging winds and seas, the Batavia became stuck fast to a reef; attempts to lighten the ship and free her were unsuccessful. The Batavia was doomed. Many of the passengers were put on two small islands where they had to fend for themselves in the search for food and water. The ships commander and officers, forty-eight in all, set out in a small boat to Djakarta and it was three months before a rescue ship returned. They found only half the number of people who had been left behind; there had been a mutiny and most of the people had been murdered. The perpetrators were hanged immediately. It wouldn't be until the 1960s that parts of the wreck and human remains were discovered.

The remains were excavated by archaeologists in the 1970s then carefully treated to conserve as much material as possible. The pieces were painstakingly reassembled in the gallery. The remaining quarter of the Batavia is the centerpiece of the museum. I walked into the quiet gallery in subdued lighting and felt like I was witness to a graveyard which is exactly what it is. The aged timbers of the ship rose from the floor, ever so delicately assembled and suspended above me. It is such a very old ship, a battered ship – I wondered how these wooden pieces had managed to survive for almost four hundred years. This ship is almost three times as old as my country! Also on display, in this quiet chamber, is the skeleton of one of the people who was murdered on the island. He lies in repose, preserved in the coral reef for centuries. His right foot is missing, his right shoulder blade is broken and his skull is fractured – perhaps damage suffered under the heavy blows of a sword? I couldn't imagine the hardships he had faced on the voyage and the untimely end he had come to. I was awed to be in his presence and felt a bit like an intruder. The few other visitors spoke in whispers – it was a place of quiet respect and wonder. A replica of the commander's journal is also on display telling the world the gruesome story of the tragedy.

The original steam engine of the Batavia sits in another room. Part of the entry fee is channeled to a fund used in the restoration of the three hundred eighty year old engine. Almost every part of this engine is being reused in the project.

After the shipwreck museum I hopped on the free bus and toured around Fremantle, noting the places I wanted to see later. Fremantle has a large number of heritage buildings giving the city an historic look. The architecture is varied and much of it built with limestone and has ornate details. The oldest remaining building in Australia is the Round House that was built as a jail in 1830-31 by convicts. It is a stout building with eight sides crafted from roughly rectangular, grey stones. With the arrival, twenty years later, of seventy-five convicts, it was quickly realized that the Round House could not hold them all so the convicts were set to work on a new, much larger jail that was used as Fremantle's prison until 1991. I walked to the jail, an imposing building with a large square tower on each side of the arched gateway. I didn't want to go inside. To enter such a building would put in my mind a place of hardship and sorrow. Try as I might to suppress the memory, I know it would come to mind later. I just didn't want that memory inside my head.

I caught the bus again and headed to the Fremantle Arts Center. The building is another constructed by convicts in the 1860s. It's a large building with three gabled roof sections that are joined by flat-roofed sections. An imposing building, it rises two stories from the street. It is a light brown color – made from limestone found in the area. While I liked roaming around: along halls, up and down creaky wooden stairs, through display rooms, the most fascinating thing was the history of the building. This Fremantle landmark building was used as: a lunatic asylum, the land base of the U. S. Navy during World War II, a shelter for homeless women, a midwifery school, a technical school, the Maritime Museum and the Immigration Museum. It is said to be haunted by several ghosts from its days as a psychiatric hospital. One ghost in particular has been seen many times as she wanders the halls in her never-ending search for her abducted daughter. While I didn't hear her screams or footsteps, I could imagine her presence. The Arts Center is known as 'the most haunted building in the Southern Hemisphere.' In the 1970's it became home to the Fremantle Arts Center. After my look around, I spent some time sitting in the shade of the many trees in the courtyard. It is often used for free concerts on Sunday afternoons in the summer time.

The free bus took me back to the station where I caught the train back to Perth. I was back at the hostel by late afternoon in plenty of time for supper. This was no ordinary supper, but one of The Emperor's Crown's special activities. Tonight was Bin Bag BBQ supper. I wasn't even sure what a bin bag was when I had signed up two days previously. But for eight dollars, it sounded like a good way to enjoy a barbeque with fellow travellers. A bin bag is simply a garbage bag. We were each given a large black bin bag with which to fashion our attire. There were some very creative designs from both the males and females; the styles varied from a girls' elaborate multi-layered evening dress to a simple Speedo swimsuit by one of the guys. There were several caped crusaders and one fellow even wore a top hat and tie. Mine was the most simple of designs. I chose the classic high Empire Waist line. First, I cut a two inch wide strip from the top of the bag so I had a strip of plastic about five feet long. Then I simply placed the bag on the front of my body and wrapped the strip around my high waist and tied it in a bow. I taped the two top corners of the bin bag to my shoulders to keep it in place and voila - I was ready. There were eighteen of us dressed in bin bag outfits. We had the back patio to ourselves where staff barbequed hamburgers and sausages. Salads, bread and cut veggies completed the meal. There I was at fifty-eight enjoying the company of all these kids in their twenties. I'm glad that I didn't think I was too old for this fun activity. A good time was had by all.

The next morning was bright and beautiful, another wonderful summer day. I returned to the travel clinic to receive my injection. This doctors' method was different than that of my family doctor, Gord. When Gord had first injected my knee two weeks before I left Canada, he did it with one shot above my knee. All done, and relatively pain-free.

"This will sting" – uh oh, a warning from my Perth doctor! Never a good sign of things to come. The doctor first injected freezing to the area below my knee in three shots. He was absolutely right – it did sting – all three times! After waiting a very short time it was time for the cortisone injection. It was, let's just say uncomfortable, so I was glad to have had the freezing. He carefully wrapped a bandage around my knee to keep the four little puncture wounds clean. Then my inner child came out. I figured that I couldn't really get a lot of sympathy with just the bandage so I borrowed his red felt pen and drew enough 'blood' on the bandage to make it noticeable. So we laughed together about that, then I thanked him and was on my way, limping out of the clinic with new life in my knee joint. I thought that was pretty good service to get in to see a doctor and get the injection in only three days! (Travel Luck)

I'm sure the walking helped the cortisone spread through my knee joint. I was walking the few blocks to the car rental office where I was matched with my new Toyota. I drove up the hill to King's Park and was quite amazed at how far I had walked just three days ago. I parked the car much further into the park than I had gone on my first visit. It was now a day to see what I had missed before.

Right next to the car park is one of the most amazing trees I have seen – and you know by now how I love trees. The tree is Gija Jumulu, a seven hundred fifty year old boab tree. That in itself is not that amazing – well, actually, I guess it is amazing! How it got to be at the park is really amazing too. I read the fascinating story of its journey from the information sign next to the tree. The tree was in the path of a new highway in the Kimberley region, three thousand two hundred kilometres away from Perth. Facing destruction, the local Gija Aborigines gave the tree to the Nyoongar people, the traditional owners of the King's Park area. In a special smoke ceremony, the Gija prepared the tree for the move. Huge diggers and cranes were brought in to unearth a large root ball and load it onto a huge flat bed trailer. This part of the operation took three days. Many branches were removed to pare the tree down to an eight meter width making it possible to travel the roads to Perth, but even at this width it commanded two lanes of traffic. At thirty-seven tons and being fourteen meters long, it was an extra-wide load, requiring pilot vehicles and a police escort during its seven day journey to King's Park. With the Nyoongar people holding a traditional welcoming ceremony for the tree, it was replanted near fourteen young boab trees already in the park. The tree had been here only nine months but was showing leafy signs of growth already. It made me happy to see that it seems to have survived its uprooting and long journey. Boab trees can live up to two thousand years – I hope this one makes it that long. Botanists will collect pods from the boab and grow two hundred seedlings to send back to the Kimberley. I don't know why the tree had to be moved as it seems to me that there is a lot of space in Australia. Why couldn't the road have taken a bend around it? Obviously, I'm not a road engineer.

The Lotterywest Federation Walkway began near the boab tree and soon I was walking along this wonderful path. The walkway is six hundred twenty meters long, a combination of ground-level and elevated paths. It loops through the Botanic Garden that is loaded with over two thousand species of Western Australia flora. Some informational signs can be pretty boring, but not here. The signs are individual works of art; created with colourful paintings of plants and animals, styled by Aboriginal artistry, and using simple explanations, I found myself drawn to them. Dwellingup Mallee – interesting heading. Here I read the story of this lone tree. There is only one of these hybrid trees known to exist in the wilds of Australia. Scientists have used DNA fingerprinting and tissue cultures to preserve this unique specimen. This garden is one of a worldwide network of gardens where there is a commitment to plant conservation.

The path has an elevated section that rises gently through the trees. The boardwalk is wide enough for four people to walk side by side. The protective side walls are constructed of steel, steel that has rusted to that reddish-brown color that blends in with nature. The supporting pylons of the walkway are also made of rusting steel which serves as a reminder of the rusted steel that was evident in mines, camps and farms in Western Australia at the time of Federation. A hundred meters along the path the steel sides gave way to glass. Arching sixteen meters above the ground, the glass and steel bridge welcomed me. The bridge is half a football field long. Its sides are made up of fifty-two thick glass panels on each of its sides. I was passing through a forest of Tingle, Jarrah, Karri and Marri, trees. Don't you think that sounds like a law firm? I climbed to the middle where I stopped for a time and took in the spectacular view of the Swan and Canning Rivers. The air smelled of ocean, trees, bushes and flowers.

As I got near the far side of the bridge I stopped to watch an approaching group of school children, parents and teachers. The students looked to be around eight years old. They wore uniforms: red shorts, white shirts and navy baseball-style caps with a piece of material that hung down and sheltered their necks from the sun. They seemed happy to be out of the classroom on a field trip. As a teacher, I know that I always looked forward to field trips too. I was happy to see them and said hi to several of the kids and their supervisors. They were a pulsation of happy vibes that passed my way – fun!

At the end of the walkway I turned right and came to the Beedawong (celebration) Meeting Place. This is a lovely, small, stone, amphitheatre that seats about a hundred people. It is a venue for Nyoongar activities such as storytelling, dance and other performances. It is a very quiet place, nestled into the garden and I stayed for a few minutes of quiet contemplation.

The Water Garden took me away from Perth and put me in the Darling Range far to the east. The path meanders along a re-created creek that flows down and around massive granite boulders. I love flowing water – the sight, the sound, the smell of fresh water. The creek is planted with native reeds and sedges which help keep the water healthy. This is an area that celebrates women. There are sculptures created by female artists that link natural and human worlds. Fifty-three brass plaques tell of women's associations that played pivotal roles in the community during the hundred years after Suffrage.

Across the creek is the Acacia Garden with showy species of wattle, Australia's floral emblem. Other wattles grown here include those used by Aboriginals for medicine, food or to make tools or spears. The feature I liked most was a most beautiful organic staircase. The staircase is like a dry, narrow riverbed that flows in gentle cascades. I walked up the stairs through a horticultural time warp. On the bottom stair, artist Stuart Green has inlayed a mosaic of an ancient species, Brown's wattle (acacia). Stuart depicts the flowers, leaves and even the seedpods of different acacias that have grown in Australia over thousands of years. This was a slow walk, not because of my knee, but because I stopped on most stairs to admire his work.

As I strolled across the large, grassy, Peppermint Lawn, I observed fifty or so people in the area: walking, talking, playing, having lunch. It reminded me of a hole on a well-maintained golf course. It was just a lovely place to spend some time.

With its spectacular views, walkways, varied works of art, fascinating trees, flowers, meandering creek, ponds, birdlife, lawns and bushland, King's Park was a great time investment. I had immersed myself, just being in the moment, enjoying snippets of nature and taking pictures. It was wonderful!

Back in the car, I drove to Cliff Street, the boundary of King's Park, and parked the car. My new quest was to visit Jacob's ladder. It is a collection of stairs, two hundred forty-two in all, that lead from Cliff Street down to Mounts Bay Road. I had heard about it from a few people in the hostel and while I didn't think I'd try to climb it, I was hoping I could watch others do it. I was not disappointed. There were about twenty people at various stages of going up or down the stairs. I stayed at the lookout long enough to watch several of these hardy souls do multiple climbs. No - not a place to take my knee – not at all. (Little did I realize that three days later I would climb many more stairs than this while visiting a cave.)

There was still time to take an afternoon drive out to the Aquarium of Western Australia which is only twenty minutes from Perth. The coastline of Western Australia is over twelve thousand kilometres long – the aquarium would let me explore all of it in an afternoon. The aquarium is divided into five sections from the tropical coral reefs of the north to the giant kelp forests of the Great Southern Coast. Complex marine environments have been skilfully re-created right down to growing their own coral, a feat hardly contemplated by other aquariums.

I love to visit aquariums. I can sit captivated for hours watching the marine animals silently glide past me. I am easily amused. They all have routines, just like I do. I have found that if I watch a fish for long enough, I can see a clockwork pattern unfold before me. I have timed the routines of some fish and it is an exact path they follow. Even though the tanks are huge by our human standards, they are impossibly small when comparing them to the ocean. Still, this is their habitat and their needs are being met. The largest tank is home to over four hundred species who share the three dimensional space and three million litres of sea water.

My self-guided tour started with small tanks that contained one or just a few compatible species. The sea dragons are definitely one of my favourite animals. This most unusual fish lives only in the waters off Western Australia. Unless you know that they look like the seaweed they live in, you would never notice them. Fortunately the tank had a picture along with some information and it was then easy to find them. They look like very large sea-horses, are a beautiful rich yellow and have many appendages that float in the water like the leaves on seaweed. Only the tiny move-ments of fins or an eye gave away their location. They moved as if guided by an invisible hand that bobbled them first this way then that – gently tossed by the currents.

Australia has more than its fair share of dangerous animals. In one tank there lived an exquisite, tiny, Blue-ringed Octopus. His body, a pale yel-low, was lavished with impossibly gorgeous turquoise-blue rings outlined with black. The centers of the rings were a golden brown, the shade of a perfectly cooked pancake. When provoked they turn a bright yellow color and use water propulsion to send themselves away from the attack-er. Even though they are only about the size of your hand, they carry enough venom to kill about twenty-five adults. They are one of the most venomous animals on the planet. Why on earth this little guy needs so much venom is a mystery, but that's just the way it is with some creatures. If a person is unlucky enough to be bitten, they might not even be aware of it as the bites are small and do not sting. It is only when the venom starts to take effect and paralysis begins that a person might know what happened. There is no anti-venom. The paralysis disables respiratory muscles and unless rescue breathing is used or the person is put on a ven-tilator, death is imminent. The poisoned person is fully conscious – just unable to breathe. So quite a dangerous, but awesome creature!

Another dangerous sea animal that I saw was the box jellyfish. You may recall that these little see-through animals caused me to wear a stinger suit when I was diving at the Great Barrier Reef. The ones in the tank had cube-shaped bells about six to ten centimetres across and perhaps an average of twenty tentacles. Each tentacle can have up to half a million little 'needles' that are activated by chemicals on their prey's skin. The injection of their strong venom can cause heart and respiratory problems and is often fatal if not treated immediately. Floating in their aquarium they looked surreally beautiful and peaceful. I'm so glad that I was able to observe them and I marvelled at how something so beautiful could be so deadly.

The largest tank in the aquarium lies beside and over an arching acrylic tunnel that lies in roughly an oval shape and is ninety-eight meters long. I stepped into the entrance to the tunnel and found that it took no ef-fort on my part to move as the floor silently glides along. My only con-cern was keeping my balance which I did quite well, with the occasional touching of the handrail. It became a dreamlike state – subdued lighting, hundreds of marine animals – just standing there, alone for the most part. We watched each other, the sharks, rays, turtles, fish and me. My mind took me back to The Great Barrier Reef and my diving experience there. The concentration of life here at the aquarium was heavier. I hadn't seen sharks or rays on the reef and only one turtle but here I got to see a lot of them and was able to be within a few meters of them. The re-created coral reef was very well done. Four hundred meters of observations later, I left the tunnel in a very mellow mood. I had really enjoyed my underwater adventure and was thankful that I had the opportunity to see the variety of sea life that exists off Western Australia.

Taking the main highway sounded like a good way to get back into Perth. It's too bad that I got 'temporarily misplaced' (I never call myself lost) and ended up taking an hour long route back to the Emperor's Crown. People were friendly and gave me good directions when at last I stopped to ask.

I had supper at the Murray Street Mall then packed up my gear and loaded most of it into the car. After four wonderful, sunny days here, I would leave Perth the next morning.

DOLPHINS AND WEDDINGS

A restful sleep and a leisurely breakfast had me leaving the hostel around ten thirty the next morning. On this, my first Saturday on the west coast, I drove south from Perth along the coastal highway to Bunbury arriving shortly after two which gave me the rest of the day to explore the area. Bunbury is located on a peninsula so has water on three sides. There are beaches everywhere that create a multitude of possibilities for recreation. I found the hostel and claimed a bottom bunk before I set out to look around. As usual I sought out the highest point in town to get oriented to the area, so drove the short distance to Marlston Hill lookout tower. The stairs up to the observation deck were fairly short and easy to climb. The view was great of course; I could see the whole city from up there, stretching back along the peninsula. Something I really loved in the northern end of Bunbury was the variation in the rooftops. If there were identical roofs, I did not see them. The roofs are not at all straightforward. Each one was a myriad of peaks and valleys; on one house I counted thirty roof sections, all assembled and working together to make a remarkable piece of architecture. The roofs were finished with rusty red, black or blue tiles or a smooth finish that I was unfamiliar with, in white, grey or black. Beyond the buildings was the beautiful blue ocean, stretching across the harbour and Koombana Bay and over the Indian Ocean to 'infinity' in the west. The Bunbury Tower dominates the downtown area, a seventy meter tall, modernistic structure that locals call The Milk Carton. With a blue and white exterior and triangular rooftop tipping skyward, it does indeed look like an open milk carton. I walked down the tower and noticed two girls who had Canadian flags on their backpacks. Naturally I went over to them and had a short chat with them. They were from Ontario and were travelling around Australia for three months together before they had to go back home to work. They reminded me of the ten weeks my friend, Lyn and I spent backpacking around Europe when we were twenty. We had such a good time doing that! The town's geography now set in my mind, I left the lookout and drove to the lighthouse, a short distance away. This is the first lighthouse I saw that wasn't painted just white on the tower; it sports a unique black and white checkerboard pattern. It stands twenty-five meters tall and its light can be seen from twenty-seven kilometres away.

Ocean Drive is spectacular and I drove along it until I came to Back Beach, a natural treasure and one of the most popular beaches in the area. With its white sandy beach, rocky outcrops and gentle surf, it is a playground for swimmers, strollers, boogie-boarders, snorkelers, fishermen, surfers and sand castle makers. During my time at this beach I observed all of the above! When I arrived and had parked the car I witnessed a wedding ceremony that was held on a grassy area right next to the beach. About a hundred people had gathered for the wedding and for twenty minutes I stood back and watch the tale unfold. It was a perfect sunny afternoon. Wedding pictures were taken on the beach, and then the bridal party and guests climbed into vehicles and headed to the reception. I strolled out to the beach and waded along in the warm water. Fifteen minutes later another wedding party showed up to have pictures taken on the beach. The bride was a beautiful brunette and was stunning in her gown. Her four bridesmaids each wore a dress in shades of blue. Standing along the top of a rock outcrop in white and blue, they looked like an extension of the ocean and the surf. It was late afternoon so the lighting was perfectly soft. Later on the beach I was talking to a fellow who told me that there had been eight weddings in Bunbury on that Saturday!

I gave the award for most fun at the beach to four teenage boys who were playing in the surf with their boogie boards. I had never seen what these boys were doing and my first reaction was "Are these guys nuts? Don't they know how dangerous it is?" But of course that was before I spent twenty minutes watching them in the waves. It was perhaps only chest deep water where they were playing. It was the rocks that made it look dangerous. Yes, they were playing in front of a rock wall that was just over two meters high. They paddled off shore until they caught a wave that carried them towards the rocks. Just when I thought they would be smashed into oblivion, another wave would be rebounding back off the rocks towards the open sea and would catch them and send them safely away from the rocks. Sometimes they would stand on the rocks, and timing it perfectly, take a flying leap into the retreating wave and be carried out to sea. They were having a blast and I loved watching them.

I walked further along the beach and was fortunate enough to see a dolphin swim by. A lot of dolphins live in the water around Bunbury - they are the main attraction of this lovely town. My last pictures of the day were of the sunset over the Indian Ocean. There were just enough clouds to make it interesting.

Darkness upon me, I drove back into town and bought a light supper in a restaurant. I wanted some mindless comedic entertainment so caught an early movie, Paul Blart, Mall Cop. It fit the bill perfectly.

I was up early the next day and arrived at the Dolphin Discovery Centre on Koombana Bay at seven forty-five. Groups of dolphins can often be seen in the interactive zone in front of the centre. There are usually some that swim by the centre around eight o'clock each morning and I wanted to be in the water if they decided to come by. Unfortunately they did not arrive that morning, so I was a bit disappointed. (Eleven days later I would get this opportunity again). I booked an eco-tour on the bay for eleven o'clock.

A short distance across the road from the Discovery Centre is the Mangrove Boardwalk. I thought this would be a good way to spend some of my time while waiting for the boat tour. This walk passes through the remains of white mangroves that used to grow here twenty thousand years ago. This type of mangrove is found eight hundred kilometres to the north so this area of isolated growth is very unusual and it is being conserved. The boardwalk makes the impassable, passable - I was able to get a close up view of the vegetation that grows in this protected tidal wetland. I had the two hundred meter boardwalk to myself for the most part, only passing one dad and daughter on the walk. There are several roofed observation platforms along the way. The uprights that hold the roof in place are carved wooden figures that are picture worthy. I wished there had been a bit of information about the artists and the meaning of the figures. There were only a small number of waterfowl in the area but the water level was low when I visited. This is an important wetland for migratory birds and they are protected with international agreements. We have protected wetlands at home in Victoria, one in particular that is used as an education center. I think it's vital that wetlands are protected worldwide.

Back over at the discovery center I still had a half hour to wait so headed off down the beach. Wading knee-deep and reaching down to catch the wave tips was Jack, a very cute two year old boy - curly, blonde hair, orange and white striped tee shirt, soggy diaper, huge smile and laughter. With his colourful shirt, Jack brought the Disney fish, Nemo to mind as he played in the water. His mom and I shared the great time Jack was having. We talked about our childhood experiences and of my kids when they were little. The beach is a delightful place to play. Water always draws people to it with its hypnotic power. Jack was feeling independent like a big boy. He was happy to lead me through the knee high (his knees, not mine) waves and showed me how to catch the water in my hands. He was just adorable and I relished the time we played together. A picture of him is one of my favourites; sweet, innocent, just living in the moment and loving it. I thanked Jacks' mom for the time together before I turned and waded back along the beach.

The Dolphin Discovery Centre is a non-profit organization that is committed to tourism, research, education and conservation. The centre has a small theatre where I watched some of the short films they have about dolphins; these were entertaining and informational. I walked around the interpretive centre and read more about dolphins particularly liking the skeleton they had on display. I always find it interesting to see the similarities and differences between animals and humans. With one last look at the souvenirs and Aboriginal art, I headed out the back door and across the sand to the water.

My boat would leave in ten minutes from in front of the Discovery Center. I waded out, was welcomed on board by Marty, our skipper, and found a seat at the starboard bow. As Koombana Bay is home to about a hundred twenty Bottlenose dolphins, Marty said that it was pretty much a certainty we would see some on our trip. He was very familiar with the bay and the dolphin population, having lived in Bunbury all his life and had worked at the center for a number of years. We motored slowly out into the bay, each of us looking in a different direction trying to spot a little puff of 'smoke' or a dorsal fin or two. "Thar she blows! Off the port side at ten o'clock." We were all excited at our first glimpse of the dolphins. Marty changed course slightly and we headed for the group. The boat stopped about fifty meters from the dolphins so as not to intrude. One of the dolphin interaction regulations is that "At all times the dolphins must have a choice to interact or not." We did not approach the dolphins closely, but being very curious animals they came over to have a look at us. Soon it was necessary for Marty to steer our boat away from the pod to try to keep fifty yards away. They simply followed us so the boat was stopped. The group of seven dolphins came within two meters of us which allowed for some great contact and photo opportunities. The highlight was a mom with her new baby; they were constantly close to each other and mom would look back often at her baby. They rose to the surface in unison to breathe then would swim along about a meter under the surface. They followed us for about fifteen minutes before peeling off in formation. We continued across the bay to the far shore where the skipper turned and slowed the boat to just above an idle. With the shore on our left it wasn't too long before we spotted some more dolphins straight ahead of us. Once again, we couldn't keep far away from the curious animals. Three of the dolphins did some surfing in the bow wave of our boat which was fun to watch. We had two more opportunities to watch the dolphins at close range before it was time to head back to shore. All in all it was a great experience to see the dolphins in the wild. It's good to know their existence is highly valued here and that they live a good and protected life here in Koombana Bay. I had lunch in the dolphin center before leaving Bunbury.

ALONG THE SNOUT

If you look at a map of the south-west corner of Australia, perhaps you can imagine a profile of a pig's head looking to the left. If Bunbury is the pigs' eye then the town of Busselton is at the top right corner of the 'snout'. The Busselton Jetty, the longest wooden pier in the southern hemisphere, was the reason I stopped here. In 1853 the first ships were moored at the jetty, the place to load and unload goods in Geographe Bay. Over the next century the jetty was lengthened as drifting sands made the water too shallow for mooring. The jetty grew to an astonishing eighteen hundred forty-one meters by the 1960s. In 1971 the last commercial ship left the jetty and government funding and maintenance left as well. Since then, the jetty has been under attack from insects, rot, fires and cyclones and has fallen into disrepair.

I walked out onto the jetty and entered the interpretive center. It is housed fifty meters along the jetty in four blue buildings that look like boatsheds. I looked at the photographs and read about the history of the jetty and the marine environment. Out in the fresh air I walked along the first two hundred meters of the jetty, the only part still open to the public. The jetty makes a gentle right turn and stretches out into the ocean and I found myself a bit disappointed that I was not able to walk out to the end of it, or to have taken the train out to the end, or to have visited the underwater observation center near the end of it. These were now features of the past, but were under repair. It is only recently that sufficient funds have been raised to repair the jetty to its former glory with the work scheduled to be finished a year after my visit. If I ever get back to Western Australia it will be on my top ten places to visit.

I was now driving along the top of the 'snout' and would soon turn south and travel halfway down the 'snout' to Margaret River. It had been quite awhile since I last couch surfed and I was looking forward to my stay with Jack and Carrol.

Their Current Mission: *"To maximise my interests, namely classical music, cooking, tennis, camping and travelling, making new friends and maintaining contact with old friends, largely over the internet."*

I really liked their profile which gave me a lot of information about them and Margaret River. About couch surfing; "Absolutely brilliant: its concept, website layout and attention to detail. As a back packer from the 60's, I would have enjoyed a Couchsurfer type organisation back then, but then again, Youth Hostels were pretty hard to beat. Now Carroll and I tune into today's traveling youth by hosting couch surfers. It's marvellous!" I wasn't one of today's traveling youth but I'm young at heart and they were willing to host me.

They get four or five requests each month and cannot accommodate everyone. They are comfortable with two or perhaps three surfers per month and ask that surfers contact them at least a week in advance which I had. "We lead busy lives and wish to make time available to welcome and get to know our guests which is not always possible on short notice." I like to get at least two weeks' notice for my visitors. Jack told me that there are twenty-three potential hosts in Margaret River but only five of those are actually hosting travellers.

Here's what Jack has to say in his profile. "My wife, Carroll, and I live in the SE part of town about a fifteen minute walk from the centre. We have no pets and do not smoke. There are taxis in town and bicycles can be rented. There are many things to do as this is very much a tourist oriented town: many outdoor/indoor cafes and coffee shops, restaurants, clothes and souvenir shops, many wineries close to Margaret River and some distance away-some with food facilities-- three breweries, limestone caves, hiking trails in the forests, wind, body and board surfing, beaches, diving, fishing and plenty of scenery! Sometimes we are happy to show people around. We are both retired, but lead active lives, so are not available to show people around every day. We generally go to bed by 10pm. We can generally host anytime. We have plenty of blankets. Two or three days is probably an adequate amount of time we'd like to host visitors. Share: My love of Classical music, cooking, good wines, tennis, and good films. Carroll's love of gardening, environmental issues, reading and keeping fit. Easy going, easy to get along with, friendly, but not in an extroverted way. Liberal in my outlook not always as conservative as my wife would like me to be."

Jack showed me to the guest room that had a double bed. I put my gear in my room and then we went out to the back deck where we talked about travelling and families. Jack excused himself to prepare dinner. He is an amazing cook and tries three or four new recipes each week. I, on the other hand, may try a new recipe perhaps three or four times a year. I have a number of menus I like and I tend to stick to the 'tried and true'. I thought that when I retired I would find more time to try new things but then retirement came and you know what? I don't really care about new recipes. Also, I like simple things. If it's got more than four ingredients, I tend to shy away from it. I offered my help and was assigned to set the table. The three of us enjoyed Jacks creation of lamb, green beans with almonds and spicy, oven-baked potatoes. Yummy!

After dinner we went out to a movie. Margaret River does not have a movie theatre, but Jack and Carroll are members of a group that bring movies to town twice a week. We went to the community center and watched Milk, starring Shawn Penn. He is one of my favourite actors and his performance in Milk was amazing! He won the Oscar for best actor in a motion picture for his portrayal of Harvey Milk, California's first openly gay elected official. We were all moved by the story of this political trailblazer in the 60s and 70s in San Francisco. After the show, the three of us helped stack the chairs at the back of the room and then we talked with some of Jack and Carroll's friends. By the time we got back home, it was time for bed.

As you may recall, Margaret River is in the center of the 'pig's snout'. This first Monday on the west coast, I would drive west to access Caves Road which runs about a hundred thirty kilometres north – south, parallel to and a bit inland from the coast. At Caves Road I planned to go south a bit, then loop back to the northern tip of the 'snout' and return to Jack and Carroll's for the night. The goal was to visit two caves and several surfing beaches. I got an early start after a scrumptious breakfast made by Jack. I turned left off Bussell Highway onto Wallcliff Road, one of the many cross roads that join Bussell Highway and Caves Road. Ten minutes later I made a left turn onto Caves Road and I was now only five minutes away from my first stop.

In the limestone ridge that runs under the area around Margaret River lie over three hundred caves. Of these there are four major caves that are open to the public. Mammoth Cave is just a fifteen minute drive from Jack and Carroll's place so I got a jump start on the day's activities. This cave has a tour, but no guides. When I got my entry ticket, it came with an MP3 player and headphones. I could take my time; stop as often and for as long as I wanted. I would enjoy this independent aspect of the tour. I began by walking along a well maintained trail and boardwalk – this is one of the few caves that are wheel chair accessible allowing passage into the first chamber. After crossing Mammoth Creek it was just a short distance into the first chamber, open to the public since 1904. The entrance allows for a lot of natural light here which is usually not the norm in caves. It's a cave that seems quite liveable due to this light, a place to seek refuge from the elements and get a degree of comfort and safety. It was lovely to have natural light showing off the myriad of formations.

Come with me. Hold on to the rail as we descend our first sets of stairs. Step onto a small landing and then on to the next set of stairs that angle sharply off the first set. Two hands now, as the stairs are narrow and steep and at times we are way too busy looking around to pay enough attention to our footing. Another landing, another set of stairs, another landing, another set of stairs, this last one being fifteen stairs long. Now we stand side by side on a viewing platform about four meters square. We are more or less in the center of a giant sphere of wonder – a huge chamber in which we feel quite insignificant. From our position we look above, below and all around us trying to take in all we see. We just can't do it. There are thousands of formations from this vantage point. Our minds get some specific ideas, but most of the information is processed as a huge tapestry of blurred images, all fantastic, but only a few that really stand out enough for our brains to really focus on and retain. That is why I take a lot of pictures. I look at all my pictures as I am writing and they give me the chance to see details that I missed – it was just too much sensory information to process and remember at the time. Now we breathe deeply after almost forgetting to breathe as we gazed at the awesome formations surrounding us. Another full turn of our bodies and we have seen it all four times. Head to the right hand side of the platform – find the next set of stairs – two hands on the railings again – wouldn't want to take a fall here. The five hundred meter long walkway is only a few feet wide. On the more level parts there is one handrail while on the many sets of stairs, there are usually two handrails. Holding the handrails made it possible for me to look around as I walked - I loved that security. The views of the formations were spectacular and gave me a wondrous and ever-changing perspective as I passed by.

To travel through this cave is to travel through time – to learn about the animals, plants and climate that were here long ago. It is the home of thousands of ancient fossil remains, some of which are thirty-five thousand years old. Palaeontologists have found remains of a Tasmanian tiger and a huge wombat-like creature from that time. The scientists continue to visit the caves and always learn something new. At many places there are carefully lit fossils and animal bones where I stopped and listened to the stories about the amazing mammals that once lived here.

The formations played with my imagination and I searched them for images, just I often search clouds for any recognizable shapes. There was a tall stack of nesting Russian dolls, a Thai princess with elaborate towering head dress, dwarfs, lions, a caramel sundae, fountains, robed Arabs, dragon's teeth, and monsters. There was a huge forest of Karri trees, row upon row lying one on top of another, frozen in time, intricate trunks and branches supporting their interwoven canopy.

Almost done now, I could see the natural light that creeps through the large sinkhole that is the exit from Mammoth Cave. As I came closer to the exit I could see the stairs, ah yes, stairs, many sets of stairs that would lead me to the surface. Get your imagination ready. Imagine your coffee mug doesn't have a bottom. Take the resulting hollow tube and slant it up off the table at a forty-five degree angle. This is a giant sinkhole, an area where the ceiling of the cave has fallen and left a large hole that allows natural light in. The bottom of the mug is where we walked to at the end of the cave tour. The top of the mug is the opening to the world and our target area. Now add a large number of stairs attached to the inside of the mug. They climb in sets that are not spaced evenly. They turn at a great number of angles. They cling somehow to the side of the mug, all skilfully built to carry visitors safely. Perhaps you are breathing more heavily by now with the climb – I was. Finally the last stair is behind us and we stop, turn and have one last look at the end of this marvellous and intriguing adventure.

There were two options to get back to my car. The first was a direct path, the second a trail through the Marri forest. It was no choice for me – I took the longer, more scenic route. The Marri tree is a common eucalyptus that is only found in the south west corner of Western Australia. The name marri comes from the Nyoongar Aboriginal word for blood. It 'bleeds' a dark red gum and was once called the red gum tree. The path winds its way through the forty meter tall trees, trunks devoid of lower branches as neighbours compete for space. Like the cave, it was a quiet and peaceful place to be. I found it kind of magical to have just stepped out of a huge cave and now to be walking above ground through a forest; I loved the contrast. This forest is a very important habitat; blossoms and nectar are produced in large amounts, hollows in mature trees offer nesting sites for birds and animals including possums, owls and black cockatoos. I had learned that the Nyoongar people called this tree the 'medicine tree.' Gum powder was sprinkled on wounds to stop bleeding and was mixed with water and used as a disinfectant and a mouthwash. A sweet tea was made by soaking the blossoms. The gum and seeds were used as a cure for diarrhoea. The powder was used to tan kangaroo hides. I stood at the base of these 'convenience stores' and tried to imagine how the Aboriginals looked upon these useful trees.

Back in my car I drove five minutes south along Caves Road to Lake Cave, my next stop. After buying my tour ticket, I walked a few paces to the huge sinkhole that is the entrance to the cave. I thought that Mammoth Cave had quite a few stairs and that is true – but nothing compared to those at Lake Cave. I gazed into the sinkhole and was awestruck by its magnitude. I was looking into a massive, rocky bowl, white limestone cliffs rising vertically to form its sides. Huge karri trees grew from its depths with ferns and grasses filling in spaces in the forest. The roof of the cave had collapsed, leaving a pile of rocky rubble over which I would pass. Through the trees, I caught glimpses of people far below, people on stairs making their way either up or down to begin or complete their tour. In fifteen minutes our guide would meet us at a platform halfway down the stairs so it was time to head down. The descent was slow for two reasons: sometimes I had to wait and let people pass and I liked looking around at all the details. I stopped on the halfway platform where I joined a few others. We in turn were joined by more people and then our guide, James. James spent some time talking about the formation of the cave, the sinkhole entrance and the plant life. "I'll meet you down at the bottom of the stairs. There is a large area that we'll stop at." Off we went, single file, down to the bottom of the wooden stairs where we gathered in the large rusty red and grey bricked area. Then I looked up. What have I done? For some reason I had counted the stairs and I now looked up and thought about the climb back out – a climb of three hundred forty-two stairs! Lots of stairs in caves – lots and lots of stairs. Well, not to worry.

We listened to James as he went over the tour guidelines: take your time, use the handrails, don't touch the formations as it pollutes them, you can take as many pictures as you want. Now it was time to follow to James. I walked to the far end of the meeting place, turned left, and grabbed a handrail in each hand. We walked in single file down the steep wooden stairs and soon were swallowed by the darkness. James turned on some lights which allowed us to see where we were going. My eyes soon adjusted to the darkness and I could see the formations of the cave. Lake Cave is quite small, only ninety meters long – a little shorter than a football field. 'Good things come in small packages.' This is so very true of this most gorgeous cave. Imagine looking up and seeing thousands of pure white limestone formations hanging from the ceiling. It is mesmerizing and I found myself smiling and looking around in silent wonder. Now imagine a mirror image, not only doubling but somehow more than tripling the beauty. This is the reflective power of the large lake from which the cave takes its name.

We slowly passed along one side of the lake on a wooden walkway that had a handrail on one side. The water was perfectly still except for small ripples formed when a drop of water fell off a stalactite into the lake. The only other sound was the drip dripping of those tiny drops. There was a reverence among us – a few hushed whispers, 'oohs' and 'aahs', and some pictures taken. It was an incredible place of peace. James talked about the history, geology, hydrology and ecology of Lake Cave. Then he put on a light show. Along with the usual white light, the cave has been set up with green, red, blue and yellow lighting. With the controls in hand James changed the lighting in a rainbow effect that elicited many more 'oohs' and 'aahs' from everyone in our group. While the light show was pretty and I'm glad I saw it, I much prefer the true and natural colors of the cave.

We continued along side the lake, rounded a bend and came to the most incredibly stunning showcase of this cave. I was speechless and a burst of happy shot through me. What magic trick of nature is this? "This is the Suspended Table. The table is a huge piece of calcite that formed at the base of the two massive columns you see. Over time, the material below the table was carried away by water, leaving it suspended about twenty centimetres above the lake. As you can see, the water level in this cave is going down and sometime in the future it may become a dry cave." As he watched us, James face lit up in a huge smile. I could see that through us, he was re-living the first time he laid his eyes on the table.

James led us deeper into the cave turning on then off the subdued lighting as we went. It did not take us long to get to the end of the cave and we turned, retracing our steps. Back beside the table we paused as a group once more. James took this opportunity to turn off all the lights and we stood there in the absolute darkness. I could see nothing of course. I thought about all the beautiful formations around me that I couldn't see. I wondered at the courage of the first cave explorers all over the world. I wondered how many undiscovered thousands of caves there must be on the planet. What else will come to 'light' in the future? What does the darkness hold?

Lights back on, we headed to the exit, out into the natural light and up the steep stairs to the meeting place. I thanked James for a wonderful hour of discovery. Before I started my climb I took some pictures of the next group heading down the entrance stairs to their underground adventure. For a few seconds I considered joining them for a second look, but I knew that I should get on with the rest of the day.

The stairs back to the rim of the sinkhole are divided into many sections that regularly change directions to follow the incline skyward. I climbed them in three stages, about a hundred steps at a time having a short rest between them. It was a much easier task than I had thought and I made it to the top in good time.

Now it was time to drive north along Caves Road along the flat end of the 'pig's snout'. Caves Road is a delightful country road. It is quiet with heavier traffic travelling on the Bussell Highway which runs inland and parallel to Caves Road. The road is sealed but narrow. The scenery changes from farms and pastures, ponds and creeks, to large valleys filled with forests of karri and jarrah trees. There is native bushland, rocky coastline and gorgeous beaches. At times I felt as if I were in a canyon - a canyon of gum trees. Their trunks were only a meter or two off the side of the road; the trees towered above me. In many places overhead, their branches reached across the road and formed 'tree tunnels'. It was as if I was being watched over by Mother Nature which gave me a sense of peace and well being.

The road sweeps through rolling farmlands and forests and is never far from the ocean. I turned west on several side roads and after a short drive would find myself at yet another remarkable beach. Most of the coastline is protected in Leeuwin-Naturaliste National Park; it was good to know that the area would be preserved for decades to come. This coastline is a surfer's paradise offering opportunities for beginners and advanced surfers alike with seventy-five surfing beaches along the coast. Surfers come here for the consistent, high quality breakers that are born on ocean swells in the Southern and Indian Oceans. Frequently I saw cars and vans laden with a variety of surf boards. I saw surfers at every place I stopped and spent time watching them play in the waves.

After three hours of driving and visiting beaches, I arrived at Cape Naturaliste to find the lighthouse closed. The surrounding area was scorched and still smoking and hot in places from a fire that had rushed over the area that week. I was a little bit disappointed that I would not be able to climb the fifty-nine teak stairs to the top of this haunted lighthouse. As the fire hazard was extreme, the trails along the headland were closed too. I drove back along the road for a few minutes until I found a side road to a beach not far away. A short downhill walk and I was wading in a beautiful little cove. The gum trees along the coast have been shaped by blasting winds of the 'Roaring Forties' and some looked like huge bonsai-beautiful trees. It was a lovely place to walk and spend some time sitting on the rocks, listening to the waves come and go and watching the birds overhead.

Now it was time to head south towards Margaret River. I had only travelled fifty kilometres north so the return trip didn't take long. At Jack and Carroll's recommendation I made one last trip out to the ocean and stopped at Prevelly Beach, one of the top surfing beaches on the coast. I had just missed a huge international competition which had been held over the weekend and there were still markers in the ocean and many of the bleachers were still in place. Perhaps a hundred people were at the site, some eating supper, but most just sitting on the grass or a log or chair. We knew what was coming soon and I was going to wait for it too. I called Jack to let him know where I was and when I expected to be home. He said that he'd have supper ready in 'about an hour'. So I ended this marvellous first Monday on the west coast with a bunch of strangers watching as the sun set over the Indian Ocean – too cool.

I arrived home and was in time to help Jack with food preparations and I set the table as well. Jack cooks and Carroll cleans up. As with the previous night's supper we had a lovely bottle of wine from a local vineyard. The area around Margaret River accounts for twenty percent of Australia's premium wines. I don't drink alcohol very often, maybe four or five times a year. With all the fine wines of New Zealand and Australia I was way past that number by now and really enjoying it all. After another great meal I cleared the table and washed the dishes. I always try to pitch in where ever I can; it's just part of being a good guest.

After supper I was talking with Jack about my camera and asked if he could transfer shots from my memory card to a flash drive that I bought in Perth. It was either that or I would need stop and buy another memory card the next day. Jack had only recently learned to do this (I had no idea) but dove into the task. As we all know, computers and humans have a love-hate relationship; this was time for the latter. Jack tried valiantly for quite some time but with no success. He contacted a friend and became quite optimistic, but still no luck by bedtime. I told him that I could buy a new card for the camera so went off to sleep. When I got up the next morning Jack and Carroll were at the computer just finishing up the transfer of all my photos to the flash drive. They had been up early and figured out how to accomplish the task. So a huge thank you goes out to them for the extra time and effort that they put into the job!

Jack and Carroll were wonderful people to stay with and I could easily have stayed several extra days, but as you have noticed I say that of most places I visit. Every place would take longer than a few days to adequately explore and every family I stayed with had things to offer. I left them standing in the driveway, waving their goodbyes to this new surfer.

A CAVE, A LIGHTHOUSE
AND FORESTS

I drove back to Caves Road and headed south, past Mammoth Cave and Lake Cave. The forest drive was amazing and relaxing – toddling along at forty or so kilometres per hour – slow enough to be safe while gawking at the trees. The road was mottled with patches of sunny asphalt mixed with shady areas. I made a few stops and walked in amongst the trees, became surrounded by them, let them engulf my senses with their aroma and size. It was magical.

At the lower end of this coastline, Hamelin Bay is an awesome sweep of beach, with pure white sand that steps down gently into the waves. At the southern end, where the stout piles of a disintegrating pier frame the bay, southern bat rays and thorntail stingrays have come to depend on the scraps from the fishermen and they hover to be hand-fed just a couple of metres out from the shore. If you step out into the water a thorntail ray might suck your ankles, which apparently is a pretty weird sensation

Just an hour after I left Margaret River I was at Jewel Cave, the next stop on my itinerary. Jewel Cave is the largest cave open to tourists in Western Australia and I found it to be the most spectacular of the three caves I visited. One surprising find made here were the fossil remains of a Tasmanian tiger which are stored in the Museum of Western Australia.

We followed Rox, our guide, down the first descent, a long, narrow tunnel which opened up into a massive cavern. I felt somewhat dwarfed by it all and was immediately awed by the size of it and the formations all around me. This was the start of our seven hundred meter journey that would take us to a depth of forty-two meters. Shortly after this spot we came to the showcase formation of Jewel Cave. You might be thinking that it would be a massive formation and you would be wrong. While the formation is an incredible five hundred forty centimeters long – about as long as seven two year olds or three eighteen year olds lying end to end – it is only about as round as your thumb and is hollow. This is a straw stalactite, an incredibly delicate formation that hangs from the ceiling of the cave. One of the longest straw stalactites in the world, it is the rock star of the hundreds that have formed here over thousands of years.

Rox led us through the cave, pointing out various formations along the way. There were places with low overhead where I had to duck and of course there were stairs, but not many, only two hundred sixty of them – child's play. The cave had a warm, soft, golden glow with subdued lighting around the many interesting features. Being a fan of engineering I was once again amazed at the amount of material that was brought into this cave to make it user friendly. Miles of wiring and switches had to be carried in and installed. The amount of timber and metal supports and handrails is staggering. This all had to be carried in – there is no highway for vehicles, no train, not even room for a golf cart. Then after getting everything underground it all had to be put together with precision to make it a safe place to travel. The concrete was carried in on the backs of men in inner tubes - thousands of trips. My hat's off to all the people who worked in all the caves I visited so that I could have such great experiences.

Rox had us stop at different locations, sometimes on a proper platform that was suspended on the side of a cavern, sometimes at a place where the path widened. "This is one of our largest canyons here. Can anyone guess what it might be called?" "The Grand Canyon" someone said. "That's a really good guess because it is quite large but that's not it. Any other guesses? No? Well, it's called Lake Canyon. Look over there where I'm shining my torch. You see the line that goes across the wall over there? That's the water line from the lake that was once here. The cave is drying up and the lake is gone now. Because water doesn't get down here very often, the formations will not grow any more. It's really important that we protect what we have here."

As we continued, Rox would gather us and ask us to search a certain area for the giant shawl, organ pipes, ghost, jewellery box, Jedi warrior and other shapes. After a short time she would shine her torch on the formation she was talking about and we could all then easily see what she had mentioned. My imagination was fully engaged and I was able to pick out many other things in the cave. One of my favorites is a larger than life horse. This is a knight's horse, a horse which is draped with a many-pleated tapestry that touches the ground along his flanks then shortens along his neck. There are some short pieces of 'mane' just around his ears. His long head sticks out of the tapestry, eyes half closed, resting here for all time – waiting for a rider who will never come.

Imagine a rocky outcrop shaped like a wizard's hat. Now cover it with gum trees, six layers in all that climb in steps and surround the 'hat'. At the next stop imagine the soft, round bodies of gigantic, fat, caterpillars – like the front of a volcanic flow, but now frozen flow stone. Above this hang hundreds of pointy stalactites – a really neat contrast in shapes. Turn another corner and think perhaps for a second that you are under water.

What you are looking at now has to be coral – and it is – it is cave coral. Several stops reveal helictites – those extremely delicate features that look like something went very wrong at the crazy string factory. They jut out sideways, travel upward for a time before taking off in a different direction, then another and another. They brought to mind an elementary school art project. In grade three I placed several watery blobs of colorful paint on my white paper then took a straw and blew the paint out in different directions. How do I remember I was in grade three? I remember it was grade three because I had my mom as my teacher that year and I would always see that project displayed on her classroom walls year after year. You can try this by simply placing some large drops of water on your newspaper then blowing them all over the place. This is the craziness of helictites. I was totally immersed in the whole experience – loved it all.

At the end of the tour I thanked Rox for an informative tour. I always make a point to talk to each guide I encounter and give them feedback. When going to university I had the best summer job ever. I got to take people on hikes at Lake Louise in the Rocky Mountains and give campfire talks at campgrounds in the area. I always appreciated a thank you at the end of my walks and talks. The feedback I received from kids to grandparents was a fantastic learning opportunity too.

Cape Leeuwin is the most south-westerly tip of Australia so it was a 'must visit' for me. I drove down the hill and saw the lighthouse at the end of the small peninsula – a lone sentinel standing on guard for over a hundred years and for at least a hundred more I imagine. The keeper's cottages and other buildings stand several hundred meters before the lighthouse on fairly large level area. I walked past the three large buildings on my left and four small service buildings on my right. The lighthouse is at the end of a paved road and a slight uphill climb. While I was waiting for my tour I walked around the lighthouse and stopped on an observation deck on its sea side. From here I could see the meeting of the Southern Ocean on my left and the Indian Ocean on my right. This reminded me of Cape Reinga on New Zealand's most north-western tip where I had watched the clashing of the Tasman Sea and Pacific Ocean. The meeting of waters here was very civilized at the moment. The only white water happened where some waves ran into a few small rocks. A bronze direction indicator told me that I was three thousand ninety-eight kilometers from the South Pole. (I like geographical things.)

Finally tour time came and I met Bruce who would lead us up the one hundred seventy-six steps, with two stops on the way up. He told us about the history of the lighthouse as we made our climb. "It was built from 1895 to 1896 after thinking about it for fifteen years. The tower and the cottages are made of local limestone that is found all over the region. The lighthouse was manned until 1992 when it became automated. With an elevation of fifty-six meters and a height of thirty-nine meters it can be seen as far away as twenty-five nautical miles. It is still a very important lighthouse and is used to gather meteorological data. There are a lot of reefs here and strong currents so there is an eight kilometer wide 'no boat, safety zone' around the Cape. When you leave here, it's worth making a stop just up the road at the old waterwheel. I hope you enjoy the view."

I really did enjoy the view. With my hair blowing madly about I 'stole' a man's wife and had him take a picture of the two of us ladies at the top of the lighthouse – another picture for my 'me and a perfect stranger' photo collection. Then I took a picture of them, and then he took another of me with Bruce.

A short time after I left the lighthouse, I was at the water wheel. It had been made to bring fresh water to the lighthouse. It's not large for a waterwheel, only a few meters across. This is an old wheel, a wheel that doesn't turn anymore. It is frozen in place, calcified by salts and minerals that have built up on the wheel itself and on the stone base built for it. I could see bare wood in only a few spots. It was interesting to see that a rivulet of fresh water still trickles here.

It was well after lunch time and time to do some driving. I drove east along the South Coast Highway through thick forests until coming back out to the coast at Walpole. From this point on I was able to see the ocean again and enjoyed the quiet drive east to Albany, the first European settlement in Western Australia. I secured a lower bunk in a hostel then drove around the town and found a small restaurant where I had supper. It was dark by this time so I headed back to the hostel where I did some reading about Albany and the route I would take the next day to Esperance.

The next morning I drove around town and looked at a number of historic Victorian buildings before driving up Apex Drive to the top of Mt. Clarence. Part of the roadway is lined with trees, planted in precise rows, standing three deep in places. I parked my car on the side of the road and walked among them. At the base of each tree is a bronze plaque that tells a short tale;

In Honor of
Pte.William.R.Richardson
28-BN
Killed in Action
France
6th August, 1916, Age 24

Back in the car I sat for awhile and soaked in the magnitude of what I had just seen. I had read a lot of names and I thought of my son, Jason, now twenty-eight, and how impossibly hard it would have been to have lost him. These young men just didn't have a chance to live their lives. It made me sad to think about it, the great loss of life in all the wars. But I love that there is a tree growing for each fallen man. And I love the peaceful location of the trees, high on Mt. Clarence. The harbor and Mt.

Clarence were the last sight of Australia as troops sailed off to war – many never to return.

I continued climbing to the end of the road and parked once more. It is a short walk to a life sized statue of two light horsemen and their mounts from the First AIF Desert Corps in 1915. This statue is a replica of a memorial that was unveiled in Egypt in 1932. The men and horses are in the middle of the action, one horse on its hind legs, both men staring ahead, wondering what might come next.

I continued up a short path that led to the summit. Mt Clarence offers spectacular views of Albany, its' beautiful harbor, King George Sound and outer islands. Across the harbor I could see a dozen wind turbines lined up on the hilltop - they produce seventy-five percent of Albany's power. It seems like a good source of energy to me; no rivers dammed and land flooded, no coal mined and burned, no oil sands dug up and processed, no broken oil pipelines, no tankers spilling oil into the environment, no oil rigs sinking in our oceans, no running out of wind.

Now it was time to cover almost five hundred kilometers to Esperance, the 'jewel of the south." The South Coast Highway runs inland for this part of the trip. Gone were the heavily forested areas and the coastal scenery. The landscape became drier which is more typical of Western Australia and was now a patchwork of agricultural land. Some thirty kilometers to my left I saw the Stirling Range pop out of the flat landscape. It is a sixty kilometer long collection of mountains and hills – a protected area that is well known for its vast array of plants and its hiking opportunities. If I had an extra day . . . .

ESPERANCE –
UNPARALLELED BEACHES

I arrived at Esperance late in the afternoon and checked into the hostel. I was in a room with two sets of bunk beds so secured a bottom bunk – I had two girls check in later who became my roommates.

I set out to drive around Esperance. The Great Ocean Drive is a thirty-nine kilometre loop that showcases some of the most fantabulous coastal scenery Australia has to offer. I was really looking forward to driving the loop and getting oriented to the area. The loop starts across the road from the hostel I was staying in so I hopped in the car, drove to the end of the driveway and turned right. The town is only a few hundred meters from the hostel so that's how the loop started for me. Just a short distance into the drive a jetty came into view on my left. The Tanker Jetty is an icon of Esperance, being the largest – at least longest - man-made feature in town. I would visit it later.

I continued on Twilight Beach Road and turned left on Doust Street, to climb to my first stop at Rotary Lookout. As you know I always seek a high observation point to get oriented to a new area. The lookout has a spiral staircase which wound around the supporting tower a few times to the observation platform above. The three hundred sixty degree view was fabulous! From this granite outcrop I looked over Esperance, along the coast to gorgeous beaches, over the water to the many islands off shore – Bay of Isles - and to farmland in the distance. It was a spectacular panorama and gave me a lot of information about the drive I was embarking on. The next eleven kilometres of the loop is the most spectacular collection of beaches I have ever seen!

Imagine you have a slab of light-colored butterscotch cake on the table in front of you. This slab is about a half meter long. Now take a knife and cut a forty-five degree angle along the edge nearest you. Take a monstrous bite out of the right hand side of the cake – leave some cake between this bite and the next huge bite. Moving to your left, repeat the process of taking bites and leaving some cake jutting out between the bites. Now, where you have taken bites from the cake, take some flour and sprinkle it several millimetres thick in a crescent shape. Now mix up the most gorgeous turquoise blue, clear icing possible and spread it out in a thin layer, not on the cake, but in front of the cake, on the table. Voila! You have a general model of the beaches around Esperance. West Beach, Blue Haven, Salmon, Fourth, Twilight, Nine Mile, Ten Mile, Eleven Mile – all pristine, drop-dead gorgeous beaches that are the 'bites' in your cake.

The rocky headlands that jut out into the ocean form the dramatic ends to the brilliant white beaches. The ocean is incredibly clear and the aqua marine and the turquoise blues are magical with their commitment to color. I was absolutely blown away by the beauty of it all! At West Beach there were two people swimming at the east end, near house-sized boulders that had broken away from the high cliff and toppled down to cascade into the ocean. I stopped at each and every beach. Well-crafted sets of stairs allowed access to the beaches – some beaches were only a few steps down, most were several sets of stairs away. Twilight Beach was the busiest with about twenty people enjoying this, the most sheltered beach. About eighty meters off shore, huge granite rocks look like a dinosaur has laid down for a rest in the water, only the top half of his back and head visible. His enormous 'eye' keeps track of any would be intruders. Two of the beaches I had to myself – unbelievable! The sand is as white and as fine as flour. It makes a squeaking noise when walked upon. There I was, sandals in hand, wading slowly along, one beach after the other. A huge burst of contentment and peace settled over me as I was one with nature. I didn't think about anything else at the time, just where I was and what I was doing.

I saw several people fishing out on the rocks – some having taken all but invisible paths down the cliffs to reach their favourite spot. I read the warning signs about the slipperiness of the rocks and the waves that could unexpectedly rise up and grab you and carry you out to sea – "others have died." So I didn't join any of them, just observed from my elevated position.

The Great Ocean Pathway is a paved path, wide enough for two cyclists to pass comfortably. It is twelve kilometres long and runs between the road and the ocean. It begins in Esperance and ends at Twilight Beach. I walked along it for a short distance and thought it would be a spectacular day outing on a bicycle. I saw only a few others on it, walking and cycling. Back home in Victoria there is The Galloping Goose / Lochside Trail, an eighty-four kilometre long trail that runs from the ferry terminal near my home, through Victoria and west out to the town of Sooke. It is heavily used both for recreation and to commute to and from work. I love the ideas of these multi-use trails and am always happy when I see one.

About halfway into the loop, I turned right and headed up into the hills a short distance. I parked the car and walked up to observe the wind turbines that supply power to Esperance. It was a nice change of pace from the beaches.

Shortly after the wind farm, the road turns away from the ocean and meanders through the countryside, not nearly as dramatic as the coast, but pleasant none the less. I passed Pink Lake on my left, which to my disappointment wasn't pink at the time of my visit. The pink algae only bloom in specific conditions and it just wasn't the right time for them. I had a quick look at the Pink Lake Country Club on my right as I passed. Seeing a golf course here solidified that, "Yes, I could live in Esperance." Six kilometres later and I was back at the hostel and it was dinner time. I used the communal kitchen to make a chicken stir fry - my 'go to' dish. I sat with others and talked for awhile and told them about the Ocean Drive - just this stretch of road would have made the whole trip out to Western Australia worthwhile. The next day would offer more of the same.

I had seen her picture in brochures and on postcards and some travel posters. She is lying on an impossibly white beach with her back to the sun and the turquoise ocean. She is lounging comfortably on her right hip, long, brown legs stretched out and crossed on the sand. Supported by her forearms she is gazing to the left. She is so very relaxed, this kangaroo lying on Lucky Beach. I was immediately taken in by this picture and set a goal to join her on that beautiful stretch of beach in Cape le Grand National Park.

I set off from Esperance the next morning and drove fifty-six kilometres east towards the Grand National Park. The countryside was fairly flat with low-lying bushes dotting the landscape. The most surprising thing on the way was the emus, lots of emus – I saw at least twenty of them. They were sometimes close to the road but more often at least a hundred meters away. They are as wary as the sheep I met in New Zealand and I learned to walk very slowly and just a short distance towards them. They would turn and stride away at the first feeling of uneasiness. I did manage to get some good pictures of these birds in the wild so that was pretty exciting for me. This is also cattle country and I have a few shots of small groups of black cattle staring at me with their big, brown eyes from behind the protection of their fences.

Once inside the park, the road passes by Frenchman Peak, a granite outcrop that rises two hundred sixty-two meters. The trail to the top would be too demanding of me and my knees and, being on my own, I wouldn't want to try it. Its most intriguing feature is a long, slit-shaped hole that is near the summit. I would have really liked to climb up there and sit in the cave – I think the opportunity to be truly alone in this spot would have been as magnificent as the view it offers.

I followed the signs to Lucky Beach and pulled into a parking spot near the campground. Going barefoot, I walked the short distance to the access path to Lucky Beach, camera at the ready. No, I didn't see the kangaroo sunning herself on the beach, but there were four small kangaroos

off to my right. This end of Lucky Beach was lying under a half meter of
sea grass that had washed up. The kangaroos were foraging through this.
I was so happy to see them so close and started taking pictures of them,
inching ever closer. Again, I need not have worried about them hopping
away as they are very used to human interaction. I approached to within
a few meters and observed them for about twenty minutes. There was a
pair that hung out together and I have several shots of them nose to nose
checking out the sea grass. They were just so very amazing to watch. It
was a peaceful interaction that I put high on my list of nature contacts.

Lucky Beach and its surrounds are incredibly beautiful! Another brilliant white sand beach that squeaked when I walked – the experience still
makes me smile. In 2009, Whitehaven Beach in the Whitsundays chal-
lenged the sand of Lucky Beach for being the whitest in the nation, a title
held by Lucky Beach since 2006. I had been on both beaches and remember Whitehaven as being brilliantly white too – but unless I was holding
samples next to each other, I would be at a loss to declare a winner. In a
media statement in January of 2009 the National Committee on Soil and
Terrain declared the sand of Lucky Beach to still hold the top honour of
having Australia's whitest beach. And there is a lot of sand here, extending
between granite headlands about four kilometres apart.

As I waded along I gazed out to sea, the horizon dotted with so many
islands that it was difficult to find a clear sight path to the open ocean. The
ocean was absolutely clear near the shore then changed to darker shades
of aqua and turquoise as it got deeper. About half way down the beach I
found a spot where I sat and just soaked it all in. I had planned to go to
several beaches in the park but sitting there on Lucky Beach I figured it
just couldn't get any better so I scrunched down into my seat and lay there
for a time. I closed my eyes and entered a somewhat meditative state in
this magical place. Finally I stood up and walked back towards the car
and spent a bit more time looking at the kangaroos. Back in the car, I
drove around the campsite appreciating what a great place this would be
to spend a week or more. I drove up to the headland at the west end of
the bay, parked the car and set out on a path over the granite outcrop. The
views were mind boggling! I sat on the rocks for about fifteen minutes
looking at the full arc that is Lucky Beach, noting the kangaroos, where
I had walked to, sat, walked back. I was very content at what I had been
able to experience here – one of the best beaches in the world, the kangaroos, and the blue palette of the ocean. It was with a bit of reluctance that
I finally got back in the car and drove away and back to Esperance.

I started a laundry then dined on my leftover chicken stir fry. After supper I joined a group in the common area where we watched some TV and
talked about our travels.

After breakfast the next morning I headed off to Tanker Jetty. I pulled
the car into the parking area and camera in hand I was ready to enjoy a
walk on the pier. There is a nice picnic area at the base of the jetty and

families were already enjoying themselves at the picnic tables on the grass and down at the beach. The pier extends seaward for about four football fields, then takes a gentle right turn and continues for two more fields – six hundred seventy meters long.

The jetty was built in the 1930s during the depression, by men who desperately needed the work. The farming industry was expanding in the area around Esperance at that time and a new jetty was needed to accommodate the tankers which would arrive with goods and depart with grain, salt and other minerals. Over eighty wooden piers were built in Western Australia and Tanker Jetty is one of only four that remain more or less intact. It was used for commercial purposes until 1980s when a new pier took over that job. Now it is a much loved recreational area that is used by locals and tourists for fishing and walking. It is maintained by Save the Tanker Jetty group above sea level. Below sea level much work has been done by volunteer divers to create an artificial reef where marine life is thriving.

I walked out onto the wooden deck of the jetty, metal handrail on my left and open side on my right. The wooden surface soon turned to concrete which had been poured to help preserve the walking surface. It was a gorgeous, sunny day and this was the next best thing to being out in a boat. I strolled to the end of the pier where there is a gap of a few hundred meters, and then the final part of the jetty rises from the water. The jetty was becoming unsafe, so a section was demolished - the furthest piece remains to give an idea of just how long the jetty once was.

On my way back to shore I stopped where the jetty makes its turn. There was a group of eight young boys, about ten years old, sitting lined up on the edge of the jetty. They wore bare feet, shorts, tee shirts and baseball style hats. Rods in hand, they were trying their hand at fishing. I stopped to talk with them and the two adult males who were with them. The boys were in town to participate in a motor bike race over the coming weekend. But for today, it was all about fishing. They were all very happy and excited to be fishing – two told me that it was their very first time trying it out. In talking with one of the adults, he said that the two boys had a hard home life and there was just never a man around to take them fishing. He couldn't understand it himself and I could tell by the way he talked that he was bothered about it. He was so happy that the boys were finally having the chance to try it. I asked the boys if I could take a few pictures of them, "Ya, sure!" I love those pictures – anglers in the making - simple pleasures.

There is a fish cleaning station on the jetty where I made my next stop. A fellow at the station was cleaning his catch of the day tossing heads and entrails over the side. Then I noticed Sammy. Sammy is a seal that has 'the good life.' He hangs around the pier and when anyone stops or even slows down by the fish cleaning station he 'torpedoes' his way to the water below it. Sammy swims in little circles and bobs his head about to attract attention. He usually has his head poking above the surface, watching and waiting. He is often rewarded as is apparent by his massive belly. It's a good thing he's in the water most of the time where the buoyancy makes it easier to move than when he ventures onto the beach. He is definitely a well fed animal. There is a bronze statue of Sammy near the walkway to the jetty, his nose kept shiny by the pats of hundreds of people. The statue is of a very small Sammy, perhaps only a quarter the size of the Sammy I saw. Perhaps the Sammy I saw was a sea lion.

I really enjoyed my two hours on the jetty; I met lots of people, petted several dogs, took lots of pictures, loved the scenery and saw lots of fish.

After my stop at the jetty, I headed back up to Rotary Lookout as the view would be just as good today as it was yesterday. When I was up there, I met three fellow travellers from the hostel and we struck up a conversation. They had walked into town and up to the lookout. I had shared my dorm with the blonde girl the night before. I told them about the Great Ocean Loop and offered to take them where I had been yesterday. It was fun to be a tour guide to the young Asian couple who were travelling together and the girl from Germany. We were lucky enough to talk to a local who was fishing on one of the beaches and he told us all about surf casting and showed us his 'catch of the day'. We all had a really good time together. After we got back to the hostel we decided that pizza would be great for supper, so off we went into town and half an hour later brought two pizzas back to the hostel where we devoured them. Just a fun afternoon. It had been a laid back day; a day of rest that I really appreciated as travelling can be very tiring.

The previous night I had shared the room with one other girl – tonight both sets of bunk beds were full so there were four of us. We got into bed, had talked awhile, said our good nights and were settling in to sleep. We heard the boys next door enter their room a few minutes later. They went to bed quickly and it was then that we realized how very thin the separating wall was. My bed was next to the wall meaning that one of the fellows was lying only about a pillow width away. The wall was so thin that I could hear him breathing! We soon became part of their conversation about their day in Esperance and added our experiences. About fifteen minutes later, we all turned in for the night. I just hope that I didn't snore.

THE WAVE

This Saturday I would drive for eight and a half hours and cover about seven hundred kilometres heading northwest to Perth. The roads here are relatively straight, running along through natural bushland landscapes with much the same scenery for hours. There is one place of interest I wanted to visit and it is conveniently located about half between Esperance and Perth. It is a natural rock formation, a huge wave. Wave Rock in Hyden is visited by more than a hundred forty thousand visitors each year and I would be one of them in 2009. Seemed like a pretty straight forward day to me. Yes, those long, straight stretches of road. It happened many times – I would look at the speedometer and be surprised that I was cruising along at a hundred thirty kilometres an hour where the limit was one hundred ten. This rental car didn't have cruise control and apparently my foot must have gained weight and pressed too hard on the gas pedal. Anyway, that's what I told the police officer when he waved me over. He and his partner were talking to another motorist when I hit their radar. "Do you know how fast you were going?" "I think about a hundred twenty-five." "Actually we clocked you at one hundred twenty-nine – it's just too fast and I'll have to give you a ticket." Sigh. So we had a short chat before we parted company. I stayed to the speed limit for at least ten minutes. What did you expect? The roads are so straight and empty . . . . I didn't pay the ticket until six weeks after I got back home when I received a reminder in the mail. I was thinking about not paying it - one hundred fifty dollars had now climbed to two hundred. I mean, really, what could they do to me? They couldn't put points on my licence or anything. But, honesty being what it is with me, I sent off a check and settled the ticket.

It was in the tiny town of Lake King that I entered The Wave Zone. In the Shire of Lake Grace this zone consists of a series of signs placed in each of the major entrances to the Shire: 'If you wave, people will wave hello.' 'Please wave safely.' 'You are leaving the wave zone.' 'We hope you enjoyed your wave.' I tried it and sure enough received a wave back from almost every car I waved to. It just gave such a friendly feel to the place, interacting with people without even having to pull the car over and stop. I thought it was a very cool thing to have in place.

So I sped on to Hyden and found Wave Rock. I parked my car and headed out on the short path to the wave. Rounding the last bend in the path the wave was suddenly right there in front of me. Wow! It was amazing to see this huge granite outcrop towering fifteen meters into the clear blue sky and curving away to the right, a little longer than a football field. It looks just like a massive breaker, the kind you see only the best surfers in the world attempt - the kind of wave where jet skis are used to tow surfers, the kind of waves found at Jaws in Hawaii. Of course its coloring is anti-water; the beige rock is streaked with black, grey, red and yellow, a result of rain carrying chemical deposits down its surface. I walked straight ahead and was on the wave and climbing it, a short lived venture as it becomes steep very quickly. The other visitors and I had to be content with our limited success getting up maybe a tenth of it. I walked along the length of the wave then halfway back. I talked with several people and we did the 'I'll take your picture if you take my picture routine.' It seemed as though everyone added several surfer poses to their cameras memory cards at Wave Rock – I have six.

Wave Rock was formed by chemical weathering millions of years ago while it was still underground; the erosion resulted in an undercut base with a round overhang. Now Hyden Rock is exposed with the wave being the north face. I walked to the far end again and past the wave. The entire rock is about as large as two football fields and I took a path that follows a fairly easy gradient to the top of the rock which was fairly flat and was easy to walk over. I noticed a very short retaining wall coursing around the edge of the rock higher up and thought that it wasn't high enough to keep even a rolling baby safe. Someone told me it has been built to channel rainwater to a storage dam and water reservoir used by the town of Hyden. There it was, a fenced off area surrounding the reservoir. It was quite contradictory to be in an arid land, high up on a huge rock and find a water reservoir.(You don't know what you don't know)

When I saw the view from the west side I was even more surprised. My eye was caught by a tiny patch of green, bright green, a small rectangle of green – what the heck? Below me, hugging the curves of the brown hills was a golf course! I scanned the landscape and was able to pick out two more or less circular, black areas – and on each was a flag stick with a little yellow flag marking the hole. Another outback course – I took a few pictures to show to my golfing family and friends back home.

I came off the rock after walking all around the top of it. The path came down close to the wave where I took another long look before returning to the car. I drove a short distance to the Hippo's Yawn and it looks just like it sounds, a gaping mouth under a rock that does indeed look like a hippo's snout. I ate my picnic lunch here, a PB&J sandwich, apple and a ginger beer – it's simple to make, travels well, and I like the taste.

Wave seen, legs stretched, yawn looked at and lunch eaten, it was time to get back into the car and drive. Hyden was very busy and crowded with people and bicycles everywhere, in town for a weekend of dirt bike racing. I pulled over in town to look at some life sized metal sculptures: Johnny The Mechanic works on a transmission, Calvin, Darrell and R.Tipps ride bicycles to power the town, Toby with his spring-created mane hauls Hayley in a large wagon, townspeople go about their daily chores. Apparently there are a lot more metal sculptures around town, a fact I only learned about later. It would have been interesting to have seen more of them, this art from found objects.

A few kilometres out of town I was looking at the road ahead trying to figure out which way it might turn. It seemed to go straight ahead and run into a line of bushes – hmmm. Then the most beautiful smell of eucalyptus enveloped me and as I approached the 'bushes' I saw that a huge tree had snapped and fallen across the road. Actually it was the last of three trunks that used to make up a larger tree. It was on the right side of the road and now this last part of the tree was blocking both lanes of traffic. There were several of us stopped on each side and I got out and took a picture before getting back in the car. On the far left, there were a few sets of tire tracks straddling the shoulder and the incline off the roadside. Yes, definitely wide enough for most vehicles. While some other people turned their vehicles around, I simply went to the left, around the crown of the tree and was on my way.

PRINCE LEONARD
AND PRINCESS SHIRLEY

Averaging about a hundred twenty kilometres an hour, the distance to Perth was steadily eroded and I arrived back at the Emperor's Crown hostel. All the dorms were full so I booked into a suite with a double bed – rather luxurious for hostelling.

It is the journey not the destination. This I found to be no truer than while driving the thirteen hundred kilometres north from Perth to Exmouth the next day. The reason that I was willing to drive over twenty five hundred kilometres was to swim with whales sharks. I didn't have any idea of the most wonderful places that I would find along the way, from spectacular beaches to rocky headlands to an independent country within Australia. Then again the destination was immensely spectacular too, so I like to say, it's the journey and the destination.

My first night north of Perth, I spent in Geraldton, the capital of the Midwest. Geraldton is a wonderful seaside town in which you can wander the beaches, visit the cathedral of St. Francis Xavier, enjoy the ambience and food of local pubs, explore fisherman's wharf, buy arts and crafts and hear the dreamtime stories of the local indigenous people.

The only room available in the hostel was a double, private room which would cost me three times more than I had anticipated. As I brought my bag to my room I began to talk to the young people in the dorm room next door. I asked them if they booked ahead and yes, they had booked a room for four people. One of their foursome had not been able to make the trip so they offered me the opportunity to share the dorm room with them, which I thought would be a good idea. I went back to the desk and got a refund for my room then put my gear in my new dorm. The four of us fell into easy conversation and spent a pleasant evening having Easter dinner together, walking along the waterfront and sharing our room. During this time with 'the kids', I found out that my new Malaysian friends were in fact, three doctors working for a year in various hospitals in the Perth area and were in the area on a week long holiday. Now I have three new friends to couch surf with if I ever get to Malaysia and they of course are welcome to surf at my place anytime they might come to Canada.

The next morning brought another beautiful day so we had breakfast outside on the back patio. We shared a table with Fynn, a gregarious Kiwi, who is living at the hostel while working in the area. He told us of a place, a country within the country of Australia, called the Principality of Hutt River. Prince Leonard and Princess Shirley Casley were farmers, who seceded from the Commonwealth of Australia in 1970 because of new government quotas on wheat production. Fynn talked with such passion about Hutt River that I knew I wanted to visit the Prince and Princess. After breakfast I said my goodbyes to my new friends and set out from Geraldton. Originally I had planned to drive straight north along the Coastal Highway until I reached the turnoff to Denham and Monkey Mia. Armed with new information about Hutt River, I took a detour from the highway and turned west an hour north of Geraldton. Around fifteen kilometres later the road became unsealed. I soon turned left onto Box Road and drove the last few kilometres into the Principality of Hutt River.

The small gathering of buildings is not impressive in and of themselves. They are made of brick for the most part and are surrounded by an arid landscape where wisps of groundcover were all that remained after a long, hot summer. There were quite a few trees on the property that provided some shade. I noticed a few caravans parked in the camping area past the buildings. I pulled the car to the left and parked in front of the nearest building. I was glad to be getting out of the car and walked up the four concrete steps, onto the front porch and then into the post office. Behind the counter I saw Prince Leonard – an elderly man in his eighties, receding hairline, about five foot six, slim build, wearing grey slacks and a white, dress shirt with sleeves rolled up to his elbows. The prince was talking to three young visitors, telling them about the post office and their passports. They all were captivated by him, as I came to be. The prince had a twinkle in his eye and a vibrant smile and I could tell he has talked and held the attention of thousands of visitors before us. Others joined us by twos and threes as he told and retold us about the story of the post office and mint. Hutt River has issued over fifty sets of stamps since 1973 and has minted over two hundred coins, all of which are collected worldwide. I bought a set of current issue stamps, coins and paper money from his highness. He was like a magician as he took each of our passports and told us about things we could never notice; I didn't know that there was an image of me that could only be seen when exposed to a black light. The prince stamped our passports for entry then asked who was leaving the same day so he could stamp those with an exit stamp as well. After holding our attention here, he led us next door to the church where he told us of visiting dignitaries and film crews. We spent about ten minutes here with the prince, most of us having our pictures taken with him at the front of the church. I also have a picture of me sitting in Princess Shirley's chair – so regal!

Then he led us outside and talked about the mint green pyramid - yes, Prince Leonard has built a hollow pyramid that is about four meters high - and its energizing powers. He often spends time in the pyramid and takes objects with him, such as crystals, to be energized. These can be bought as souvenirs. No planes are to fly over his pyramid as the energy given off might interfere with their instrumentation.

Leonard Casley is a former mathematician and physicist. He worked for NASA in the 1950's and has a star named after him. He has authored many papers involving mathematics and religion and has sent some of his works to world leaders, including President Obama. It would have been so interesting to have a few days to talk with Prince Leonard – what a remarkable man!

I walked and talked with him on our way to the last stop, the gift shop. Inside, behind the counter was Princess Shirley - his wife of over sixty years, mother of seven children - manning the store. The prince went behind the counter and picked a souvenir pen off a rack and motioned to me, "Here, a gift for you to take back to Canada." I was very pleased at this gesture. The burgundy and gold pen has a permanent resting place on my kitchen table and I think of him each time I use it, which is pretty much every day.

The national anthem of the Principality of Hutt River:
It's a hard land but it's our land.
Built with love and dedication.
Self-assurance is our small nation.
One man's dream of independence.
God bless the Prince of The Hutt River Province.
God bless the man whose dream has come true.
God bless this land where dreams can come true.
God bless the Prince of the Hutt River Province.
God bless this man whose dream has come true.
God bless this land where dreams can come true.

The Prince said his goodbyes as he headed off back to the post office to begin the tour with new visitors. I took some more pictures of sculptures made from cast-off metal pieces and one of a meter and a half tall bust of the prince. It had been carved from rock by a visitor as a tribute to the man. I'm so glad that I had met Fynn at breakfast and had made the detour.

Now I headed back on Box Road and turned left at the next junction, towards the ocean forty kilometers away. The road didn't have a single curve for the next twenty kilometers. It was a reddish, gravel alley in a gently rolling landscape with low brush growing on each side A generous two lanes wide, it rolled gently up and down and carried me to the west before angling to the north and out to the coast and Kalbarri National Park. I had picked up a brochure about the area while in Perth and had hoped I might have time to take the detour to see it. With the trip to Hutt River, I was already on the road to Kalbarri so it became a 'no-brainer' to continue on this side road.

I was travelling along a supremely stunning, rugged piece of coastline that is the western boundary of Kalbarri National Park. The scenery rivals that of the Great Ocean Road. The relentless poundings of waves and wind have carved towering cliffs that are made of irregular layers of colored silt and sand. The cliffs look like rough cut edges of a 'ginormous' lasagna, with yellowy cottage cheese and sauce dripping out between the layers of wrinkle-edged noodles. They continue up and down the coast, gorgeous seascapes one after another. The cliffs are a hundred meters high in places – as tall as a football field is long. There are secluded beaches, strange rock shapes and natural arches to be seen. I made five stops along the coast – every view was added to my camera – each as stunning as the ones before.

The town of Kalbarri really jumped out at me as I rounded a bend and found myself at a lookout. Below me the Murchison River flowed parallel to the ocean then took a sharp right-angled turn into the Indian Ocean. This creates a much-protected shoreline for Kalbarri. There is a large park that runs along the river and I saw many people relaxing and playing on the green grass, such a contrast from the dry landscape I had been driving through. People were playing cricket, tossing Frisbees, playing catch. A band of brush separates the grass from the sandy beach where twenty or so people were playing in the water, swimming and piloting toy boats. There were small piers jutting out along the shoreline, some with boats tied to them, some with people fishing. A white sand beach runs along the riverside and I could see the buildings of Kalbarri stretched along the river. Kalbarri has much to offer and I think it would be a lovely place to spend a holiday.

After Kalbarri the road headed east and in just over an hour I was back on the main highway heading north. The road passed through endless kilometers of brush-covered red earth. Warning signs featured silhouettes of cattle and kangaroos – Caution, Stray Animals, Next 130 km. I passed some cattle in dribs and drabs of several head but saw only the remains of kangaroos who had met an untimely death on the road.

SHARK BAY

A few hours of travelling north brought me to an intersection where once again I turned and headed west towards the ocean to an incredibly mind-blowing area. Imagine a capital W shaped piece of land that hangs off the west coast of Australia. The W is made up of two peninsulas and islands and the protected water inside the W is home to features that help make the area a World Heritage Site.

In 1991 the Shark Bay area was added to the list of World Heritage sites with these words: 'at the most westerly point of the Australian continent, Shark Bay, with its islands and the land surrounding it, has three exceptional natural features: its vast sea grass beds, which are the largest (4800 sq. km) and richest in the world; its dugong ('sea cow') population; and its stromatolites (colonies of algae which form hard, dome-shaped deposits and are among the oldest forms of life on earth). Shark Bay is also home to five species of endangered mammals.' Over the next four days I learned about this heritage designation first hand.

A sweeping left turn down a hill brought me into the tiny coastal town of Denham, Australia's most westerly town. Welcome to Denham was spelled out in blue mosaic tiles on the low brick wall near the center of the roundabout. Three palm trees stood in the center, the flat blue horizon of the ocean just beyond while a smaller sign pointed to town center and Heritage Drive. I entered the roundabout at six o'clock, drove round and exited at three o'clock and continued along Heritage Drive. Being a town of less than two thousand people it didn't take long to drive the length of the Denham waterfront. Denham has all the amenities that anyone really needs and serves as the base for the Shark Bay area. I headed back along the waterfront and through the roundabout some fifty yards to my hostel. Each unit at this hostel is set up like a small three bedroom apartment. Each bedroom has two sets of bunk beds accommodating twelve people in total. We shared the living room, bathroom and kitchen. Six of the young people were living there long-term while working in the area. One of the girls, Lauren, a twenty-two year-old girl from Canada lives right next to my home golf course. When I got home I called her parents and gave them the message from Lauren , "I love you, I miss you, and I'm using my SPF 40 sunscreen every day."

I drove back into town where I spent the rest of the evening walking along the foreshore. I was delighted to find tame emus that make Denham their home. I had only seen emus at quite a distance in the wild so I was happy to add some close up photos of them to my collection. Their feathers look more like fur from a woolly mammoth than feathers, parted down the center of their backs and flowing down below their bodies. Their eyes are beautifully large and brown; short, black feathers sprout upwards from their heads in an afro style. There were two that stayed close to each other, striding along at a leisurely pace on their long legs. I took a lesson from them and continued along the seafront walkway at a slow pace.

I got back to the hostel just before sunset, met some more room mates, then we all walked across the road. We stood on the beach together, watching the sun dip down into the Indian Ocean from the most western town in Australia. It had been a good day.

After breakfast the next day, I drove a few kilometres north of town to Little Lagoon. A beautiful white beach surrounds the lagoon and it was gorgeous: the beach, clear turquoise water, surrounding bush land and brilliant blue sky. Little Lagoon is sheltered and provides an excellent place for swimming, fishing and playing in the water. The water had small ripples from a light wind. Two children, knee deep in the water, were striding along after a runaway air mattress; it had been caught by the breeze and was on its way across the lagoon. Dad came to the rescue and managed to catch up to the wayward play thing. There were only eleven others to share the lagoon with so it was a quiet and peaceful place to be. Both the adults and the children I saw playing were having a great time. I spent a half hour there walking along the shell strewn beach before heading back to the car. It was a great way to start the day.

Ocean Park Aquarium is eight kilometres south of Denham and was next on my list. This small tourist attraction sits on the shore of Denham Sound and uses a combination of sea and fresh water in their tanks and pools. I entered the first building and walked over to a tank where a guide was talking to a few others. Cutie pie Duncan, dressed in khaki shirt and shorts and stylish hat, was holding a dinner plate sized turtle for us to see. The little turtle was a mixture of brick reds, and browns, with thick black lines separating the sixteen different plates on his back. He 'swam' in the air, all four legs paddling at once, as Duncan held him and talked about turtles in the area.

We moved from tank to tank in this building, Duncan telling us about the creatures in each one. We saw sea snakes, which are gorgeous when met under these controlled circumstances. Had I met one while swimming, I'm sure the experience would have taken on a whole different tone. I loved watching the little squids as they fluttered along just under the surface of the water. I took a really close-up look and noticed their bodies look like a million pixels of nature that can change color as easily as a picture on a monitor. They are masters of camouflage and their colors ripple along their bodies as they adapt to new circumstances. The stonefish has amazing camouflage making it difficult to find even in a fairly small tank. This fish blended in perfectly with the bottom of the tank and I could not make it out until it moved; I was able to pick it out only because I knew it was there. There would be no chance to see this deadly fish when in the ocean.

We moved to a large outdoor pool where Duncan lured its occupants with food. It was interesting to be introduced to the many different fish that live in the area. Unless you are an avid snorkeler or a diver, you'd never get the chance to see the marine life that Ocean Park has to offer. Duncan told us about each of the fish and explained its place in the ocean ecosystem.

The most exciting of the exhibitions was the shark pool. There was a raised, wooden walkway that led to a circular platform in the center of the pool. Here, Duncan told us about the hammerhead, tiger and bronze whaler sharks that inhabit the pool. We could see them swimming around the pool, some only a meter in length, with the largest about three meters. The sharks are lured to the walkway by food hung into the pool on a line. The line runs through the offered meat, one end tied to a rod in Duncan's left hand and the other end held in his right hand. Duncan stood leaning over the edge and guiding the meat like a puppeteer brought the sharks into perfect view. They rose from the water, jaws agape, and one after another took food from the line.

That concluded the tour. I passed through the small gift shop on my way back to the car, happy that I had come here. It had been a relaxed tour with an informal style – entertaining and educational.

Forty minutes later I was strolling along the cliff top at Eagle Bluff, an area for viewing marine life. There is a new walkway along the cliff with a sturdy safety rail making it much safer for everyone, especially children. From the bluff I had a bird's eye view of the water below. I could see a few small islands that were populated with birds and I saw several rays and a shark swimming along looking for prey, totally unaware of their human visitors high above. The water within a hundred meters or so of the shore is a gorgeous turquoise green and clear. Past this, the water darkens suddenly and dramatically to a dark blue, where the massive beds of sea grass take over the ocean. In the distance the shoreline was white. I learned the next day that this is an area of salt harvesting. I spent twenty minutes here at this wonderful vantage point, walking the length of the pathway and back. Eagle Bluff is the spot where Captain Denham landed in 1858 and carved his name into a rock on the bluff. That is where the town of Denham gets its name. The rock has been removed from cliff as it was beginning to break away and now has a home in Pioneer Park in Denham.

It was a twenty minute drive to my next destination, Shell Beach. 'You don't know what you don't know', so I had never pondered the existence of the likes of Shell Beach in Western Australia. From a young age I had a picture of white sandy beaches in a tropical setting with warm water and swaying palm trees. I had never lived this vision until only a year previously when I took a trip to Hawaii. When I heard of the name, I imagined a beach where you could find a lot of, well, shells. But I imagined a sandy beach upon which I would find different shells of tropical bivalves perhaps as many as two or three hundred in total. Well, I never expected that shells is all I would find at this beach, nothing but shells, over one hundred kilometres long and in places up to an astounding depth of ten meters, nothing but tiny white coquina bivalve sea shells, billions and billions of them. There is no sand at Shell Beach. The shells are small: they are about the size of a large pea, a child's finger nail; you can arrange three of them on a quarter. Due to high salinity these tiny shell fish have no predators here and they have flourished in massive numbers for thousands of years and when they die natural deaths they are washed ashore.

To hear about Shell Beach was amazing, to visit it astounding. From the parking lot, I walked along the short path onto a white undulating plain, a plain frozen by time into three foot high sea swells set some forty feet apart. I roller-coastered my way to the ocean's edge, the aqua blue water so clear and calm that it invited people to wade out into the bay. I sat atop the shell swell closest to the water - from a distance the beach was a huge white plain, an entity unto itself. Upon closer examination it became a collection of billions of individuals, all combining to form this wondrous beach much as the stars form our universe, the trees form the forest, and people form humanity. As thousands have before me, I scooped up handfuls of the miniscule shells and sat mesmerized as I marvelled at their design and the vast numbers lying in my proximity. I poured them from hand to hand, I smelled them, I listened to their gentle wind chime noise as they fell, I buried my legs in them, and I examined them one by one in first one hand then the other. I formed the letters Shell Beach on my leg and watched them blow away before I had any chance at a picture. I took macro pictures of individuals – I even found three shells that were not like the billions, but rather spiral shaped and a light purple color. I watched as other people went through similar processes. The shells do get crushed somewhat over time and become compressed and hardened so much so that they can be sawed into blocks, quarried and have been used as construction materials for buildings in Denham and on surrounding stations. Today, special licences are required for the removal of the shells and they are used for the production of calcium for poultry feed and mulch for specialized gardens and planters. Shell Beach is one of only two beaches like it in the world. I felt privileged to have been allowed to sit and wonder at this amazing beach. I am easily amused.

I got back to the hostel at supper time where I made a chicken stir fry. An hour later I was back walking along the waterfront in town. I went to a pier and talked with the people who were fishing for squid and fish. They shared their stories and showed me their catch of the day. It seemed a perfect social thing to be doing on a Tuesday night – much like people back home would be doing when summer came back to Canada. Another colourful sunset and the day was pretty much over. I planned out the next day then hung out in the living room with some of the others who were at the hostel before retiring for the night.

I packed up the car the next morning and had a quick look around as I do each morning. Another flat tire! I haven't had two flat tires back home in ten years – guess I had to come to Australia to catch up? It wasn't entirely flat so I was able to drive it to the tire repair shop in town. They had it fixed for me in quick time – half a wood screw had gone through it. Same thing at Lakes Entrance – a screw was the cause of the leak. I guess there's a lot of construction going on everywhere.

I had seen them parked on the side of the main street when I had driven into town the previous day. All shiny and red - "C'mon, you know you want to come with us. You'll love it! Imagine the wind in your hair, the power, the sunshine and the sights. C'mon, give us a try." Anyway, that's what I heard - I answered the call. Parking the car I ambled over to Rick, the rotund man in charge who was taking money and getting people to sign legal waivers. Yes, waivers. Those pieces of paper that absolve the company of blame should I have an 'incident'. I mean what could go wrong? Well, there is a long list of what could go wrong actually - a very long list. I could fall off at low or high speed, arms, legs and head somersaulting through the air - spinning, turning, coming to a crashing halt against the ground, a tree, a building. I could run into or be struck by a vehicle. I could leave the path and end up in the ocean. Who cares? Not me! I could have a lot of fun! I had always wanted to try it, now was my time. No hesitation, just sign the form, pay the man and come back in a half hour for departure. I was in! I walked along the waterfront for twenty minutes then came back to our starting point ten minutes before we were to depart. I was going on a three hour quad bike tour.

I donned my helmet and my reflective safety vest, grabbed the handlebars and lifting my right leg up and over the 'beast' to land on the black, vinyl seat of my four wheeled vehicle. Eight quads in all, three of us riding solo. Rick led the way as one by one we manoeuvred our quads off the curb and onto the street. We were a parade of novices, riding single file down the street. I'm sure everyone was watching us as we passed. Some of them must have looked at the last person in the line; a lone female rider, smile already plastered on her face.

A few hundred meters later we left the paved road and turned onto a narrow, sandy road. We travelled slowly, under control for the moment. I was at the rear of the group, so fell back a little to let the sandy dust settle or blow away. A sense of power and freedom came to me. This brought back memories of galloping my horse, Blaze through the forests and fields back home. When I was nearing my sixteenth birthday my dad had asked me what I wanted for my present. He wasn't at all happy with my answer. "No daughter of mine is going to be caught riding a motorcycle! There must be something else you want." That's how I ended up with a horse. But Blaze wasn't as fast as a quad and he tired after a time. This quad could take me faster and further than he ever had. Dad had been right about the motorcycle of course. I spent years having wonderful times riding Blaze in the thousands of acres around Kimberley. Looking back I would not have traded him for any motorcycle. Now I rode a quad; safe but exciting.

The road turned down to the beach which we travelled along until we came to the entrance to Little Lagoon, five kilometres from Denham. I had just visited here the day before but now got to approach it from the other side which was cool. Little Lagoon is a circular, shallow body of water and from the air would look like a capital letter Q with the tail being the entrance channel from the ocean. We turned inland and travelled alongside the channel towards the lagoon. We stopped at an observation area where we were fortunate enough to see eagles, oyster catchers and other birds. I felt a bit guilty riding my bike and making noise - it became such a peaceful place once we had turned off our bikes. A father and son were trying their luck at fishing – nothing yet but they were enjoying the outing. There is a fishing platform that is wheelchair accessible which I think is a great idea.

After a short stay we continued to the lagoon. We travelled half way around the lagoon then turned and crossed the sealed road that leads further north.

We now travelled on a sandy track uphill and away from Little Lagoon. We stopped when we got to the summit and looked back over the lagoon and towards Denham - another great view of land and sea. We also got to see the golf course from here. I golf at Cordova Bay Golf Course back in Victoria. It is a very well maintained and beautiful course. This golf course was about as opposite my home course as you can get. There was not a single blade of grass in sight in this arid landscape. The first hole is four hundred twenty-four yards long. Your tee shot is over an expanse of meter-tall bushes. If you hit your ball properly you may or may not find it if it lands on the fairway. The fairways are mostly sandy dirt, overtaken with small plants and rocks. The 'greens' were only somewhat more manicured than the fairways meaning they were mostly sand - but each had a rake and smoothing tool. It would have been interesting to play there, but not in the summer heat of thirty plus degrees.

We continued along the track travelling parallel to the ocean but inland. We had the chance to increase our speed and I was quite happy to get up to forty kilometres an hour – the top speed that Rick said we would attain. The track ran alongside the highway for a kilometre or so and this is where I decided I wanted to go much faster than forty. I slowed to a crawl and let the others get a few hundred meters ahead – then I opened the throttle and bounced along, the wind in my face, the bush a blur. Quite a rush at seventy kilometres per hour! I slowed and joined the rest of the group as they waited to safely cross the highway. We were now south of Denham on the rugged bush track that would take us over bushland and out to the red cliffs south of Denham. The track was a lot of fun to ride along, with twists, tight turns and bumps making it seem like a theme park ride. Again, I let the others get ahead and throwing caution to the wind gunned it almost losing control a few times. I didn't care that I might take a spill. I just wanted an adrenalin rush.

We reached the top of a cliff and stopped the bikes. We dismounted and listened to Rick. "Right across the bay from us is Useless Loop, a salt mining town. We can see it from here, but if you want to drive there you have to have a four wheel drive vehicle and it's two hundred fifty kilometres away. There are huge ponds that are flooded with sea water again and again. Through evaporation the salt concentration increases and eventually the water disappears leaving the salt behind. The salt, the purest grade in the world, is then scooped up and loaded on to ships for export. Just to the right is Dirk Hartog Island which is the western boundary of Shark Bay Heritage site. Captain Hartog, the first European to set foot on Australian soil, landed there in 1616 and Hartog homestead is on the island. It is a valued nesting site for loggerhead turtles and has a great variety of wildlife."

We got back on the bikes and continued along the cliff top until we came to a place where we rode downhill, ending up on the beach where we stopped again. We stopped here for about twenty minutes so a father and son stripped to their boxers and went for a quick swim. The rest of us just enjoyed the spectacular scenery. The cliffs are a gorgeous orangey-red color and tumble down to meet the light coloured sand. The water is pristine, absolutely clear, and a dark turquoise on the horizon.

There was a lot of brown sea grass on the beach and in the water, remnants of the giant sea grass beds in the bay. Rick told us about this remarkable plant – twelve different types in the area. It's taken five thousand years to attain this size. The sea grass is the foundation of Shark Bay's ecosystem, providing life to the whole area. The sea grass banks here are the largest in the world, covering over four thousand square kilometres. That's the size of a one kilometre wide strip going across the United States. It's a lot of area! The banks stretch for one hundred thirty kilometres along the coast and are a major food source and habitat for many different animals including dugongs, turtles, fish, oysters, scallops, sharks and prawns.

Back on the bikes now, it was only fifteen minutes until Denham came into view and soon we were back where we started. The three hour trip was a wonderful adventure. It allowed me to go to places that I couldn't have reached otherwise.

MONKEY MIA

Iwalked along the street until I found a small restaurant that Lauren had recommended and went in and had lunch. It was now mid afternoon and time to drive twenty-six kilometres up the peninsula to Monkey Mia, (pronounced My-ah) I didn't want you to read along pronouncing it Monkey Mee-ah, and then having the song 'Momma Mia' popping up in your head, and having to live with that distraction – I had to live with that distraction. Anyway, so much for that. As I was saying, Monkey Mia is a resort close to Denham. Perhaps the name Monkey comes from a schooner that anchored in Shark Bay in the 1830's when there was a pearl industry; no one knows for sure. Mia is an aboriginal name for a temporary shelter. The resort is set on Dolphin Beach in Shark Bay with pristine turquoise water lapping at the white sand shore. It is an oasis for travellers from all over the world. The resort is the only facility in the area and has a variety of accommodations from beach front villas to a camp-ground. I checked into Dolphin Lodge, the hostel building of the resort, and secured a bottom bunk in a seven bed co-ed dorm. All guests have free use of the swimming pool, hot tub, bars and cafes.

Monkey Mia is located in a pollution free region – there is no industry, no over-development, and other than the resort, no development of any kind. It boasts three hundred twenty sunshiny days each year and sits on a pristine beach with water to match. Originally a pearling camp and fish-ing base, Monkey Mia provided the only place where the water was deep enough for boats at low tide.

I headed out to the beach, just a few meters away. "Wow, I am so lucky to be here right now. This is an incredible place, very low-key and peace-ful." I walked down the beach along the front of the resort to the gift shop and ticket center at the far end. I had picked up a pamphlet somewhere along the way about walks offered with an Aboriginal guide, Darren Capewell. I purchased a ticket for his night time walk that evening and for his day time walk the next morning. I also got a ticket for a wildlife cruise the next day and as a perk for purchasing this ticket, I was entitled to an evening cruise in the bay. This would leave in twenty minutes from the pier at this end of the beach. (Travel Luck)

I walked up the short ramp onto Aristocat 2, a sailing catamaran. About twenty of us had come aboard for the evening cruise, an hour and a half leisurely sail in Shark Bay. We motored a short distance out into the bay then the sails were raised. We had a slow sail as the winds were light but it was a perfectly relaxing evening with the sun getting lower on the horizon every second. The lighting was perfectly magical and softened everything it touched. I sat on a bench near the bow and began talking to two couples who were in my age bracket. They were here on a five day trip from Perth. We shared good conversation and a fine bottle of wine. It was a very pleasant way to spend the early evening.

The communal kitchen in the hostel is large and well maintained but except for two pots and a frying pan is barren of cookware. Not a knife, fork, spoon, bowl, plate, dish towel or soap – absolutely nothing! This was the first hostel I had encountered that had so little in the kitchen. I managed to find a wayward spoon that was in decent shape and I would hoard it over the next two days. I had leftovers for supper which I heated in the microwave and ate with 'my' spoon. After supper I walked down the beach to the amphitheatre for my evening walk with Darren. I sat alone in the darkening light waiting for him. There was a group of tweens and teens wandering around, spending this summer evening with new found friends. They passed by several times over the next hour, always looking for something to do and trying to find their place in the group. A couple with two young children joined me and waited for Darren and his walk. After forty minutes we agreed that Darren was a no-show for tonight – I headed back to the far end of the beach. I went onto the deck in front of the bar where I sat and listened to live music by two young fellows who played guitar and sang. I saw Darren at one of the tables so knew that he was okay and thought I'd most likely see him the next day.

There are about three hundred wild bottlenose dolphins living in Shark Bay – about a hundred twenty have been named and studied. The dolphins have been fed by humans since the 1960's, first from fishing boats and docks and more recently from shore. A small number of these, five females and two male calves when I visited, come to the resort each morning for feeding. This is an incredible, free opportunity for dolphin human interaction. The dolphins set their own schedule, usually showing up in the morning around 8:30. I walked the fifty meters to the beach and then down about a hundred meters to where like-minded people had gathered. There were rangers to monitor the interaction and to give us information about the dolphins. As we waited, Jenny told us a bit more about the marine life in Shark Bay. "This mutually beneficial ritual happens almost every day of the year, the dolphins having only missed four days in the past five years. This is the best place on the planet for a natural dolphin experience. The dolphins have been visiting the beach since the 1960's.

They are wild, live the area and visit of their own accord and are fed every day of the year. Monkey Mia is the top behavioural site in the world for bottlenose dolphins and tiger sharks. Scientists from all over the world come to Monkey Mia to do research and there have been a lot of documentaries filmed here, some for the Discovery Channel and for National Geographic. In addition to studying the dolphins and sharks, research is also done on dugongs, turtles, rays and sea snakes." I love watching nature documentaries and I was thinking that I probably had seen some footage from Shark Bay – at least I claimed that familiarity as I stood on the beach.

We entered the water and stood knee deep waiting for their arrival. Right on schedule they showed up, little puffs of water blown into the sky, dorsal fins and bodies cutting the surface. Bella, the dominant female ventured the closest. She came in and swam parallel to the shore about a meter or two away from us, swimming on her side, one eye out of the water so she could watch us as well as we could watch her. Jenny walked ahead of her and Bella followed along the shore passing the people who had come to see her. After a short time, four other rangers with shiny metal buckets appeared and waded in to the water. They spread out along the beach so that each of the females had their own place to get some fish. So that the dolphins would not become dependent on people for food, each ranger had just a very small amount of fish, four tiny servings, each about the size of a small orange segment. A few lucky visitors got to wade out and get a piece of fish from the bucket and offer it to a dolphin. This was synchronized because Bella was apt to charge over and butt another dolphin out of the way to take their food if she had the chance. The other dolphins had eaten their small morsels as Bella was held captive by the promise of one last tasty bit from her bucket. As soon as the rangers rinsed out their buckets and held them above their heads, signalling that the other females had finished, Bella was given her last piece of fish, then she turned and headed off shore and just as they had magically appeared, they now vanished.

As the dolphins had dispersed, so now did all the visitors who were scheduled to leave on their morning buses. This brought the number of people down to about thirty from over a hundred. The dolphins come in for a second feed about an hour after the first one, so I got to experience it again. They would return again the following morning – I would be there.

Immediately after my dolphin encounter I ambled a few yards to the canvas covered amphitheatre to take a tour with Darren "Capes" Capewell, a local Malgana tribe member. There was the couple with their young boy and girl from the previous evening and me, so another small group. (Travel Luck) Capes walked into the amphitheater: a nice looking fellow wearing a white sleeveless shirt, navy shorts, worn brown boots with black socks and a gold necklace, all topped with a wide brimmed straw hat. He had a calm unhurried manner about him and I already felt a connection with him. Capes first words to us were "Wula guda nyinda" which translates to "you come this way", an Aboriginal term for the sharing of stories – both between generations and cultures. Capes walks are a combination of eco-tourism and cultural tourism. This notion of intercultural sharing extends into every aspect of the tours, which operate under the philosophy of education, understanding and respect – EUR. The aim of his tours is to foster an understanding of the natural land, wildlife, stories and traditions of the region. "Learn the secrets of my people and how we relate to the land, ocean and spirit of country," said Capes.

Aboriginal people, when speaking in English of this connection, often refer to land as "country". Anthropologist Deborah Bird Rose has described 'country' in this way:

"People talk about country in the same way that they would talk about a person: they speak to country, sing to country, visit country, worry about country, feel sorry for country, and long for country. People say that country knows, hears, smells, takes notice, takes care, is sorry or happy. Country is a living entity with a yesterday, today and tomorrow, with a consciousness, and a will toward life. Because of this richness, country is home, and peace; nourishment for body, mind, and spirit; heart's ease." Wherever I travel, it is the same message passed on by the people who first inhabited the land. "Our elders remind us that if we take care of the land, the land will take care of us. It feeds us clothes us and keeps us warm." Grand Chief Ed John – First Nations, British Columbia

Capes told us that "When you visit Monkey Mia it is easy to 'see' country, but to truly take something away with you – you need to feel the spirit of country. This is what I share with visitors. People walk away with a deeper appreciation of what country means to my people. I guarantee you will leave feeling and seeing country from a different perspective."

He had me at "Wula guda nyinda". I immediately felt deeply connected to Capes and was eager to walk with him and learn everything he would share about this place. I was feeling somewhat low in spirit, reliving the tough times Jenna had gone through. Sometimes the feelings and images from her long illness come back and pound me into the ground; it usually takes several days to get them out of my mind. Capes looked into my eyes and seemed to pick up on this right away. We didn't talk about it, he just knew – we connected. He became the care giver, I the receiver. I decided to stay close by his side for the rest of the time. There was nothing hurried or rushed about Capes and his walk. He slowly began to move away from the resort and across the road and soon we were on a path on the white sand that lies near the sea. I heard words in a language I did not know, words that had passed through generations. I was able to pick out his name once but did not know the context. Capes was talking to the land as he walked.

Capes had said that this was a walk through red sand country and white sand country, where desert meets the ocean. It didn't take long to understand what he meant. We gathered a few meters up the path and Capes had us scoop up a handful of the white, sandy earth from underfoot.

"This is white sand. Say hello to it. Introduce yourself to it. Rub it between your hands and on your arms. Say why you are here," said Capes. "This is what you should do anywhere you visit."

Nature holds a deep place in my heart and soul, so I didn't hesitate to rub the sand over my hands then onto one arm and the other. I was captivated with the land and with Capes. This was the first part of the teachings of the profound relationship between the nature and humankind that Capes shared with us.

Where I saw only sparse growth, Capes showed us bush tucker (native edible plants) and plants used as medicine. He taught us new Aboriginal words that my mind had trouble processing and remembering. He would repeat them then quiz us along the way so we could better retain them.

Markings in the earth were woven into stories of the animals that had made them. "This lizard was taking his time. That one was running beside another. An emu passed this way this morning."

"These are the ways country talks to you."

Sacred stories, legends and traditions told us of the strong cultural history of the Nhanda and Malgana people of his heritage.

We walked along the path of white sand until we came to a slope where a dramatic change unfolded. The white sand stopped and was overtaken by red sand, this country where desert meets the sea. "This is red sand country. Scoop up a handful of red sand and introduce yourself." And we did.

We walked along the hillside for a bit then gathered around Capes. He pointed out a shallow cave just above us that had been excavated in the 1980's by archaeologists. Evidence of charcoal on the roof and remains of shellfish on the floor showed that this cave had been used by Aborigines over a thousand years ago.

We continued up through the red earth, hillside trail and went on for a bit, and then Capes had us stop. He smoothed three meter square area with a stick. Then with a single stroke, began a drawing of the western coast of Australia. Explaining as he drew, we soon had a large map before us of the country and of all the different Aboriginal tribal regions. These tribes had had lived in the area for thousands of years and this land had sustained them. He told us of cultural traditions and ways such as those that govern the marriage between tribes. It was all so very interesting.

We continued to a lookout that gave us magnificent views of Shark Bay below. When it was time to continue, we walked down the front of the lookout through red sand. Red soon turned to white beneath my sandals and I knew that the walk would soon be over.

"This has been a healing walk for me. I'm really looking forward to coming out with you tonight on your evening walk, Capes. Thanks so very much!" I said.

I went back to Dolphin Lodge and made a sandwich for lunch, good old PB & J. It was back down the beach by one thirty to go on an afternoon wildlife cruise in the bay. I re-boarded the Aristocat 2 and we were soon motoring out on the bay for our three hour cruise. (Did you start singing the Gilligan's Island song too? Yes, a threeeee hooouuur cruise). This was pretty much an ideal way to spend the afternoon. I always love being out on the water, perhaps due in part to my childhood. Growing up in the Rocky Mountains, we had a summer cabin at a lake only a half hour drive from my home town of Kimberley. We spent endless days at the lake, much of the time either in the water or paddling along it. One winter my dad painstakingly built a canoe of fibre glass laid over a plywood frame, in our basement. I can still remember the day the fibre glass was put on the wooden frame – a fast and frantic blur of action – the words "Joan, get out of the way!" burned into my brain. I think I was about four at the time. That summer, while our friends roared by in power boats, my family paddled the canoe. In the moment, my brothers and I wanted a power boat to go fast and to water ski. In the long run, of course my dad had been right and I think we had more fun in the canoe than we would have had in a power boat. So any time I am out on a boat, I feel a sense of peace, just as I did when out on the lake back home.

We criss-crossed the bay, looking for wildlife. We saw a few porpoises in the distance but none close to the boat. I had been hoping that some might come by and surf the bow wave, but no luck with that today. We were lucky enough to get a few glimpses of a dugong and her calf. Dugongs look similar to manatees and about fourteen thousand live in Shark Bay. They can be quite shy and even though their numbers are large, not every cruise results in a sighting of them. It was nice to see the two of them together, swimming under the surface then rising for a breath of air before disappearing again. Awhile later we caught sight of a lone male dugong as well. Two turtles were close enough to get a good look at and I immediately thought of the other times I had seen them in the wild: first snorkelling off Maui in Hawaii, then at the Great Barrier Reef. The Aristocat 2 has a fishing licence so the crew took a few rods to the stern for us to take turns. While I could have put the rod in a holder I chose to hold it – that way I could feel each tiny move of the bait. None of us caught any fish, but one person snagged a sea snake. The snake was carefully brought on board and freed from the hook that had pierced his upper body – not a serious wound. We all found him to be very beautiful and I was happy to see that only two small children were uneasy about him. We watched him swim away with a multitude of S-shaped wriggles and wished him the best.

The one stop on the cruise was at the Blue Lagoon Pearl Farm. The farm can be seen from Monkey Mia and is about a ten minute boat ride across the blue water. We approached it from sea side, came alongside and stepped onto the pontoon. About half the Sea Lab pontoon is open but under cover; the other half is enclosed and includes a gift shop. We started our tour on the open deck where an employee told us about pearl production both in the wild and on farms. "In the wild, a pearl is formed when a small particle enters the oyster. The irritant causes pearl producing cells to dislodge and more layers are added to cover the particle over time, producing a pearl. On a pearl farm, every oyster undergoes a special procedure. We use Mississippi Mussel shells and place a small piece into the body of the oyster. We cover this with a piece from another oyster - the part of the oyster that produces the pearls. We have a favourite person who comes here and seeds our oysters. She is Asian and has small hands that she uses with speed and dexterity. It is an exact science and takes years to develop the necessary skill. On a good day she can earn five thousand dollars; good pay for an excellent surgeon. Then the oysters are taken out to beds and we wait for the pearls to be produced." After talking about how pearls are formed he got an oyster and opened it to reveal a pearl. It was not the perfect sphere I was expecting, but rather an oval shape. He opened a second oyster and showed us the pearl inside. This one was attached to the shell – it looked like a small hill on a flat plain.

The jewellery is a collection of unique loveliness. There are pearls inset with opals, diamonds and gold. There are blue, green, white, pink and black pearls. There are necklaces, pendants, earrings, rings, bracelets and show pieces. It is a small gift shop but packed with hundreds of thousands of dollars of 'art.' It was all lovely to look at but quite out of my price range with rings starting at nine hundred dollars and one gorgeous pendant going for forty thousand dollars. Who knows what else they have that was not on display. We stayed for a half hour then got back on board our boat.

Our captain headed back out into the bay for the final hour of our trip. I didn't know what a boom net was but found out in quick time. A cargo net is strung between the pontoons at the stern – sort of looks like a huge hammock, big enough for eight or ten people to sit in. Those who choose to sit here are guaranteed to get soaked, rather refreshing on a hot day. Two adults and six youngsters were enjoying the fun when suddenly, one of the girls let out a yelp. "Ow – I've been stung!" More yells from some others too. All quickly rose to their feet and clambered over to the side and out of the net. We had passed through some jelly fish and several people showed twig-shaped red welts where contact had been made. That was the end of sitting in the boom net for the trip.

We wandered about the bay before turning back to Monkey Mia and putting up the sail for this final leg. It was a beautiful ending to my three hour tour.

I was walking along the beachfront path, heading back towards Dolphin Lodge, when a fellow caught my attention. "Hey! It looks like you could use a beer. Come and join us." This was a couple who had been on the quad bike tour with me the day before. Their sons were playing down on the beach and mom and dad were sitting on the lawn keeping an eye on them. I don't drink very often, but the chance of a cold beer was appealing to me so I sat down and spent a pleasant hour with them. I really felt like I was on the other side of the world, in Australia. It was really nice. The boys came up from the beach, "What's for supper?" At the same time a teenage boy caught my attention, "Hey, was that shot in or out?" We had also been watching four teens play volleyball in front of us. They couldn't agree on a call so asked my opinion. "It was out for sure." "Do you want to ref our game?" "Sure." That's how I ended up standing on the raised walkway refereeing a volleyball game that grew to eight players, four girls and four boys. I have a wonderful picture of them posing on the sand court at the end of the game, all smiles and relaxed. Duties completed, I went back to Dolphin Lodge where I had the last portion of my stir fry, eaten with my 'found' spoon.

I was back in the amphitheatre at eight that evening. "Wula guda ny-inda" said Capes. And so began my second walk with him. Twenty–two people were there for this adventure. I sidestepped the others and took my place at his side as we began this evening trip; I just wanted to be near Capes. I felt I could lean on him and he would somehow help me find my way. He took me aside almost immediately and told me to take my time, to be in the moment and to slowly rub the white sand and the red sand on my hands and arms and that it would help. I believed him.

We walked in reverse direction to the morning walk; white sand to red sand and up the hill to the lookout. When we got to the top we continued for a short distance then came to a small campfire. Capes had started the fire before he came to meet us at the amphitheatre at this gnurra (Aboriginal camp). Behind the fire and where Capes sat was a semi-spherical shaped Mia Mia (Aboriginal hut). It was made of branches gathered from red sand country.

He asked us to form a semicircle around the fire and we each found our place in the red sand. It was a surreal place to be: in the desert, at night, the crackling fire making the red sand dance. An so very quiet and peaceful. The warm air embraced me, the earthy smell surrounded me. And then there was the voice of Capes, once again telling us of his heritage with his map, a calm voice, a strong voice, a knowing voice. He spoke of his ancestors camping at this very spot. So very long ago. There was a turtle shell at the camp which was used for carrying water and other food. I blew on a conch shell with some success - another few minutes and I think I would have the right position of my mouth on the shell and the right amount of force to blow with to make a descent sound. A hollow Emu egg was shown to be a water vessel.

Then there was the music. Capes had two clap sticks which are a traditional Aboriginal percussion instrument. They were made of hardwood and gave a deep resonant sound when hit together. They are used in ceremonial and everyday singing.

Capes also had a didgeridoo, that termite-hollowed, iconic Australian instrument. To have it played by Capes in the desert night was perfectly surreal. We guessed at the animal sounds he played: a lizard here, an emu there, a bird, even a story of a kangaroo and her joey hopping alongside. To me, it was the same feeling as canoeing on a Canadian lake in the mist of the early morning and hearing loons calling. I was just immersed in the moment. Time stood still, every cell of my being was listening to the didgeridoo; its' vibrations travelled through my mind and body – there was nothing else. It was a feeling of total peace and well being. I was out of harms' way. I'll never forget it.

On this evening trip Capes had brought some fish with him and now he placed these in the amber coals of the fire. A short time later, we all got to savour these delicious fish, cooked in the fire, the same way as has been done for generations. I felt a real connection to his culture. I have eaten salmon cooked traditionally by First Nations people in Canada and thought of them at this time. Capes had travelled to Canada and spent time with the First Nations people there - cross culture sharing.

Once again I scooped handfuls of red sand and rubbed it over my hands, arms and now my legs too. Capes brought a smouldering branch from the fire. He told us to pass it around and inhale the smoke that skirted upwards from its tip. He told me to take my time with it and I did, deeply inhaling the smoky eucalyptus spirals that made me more relaxed, allowed me to become more entwined with the experience and gave me a chance to heal. Then I passed it on but the aroma lingered with me awhile. Good medicine. Next to me a father held his sleeping son, his wife their tired daughter. Everyone was still and silent, the only motion was from the fire and from the passing of the branch.

Too soon, it was time – ten thirty - to leave our campfire. I used my 'roll to one side and push off with my good knee manoeuvre' to get up from the ground. I stretched and got ready to leave this enchanting place. We walked quietly in single file, following Capes the way we had come, tiny headlamps lighting our way. We passed through red sand then into white sand country where I scooped up the white sand and rubbed it on my hands and arms. "Hi, I'm Joan and I'm here to find some peace."

We stopped one last time in the desert night to look skyward. This was so incredible for different reasons. The stars were incredibly bright in this place with no light pollution. They are totally different stars than what I am used to seeing in the northern hemisphere and Capes pointed out new constellations to us. But the most interesting formation in the night sky was not of stars but of a space where very few stars shone - this area took the form of a gigantic galactic emu, stretching up and to the right. Too cool!

We made our way along the path and across the road that marked the end of our trip. Handing in our headlamps, I hung back until the others had left. I told Capes what a moving experience I had with him both on the morning and on the evening walks. He had made a difference in my life. He smiled and nodded knowingly.

My time with Capes was the ultimate enriching experience of my stay at Monkey Mia. Come this way.

I entered my room quietly using only the faint light from outside to guide me. It was after eleven and this is just common courtesy. I was soon in bed and fell asleep easily after an incredibly full day. The knocking came at two in the morning. Someone was knocking at the door so I got up to let them in. When I opened the door I saw three young fellows, the one in the center being propped up by his buddies. I showed them to his bed where they poured him for the night. Their friend safely in bed they left and headed off to their dorm. I was quite surprised the next morning when I was having breakfast. The three young men came over and joined me. "Hey, thanks for last night. It was cool that you didn't get pissed off with us coming and waking you up in the middle of the night like that. We find it kind of hard to believe that you welcomed us in with our buddy." I told them that I thought it was great that they were looking out for each other and had made sure that he was safe for the night. That's what friends are for. We had breakfast together and enjoyed our conversation about travel and friends. I washed out my plastic container that had served as my cereal bowl and washed the spoon that I had borrowed for the past few days. I left the spoon on the counter where I had found it, perhaps to be used by someone else like me who had come unprepared.

I packed up the car and headed to the beach for the last time. I arrived a few minutes before Bella swam in with her crew and was once again entranced by their presence. It was a fitting farewell to Monkey Mia. I shall never forget it.

It was with some sadness that I left this place and I hope that someday I can go back and spend a few weeks there. It was mystical to be on the edge of the continent, where red sand meets white sand, meets ocean, where there is no pollution, where nature is cherished and respected. Whatever I had been missing, I had found it, and I was feeling well once again.

SINCE THE BEGINNING OF TIME

Stromato-whats? I had never heard of stromatolites, but visiting them was mentioned as one of the things one should do while in the area. They are one of the reasons that Shark Bay is a World Heritage Site. So with an open and curious mind I turned left off the road and drove the short distance to the parking lot at Hamelin Pool. I entered the small onsite building which acted as the site entrance as well as local store and camping office. Armed with some basic information and simple directions I stepped out the side door of the building, turned right and began a slightly uphill walk. This took me to a viewpoint with chairs and a bench. This is where I would come if I was staying here for any length of time, just 'kick it back' and take in the view. A short downhill walk took me to a seashell block quarry just as I had seen at Shell Beach. I continued to my left along a path that paralleled the ocean on my right. The air had a nautical scent, the sun was warm and it was quiet. I could see the ocean boardwalk when I came to the first of several informational signs.

Stromatolites are the earliest known form of life on Earth. At one time, they were the only life form on Earth. They are known as 'living fossils'. I did not know that. I also learned that the water in this area is twice as salty as normal seawater. This is because the area has a low tidal flow. "Stromatolites grow at a rate of less than 1mm per year - that's one tenth as much as coral. A microorganism, cyan bacteria build up, trapping fine sediment particles from the warm water and binding it together with mucus. This unusual life form grows to about 60cm tall and looks like mushroom-shaped rocky domes. The discovery of these living fossils was akin to finding a live dinosaur. "

So armed with a new respect for what I was going to see, I was soon at the boardwalk where two other people were looking into the water. The water was crystal clear. There were thousands of dark rocky domes that forested the ocean floor, contrasting against the white sandy bottom. Schools of small, white fish were darting about in this unique habitat, having adapted to life in this area of high salinity. Nope, there were no spectacular things that the stromatolites were doing, nothing to catch my immediate attention. But when I stopped and took the time to look close-ly I could see tiny bubbles of oxygen bubbling to the surface everywhere – a result of the billions of tiny organisms. Then the magnitude hit me. These wee, tiny things had made it possible for other life forms to exist on Earth by pumping out oxygen for billions of years and they were still here, doing the same thing right here and now. How cool is that? Well, I thought it was pretty cool. And so I walked along the looping boardwalk, stopping frequently to look at stromatolites. This is the only place on the planet that I could come to walk so close to them. Going back to the car I thought to myself that I probably won't ever get a chance like that again! What a wonderful place to have visited!

Nature has provided so much that is worth protecting. I have been to five of the twenty World Heritage designated areas that meet all four crite-ria for natural places, three of them in Australia; Shark Bay, the Great Bar-rier Reef and Queensland's Wet Tropics. I have also been to the Grand Canyon and Yellowstone Park in the United States.

It wasn't long before I was back to the main highway where I turned left and continued north towards Exmouth. Today I would drive seven hundred fifty kilometres to my destination. The highway travels inland for the most part so there were no beach distractions and the landscape was not remarkable. I did get to see a lot of animals though. There was a lot of road kill which attracted eagles and I saw nine of them eating at their very own roadside buffet. The cattle stations are huge and are fenced east – west. This meant that there are no fences keeping animals off the road and they are the biggest hazard to driving. There were a lot of places where I had to slow drastically and one spot where I had to stop and wait for some cattle to get off the road. I saw the remains of at least a hundred animals over a hundred kilometre stretch so there must be thousands liv-ing in the region. I passed goats, cattle and sheep crossing the road or standing next to it.

I love the solitude of driving and find it therapeutic, so I found that the time passed quickly. After five hours I turned off the highway and drove west to the tiny, ocean front town of Coral Bay. Coral Bay has about two hundred residents and is a tourism town. It was time for lunch so I parked next to the beach and began walking north along the sand. The bay is ab-solutely gorgeous – an expansive arc of white sand bordering incredibly turquoise waters. Coral Bay is a place where you can don snorkel gear, step into the water and soon be swimming over a coral reef. Thousands of people visit each year to enjoy the reef: swimming, diving, boating and fishing. It was another glorious summer day with the temperature in the high twenties. Along the beach I noticed a few small shelters and headed for one of them. The shelter consisted of four upright poles supporting a roof and that was it – simply a place to seek some relief from the sun. I pulled out my sandwich, banana and ginger beer and began eating my pic-nic lunch. There were three girls in the shelter and it wasn't long before their conversation drew me in to talking with them. They were in Coral Bay for two months as part of a marine research team – what a great way to spend a summer! They told me about their jobs and backgrounds and I loved it. As one girl described her work she said she was 'engasped' by what she was seeing under a microscope. Her friends were quick to point out that there was no such word as 'engasped'. I asked her to define it. "Well, it was just so incredible that I was totally engaged by what I was seeing and I gasped when I saw how beautiful it was. So, you know, I was 'engasped.'" I encouraged her to keep the word in her vocabulary and for her friends to add it to theirs as this is how language evolves. They were just so young and enthusiastic and were having a good time together.

Now I was only an hour and a half from Exmouth. At some point it became apparent to me that there were some unusual mounds dominating the landscape. These became more numerous as I continued north. I was driving through termite territory - thousands of rusty red, person-high mounds, rising from the ground like loose stacks of hay after a harvest. This required closer inspection so I pulled the car to the side of the road and walked over to one about thirty meters off the road. The walk was interesting as the ground had an abundance of defensive plants. The most common plant looked like a hedgehog on steroids. These plants are a mass of long thorns that jut out in every direction so no plan of attack on it is possible. Contact with these thorns is, as you may have guessed, quite uncomfortable. Trying to protect my legs, I walked a zig-zaggy path on the red earth towards the termite mound. I touched the mound and found it as hard as a rock, baked by the sun over many years. I was quite impressed by the size of the structure, but at the time was unaware of just how amazing a termite mound is. When I was back in Perth I learned more about the mounds and the termites when I visited the museum. The reason the mounds are so hard on the outside is that the little bugs mix together saliva and mud that hardens to form a cement-like substance. A cut-away view revealed a honeycomb of tunnels and chambers in the outer storage zone where grass is stored. The next layer is made of termite feces and earth – this is where the nurseries are where workers take care of eggs and newly hatched nymphs. While the internal structure of the mound is expanded as the need arises, the mounds above ground level do not change much and like an iceberg, most of the community is underground and unseen. Mounds are formed over decades and can house several million of these insects. I didn't see a single termite out in the heat of the day. Some tunnels and chambers have been found as deep as ten meters underground. The whole thing is air conditioned via a maze of underground tunnels that direct hot air up and out of the mound and draw air inside where it is cooled before being directed through the colony. Termite mounds are the tallest non man-made structures on Earth. Amazing engineering when you think about it. It is estimated that the mass of termites is ten times greater than the mass of all the people on Earth! We've all heard that cattle are responsible for a great percentage of methane gas released into our atmosphere each year. I was really surprised to learn that termites are thought to be responsible for forty percent of methane - power in numbers! (You don't know what you don't know)

I managed to get back to the car with only minor scratches on my legs, a result of my first unwary contact with the hardy plant I later learned is spinafix. The concentration of the termite mounds increased as I drove farther north and then decreased as I got closer to Exmouth.

THE WORLD'S BIGGEST FISH

The hostel was easy to find and I had a room with a bunk bed, my own bathroom, a small fridge and even a television. No roommate showed up, so I had the luxury of the room to myself. It had been a long day and I didn't feel like going out food shopping. I walked up to the liquor outlet at the front of the hostel and asked them about fast food delivery. They recommended a pizza place so I ordered my supper and walked back to my room, gathered a load of laundry and put it in the wash. About twenty minutes later I walked back to the front and picked up my pizza. So there I was in the lap of luxury: sitting on my bed, eating pizza and watching TV – at least it was pretty luxurious to me. Laundry washed and dried, I went to sleep as soon as possible as I had to get up early the next day for my new adventure.

I sat quietly on the bench and waited for him to come around again. The first time I saw him I was in awe and knew that I would be here for some time just waiting for the chance to see him again and again, short periods in time that would stay with me for the rest of my life. I was in the Osaka Aquarium in Japan. It was 1991. I had never imagined a fish as large and fascinating as the whale shark. He circled the huge tank with the regularity dictated by his confines. When I was researching the numerous activities to do on my trip I found that there was a place in Western Australia that I would actually be able to swim alongside the world's largest fish. That was the main attraction for me in Western Australia. I knew it would add over three thousand kilometres to my trip, but I also knew that I would forever regret it if I didn't make the attempt.

I was very lucky to have a spot on the boat as I booked the trip just four days earlier when I was in Denham. Naively, I thought that would be plenty of time to get on a boat but once again I realized that booking further in advance might be a good idea. Sadly, during pre-purchase research, this crucial info nugget was somehow overlooked. Apparently I had missed the advice to "book your tour well in advance especially during peak season" this being April through July. The visitor centers are staffed with wonderful people and Lisa was superb in making calls for me. I was told to come back in two hours when I would find out whether or not I had a spot on our boat. When I realized that I might not be able to fit this trip in to my schedule I was profoundly disappointed. I spent the next two hours walking along the waterfront of Denham. I returned to good news from Lisa. She had heard back from Three Islands Marine Charters and they had a space for me on the date that I wanted.

The van arrived shortly after seven and I quickly joined the others already on board. We made two other stops then headed north along the Cape road. Several kilometres later we began to see on the horizon, the thirteen naval communication towers that were, in 1967, jointly constructed for use by the Australian and United States navies. The towers are taller than Frances' Eiffel Tower, the tallest being almost four hundred meters. The town of Exmouth was built as a support town for the naval presence at that time.

We then turned to the west and headed out to the west coast of the Cape to Ningaloo Reef which runs some two hundred sixty miles along the North West Cape. The west coast of Australia is a meeting place of cold water coming north from the Antarctic and of warm water that comes south from the equator. It is this confluence of waters that helps provide the perfect habitat for Ningaloo Reef marine life. Ningaloo Reef is one of Australia's most beautiful reefs and it is a protected sanctuary for marine life. It is a wellspring of life, an exquisite area with crystal clear turquoise water that is host to an amazing array of marine life. There are over two hundred fifty species of coral and five hundred species of fish in Ningaloo Marine Park. The reef forms a protected lagoon around the North West Cape which averages two to four meters in depth. Exploring this marine wilderness can be done simply by walking in from the beach or entering from water craft. There are limitless snorkelling areas around the reef. The reef is a very important fringing reef, one of only two coral reefs in the world to have been formed on the west coast of a continent. It is a tropical paradise of corals, warm waters, impossibly bright coloured fish, manta rays, dolphins, turtles, dugongs and during April through July a feeding area for whale sharks. They are the reason I have come here.

I was on a full day adventure with Three Islands Marine Charters. The price tag was the most expensive of my trip but I was only going to do this once in my life and it was great value for the dollar. To snorkel in this area was an ultimate thrill and the experience of a lifetime.

We arrived at Tantabiddi Marine Sanctuary where our boat, Draw Card was moored and were soon being ferried out to the seventeen meter boat in groups of five. I felt immediately welcome on board by the outgoing, friendly staff. Most of the boat is a large shaded deck area with full width water access area at the stern. Once all onboard, we headed out into the lagoon for a kilometre or so. Lifejackets and other floatation devices were on hand for those who wanted to add a bit more buoyancy when snorkelling. Andy is a gregarious Aussie, a retired navy diver and would be our videographer for the day. We were inside the reef where we had a briefing of how the day would unfold, safety features and the procedure for swimming with the whale sharks.

We got snorkelling gear and soon stepped off the stern into the water for our first session in the pristine lagoon. A safety tender launched with us each time we were in the water. I had loved the Great Barrier Reef, but this magical place seemed even more spectacular! First, we only had a ten minute boat ride to our first site. Second, there appeared to be more fish here. Third, we didn't have to wear stinger suits. It was absolute sensory overload and I loved it! I was immersed in the world's largest 'aquarium', surrounded by a living spectacle of blue and orange butterfly fish, green turtles, translucent wrasse, sponges, grouper fish, long and slender bright yellow trumpet fish, orange and white clown fish, black-and-white angelfish, red and white coral, sponges, brain coral, giant clams, parrotfish, crabs, sea cucumbers, puffer fish, blue devilfish yellow goldfish, black and yellow angelfish and pipe fish that could change color. The water was warm and calm and I swam slowly along the surface during this surreal experience. It's impossible to find the words to explain how happy I was at this moment in time - just a big burst of happy enveloped me.

There were clown fish hovering in anemones, lionfish, and moray eels peeking from nooks in the coral, star fish, and darts of brilliant blue, dashes of yellow and orange all against the white sand ocean floor. We all agreed that this area was one of spectacular beauty and considered ourselves most fortunate to be here. This initial snorkelling session was followed by morning tea as we rode along to the second snorkel site. With a splash, we were soon swimming again literally immersed in the beauty of it all.

We re-boarded after about forty-five minutes, and headed out through an opening in the reef to the open sea. The whale sharks are an open sea fish. They are attracted to the Ningaloo Reef because of the annual coral spawn which occurs during a full moon in April. This is only one of two places in the world that the whale sharks can be seen in large numbers. The tourism generated by their presence offers the opportunity to raise awareness of this threatened species. High concentrations of zooplankton are associated with the coral spawn and these gentle giants of the sea come here for the rich buffet it affords them, existing for the most part on microscopic organisms that they suck into their mouths. Food that is larger than two millimetres gets trapped by denticles, a fine sieve like device and any liquids are then passed through the gills. As the whale sharks open their mouths a vacuum is created, so larger prey such as small fish, squid the occasional octopus may also be taken in.

Wait. Wait. It was now time for the waiting game. The whale shark tour companies have associated spotting planes flying overhead in search of the main attraction. Spotting whale sharks from a boat is nearly impossible so planes provide their positions. Time was passed orienting us to the procedure for our adventurous swim with these passive creatures. Whale sharks are an endangered and protected species and their interaction with humans is regulated, licences being issued by the Department of Environment and Conservation. Recreation and conservation have been harmonized here as in many other marine parks. Only ten people at a time can be in the water with the whale shark. A whale shark spotter is required to be with us at all times. Regulations require that once in the water we do not swim in front of him, swim no closer than three meters from the side of the whale shark and no closer than four meters when at the rear. Working in tandem with another tour boat we would share the time swimming with the whale sharks we found. Daily limits of one and a half hours of human contact with any one whale shark are set requiring the companies to work closely together timing their swims in synchronization with each other.

"Group one, get your gear on as quickly as possible and get to the back of the boat. We have a whale shark."

The plane had spotted a whale shark and Draw Card made its way to its location as we got ready for our first encounter.

A flurry of activity followed as I and the rest of the group made our way to the stern and hurriedly donned fins, mask and snorkel.

"Go. Go. Go. Get in the water!"

Five of us on each side of the stern splashed in and made our way to the left and to the right separating our two groups by about fifteen meters forming a corridor through which the whale shark hopefully would travel. The boat had dropped us off about fifty meters in front of the whale shark and now we waited in the water as he approached, the idea to have half of us swimming on each side of him. I was really excited waiting in the warm water. Then in the distance I saw him coming in our direction, a shape becoming larger and more clearly defined with each meter he swam towards me. This huge fish, with an impossibly large mouth agape, was gliding through the turquoise water. Wow, I mean, wow, I mean . . . I was without words, just in awe of where I was and what I was doing. It was as if I were swimming in the midst of a dream! I turned to parallel the shark and swam as fast as I could, staying the required three meters from his side, so I hoped. I didn't want to get too close and become the person who caused the shark to seek refuge in the depths, diving out of view of both our group and the others to follow.

He was brownish and marked with the whale sharks distinctive pattern of pale vertical and horizontal stripes enclosing creamy white spots. These spots dominate the head. He was a big fish, not a big whale shark, being perhaps seven meters long, but he was a big fish and I was swimming right there beside him so he was immense to me. Whale sharks can be as long as twenty meters so this juvenile has some growing to do. He was not alone. Remoras glided around him in the habitat that he provided. I was just in this magnificent moment, in this surreal place on the other side of the planet doing something that I could not have imagined was possible. It was magical and mystical, one of life's highlights for me, something to cross off the bucket list. Here I was, kicking hard and using my arms for extra thrust and breathing harder at every stroke. He, of course, was streamlining through the water, his massive tail propelling him effortlessly as we all began to slip rearward, first beside the pectoral fins, then the dorsals, then the tail and ending up behind him watching the rhythmic back and forth of his massive tail carry him away. This first encounter lasted perhaps a minute but such an intense minute that I could never forget it. Our group gathered and shared our excitement while bobbing in the warm water. We had just shared a mind blowing experience, something that created a bond.

Group two was now in the water waiting for the whale shark to swim to them so they too could feel the rush, relish the time spent swimming with this very large, very gentle fish. Draw Card swung around and slowly motored back and picked us up. From the deck we watched as people on a second tour boat had time with the whale shark.

After a half hour or so it was "Group one. Get your gear and get to the back of the boat. It's time for your second swim!"

Again the routine was followed allowing each of us another amazing swim with the shark. Then it was time for our group to get out of the water and back onto the boat. While we were waiting for our third and final swim we enjoyed lunch, which was prepared the night before by Joanna who works behind the scenes. Food buried the table: salads, cold cuts, breads, desserts and beverages. As with any meal outdoors, it just seemed to taste better. I know it really tasted good with a side serving of adrenalin. We were lucky enough to see a lone dugong during our lunch time

About twenty minutes after finishing lunch, we got our third call to get into the water. So away I went with my group and had my third swim with this largest of fish. That third swim was just as great and as exciting as the very first swim. Just amazing! When the whale shark pulled away from us for this last time I found myself somewhat alone about thirty meters from the others. I was just floating in the water and looking down into the sixty plus meter depths. When water is that deep there is nothing else to see, just deep grey blue water. By some illusion there seemed to be rays of pale blue light that radiated from the bottom towards the surface. I closed my eyes, was breathing slowly and was bobbing there alone, totally relaxed going over the three amazing contacts with the whale sharks. It was at this moment that I was thinking how surreal this had actually been. I felt at peace with the universe in this state of sensory deprivation. Then it got a little weird.

When I opened my eyes I saw a few meters below me, rising from the depths and moving away from me, a shark, a grey shark, the kind that might just be curious or might come along and take a nibble of something.

He was beautiful, and I watched him with guarded admiration. At three meters in length, he was large enough to do some damage if those were his intentions. I didn't know what type of shark he was, but he was approaching the surface and heading towards the rest of my group. I had a choice to make. I could continue watching him until he faded away in the distance, which would have been my preference. Or I could alert the safety boat. I didn't want to take any chances so I waved over the safety boat and told Mike what was happening. He asked me if I was all right to swim over and join the rest of the group and I told him I was just fine and could definitely swim over to join my group. I just felt I needed to tell him about the shark in case something might happen to someone else in our group. When I did swim over to the rest of our group our guide had us in a very tight circle and he kept on checking the water beneath us to see if we were indeed safe.

Safely back on board Draw Card one of our shark spotters had said that she too had seen the shark and it was a Dusky Whaler. They said this type of shark poses no real danger to people, and he was most likely just curious as to what was going on. I found it very interesting when the next day a local fisherman in Geraldton told me the Dusky Whalers are indeed responsible for most of the shark-human interactions that they get on the coast. So who to believe? At any rate, it was quite an encounter and a really good way to end my swimming with whale sharks on a beautiful day on the west coast of Australia.

With a third and final headcount, assuring we were all safely on board, our captain turned the boat back towards the opening in the reef. On the way we spotted one of the many dugongs that live in the area. We travelled through the channel to the inner reef and soon were over the white sandy floor of the Ningaloo corals. Then we were treated to an afternoon fruit platter, which was sumptuous. Donning snorkel and fins one last time, we headed for our last swim in the pristine waters of the Ningaloo Reef. I swam leisurely and with confidence. An hour later, it was with reluctance that I took off my fins and mask and climbed back on to the waiting deck of Draw Card.

Andy showed us all the footage he had taken of our underwater adventure that day. From the numerous angles and depths that he had recorded from, I came to understand what a good videographer, diver and swimmer he is. When I received my recording in the mail some weeks later, I relived the experience again and again and was able to share it with family and friends.

INTENSE DRIVING TO A GRUNGY HOSTEL AND A MOUSE IN THE HOUSE

In retrospect I should have stayed another night in Exmouth. I had been up early and had a full day of adventure out on the water. It seemed like a good idea to complete the first three hundred kilometres of my trip back to Perth that evening. That would leave two days of easy driving to look forward to. Yes, it seemed like a good idea at the time - well, at least plausible. Shortly after I was dropped off at the hostel I was in my car and heading south. I had passed The Tropic of Capricorn sign on my way north, but was past it before I realized it. Today I stopped and took a picture of it – this globally famous line of latitude that marks the southern border of The Tropics. The landscape is typical of Western Australia: expansive, dry, spotty vegetation, red soil and animals, lots of animals. Yellow warning signs were posted at irregular intervals – black silhouettes of cattle, sheep and kangaroos. The amount of animal remains was staggering! I saw over a hundred carcasses in various stages of decomposition on the sides of the road. I wondered how many more had been struck by vehicles and had died some distance from the road. The road kill provides and endless buffet for scavengers. This allowed me to stop and again watch eagles, huge, magnificent birds. It reminded me of the bald eagles at home where each fall they gather by the hundreds to gorge on salmon carcasses during spawning season.

My car was a compact size and I knew that if I hit a kangaroo or steer that I would be in serious trouble. My little car would crumple like a cheap accordion on impact. I was constantly scanning the road ahead as well as several meters on each side. In daylight it was fairly easy to see animals up ahead and I had no trouble when driving north the previous day. Now the light was changing, fading away into the night – a much more dangerous time to be driving. This is when animals become active after resting in the shade for the day. During this leg of the trip I saw all the animals that I had before plus kangaroos, a feral cat and a fox. The roadsides are heavily populated with reflectors on meter and a half tall posts. In my headlights they lit up like an airport runway and showed me where the road was and if there was a turn coming up. The closest animal contact came when I saw one of these reflectors 'disappear.' Basic physics told me that something must have crossed in front of it, blocking it from my sight. I immediately braked firmly and slowed to twenty. Moments later my headlights revealed a small group of cattle and I came to a complete stop as they crossed the road one by one right in front of me. I'm pretty sure I would have hit one if not for the warning of the 'disappearing' reflector. As it grew even darker I caught up to a pair of road trains. Yes, road trains. These are like the biggest eighteen-wheelers back home except that these are seventy-four or eighty-six wheelers! The cabs pull three or more trailers behind them. These are huge trucks, fifty-three meters long! Great care has to be taken if you ever think about passing a road train. The two road trains and the space between them were as long as a football field and a half. Tucking in behind the rear train seemed like a safe place to travel. The trucks are equipped with heavy impact bars at the front of the cabs. Any animal hit is instantly killed and tossed up and away from the road. This created a 'no animal' zone behind each of the trucks, taking away the most dangerous aspect of the drive. It was very intensive driving and the trucks 'towed' me along at speeds I wasn't really comfortable with and an hour was all I managed with them. I knew I was close to Carnarvon by now so relaxed and took my foot off the gas to slow to the speed limit. Only then, when my whole body relaxed did I realize what a lot of concentration had been entailed in that drive. Yes, it would have been a good idea to have stayed in Exmouth for another night.

On a side note, it was a week later when I read the fine print of my next rental car to discover that the collision insurance did not cover any animal strikes after sundown. Makes sense to me. I didn't do any more night driving on my trip.

Here I was then in Carnarvon, three hundred sixty-seven kilometres south of Exmouth. It was easy to find the hostel, but what I found didn't impress me at all. The first sign – it is not staffed in the evening, but there was a phone number posted on the door. My two phone calls were met with an answering machine and I didn't get a return call during the next fifteen minutes. I went in to the building and found all young occupants who told me that they were working in the area. This was definitely an ill-maintained hostel: unkempt, dirty kitchen and bathroom. I would call it a grungy place. So, no thanks – yes, staying in Exmouth would have been a good idea. The Carnarvon Hotel was the only place I came to on the main street so I checked in there five minutes later. When I asked the clerk about parking – "Should I just leave my car on the street out front?" "Oh, no, you don't want to do that, dear. We have a compound out back for cars. It's already locked, but here's the key. Just bring it back after you have your car safely inside. We unlock it early in the morning."

Armed with new knowledge and the keys to the compound and my room I drove my car around the back of the hotel and secured it for the night. I must say that when I heard groups of loud and apparently drunk people in the wee hours, I was glad to have my car off the street. My room was basic but clean and had a fridge and TV. It also came with animal interaction. I was lying on the bed watching TV when a movement caught the corner of my eye. What the heck? Did I just imagine that? Was that, could it have been a mouse? Eyes now off the TV, I waited and sure enough a wee brown mouse flashed by again. I put a few granola bits on the floor by the fridge and waited her out. I have pictures of her very cute self, picnicking on my food in my room. I have proof that I was charged for a separate room but ended up sharing with another occupant! I briefly thought about asking for a rodent discount the next morning but didn't. I thought they might trap and kill her and I didn't really want that to happen; maybe she was looking after a family . . . .

So that was my Carnarvon experience – enough said.

THE EMPEROR'S CROWN REVISITED

It was a 'pedal to the metal' day, driving just over seven hundred kilometres from Carnarvon to Perth. I passed by the turnoffs to Monkey Mia, Kalbarri and the Principality of Hutt River and relived my experiences at each place as I drove. I pulled off the highway into Geraldton and headed to a beach that I hadn't visited during my previous stay. I ate my peanut butter and passion fruit jam sandwich and drank my ginger beer on the beach. I saw a man who was just getting his boat out of the water so I went over to him and began to talk. Like me, he was a science teacher and had been enjoying his Sunday off work by going out to check his traps. He showed me his catch of three lobsters – he would eat well tonight. I told him about swimming with the whale shark and about seeing the dusky whaler shark. He is the person who told me about dusky whalers being involved in most encounters with humans on the coast. At any rate, we had a nice chat. I continued to walk for a half hour more, then, legs stretched, I was ready to resume the drive to Perth.

The rolling countryside around Geraldton is the Shire of Greenough. I began to notice some trees that were quite unique. The first one I saw, I simply passed by. I thought it was a tree that had been damaged and broken by the wind. Then I saw another, and another. All over the shire I was seeing these trees that grow skyward for a few meters then take a right angle turn and grow parallel to the ground, their branches and foliage 'sweeping' the earth. I had discovered The Greenough Leaning Trees, an icon of the area. As I drove along the Brand Highway, there were places where I pulled off to the side of the road and get a longer and closer look at these intriguing trees and of course take pictures. You know how I love trees. An informational sign was near one that I stopped at: "The trees belong to a native Western Australia species of River Gum. Their characteristic 'lean' is caused by strong southerly winds that burn off the growth on the windward side (flagging). This eucalypt is known to be a very hardy grower, though it has weak branches."

Perth was another four and a half hour drive and it was like coming home when I entered the city for the third time. The Emperor's Crown had a bed reserved for me for the following night, but nothing was available for this evening. They told me about a hostel that was just two blocks away, and said that if I couldn't find a bed there, I could sleep on a couch in the TV room. I found myself checking into the Swan Barracks.

The Old Swan Barracks was built in 1896 as a drill hall for the growing Volunteer's Movement. It was used as such until 1992 when the military left it and the site was sold. It has heritage protection. I parked out front and looked up at the stone tower that is the main entrance. It looks like the front of a castle, a fortress, with the grey stone walls rising ten meters above me. A large arch forms the entrance which I walked through carrying my overnight bag. Once inside the lobby, it was much like checking into a hotel. The long wooden counter on the left, international clocks mounted above it, was manned by two people. "Hi. I need a bed, just for one night. Preferably a female dorm and a bottom bunk, please." There were no bottom bunks available, but at least I had a place to stay. I got my room key, climbed the stairs and walked down a long corridor to my room. Bed secured I ventured back to the lobby area and went into the Great Hall. This room is very large, as a drill hall would have to be. It is a huge, multi-use social area that has a bar, lots of seating around illuminated whiskey barrel tables, pool tables, a foosball table, internet, video games along the walls and a ginormous television. Well, it's not really a television. A wall acts as the screen. Whenever I came into the hall, sports events were projected on it, and they were pretty much life sized. Sitting here was like sitting in a castle with the stone wall of the central tower rising up into the darkness. I found it a bit overwhelming after all the small places I had stayed in and didn't stay long. The barracks had an overhaul in 2008, but I'm pretty sure they didn't get to my dorm. I actually took one of my sheets and tied it over the dusty window as there were no window coverings of any kind. My room was right over the street and it was quite noisy, but I managed to get a half decent sleep with only one trip down and up the ladder in the middle of the night. I went into the kitchen the next morning and had the free breakfast that was offered: toast and cereal. Then it was farewell to the barracks and back to the Emperor's Crown – ah, what an improvement!

Monday was a day of leisure, no travelling to do, no big plans. As I had driven through to Perth on Sunday this was a 'bonus' day as I thought I'd be driving the last leg of my trip back from Exmouth. I caught up on emails and paid some bills online. Thousands of miles from home, but there were still things to look after. I would fly out of Perth on Tuesday so cleaned   the car and repacked all my worldly goods. It was good to have the chores finished in the morning. I took the afternoon and drove around some areas of Perth that I hadn't been before. One stop I made was to Russell Square that I had passed many times on the Red Cat bus. The park is not large, maybe the size of a football field, but it has some huge fig trees that called to me to have their pictures taken. It was very peaceful sitting in this little park, people watching and enjoying the shade and majesty of the trees. Next I drove down to the waterfront then caught the ferry across the Swan River to South Perth. I didn't go for any particular reason and if there were some touristy places to see, I surely missed them. I found a little place for a late lunch and walked around the area near the ferry terminal. I could have easily driven over the bridge just a kilometre or so downriver, but it was pleasant to be out on the water even if only on a passenger ferry. I think it gave me more of a feeling for the day to day commuters of Perth. I returned to The Emperor's Crown and parked the car for the night. There is a cafe next door so I went in to see what I might be able to get for supper. They were closing in fifteen minutes which was lucky for me as they had bargain prices on the remaining food. I got a lovely Thai meal for four dollars, a bargain anywhere. After supper I caught the Red Cat to the Murray Street Mall and wandered around, sat on a bench or two, people watched, window shopped. With nothing else on my agenda I went to see a no-brainer movie, Seventeen Again, starring Matthew Perry and Zack Efron – well, I told you it was easy to watch. The Cat buses stop running at six o'clock so I had a short walk back to the hostel.

Today I had a reservation to fly out of Perth at five forty-five in the evening. The hostel has a good laundry facility which I used to do a wash. After I checked out of the hostel I had another relaxing day which I spent mostly in King's Park. It is a lovely place to walk, sit and read, and just enjoy nature. I spent about fifteen minutes watching two parrots that were spending the day in the rough landscape of a large palm tree. When the huge leaves fall off these trees, they leave the base of the stem attached to the trunk. These build up over the years until there are hundreds of little nooks and crannies for little animals to call home. It was like a honeycomb of tiny tree caves.

I returned my little, blue, rental car at the airport. Over nineteen days, she took me to some of the most spectacular places on the planet. We logged five thousand one hundred twenty-four kilometres on our exploration of Western Australia and what a great time I had!

My flight lifted off ahead of schedule – yes, that's what I said – ten minutes ahead of schedule. It seems as though travellers in Australia check in on time and if everyone is in the plane ahead of time and the pilot can get clearance for take-off, well, the plane takes off! Imagine that! This happened two out of the three flights I made in Australia. Hurray for Virgin Blue Airlines! We arrived in Adelaide safely and uneventfully. With the flight and the time change it was now eleven o'clock in the evening.

I had reserved a car online and now checked in at the rental counter at the airport. "Yes, your car is waiting for you, Ms. Trill. Are you going to be having a holiday driving around the Adelaide area?"

"I'll only be in Adelaide for one night. I'm going to Uluru."

"Oh, Ms. Trill, you won't be able to do that. This rental is only good if you stay in South Australia. If you are going into North Australia we don't want your business."

"Pardon me? I reserved a car with you, but there are restrictions on where I can drive it?"

"Yes, Ms. Trill. If a car breaks down on that highway, that is very serious business. We might not ever get it back."

"What do you mean?"

"Well, if a car breaks down, and you do manage to get someone to take you to the next town for help, chances are that when you got back to the car it will have been vandalized, perhaps beyond repair." Well, I tell you, that got my attention and made me think this might be quite an adventure, this long drive alone in the Outback. I looked to either side of this rental desk, to two other companies. I simultaneously asked both agents if they could get a car for me. Eurocar had one available and the agent was okay about renting it to me to take up to Uluru. This cost me two hundred dollars more as I booked it at the rental counter, but really, what choice did I have. I was just happy to have a car for the next leg of my trip. Tomorrow I would leave civilization and head into the great Australian Outback – alone, in my little, silver Kia Rio. Driving for thousands of kilometres on a sealed road seemed as though it should be perfectly safe and non-eventful to me. Now familiar with Adelaide it was very easy to get into the city and find the YHA hostel. I got the key to the compound from the front desk, parked the car for the night and was in bed before midnight.

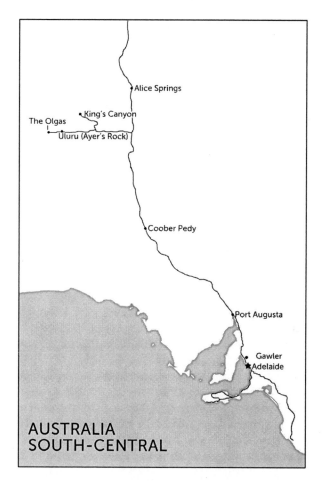

AUSTRALIA
SOUTH-CENTRAL

INTO THE OUTBACK

Arriving late the night before, I didn't have any food with me for breakfast the next morning. I went to the front desk and was able to buy an orange, cereal and milk for breakfast. I would stop in Port Augusta around lunch time and do some grocery shopping. After breakfast I washed and dried my dishes, got my gear from my room and caught the elevator to the ground floor. I tossed my linens into the laundry hamper and checked out. I had enjoyed staying at this hostel which is very well maintained and has a lot to offer.

After two relaxing days in Perth this would be a day of driving. My destination for today was Coober Pedy, eight hundred fifty-three kilometres up the Stuart Highway. I travelled along the Port Wakefield road, along the coast for a time, then inland then back out to the ocean at Port Augusta. The scenery was varied with flat lands as well as gently rolling hills along this part of the road with the Flinders Range dominating the landscape to the east. Most of the countryside was brown at the end of the long, hot, summer. Port Augusta, the `Gateway to the Outback`, is a bit over three hundred kilometres from Adelaide and is the last town of any size before getting into the enormous Outback.

I found a large grocery store and walked up and down the aisles looking for my favourites. For breakfast I bought Muesli and lemon yogurt. I bought a twelve pack of my new favourite soft drink, ginger beer. I put a loaf of brown bread into the cart along with a jar of peanut butter and a jar of passion fruit jam. From the beverage aisle I added five, four litre jugs of water. For my stir fry I bought a barbecued chicken, red pepper, broccoli, carrots and noodles. Fruit and a few snacks were added to the order and I headed to the checkout. The cashiers at this store were lucky enough to be seated on rolling chairs while they did their job. I thought this was a good idea as it must get tiring to stand in one spot for hours on end. With my groceries stowed away in my re-usable shopping bags I got back to the car and arranged my haul in the trunk.

When I left Port Augusta the car was well stocked with food and water so I knew that I wouldn't go hungry or thirsty no matter what happened. The Stuart Highway begins here and slices the continent north-south through Alice Springs and further north to Darwin. I would be turning off the highway south of Alice Springs to travel out to Uluru. I left town and was now officially entering the South Australian Outback.

The Flinders Range was on my right hand side in the distance. It didn't take long for the mountains to disappear and for the landscape to level out and the vegetation to become sparse. I loved the idea that I was in the Outback – it is such an iconic word about Australia. I was entering the great Australian Outback; a place where none of my friends and family had gone before. I was really looking forward to the hundreds of kilometres before me, to be alone, no decisions to make. "Just shut up and drive" as the song goes. I knew that I would be on a sealed road for the trip and I wasn't on a walkabout, but here I was, alone on a 'drive about' and I thought "How cool is this?" The earth was painted from a gorgeous palette of rusty reds, oranges, tans and yellows in well-defined, contrasting areas. It was as though someone had run a brush loaded with one color down on the surface and then beside that color had painted a second line using a different color or hue. The textured ground was scattered with little rocks. I was surprised at the amount of foliage in the Outback. Somehow the hardy plant life here manages to eke out a living in this, one of the harshest environments on the planet. Most scrub was less than half a meter tall but a few trees rose up to three or four meters. Tufts of grass popped through the desert at irregular intervals. On some stretches the asphalt, instead of being the dark grey most of us are used to, was a rusty-red, put together using local material. The sides of the road were lined with solid white while in the center was dash after dash of white passing lines. There were only a few areas where the lines became a double white in the center of the road where it wasn't safe to pass. I could see the shallow grooves in the surface where thousands of tires under heavy loads have left their mark. In places it looked as though the surface of the road had melted then 'puddled' into the tracks, all shiny and glossy. With temperatures approaching fifty at times, I imagine the road does tend to soften in the summer. I stopped at a few places and took pictures of these new landscapes. The only signs of habitation along the way were the roadhouses – stops along the way where you can purchase fuel and always get some hearty food.

In stark contrast to the red earth, I noticed white lakebeds here and there and stopped near one to have a closer look and take some photos. I was at Lake Hart. I found it surprising that there were any lakes at all in the Outback – I just hadn't associated it with huge bodies of water – it was counter intuitive. The water had evaporated under the relentless summer sun leaving vast expanses of white, salt flats. This saline lake has been used in the production of salt as have other lakes in the area. Remnants of the operations can be seen in a few places as faint rectangular outlines along the shore. The Ghan, a world famous rail line, runs along the shore of the lake on its way north to Darwin. Not far from Lake Hart is Pernatty Lagoon. This is the only place in the world where green selenite crystals are found. If you are someone who wants to line up their chakras, this may be the crystal to add to your home. They are said to have certain metaphysical properties that have high energy in the heart chakra and give off vibrations that shall be a positive influence in your life.

I loved the sign which told me I was at Glendambo: Population: Sheep 22,500 - Flies, 2,000,000 - Humans, 30. This is the last place where there are any facilities to buy gas until Coober Pedy, now about two hundred fifty kilometres away. I filled the car and also took the opportunity to buy a small carton of Cafe Mocha which was my tastiest driving companion - delicious and refreshing every time.

If car A leaves location 1 at eight in the morning and at the same time car B leaves location 2 and they are driven towards each other in excess of one hundred thirty kilometres per hour, what time will it be in Perth when they meet? Just a curious little Australian math problem that came to mind in the outback, a vast desert of desolation and unrelenting landscape that comprise the view for hour after hour, day after day. This continent that is some four thousand kilometres wide has only one main paved road that bisects it north to south, that road being the Stuart Highway. The remoteness could be overwhelming and perhaps even stifling to a lot of people but I rather liked driving alone, finding it somewhat therapeutic giving me a sense of space and freedom. Well, I can tell you that car A, my car, didn't meet any cars or road trains for about a half hour, so that means that the cars were at least one hundred kilometres apart at eight in the morning. The Australian outback is expansive and quite inhospitable, so much so, that much of it has never been trod upon nevertheless surveyed and mapped.

At a hundred twenty kilometres an hour, the landscape passed by pretty quickly, but I couldn't tell that from the scenery. There are no landmarks to speak of, but that didn't matter to me. It was great to be driving alone. I didn't even have any music playing and I think that helped me gain a better appreciation for the vast isolation of the Outback.

I had been driving for hours through absolutely barren, flat country where the tallest features were the bones of road kill. In the distance I began seeing little triangles punctuating the horizon. More and more little cones appeared and soon dominated the landscape. I was coming into Coober Pedy territory. Opals were discovered here by a lucky accident when Willie Hutchison, a fourteen year old, stumbled across them while searching for water. Coober Pedy, population about thirty-five hundred, is the opal capital of the world. Rock is pulverized and dug out of the ground and brought to the surface where it is processed in the search for these most fascinating of the worlds' gems. The waste dirt and rock is piled near the open shafts on the surface forming mullock heaps. Over an expansive area measuring seventy-five by thirty-five kilometres, the main field has hundreds of thousands of conical hills marking abandoned and working shafts. All the mining is done by independent prospectors; there are no mining companies in town.

I pulled off the highway to my right and drove down the main street. There were not many buildings in sight and it seemed as though I must be looking at Cooper Pedy in its entirety. I could see a few local businesses, but where were the houses? Coober Pedy is a town of extremes - temperatures can reach fifty degrees in summer and dip into single digits on a winter's night. About seventy percent of the people live underground in homes fashioned in old mine shafts or those dug specifically for living purposes. Living underground, allows for a comfortable temperature year-round in the low twenties. I was looking forward to checking into my hostel after a long day on the road.

I had booked two nights at Radeka Down Under, an underground hostel. Oliver Street runs off the main street and the hostel is about fifty meters up the road. It is located in the center of town and is close to everything. The friendly owners, Martin and Francine Smith, offer a courtesy pickup and drop-off from the nearby bus station for backpackers. Originally an opal mine, it had been converted to accommodations in the mid-1980s. It offers a variety of options, including two above ground motel rooms, as well as other underground motel rooms, budget rooms and dormitories.

I would be staying in a dormitory. I had seen Martin's picture on the internet and there he was standing behind the check-in counter. Slender, with a full, salt and pepper beard and long hair to match, topped with a broad rimmed brown hat, he looked exactly as I had seen him on their website, right down to his dark blue tank top. He had character written all over his face - the stories he must have to tell . . . . He gave me a rundown of the hostel and some information about the town. I booked an afternoon tour through him for the next day.

Francine became my orientation guide and I followed her through a back door to a set of stairs. We stepped down the thirty-four stairs and continued down a ramp until the floor levelled out. We were in a wide hall carved into the rock. The walls were stunning, with bright, rusty red streaks, marbling their way through an ivory background like so many rivers and their tributaries. As with all dugouts in Coober Pedy, the walls had been sealed with a clear finish to keep the dust at bay. We continued along this hallway then took a sharp turn to the left cutting back almost parallel to the first hall. Another twenty meters, and we were in The Dungeon - the end of the tunnel. And there in an alcove with no doors, but open to the main hall stood two sets of bunk beds. Two sets of bunk beds, just the same as my first hostel in New Zealand some ten weeks previously. We were six and a half meters underground - a very cool place, in many ways. The dormitories are not rooms but simple excavations in the rock making room for two to four sets of bunk beds in one area. Each of these areas is separated from the others by a sandstone wall. The front of each area is open to the main hallway so there is minimal privacy. Francine showed me another tunnel and set of stairs that were for emergency use only. If a fire started there would be little to burn other than mattresses and tourists, but you know, it's the smoke that usually kills you. I thanked Francine and she went on her way. The only thing I would find a bit inconvenient here was the fact that I had to walk along my hallway, make a sharp right turn and walk along the next hallway then up the ramp then the thirty-four stairs to use the washroom facilities.

I walked back up to the car and got my groceries. The kitchen was nice and clean and I had it to myself for the most part as I prepared my chicken stir fry. It was delicious as usual and I made enough for four nights. I watched some television with a few others in the common room and went off to bed around ten.

The Dungeon was near the end of the deepest part of the hostel and I had this quiet, isolated area to myself. I was given one small sheet and pillow as my bedding, the most meagre offerings at any of the hostels that I stayed at. I could have brought in my sleeping bag from the car or I could have asked for a blanket, but thought that I would be warm enough sleeping underground in my pyjamas. Well, you may have figured out already that I was wrong on that count. Although initially quite comfortable, I soon found myself cooling off and wishing that I had brought in my sleeping bag. In order to avoid the long hallway walk and climbing up the stairs I decided to use my towel as a blanket and see if I could keep warm enough that way. While the towel helped quite a bit it wasn't long before I grabbed a pillow off another bed and my small hand towel and attempted to place them over uncovered parts of my body to keep warm. So there I was in the middle of the outback of Australia, lying underground by myself in The Dungeon, huddling under a mishmash of items, trying to keep warm - that was how I first fell asleep at Radeka Down Under. When nature called in the middle of the night I went out to my car and retrieved my sleeping bag. Then I was quite happy and warm sleeping in my underground abode.

Coober Pedy is a small but very interesting place. The first place I drove to the next morning was The Big Winch. This is the highest point in town and offered me panoramic views of the whole town and it surrounds on the vast Gibber Plains of Australia.

Imagine that you are in the middle of a humongous sand and gravel pit. The rim of the pit is several hundred meters across; there are numerous piles of sand and gravel forming a gently rolling landscape. On some slopes there are hundreds of tires stacked up to hold the hillside in place. Here and there, seem to be some entrance ways cut into the hillside – what the heck? Now look at all the pipes sticking out of the ground, not ten or twenty, but hundreds. These are ventilation pipes and they mark the living quarters down below.

I was looking at the location of the subterranean suburbs of Coober Pedy. Parcels of land are divided into squares and rectangles by fences made of thousands of pieces of corrugated iron attached to metal poles. These fences are sometimes all one color, green the most common, but usually are a combination of colors as they weather in the Outback. Initially I thought they were pretty ugly fences, but then, I was used to cedar fences on the west coast of Canada. There is no forest industry here in the Outback and it made perfect sense that the metal panels were the best building material to be had in Coober Pedy. There are a great number of old vehicles that sit rusting out on properties around the town. It looks like a town that had been devastated by an unbelievably large rock and dust storm that had dumped meters of waste upon the site.

Two facts have lead to there being very little vegetation in the area. First, Coober Pedy lies on the edge of the Stuart Range and sits on beds of sand and silt stone that are more than thirty meters thick - this is topped with a rocky desert. The second reason for little plant life is the low precipitation. Some persistent residents do grow trees and shrubs by using town water and treated waste water. There was strict water rationing until 1985 when the town discovered an underground source twenty-four kilometres north of town. The water is piped to town and treated to be used by residents. It is reused as much as possible.

Ah, yes, The Big Winch. At about ten meters tall with a huge bucket hanging from it, The Big Winch is a town landmark. It had to be rebuilt after a huge storm damaged it in 1986. With big storms possible in the area, it seems like another good reason to live underground. A couple joined me a few minutes later and we went through the 'I'll take your picture if you'll take mine' routine. I wondered if building extra large things such as The Big Banana, The Big Winch, The Big Perogy and The World's Largest Hockey Stick close to my home in Canada is a worldwide phenomenon – I imagine it is.

Also on this piece of high ground is Coober Pedy's first tree. It is not a living tree, but a tree made by early miners from bits of metal scavenged from wrecked trucks. It rises about seven meters and has sixteen branches off the main trunk with smaller branches off those. It is topped with an old wheel hub. Its rusty red color fits in perfectly with the countryside.

A few meters down the road from the winch I stopped in at an interesting place. The objects in front caught my eye as I drove by the first time and I knew I would stop on my way back. It was the tall, left-behind movie props from Pitch Black that first got my attention. Rising several meters and being reddish in color, they resemble large termite mounds. They served as the entrances to the dens of meat-eating aliens in the movie. Now they acted as a lure to get people to stop and investigate. The yard also had other pieces from the movies Mad Max, Beyond Thunderdome and Red Planet. The owner is somewhat of an artist and has welded together metal remnants into interesting and unusual shapes. I always find it interesting to see how artists assemble odd pieces of junk to create new things. I was not disappointed as I wandered around outside, then inside The Junk Yard.

I drove around most of the town – it took me four minutes to travel from one end to the other. There was not really much to look at as most of the buildings are underground. One of the most important features of Coober Pedy is quite small. It is above ground on the side of Hutchison Street – a coin-operated water dispensing tap. I had barely put a dent in the five jugs of water I had brought with me so I didn't need to buy any more water. The water is very inexpensive at twenty cents for each thirty litres.

I parked downtown and started a walking tour of the main street. The entrance to the Umoona Opal Mine and Museum rises in front of a hill. It is made of brown stones and looks more like a wall than an entrance way. Over the door the wall is about four meters high and tapers off until it is only a meter high on each side. I walked through the main door and after just a few meters realized that I was underground. This was an original working opal mine, the largest underground in Coober Pedy, which offers a great variety of things to see. The stone walls are covered with photographs and interpretive signs which cover the history of Aborigines and Europeans in and around Coober Pedy and the opal mining industry in the area. I was walking along when I came to a tunnel leading off to my right. It was perfectly circular, a few meters in diameter, sloped down and had a hand rail mounted on one side. This was the starting point for the daily tours that are available. Unfortunately I did not have time to take a tour as I was already booked for an afternoon tour of the area. It would have been very interesting I'm sure, to go down into the mine and to the underground home below.

I was quite entranced by the display of opals and jewellery in the retail showroom. They have quite a grand collection of rough and cut opals and a range of opalised fossils. It was here that I learned a lot about the value of opals. Color is what it is all about. The background color is of prime importance. Ninety percent of found opals are clear and there-fore worthless. The most sought after opals are black with red 'fire' or flecks of color in them. Blue-green coloring is the next most valuable while blue is the least valuable as it occurs more often. Large sections of color are prized. Not only the color, but the patterns made by the color are of prime consideration when putting value on an opal. Of course, the larger the opal, the more value it has as well. The more expensive opals are solid. The lady behind the counter showed me three rings. One was a solid opal. The second one called a doublet was made by gluing a thin layer of opal to a layer of black backing. This dark background makes the colors stand out better. The third ring was a triplet. These are made by assembling a paper-thin slice of real opal glued to a dark background then topped with a thicker clear layer made of quartz, glass or plastic. This is the least expensive of the three because less real opal is used. I found it all so very interesting and loved looking at the exquisite pieces of jewellery and loose opals on display.

After Umoona I walked out into the parking area where I went over to a spaceship. Yes, that's right, a spaceship. When I stopped to think about the landscape in the area, it seemed like an abandoned space craft might not be so out of place after all. The area does look like a barren and desolate place, a place that perhaps some astronauts may have found themselves after landing on an inhospitable planet. This was of course, another abandoned movie prop, left here, right on the spot where filming had taken place for Pitch Black. Coober Pedy was getting more interest-ing with each step.

Between the Umoona entrance and the space ship was a door cut in to the front of a rocky hillside. It was recessed about a meter, made of corrugated metal and had a small roof projecting out over its front step. It marked the way into George Burford's dugout. He was an opal miner and buyer. The information sign told me that 'Opal buyers were expect-ed to make all travellers comfortable on the opal fields. George Burford was good at this and was known as the unofficial mayor of Coober Pedy. George was a community leader. At the age of twenty-four in 1920, he was elected first Justice of the Peace. He lived here for many years. The dugout at one time was also a Commonwealth Bank Agency. Henryk Michalczyk, a Polish opal miner, lived in this dugout for nearly fifty years. He maintained his basic lifestyle while the town grew up around him. He used to say "I still like Coober Pedy. I like the free life."

I got back in the car and drove down Old Water Tank Road to Faye's Underground Home. I parked near a cactus garden and walked up to the front door and knocked on it. The door was opened by Colin McLean. Colin is a pleasant looking older fellow and wore blue jeans, a striped polo style shirt and flip-flops. As he spoke, he often clasped his fingers together over his chest as he recited the stories of Faye and Coober Pedy. He and his wife, June, live as caretakers in the home and offer tours to people on a drop in basis six days a week. Faye Nayler had come to town to be a cook in 1961 and was part of a very small percentage of females in Coober Pedy. She bought a thirty year old, simple, one room dugout from Coober Pedy's mail truck driver. Using only picks and shovels, Faye and two female friends toiled over the next ten years to create a very impressive underground home. Faye moved to Queensland in the '90's.

I walked down three steps into the kitchen which was the original one room dugout. Dugouts have the kitchens, toilets and bathrooms situated at the front of the home to facilitate the removal of waste water. Faye's kitchen has a wooden parquet floor and all the conveniences you need. Colourful red, green, blue and yellow jars are above the stove. The microwave sits in a custom-carved recess up and to the left of the stove. Being a cook, I imagine that Faye must have spent a lot of time here in her kitchen.

Colin then continued the tour with us walking through an archway into the next room. The walls have been coated with an off-white sealer but the reddish streaks still show through. With adequate lighting the effect is of a bright but warm interior. The living room is cosy with two couches nestled along adjoining walls. As I walked along the wide, curving halls and up and down some stairs I found delightful things at each turn. One of my favourite features is a shallow recess along a hall wall that serves as a frame to a dozen boomerangs and throwing sticks. The collection occupies a space a meter by two meters – it was just totally Australian and I loved it.

The bedrooms, each with walk-in closets, are found on different levels which add a lot of interest to the layout. The three friends also dug out enough space for a billiard room, bar and a wine cellar. There is a floor to ceiling fireplace that is faced with brown, Jasper stonework. It has been sealed with a glossy finish and left me with the impression of the scales of a giant dragon that lives in the pages of some fantastic story book. Colin told me that it has never been used – with the constant temperature underground in the low twenties there has never been a need to fire it up. Also, there would be the problem of fuel as there are no trees around to provide firewood. Jasper has also been used on the counter ends in the kitchen and on the base of the bar.

But, the most surprising feature of the home was the swimming pool – yes, a swimming pool! I surely wasn't expecting to find an indoor swimming pool in a dugout. It was about four meters by eight meters in size and was filled with beautiful turquoise blue water. There were ten lawn chairs placed here and there around the edge of the pool. There must have been some great parties here over the years!

Faye was an entrepreneur and established The Opal Cave in 1963 to accommodate tourists. Colin said that she was the first person to offer tours of the area. The Opal Cave is still operating in town and I expect it will be for years to come. I would have loved the opportunity to spend some time with Faye and listen to her stories. As it was, Colin proved to be an excellent host and source of information. Homes are dug by machines nowadays. The first job is to have a bulldozer come and cut a swath out of the front of your hill. This leaves a vertical wall which is a starting point with sufficient height for ceilings and rock overhead. Next, the tunnelling machine, about the size of a Bobcat, is brought in and rotating heads mounted on an arm, start cutting away the chambers and halls forming your unique floor plan. The walls are very thick to allow for supporting the spans of rock above the living areas. In the next phase the plumbing and wiring is put in place. This is followed by the laying of a cement floor which is later finished with wood, carpet or tile. Faye had the wooden floor in her kitchen and the rest was mostly carpeted.

I walked outside and said thank you and goodbye to Colin. Faye had established an interesting garden in the front yard – hardy plants for a harsh environment. She had about a dozen different kinds of cacti thriving in the sandy, red soil and a few other spiky plants as well. I had really liked this intimate tour of Faye's Underground Home. It is unique to most homes that are open to tourists in that it is currently being lived in by Colin and June.

I drove back into town and set out to walk around. There are over thirty opal dealers in town and I only covered a small fraction of those. The gems in each shop were mesmerizing, all were beautiful in their own unique way and the shop keepers were very obliging in showing opals to me and explaining where they had been found and how much they were worth. It seems that everyone in Coober Pedy digs. As I continued around town and talked to local shopkeepers, I got the feeling that Coober Pedy has quite an international gathering of characters. They had come from around the globe to seek out their fortunes in the opal mines. Some seem to be flying 'low under the radar' and just want to be left alone to try their luck here in the Outback. One fellow told me he had come to town for a month to try his hand at mining – that had been thirty-eight years ago. I also learned that there are over forty-five different nationalities represented by the residents.

After a simple lunch at the hostel it was time to head out on a tour for the afternoon. The tour van picked four of us up at the hostel and three others at another place; so once again, it was a nice small group. Al was a gnarly man and had been in Coober Pedy for about thirty years. Like most people in town he was an opal miner and had found some good ones in his time. He was always on the prowl for the next strike. He said that everyone digs in Coober Pedy. I can see getting bitten by the 'find the opal in the rock' bug. Just dig a little more for 'my precious'.

Our first stop was just a few minutes into the tour, at the Catacomb Church. One of several underground churches, the Catacomb Church is dug into a hillside. We stepped up to the vertical rock wall and entered through a rough cut opening then through a door on the right. The interior has been cut in the shape of a huge cross. It is furnished with blue and yellow plastic chairs set in rows to accommodate about seventy-five people. There is an upright piano standing off to the left that is protected under a cloth cover. The podium is crafted from six sturdy branches of mulga wood and an old miner's winch, complete with a five gallon rust-colored bucket hanging beneath it. The whole effect is peaceful simplicity in tune with nature. I liked the style of it all. It would be a nice place to gather away from the harsh environment that lies outside the hillside.

Next we drove up to The Big Winch and had a look at the town. "The name for the town comes from two Aboriginal words, 'kupa' for white man and 'piti' for hole - Coober Pedy means "white man's hole." As we drove around the town site Al showed us the best places to eat. There are many ethnic restaurants and halls that take turns opening on different nights of the week: Greek, Italian, Croatian and Serbian among others.

The Coober Pedy graveyard was our next stop. Al told us some stories about the people who were buried there. A beer keg served as a head-stone at the grave of Karl Bratz 1940-1992. Welded on the keg were the words 'Have a drink on me.' A plain white cross marks the resting place of Crocodile Harry, 81 yrs, 13/10 2006. There is a black cartoon of a crocodile near the top of Harry's cross. A small metal crocodile leans on the cross at the base, smiling, sitting back relaxing and has his hands clasped behind his head. Several brown bottles are turned upside down, planted in the earth. There are two metal mugs that have buxom women on them. Harry loved the ladies. It is a tradition to bring a drink or two when going to the gravesites of friends so you can have a talk and share a drink with them. That's why on many of the graves, I could see the keg, bottles and mugs. Faded red and white plastic roses stand in a glass vase in the shape of a nude woman. Harry loved the ladies. We would visit Harry's dugout a bit later on in the tour. It was time to get back in the van and visit the Coober Pedy golf course.

There was no grass to be seen anywhere. It looked like a huge, uninviting sand / rock trap, nothing but red earth everywhere. We all got out of the van and Al told us about the part of the course we were looking at. ``It`s three hundred forty yards to the hole. You can`t see the hole, you can`t see the flag. They will issue you a map. From here, you should aim over the water tank over there on the hill. The hole is on the other side. If you are a good golfer your ball lands on the other side. Then you walk around and look where you think your ball landed. Most of the time you can find it. If you're not a good golfer you probably hit the bushes or the rocks and the ball bounces anywhere, everywhere. You carry a little piece of green Astroturf with you and you get to put your ball on it when you take a shot. We do have night golfing because it gets so hot here. We have glowing balls. We have four holes for tourists who want to play a few holes when they pass through here in the day or night. You can't lose the ball at night because they glow. When you're done getting on the scrape (green) and getting the ball in the hole there's a rake leaning over there. It's a two inch diameter hollow metal tube with a bunch of pointy parts sticking out of one side. It's your job to rake your footprints out of the green and then to smooth it out for the next players. The reason the greens are black is that they are made of sand mixed with oil to keep the sand from blowing away. This course at Coober Pedy is the only one in the world to have reciprocal rights with Saint Andrews in Scotland. Some tourists join the course here for that reason alone." Just as I had done at Wave Rock in Hyden, I took several pictures to show my family and golfing friends.

We headed out of town and drove a few hundred meters off on a side road to stop in the middle of a bunch of rock piles. It is not advised to go into the mine fields on your own. First it can be physically dangerous and second, you may be regarded as an interloper, a person who has come to look for opals on someone's claim. The miners in Coober Pedy tend to be secretive and can be suspicious of your intentions. Before we got out of the van Al told us a bit about safety issues. We had all seen the large signs with simple human figures on them; DANGER, Don't Run, Beware Deep Shafts, Don't Walk Backwards, Unmarked Holes. Each of the warnings came with a picture of a man falling down a huge hole. Once we got out of the van we quickly became aware of the danger. Beside each pile of waste, there is a vertical shaft yawning open nearby. There are no neat little fences or warning signs around the individual holes, they just appear everywhere. Al told us that there are over two hundred fifty thousand holes with more being drilled all the time. I was very conscious of each step I took and was surprised that even in this state of alertness, the holes just suddenly appeared. The miners use a nine inch auger when they are doing exploratory drilling. The rock is checked for opals and if none are found, they move on and drill again. Ninety-five percent of all opals are colorless and therefore worthless. If opals are found then a thirty-six inch auger is used to drill to the desired depth. Then miners enter the shaft to blast and dig sideways in search of the opals. The excess, pulverized rock is shovelled into a large tube and then vacuumed to the surface and into a huge barrel mounted at the rear of an opal mining truck. Then the contents are dumped out and form the conical waste piles. The piles vary in size from just a meter tall to over ten meters, depending on how much digging had been done at each shaft.

Al drove us to a place where miners had used an open pit method in their search for opals. It was a huge rectangular hole that had been cut out of the rock, about forty meters wide and twenty meters deep along a length of a hundred meters or so. The hole look larger than it was as all the pulverized mine waste was piled high around its edges. We had a chance here to go noodling or fossicking – look through the piles of rubble for any sign of opal. Al told us not to get our hopes up as every rock we touch has probably been touched by hundreds of people before us. One fellow in our group did manage to find a fingernail sized piece of rock that had a bit of color to it; the rest of us were out of luck.

Now we would have the chance to tour the mine and home of Crocodile Harry. The yard of his place has a collection of rusted out vehicles and odd pieces of metal, some welded together in artistic creations and others just cast aside to rust on the ground. Harry had a line-up of old vehicles along one side that had been stripped and used as planters. Now cacti and other hardy plants grew from engine compartments, through roofs and from trunks, some rising as tall as four meters. Harry dug out his mine by hand and created his unique home from abandoned tunnels as he moved around under the hill he was mining. Harry's home is very wide – you could parallel about park eight vehicles along the front. There are several recesses in the rocky hillside that could serve as entrances to his dugout. The front of the hill has been cut back to the vertical and rises a few meters before it slopes up and away. Standing in front of Harry's place, Al told us about Harry Blumentals: crocodile hunter, opal miner and ladies man. Harry had been a crocodile hunter in Northern Australia for thirteen years and had taken on the name Crocodile Harry as he liked its' uniqueness. He claimed to be a Latvian Baron who was forced to leave Latvia after World War II. He left crocodile hunting in 1975 when he moved to Coober Pedy to try his luck at opal mining.

I was visually assaulted upon entering Harry's home. He had created a number of tunnels over the years and they formed a large complex of flowing pathways and rooms. He had sealed the surface of the rock with white plaster paint so it in turn could be painted on. The walls and ceilings were entirely covered with an endless collection of colourful bras, panties, halter tops, hats, shoes and hundreds of pictures of scantily clad or nude women. Al said that the first bra was donated to Harry by Tina Turner when she was here during the filming of Mad Max Beyond the Thunderdome. Harry had carved several columns to look like nude women. Harry loved the ladies.

His bed sits in an alcove with a shelf on two sides and a rectangular opening cut through the rock at the head of it. Completely surrounding the bed were hundreds of autographs, plate sized reminders of female visitors; Thyrral, Kaylen, Deb, Maggie, Kirsten, Gerta, Juddy, Ashley,

Destiny, Mirjam, Helland, Aisling, Jo Rynne, Caro, Andrea from Canada and five Irish Sheilas in a Kingswood. It seemed like 1984 was well represented. 'Harry, it's been a very pleasurable experience meeting you – one I'll never forget! With love, The Maharaja's daughter Binna.' 'What a great place and a great guy. Thanks Harry. Love Debbie'. 'To Harry, Love Angie. I tried to resist, but how could a lady resist such excitement. May 14/00.' Harry loved the ladies.

After touring his living quarters we walked out and around one side of the hill where Harry had cut a huge cavern into the sandstone. Al figured that whenever Harry wanted some money he did a little digging in this area, found some opals and was set. Harry's home has a guardian and Al has been talking to him for a few years about doing a bit of mining here in the hill. He has yet to be taken up on the offer. It was time to leave this remarkable place and head out to The Breakaways.

Al turned the van off the highway a little north of town. Now we were rattling along a dirt road that gave a new meaning to the word washboard. The road was made by making a few passes with a grader. This left a reasonably flat surface with a little pile of rubble running along each side of the route. Al told us that Coober Pedy only gets fifteen centimetres of rain each year and it seems like it was all coming down today! The countryside and road was amazingly wet for the Outback which enhanced the colors of the soil. Al was a good driver and kept us 'sunny-side-up' all the way although he did fishtail a few times on some muddy corners.

It took about a half hour to get to the lookout over The Breakaways which is a collection of valleys and flat-topped hills, providing the most beautiful landscapes in the area. Being in such an arid area it is hard to fathom that seventy million years ago the whole area was under a vast inland ocean. The waves of color, intensified by the rain, flowed across the landscape in an artistic variety of reds, oranges, yellows and off-whites. It is here that 'Priscilla, Queen of the Desert' was filmed. In one scene, having stepped out of Priscilla, their bus, one character says "Oh my God! Where are we?" It was just an unrecognizable and surreal landscape. If a person was taken there blindfolded, they would probably not be able to guess where in the world they were – or perhaps even if they were still on Earth. We met another tour van and the driver told Al that it was impassable further down the valley. One vehicle had been stuck for a few hours that morning and he told Al that he wouldn't be able to get back up the hill if we went down into the valley. Usually, the tour would continue by driving down into the area but we had to content ourselves with the gorgeous view from the lookout.

We got safely back out to the highway and drove towards town. Our final stop was at the entrance to town where a black mining truck was mounted about four meters off the ground on metal posts so it could be seen from quite a distance. It had a large engine that was painted white, mounted on its flatbed. Sticking up and away from the rear of the flatbed at a forty-five degree angle was a huge barrel painted in three sections: black, white and blue. The barrel was joined to the flatbed with a large tube. Mine waste would be vacuumed up the tube to the barrel where it would be dumped into the waste pile on the surface. I thought it was a perfect sign for Coober Pedy. Al said that the ground under the truck is sometimes seeded with a bit of opal so a dad took his young son to check it out. Sure enough, they were very excited with their find of some 'color'. We got back in the van for the last time and headed into town.

Al had one more thing he wanted to show us – and it was green. Yes, even here in the Outback there is a grassy football oval that is kept green using 'grey' water recycled from town. The whole town gathers there during the Opal Festival which is held every Easter weekend. In October, it plays host to annual horse and camel races, a family affair. The local elementary school also has a grass football oval kept green by treated sewage water.

Al dropped me off at Radeka Down Under around five o'clock. I had a quiet evening watching a bit of TV and reading about the trip ahead of me the next day – the drive to Uluru. I shared The Dungeon with another couple who stayed next door to me. They didn't disrupt the tomblike silence at this far end of the dugout. This night I started with my sleeping bag to keep me cosy and I had a restful night's sleep.

TWO HITCHHIKERS
AND A HUGE ROCK

The outlines of two bodies appeared up ahead on the side of the road, growing larger as I approached them. Two kids looking for a ride to Uluru. Why not pick them up? Tini, nineteen, was from Germany and Francois, twenty, was from Quebec. They had met in Sydney, and they were now traveling around Australia for a month, this being their last week together. It was a nice change to have some company and we whiled away the time with conversations about our travels, families, home and listening to Australian music on some CDs that I had purchased. The only 'towns' of any note were the roadhouses along the way.

Marla, two hundred thirty-three kilometres north of Coober Pedy, is the last town before the border of the Northern Territory. There is a large billboard that outlines the geographical location of Marla in relation to well know Australian places. In green letters on a white background there were forty-two place names including: Darwin 1975 km North, Alice Springs 458 km North, Perth 3440 km West, Sydney 2610 km East, Port Augusta 770 km South and my favourite – The Outback, Right Here Mate! It seemed so very Australian – I loved it! It also had information about The Great Artesian Basin which is the source of water for the Outback and had several maps on it. It was probably the most informative 'road sign' I had ever come across. Marla is a service town for the area and has a motel and camping facilities, post office, supermarket, restaurant, pub, workshop and a police station. The road house on the highway is huge and we saw several road trains stopped in the gigantic parking area.

The Stuart Highway was still taking us through very flat landscapes with intermittent vegetation. It is real desert country. Welcome to the Northern Territory – there were complementary signs on each side of the road, each with a large rectangular base about two meters high, a meter thick and ten meters long. Just off the center of each, the base was pierced by a large triangular addition in a dark brown. These pieces were about twice as high as the base. Now in the Northern Territory the speed limit increased to one hundred thirty and my little car was up for it. Nineteen kilometres over the border we came to Kulgera, the first road house in the Northern Territory. Its' claim to fame is that it has the closest pub to the center of Australia.

With the higher speed and it being about one hundred kilometres to Erldunda, the next turn off, we were there in under an hour. We stopped here at the road house and bought drinks and gas. Erldunda is where we turned off the Stuart Highway and headed west on the Lasseter Highway. Now we had two hundred fifty or so kilometres left to get to Uluru. The roads were great and there was not much traffic. Even though we were very far away from Uluru, I found myself scanning the horizon for the red monolith rising unexpectedly out of the flat desert. Tini was the first to see an image off in the distance she thought might be it. There was a bit of excitement for just a moment, but I knew the shape was all wrong. What she had seen was Mount Conner, a large table-top mountain. It is an impressive mountain at three hundred fifty meters high and the Aborigines hold it in high esteem – but it isn't Uluru. So very close now, when would we make visual contact? Finally I saw another image in the distance and it seemed to have the outline of the famous rock – it was! We were all excited to see our goal that we had spent all day driving to. Soon we came to the park entrance where we each paid twenty-five dollars for a three day pass. It was late in the afternoon so we headed straight to Uluru.

My parents were big on books and we always had a lot of them at our house when we were growing up. One of the most phantasmagorical books I loved was called 'Around the World in 1001 Pictures'. It was in that book that I saw a small black and white picture in the top right hand corner of an early page. The picture looked like a giant hot dog bun lying on a flat prairie – what is it and why is it in this book? This Ayers Rock was in the middle of nowhere, in a country called Australia. It just seemed so out of place in that flat land. And it was big, I mean really big for a rock! I knew that I wanted to go there someday. After age six I had the chance to see Ayers Rock in other pictures so I found out that not only was it out of place and very big, but it was also red. Now it became even more fascinating – I mean red rocks on Earth? How is that even possible? The Rocky Mountains in my back yard were shades of brown and grey.

I was remembering that tiny photo from my childhood as I drove closer to Uluru. The great red icon became immense and took on such a personality as we got closer. The typical 'postcard' shot is of the west face and looks pretty smooth. But once I was there, Uluru showed me a very interesting 'face' – one of great cracks, fallen slabs of rock, weathered indentations and black streaks that were tell tale sign of where water runs. Oh, the pictures I would take. Dad always said out of a roll of thirty-six pictures, he'd be lucky to get one or two that he really liked. I am my father's daughter and I would end up keeping two hundred and twenty- seven pictures of Uluru – I forget how many I deleted. I sure do love digital cameras! We stopped at the visitor's center and got pamphlets about Uluru, the nearby Olgas and of Kings Canyon. The center is an educational place that has a lot of information about the Aborigines, the land, and the significance of Uluru to their people.

Now we drove to the west face of the rock where we parked and walked to the base. This is where the walk to the top begins. Tini and Francois wanted to climb to the summit so I assured them I would be here with their gear when they got back. They were so happy to be together and to be off on a new adventure. I watched the various climbers which told me a lot about the trail. When I saw people putting their hands down on the trail in front of them and almost crawling up - well that told me it was very steep. When I saw them stop and take frequent breaks - that told me it was a hard climb for them. When I saw them turn back and come down - that told me that they were smart enough to know when to quit. Tini and Francois used the fixed chain which runs part way up the steep ridge which is the trail. I thought they had gone almost all the way when they disappeared over the first horizon. Thought the same thing when they reappeared further up and then vanished over the sky line again. When they got back they said that they were only just a quarter of the way by that point. They returned some two hours later, just after sunset, safe and sound. It is quite a strenuous climb Uluru being some three hundred forty meters high, about the same as climbing the stairs in a ninety-five story building, and is pretty steep in places. The footing can be treacherously slippery as well. The route is just over one and a half kilometres in length. There is a fixed chain on the steep first part of the climb. Thirty five people have died while on the trail, most from heart attacks. If your goal is to climb Uluru, you may come away disappointed as the trail is sometimes closed due to high winds at the summit or due to high temperatures.

At the trail's base I met Sue whose husband, Jerry was making the climb too. We had about an hour during which we talked about our intrepid explorers on high and hoped they would be back before sunset. Jerry was the first to appear, a tiny spot in a green shirt up on the trail. We watched as he slowly found his way down to us, working his way along the fixed chain trail and taking baby steps along the way. Sue and I agreed that the trail was not one for us. Upon Jerry's return he supported Sue's decision not to climb and said she would most likely have turned back on the first steep section. As I watched people coming down, I could tell from the angle of their bodies and their meticulous and slow foot placement that my knees could not have made the descent unharmed.

Tini and Francois appeared around a half hour after Sue, Jerry and I parted. They loved the climb and were able to show me pictures of the adventure. I'll admit that I felt that somehow I had missed out and that Tini and Francois had just stood somewhere that I would never be. Perhaps if I had been in good physical shape, I too would have made the climb but not just to reach the summit – each step of the journey would have had spiritual meaning to me.

The Aborigines don't like people to climb Uluru as it is a place of spiritual significance to them. On special occasions this sacred route is taken by a few select Aboriginal males. One of the reasons they don't like others to climb is that as owners of this land, they feel responsible for victims of falls leading to injury and perhaps even death. Some say that when a non Aboriginal dies, their spirits get mixed in with their ancestor's spirits and this is not a good thing. So even if I had been physically capable of climbing Uluru, I don't know that I would have.

Tourism being what it is, it isn't really made clear that the Aborigines don't like people ascending Uluru. Driving thousands of miles to reach this unique landmark, many people treat the climb as finally reaching their destination, the summit. It was part of an agreement that gave title to the lands to the Aborigines in 1985, that the rock remains open for people to climb, so it is not against the law. Often, seeing others climbing Uluru makes it easy for the undecided to make the climb – others are doing it – why not me?

Some people say that the climb is not worth it as they are standing on the main point of interest in the area and the landscape is boring. Others say that it is the highlight of their trip to Australia. I didn't make the summit but my time at Uluru is a highlight of my adventure.

We drove to Yulara Resort, the only development in the area of Uluru, providing a welcome cocoon from the harsh reality of the outback. Yulara offers many types of accommodation from luxury condos to a camp site where I dropped Tini and Francois. I drove back the kilometre to the hostel and checked in. I was in a dorm that could accommodate twenty people in five groups of four bunk beds. Each group had a wall separating it from the others giving some modicum of privacy, but was open at the front. I claimed a lower bunk bed and had one of these areas to myself for my entire stay. The toilets, showers and laundry were in another nearby building so I had a nightly walk to this building in the wee hours – watch your step – don't get lost. It had been a great day, but a long day. I was so glad that I had three leftover meals remaining. I put two in the fridge with my other food and heated the second one up in a frying pan with a lid over it. I would have liked to use the microwave, but it wasn't working. Still, it was a tasty and nutritious meal. I was happy to see crested pigeons around the outdoor tables. I hadn't seen them before and although they are common here they were new to me. They look like your average, poop on your windows / statues, pigeons, but they had a little tuft of delicate feathers sticking out from the top of their heads. I am easily amused.

After dinner, I walked around the facilities to get oriented to my surroundings. I slipped some coins into the computer and caught up on e-mails, then plunked down at one end of a couch in a small common area to watch some TV. I wasn't expecting much in the outback, and I wasn't disappointed. There were three channels: one for sports, and two others with not much to choose from. The channel changing knob had broken off and there was no way to reach inside the cylindrical opening to change channels. Someone had shown me how to do it with a straw and I was able to do it. Three older couples from Britain came in and one fellow wanted to watch the sports channel which was fine with me. Only trouble is, he lost the straw inside the TV. I found a pen and took it apart so it would fit the small hole. Hurray for Canadian ingenuity – I had done a beautiful 'MacGyver' fix out in the Outback. Of course with a pen, I'm sure MacGyver could have done a lot more than simply change channels. So we had the sports channel on and we chatted about our trips. The six of them were on a two week holiday in Australia and had flown in to Alice Springs the previous day. They had a day and a half to explore the area and would leave the next afternoon. I thought I was so very lucky to have two months in Australia and be able to drive thousands of kilometres to get a much better feel for the country.

I had talked with several people in the hostel who had highly recommended a visit to King's Canyon. My plan for this Saturday was to do just that. I had told Tini and Francois that they were more than welcome to come with me. I would be leaving at nine in the morning and if they were at the car we would spend the day together. When I was walking to the car, I noticed fifteen dollars lying on the ground. I picked up the two bills, turned back, and went up to the reception desk in the main building. I explained where I had found the money. Both girls looked somewhat surprised that I handed in this seemingly small amount of money. Yes, it was only fifteen dollars, but if it had been lost by a person staying in the hostel it might be a significant loss for them. At any rate, it wasn't mine. The girl said to check back when I checked out in two days to see if it had been claimed. (When I did so, the money had been claimed, so it had most likely meant a lot to the person who lost it.) It was with a Good Samaritan feeling that I went back to the car to find Tini and Francois.

Driving to Kings Canyon meant backtracking about a hundred kilometres then turning north on the Luritja Road. With a six hundred kilometre round trip I hoped it would be worth it. It was. The canyon walls are over a hundred meters high which is quite impressive for a small canyon. Kings Creek flows along the bottom. There are two walks to choose from: a six kilometre, four hour trek up and around the rim and a two and a half kilometre, one hour walk along the bottom of the gorge. We would stick to the canyon floor. Tini and Francois went ahead together, while I held back and immersed myself in the land. Very close to the parking area was a trickle of water where I spent several minutes watching some small birds drink and flutter about having a bath. Water means life in this most beautiful natural oasis. Because of the creek there was a lot of plant life in the canyon. Gorgeous purple flowers were in bloom, bushes thrive, ancient ferns flourish and large gum trees grow well. The walk was well shaded along some stretches. The path follows the lay of the land and meanders up and down and between the boulders on the floor of the canyon. These huge rocks have fallen from the canyon walls to come to rest at the bottom. The red sand stone walls rise vertically on each side. Layer upon layer of sediment were laid down and formed these rocks millions of years ago under an inland sea. They are stacked up to form individual works of art: broken, sculpted and smoothed by the elements over impossibly long periods of time. I climbed a few sets of wooden stairs to reach the viewing platform that marks the end of the walk. The furthest part of the canyon is a sacred Aboriginal site and it is expected that visitors will not trespass by leaving the designated pathways.

When I take a path then return by the same route, it is like being on a whole new walk. The change in perspective is literally doing a hundred eighty degree turn and it all looks brand new. I took my time on this new walk, noticing many things I hadn't seen on my way in to the canyon. I noticed more of the hundreds of different plant species found in Kings Canyon. I watched for some time, a line of ants, marching along their super-ant highway, all on a mission of some sort. I spent more time trying to find birds by following their songs – limited success as they were well hidden most of the time by distance and foliage. I took more close-up pictures.

When I emerged from the Kings Creek Walk, I went over to the far side of the canyon, to the base of 'Heart Attack Hill'. This is the beginning of the steep, rough, uneven, rocky stairway that takes visitors to the rim of the canyon for the longer hike. It 'flows' down the hillside much like the path a stream would take, turning left and right to hug the terrain. The first sixty or so stairs could easily be seen, but after that, I had to rely on seeing other people high above me to follow the path's direction. That walk would not be taken by me as it was very long and we didn't have the time. I was a bit disappointed that I couldn't do that hike because I knew the views of the countryside and the gorge below would have been spectacular.

I met up with Tini and Francois a bit before the parking area – they had enjoyed their two hour visit too. We got back to Uluru about an hour before sunset driving straight to the 'sunset viewing' parking area, and joined an already large gathering of people. The cars were lined up along the fence, pointing straight ahead to Uluru. There is something special about sunlight at the end of the day. It has a warm, glowing feel about it and softens whatever it illuminates. Uluru was a perfectly deep, rusty-can red which deepened as the sun dipped lower. Somehow the color deepened with each passing minute. Our shadows grew ever longer and the darkness marched in steady time across the flat land in front of the rock. The shadows began to climb up Uluru and the red color became the most intense of the evening. Then the sunlight was gone and Uluru darkened to muted mauves. It had been a wonderful hour and a half watching the changing lighting on the rock. It gave me a feeling of warmth and happiness to have witnessed it all, to have been here first hand just as thousands of people have over the years.

I dropped Tini and Francois off at the campground and headed back to the hostel. I had my third meal of roasted chicken, noodles, broccoli, carrots, onion, celery and potato that I had made at Coober Pedy a few days previous. It was still a good supper and I'm glad I had the foresight to have cooked enough for four nights.

Today I planned on driving out to Kata Tjuta / The Olgas, a collection of thirty-six dome-like towering rocks that are a hundred fifty meters taller than Uluru. Kata Tjuta is on the World Heritage list. I had made a similar offer to Tini and Francois the previous evening and once again they were at the car when I went out at nine. After our trip to Kings Canyon the other day, this forty-five kilometre drive was very short. Kata Tjuta can be easily seen from Uluru and we had it in view for most of the trip. The group of rocky domes has a much more interesting profile than Uluru as there are many individuals making up the whole. Some of the domes are very close together while others are hundreds of meters apart. The name comes from the Aborigine language meaning 'many heads'. Their legends tell of mice women, snake men, a kangaroo man, a snake, a lizard sister and cannibals who are represented by the huge rocks in the area.

There are two walks to take. The shorter one takes about an hour to cover over the two and a half kilometre length. It climbs gently up a path made of rocks that were stuck together with what looked like rusty liquid iron because of the red coloration. It is a very hard, unyielding surface, so I'm glad I changed out of my sandals, put on runners and used my trekking poles! I walked on my own here as I like it that way and I'm pretty sure Tini and Francois wanted their time alone together. The path, fittingly called Walpa Gorge Walk, runs between two of the giant domes which gradually close in on each other at the far end of the path. The walls rise vertically and are weather-worn and interesting to look at. I felt a special spiritual kinship with my surroundings and had a feeling that this place was much more sacred than Uluru. Later I found this to be true. There used to be more paths to walk on, but all but two have been closed to visitors. Sacred rituals are held here and participation is limited to only a select group of Aborigines.

The Valley of the Winds Walk is a longer seven and a half kilometre circuit that takes about three hours to complete. We would not do this longer walk as Tini and Francois wanted to head out to Alice Springs a bit later and I think it would have been a bit too much to try on my own.

We were happy with our shorter walk. On the way back to Uluru I dropped Francois and Tini on the main road as they were going to hitch a ride to Alice Springs. We had enjoyed each other's company but it was nice to be on my own again. I went back to the resort and had lunch and a rest.

At three o'clock I drove to Uluru. I pulled off to the side of the road at several spots and took a closer look at the vegetation. I was surprised to see that the whole area here in the Northern Territory was home to a forest of desert oak trees. The forest is not like the evergreen forest back home, but is made up of thousands of trees spaced more widely apart. The mature trees grow to about eight or nine meters tall. Having long, feathery leaves, they have a very soft look about them. The branches spread out and form a nice bushy shape at the top of the tree. The youngsters are much like teenagers, tall and slender with wispy branches hanging down. They look a bit like soft bottle brushes. There are a lot of other plants here too and the contrast between their shades of green and the red, red earth was always striking.

There is a path that goes around the base of Uluru. It is wide, level and well-maintained. There are several parking lots around the base that allow access at various intervals and now I drove around to the east face of Uluru and parked the car in one of the sunrise parking spaces. At this point I had access to a waterhole. I walked on a small path in the direction of Uluru which was cast in afternoon shadow. Off to my left I took another short path to a collection of boulders that had long ago lost the fight with gravity and had tumbled off the rock face above. One of these huge boulders sat so that a large overhang formed a protected area that had been used as a shelter for thousands of years. I thought it was a great spot as it was very well sheltered and was close to water, that most precious of commodities in the arid environment. Once I got to the protective fence I looked closely at the walls and ceiling and could see ancient hieroglyphics that had been painted there over eons of time. There were spirals, straight lines, outlines of hands, animals – layer upon layer – knowledge and stories of the Dreaming passed on generation to generation. The ceiling was black with deposits from the many fires that had burned in this place. It had been a home to many I suppose, and here I was, a foreign visitor trying to decipher what had been passed on. Some symbols were easy to understand, some remained a mystery. All I know is that I loved the chance to be there.

I turned back and then made a left on to the main trail. The whole area was covered with foliage from simple flowers to tall trees. The path flowed like a lazy creek, left, right, straight for a bit, then more winding. That slowed the pace of everything and by the time I came to the end of the trail and stood on the platform at the waterhole, time stood still. I was alone at this place of nourishment. I stood still and listened to the trickle of water, still coming off Uluru three days after the last rain. I mean this is three days later and water was still running off the steep non-porous sides of the massive rock. I watched the water bugs below me and the birds in the trees and the sky. I marvelled at all the different plants growing along the edge of the water hole. I sat on a magnificent bench made out of beautiful wood left in a mostly natural state. Any other material just would have taken something away from the experience. It was a peaceful and somewhat spiritual place to me and I relished every moment until a small tour group came along. I stayed a few minutes more before heading back along the path until I met the bigger path that goes the nine and a half kilometres around the base of Uluru. I turned right on the main path and headed north for a time where once again I had the place to myself. I was amazed at the amount of rocks that had fallen from Uluru. There was so much evidence of massive erosive episodes everywhere. It was like a giant puzzle and I loved looking at fallen pieces and trying to match them up with the places they had fallen from. In some places huge slabs had sheared off and plunged twenty or so meters downward to remain standing on edge leaning in against Uluru. The most common features were the thousands of boulders that had seemed to pop out of the rock faces and left huge indentations in the otherwise smooth face. When I was little and looking at that black and white photo of 'Ayers Rock' I had never imagined such a weathered surface. (you don't know what you don't know) I spent more than an hour walking along the base trail. It was truly mesmerizing and I wished I had another day to walk around the base, but I was heading out the next morning.

I drove to the west side of Uluru and parked at the base of the summit trail. The trail had been closed for the day due to high winds at the summit. The winds are so strong that it is easy to literally be blown off and over the side. I got on to the base trail again and headed south on the Mala walk. The walk took me by several overhangs that created cave-like places that had been used by the Aboriginal people in the past. Each has rock art on the walls in the familiar patterns I had seen on the other side of Uluru. The loveliest place was Kantiju Gorge, a water hole at the base of a spectacular rock face.

It was shaped like a thirty foot breaker, a magnificent wave carved out of stone at the base of Uluru. Warm hues of rust and ochre were lined with darker streaks were water has trickled. The waterhole at one end lay still, reflecting the scant vegetation on one side, the rock wave on the other. The air was warm and still, the light was streaming low across the atmosphere and coloured the rock with warmth and tenderness.

I climbed a few meters up at one end of the wave and nestled into a natural rock lounger still warm from the heat of the day that was almost passed. I place my outstretched hand on the rock beside me and felt an increasing warmth pass through my hand as the past caressed my soul and my world disappeared. I don't think anyone noticed me tucked away there. I became one with Uluru, sinking into her layers and becoming unmoving like rock itself. I just lay there, at peace, barely breathing, in the moment, soaking it all in.

Later I reluctantly emerged from my cocoon and walked back to the car. It was a similar experience to see the sunset while standing at the base of Uluru as it had been to watch from a distance. But it was different too – it seemed a more intimate time when the sun's rays finally fell away from the rock. I watched my final sunset at Uluru and said farewell to the experience of a lifetime. Wanting to delay my departure, once again I drove slowly around the base of Uluru in the gathering darkness.

I spent a quiet evening around the hostel. I was leaving the next morning so I made sure I had all my gear in order.

BACK TO RADEKA DOWNUNDER

It just wasn't there. It had been there just hours before, patiently wait-ing to be taken out of the fridge. This was my green food bag, a re-useable shopping bag made of lightweight rip-stop nylon that had been a part of my life for some fifteen years. When I came in to the kitchen my last morning at Yulara Resort and looked at the glass-doored fridge, I immediately knew something was wrong. There was no green bag that caught my eye. I sighed and looked around the kitchen and in the other fridges hoping that someone had just moved my bag for some reason. But, no luck. I went to the fridge where my bag had been, opened the door and was surprised to see a familiar sight. Sitting there on the shelf was my yogurt, milk, orange, cereal and cold drinks. Someone had taken my bag, but left my food. I miss my bag but like to think that it is living a new and useful life and is enjoying seeing parts of the world that I won't ever see – just like the Travelocity gnome. In three months of travel, with the possibility many times over that things could have been taken from me, the green bag was the only thing that was ever taken from me, so that in itself is a pretty good record. (Travel luck) After being re-united with my favourite breakfast I checked out of Yulara Resort and headed east, towards the Stuart Highway and Coober Pedy.

I stopped to take pictures of the red sand and the plants that sprouted up here and there. I have a picture of a yellow sign with the outline of a steer on it – and another with the word 'grid' on it. This told me that I was driving through one of the incredibly huge cattle stations in the Northern Territory. The grid would keep the cattle in the proper station, but noth-ing kept them from crossing the road. I took pictures of steers on the edge of the road. I have a picture where the road is simply invisible as a mirage makes it look like it has melted into the blue sky.

I have a picture of a small, green, triangular sign that has the white let-ters SH and the number 80 below them. I knew I was 80 kilometres from somewhere, but didn't know where that might be. I couldn't bring to mind any town or roadhouse with those initials. Still, I found it interest-ing to mark my progress by the decreasing numbers, SH 50, SH 40, and so on until I arrived at – you guessed it – the Stuart Highway. There were many more of these little signs that helped me keep track of the trip. The last ones I saw that day had the letters CP on them. (Coober Pedy)

I took a picture of a yellow sign that said 'Floodway'. There aren't many bridges in the outback as there are very few rivers. When it rains, the water channels where ever it has the mind to and eventually crosses high-ways and roads. It has the right of way and creates a floodway. This means the road is flooded to some extent for an indeterminate period of time. If you want to continue your trip, you must have a vehicle equipped to go through the water. It seemed as though well over half the vehicles in the Outback were designed for this 'snorkelling' job. Most are sports utility vehicles and are equipped with air intakes found up at mid-windshield height. This means that the engine won't stall when you cross deep water. The signs seemed a bit out of place in the arid and dusty landscape, but even a distant cloudburst can make dry river beds become raging torrents with little or no warning. It is always a good idea to pay attention to these signs.

Five and a half hours into the drive I stopped and took a picture of an abandoned vehicle. It had been stripped of the tires and wheels, the trunk and hood were open and I'm sure things had been removed from them. The windows were only a vacant idea, with thousands of little bits of auto glass shattered onto the red earth. A red rock about the size of a softball was resting on the dented roof. Yes, maybe that rental agent lady in the Adelaide airport had a point when she told me that they didn't want my business. A half hour after that I stopped and took a photo of another ve-hicle. This one had fared even worse as it had been set on fire after being stripped and vandalized. Or perhaps the relentless rays of the sun were focussed through a piece of glass and started the fire? So I had a little sigh of relief that I had made it this far with absolutely no car problems. (Trav-el Luck) It had been a good driving day; very peaceful, the land spreading out beyond my awareness to some special infinity of the Outback.

Martin was standing behind the desk to meet me at Radeka Downunder. I got to sleep in the same lower bunk bed as before, so I felt right at home.

I met with Francine in the morning and had her show me some earrings that she had made. I was happy to find a lovely, affordable pair to take back to my Emma / house sitter, Lyndee. I also bought two small pieces of sandstone that have artistic streaks of golden yellow running around them. It was a bit sad to be leaving Coober Pedy. I think I could be kept amused for a few weeks here digging for opals and playing golf at night. But I did have to hit the road again and drive south to Gawler, a town just north of Adelaide.

An hour or so south of Coober Pedy I stopped to take a picture of a sign and the bit of highway it referred to. The sign had an outline of a plane on it and said RFDS Emergency Road Strip 500 m. Yes, this was a makeshift airport in the Outback. The road had been widened and I imagine more attention had been paid to its construction to handle aircraft. It just made perfect sense to me to have a safe place for planes to land out here. It was right at another of those little green signs marking my progress - this one said CP 150.

I stopped at Spud's Roadhouse for lunch which is in Pimba, population thirty-five. Spud's is classic Outback and is the local gathering place and watering hole. Spud was well known to locals and to those who travelled the Stuart Highway. He passed away in 2007, but his legacy lives on.

The Outback roadhouses are full of character and Spud's interior walls were covered with interesting things. The front of the long bar was a patchwork of yellow, white, blue and black licence plates, well over two hundred of them. More were mounted on the wall by the dartboard and pool table. Behind the bar, coolers stood at the ready, full of beverages and food. Above the bar, I read the chalkboard menu and ordered a burger with 'the lot'. I passed the time by walking around the interior of Spud's which is also a general store. I could buy food, drinks, fuel, oil, rope and other basic necessities. There was hardly a bare spot on the walls. There was a lot of war memorabilia, neatly arranged in large glass covered display frames. There were all kinds of pictures, flags and little reminders from tourists who stopped by. There were also surfboards. Yes, you read that right – surfboards mounted on the walls, here in the middle of the Outback.

My burger was ready. It turns out that with 'the lot' consists of a beef patty, bacon, lettuce, onions, cheese, tomato, sauce and an egg - this was a 'double-fister', three-napkin meal and for eight dollars was a bargain.

A few hours later I was near Port Augusta where I decided to visit the Australian Arid Lands Botanic Garden. I live in a temperate rainforest so my idea of a garden is one of lush, green foliage, manicured lawns, towering trees and vivid conglomerations of flowers. I thought an arid garden would be a bit boring, but then again, I've been wrong before. The garden covers around five hundred acres which is the size of around four hundred fifty football fields – so that's a pretty big area. The gardens have wonderful views of the Flinders Range and I quite liked seeing some mountains in the background once again. The garden is a showcase for hundreds of plants that live in Australia's arid regions. There are plants that serve as bush tucker and some as medicine. With twelve kilometres of trails to cover, I knew that I had time for only a tiny fraction of that, but what I saw, I enjoyed. For bird watchers there are several hides to watch from in the hopes of seeing some of the one hundred plus species of birds that live in the area. I found that to be an incredible number! The plants have to be amazingly hardy to withstand the lack of rainfall and temperature extremes from just below zero to highs in the forties. Some of the plants are endangered in the wild so have found a haven here. The garden practices conservation and research so the different plant species will always be around. I think that's a really good thing.

GAWLER

Now I had about three hundred kilometres left to drive for the day. I had arranged to couch surf with Nick and Gabrielle in Gawler. When I got in to town, I called Gabrielle and got excellent and simple directions to their house. I hadn't surfed in awhile so I was really looking forward to my stay with them.

Their current mission: "to have contact at home and away with as many people as possible to learn about our wonderful world"

I was happy to pull up in front of their house and see them in person. Gabrielle showed me to my room which had a lovely double bed. It was very luxurious after spending the previous nine nights in hostels at Uluru and Coober Pedy.

Nick and Gabrielle have been couch surfers for almost a year, just a few months longer than I had. They are a wonderful, warm and friendly couple whose children have grown and now have families of their own. We are the same age, and at similar stages in our lives. They love to travel as I think all of us who couch surf do. They lead busy and fulfilling lives with Nick working in telecommunications and Gabrielle working in a local bakery.

I went to the bakery for lunch one day and quickly understood why it was so very busy in there. Everything was delicious! We had a sumptuous soup for dinner the first night and lamb kofta and vegetable pilau the next night. I had never even heard of this delectable Indian food. Gabrielle is a fabulous cook and I really enjoyed being spoiled by her. I loved their easy Australian informality. We got along very well and I think if I lived in the area we would be good friends.

After a lovely sleep on a 'real' bed and a nice breakfast I had the house to myself as Gabrielle and Nick were both at work. Isn't it wonderful that there is that level of trust in the couch-surfing community? I did a large load of laundry and hung it up on the line in the backyard to dry. It was next to the house that I found a box of Trill Bird Feed – I didn't know I had family down here in the business of keeping birds well fed. Well, I most probably don't but you never know . . . . I also used the time to tidy the car and repack all my gear as I would be flying out to Sydney in the morning. Chores done early, that left me with the whole afternoon free to see some things in the area.

Gabrielle and Nick had grown up in the area and gave me a 'go to' list of places to visit. Armed with their tips I went to the local information center, got a map and worked out a perfect itinerary for the afternoon. I headed east from Gawler to the Barossa Valley, one of Australia's best wine regions that has been producing fine wines for over one hundred sixty years.

My first stop on the way to the valley was the Whispering Wall. Built over a hundred years ago, the new design of a tall, thin wall of concrete bent against the pressure of tons of water was unique at the time. It was featured in Scientific American and gained international attention. The reservoir wall that forms the dam is an arc, part of a perfect circle, thus giving the parabolic shaped wall unique acoustic effects. As I drove into the parking lot, four people were entering their car and were soon gone. Ah, travelling alone. There are times when another person would be good to have along. Such as when you are visiting a place where you require two people, one at each side of a dam that is one hundred and fifty meters long, to whisper to each other and see if it really works – can you actually whisper and clearly hear each other from such a distance? I enjoyed walking on to the dam and took many pictures of the reservoir, birds and the dam itself. I stationed myself at the far side of the dam and waited; after a short time I saw a couple arrive and exit their car. The wife went to the toilet while the husband strolled down to the dam.

"Pssst . . . hey you. Yes, you. What are you doing here? It's not safe to be out alone. Does your wife know where you are?"

Well, this voice out of nowhere sure got his attention! He gawked around in every direction not being able to see me as I was motionless and somewhat camouflaged by some wayward branches. Being a kind-hearted person I added "Welcome to the Whispering Wall". I gave him instructions where to walk and he was soon at the platform on the other side. We carried on a hushed conversation for a short time until his wife joined him then there were three of us proving that yes, indeed, the wall worked, just as everyone had said. Imagine that. I walked back to the other side and the husband thanked me very much for being on the far side.

"If you hadn't been there, it sure as hell would have been me that would have had to march over there!"

Shortly after, I departed and left them and some new arrivals to marvel at the bouncing waves of sound.

The Barossa Valley was absolutely beautiful with row upon row of grape vines entwining their way up and down the hillsides lit with the late afternoon glow from a low sun. A perfect light for photos and I was in my glory and once again very thankful for the invention of the digital camera.

My dad loved taking pictures but was limited to perhaps sixty or seventy-two (multiples of twelve) on a two week holiday. Then he had to wait for two weeks for the film to be sent away, developed and printed, perhaps to find out that he had another picture of his thumb, or that the lens cap had been left on. How he would have loved the instant feedback offered to me and being able to afford to take a hundred or more pictures each and every day or every hour! He always told me that if I wanted one good picture I should take at least twenty. It surprised some family and friends that I took over six thousand pictures, but why not? In retrospect, I was surprised I didn't take three times that number. I was dutiful in selecting only the best ten percent and set them up as scrapbooks for family and friends to view.

The wineries marched across the valley with precision, one after the other, making a spectacular scenic drive through the region. Wide, manicured lawns and Australian red gum trees welcome visitors. Many rustic buildings, cottage homesteads and historic churches are reminiscent of early days some one hundred sixty years ago in the Barossa Valley. There are more than sixty wineries in close proximity to one another and I passed magnificent gates and signs that marked their entrances. Signs called out to sample notable wines at enchanting vineyards such as Penfolds, Barossa Valley Estate, Eden Valley, Two Hands, Yalumbra and Jacob's Creek. Ten months later, I was sitting at home at two o'clock in the morning watching the Australian Men's final from Melbourne. I then realized what an big winery Jacob' Creek must be as I saw the name prominently displayed multiple times in the arena. It was fun to now recognize a new product.

It was high on a hillside that I found another group of marvellous outdoor sculptures. These had been worked upon by various artists, some on their own, some in pairs, over a six-week period to create a sculpture walk. The fresh fall air was scented with gum trees; I could almost taste it. It was very quiet, the late afternoon light was dramatic and warm and the leaves were green. A full sensory buffet! I continued around the valley totally immersed in the experience.

I got home safe and sound where we had dinner then rented the movie Australia. Well, I guess I rented the movie as I had wanted to see it before I left home and hadn't gotten around to it. So here I was, sitting in Australia, just a week before I would be back home, watching the DVD at Gabrielle's and Nick's. As it turns out, the DVD skipped quite badly so I missed about a third of it. We had a nice evening together anyway.

I had another good rest in that wonderful bed and was able to get up early the next morning. The three of us had breakfast together then Nick and I got ready to leave. I had everything in the car by six forty-five. With a huge thank you and hugs to match I said goodbye to Gabrielle and Nick. Nick works near the Adelaide airport so we left in our two car convoy, waving goodbye to Gabrielle who stood in the front yard. It was nice to have Nick to follow and it reminded me of following Mike and Heather out of downtown Auckland two months previously.

Nick and I honked horns and waved as our paths eventually separated, he to his job and me to the rental car parking lot. I said goodbye to my faithful little car that had carried me safely through my 'drive about'. We had logged four thousand two hundred five kilometres over the past eight days. It had been an absolutely brilliant time through some of the harshest landscapes on the planet. I had loved it all!

SEVEN HUNDRED KILOMETERS AN HOUR

I arrived an hour before my flight time to check in and get through security. At eight forty-five my plane was roaring down the east-facing runway and took to the air five minutes ahead of schedule. I know I've told you that I like seeking high points to get oriented to new locations. Flying is of course, the highest of these viewing opportunities and my window seat provided the ultimate in seeing Australia's geography. Biggest impression – it is very brown! The country is a patchwork of mostly rectangular parcels of land that have been divided up over the years. There are few trees. Every now and again there would be a dark green partly irregular patch. I learned that this was forested parkland. There were some parts that were not divided up, the arid, brown hills rolling on by kilometre after kilometre. We flew alongside the Lachlan River for part of the flight which meant more agriculture and vegetation to look at. The land was changing to a palette of greens as we went further east and it became a patchwork of all-green parcels as we approached Sydney. Coming in to Sydney the view became filled with a collection of predominantly red-roofed homes surrounded by green areas. Here and there I could make out the eighteen bright green fairways of well-kept golf courses. Then the ocean began to appear, inlets of water that made islands and peninsulas where there were thousands of homes. It was all very nice to look at.

I thought about the overland trip Roland and I had made from Sydney to Adelaide. We had taken a leisurely ten days to travel along the coast which was wonderful. At one time I had planned on driving back to Sydney from Adelaide but I saved a lot of time and money by flying back. If I had driven on the Stuart and Midwestern Highways I could have covered the fourteen hundred kilometres in two days – by flying I was there in two hours. We touched down around one o'clock local time.

SYDNEY

After picking up my two pieces of luggage I called Lyn and Tom. These are the people who I had met on the walk at Pancake Rocks in New Zealand. They had asked me to stay with them when I came through Sydney, so here I was, ten weeks later. I had added them to my e-mail group so they could keep track of me during my trip. They knew I'd be coming to Sydney during the last couple of days in April or the first few days in May.

As it turns out, I had forgotten to send a personal e-mail to update and confirm my arrival day and time; consequently, they were not home when I called them from the airport. I decided to take the airport shuttle which dropped me off in the heart of town – in the rain. Walking around town pulling a suitcase and toting an overstuffed duffle bag was not any fun at all. I managed to find a travel office where I could store my bags for twenty dollars. Unencumbered, I stepped out into the streets of Sydney. There is a blend of old and new buildings as to be found in most cities. I loved the older architecture – it reminded me of downtown Victoria, back home in Canada. I was amused to see a McDonald's housed in a Victorian style stone building – the old, the new.

It was time for lunch so I stepped in to a small cafe that seemed quite busy – usually a sign that it would be a good place to eat. It was quite cool with the rain so I had a bowl of leek and potato soup along with half a ham sandwich. My phone rang just as I was finishing lunch – it was Lyn. "Hi, Joan. We were quite surprised to get home and hear your name on our answering machine. We didn't know exactly when you were coming." I apologized for not sending an e-mail to them and then talked to Tom and got directions to their house.

A short hour after I had left my bags, I was back on the third floor of the office building retrieving them. There were no pro-rated rates, but that's okay. At ground level I stopped in a chocolate store and bought some delectable treats to take to Lyn and Tom. I was back outside in the rain where I walked a few blocks, crossed the street and went into the transit office. I bought my ticket to Dee Why, the suburb where Lyn and

Tom live. Dee Why is a thirty minute bus ride from the central business district so I got to see a lot of territory on the way to their place. I called Tom when I got off the bus in Dee Why and he drove down to pick me up. I smiled when I spotted him approaching in his car. A very short drive later we turned right in to a 'canyon' driveway. That is it had walls from other houses on each side of it and was just wide enough to let a car comfortably through. It climbed up about four meters, taking us to the lower level of the house.

I walked in the front door and was greeted with a hug and a smile from Lyn. Their foyer is at the bottom of the stairs that climb up to the living area. The bedrooms, bathroom and toilet are downstairs. The foyer is large enough that there is a cozy sitting room with a hide-a-bed in it. That's where I would be sleeping for my first night. Tom and Lyn had a couple of friends staying with them for the night, Roni and Mike. After they left the next day, I moved in to the guest room which shares a wall with the sitting area. We spent the evening talking about and sharing pictures of our respective New Zealand holidays.

Mike had a meeting to attend the next day which left Tom, Lyn, Roni and I to go to the North Head Sanctuary. The North Head marks the northern side of the entrance to Sydney Harbour. The headland has been left in its natural state with winding paths travelling through untouched bushland. After a short drive from Dee Why we parked the car and headed out on a looping path which offered many spots to look out over the ocean. The first lookout was spectacular! We were standing on the edge of dramatically plunging vertical cliffs looking north up the coastline. The waves crashed into the rocks below us making a white line of surf that separated ocean and land.

We continued along the path in a clockwise direction with Lyn and Tom showing me the different plants of the area. The best wildlife encounter happened in the middle of the path – it was a lovely, green, praying mantis. I have a few good close-ups of the insect touching Tom's hand. I had thought that mantises lived in more tropical places so it was a nice surprise to see him here near Sydney.

Half way around the loop we stopped to look at the impressive panoramic view of the Pacific Ocean, the cliffs opposite North Head, Sydney Harbour and the Sydney skyline. We had the place to ourselves and all enjoyed the serenity of the location. Here we were, standing in the peace and quiet of the area while across the water millions of people were going about their busy lives.

Next we drove about three kilometres to Manly. The Manly beach is another sweet arc of sandy waterfront with a crescent of thirty meter tall trees following the curve of the beach. A gently sloping shore and an enclosed swimming area make a wonderfully safe place for children to get in the water. The swim area is enclosed with a stinger net so people do not have to wear stinger suits. When we began our walk heading south, there were only a few people in the water which is quite unusual but it was still fairly early and as we walked along, more and more people showed up to enjoy the beach and the water. Manly Beach is very popular with locals and tourists for swimming, snorkelling, scuba diving, surfing, walking and just sitting on the beach relaxing. Many people consider Manly Beach to be the most beautiful beach in Sydney. Tom said that only Bondi Beach is more popular.

I was hardly aware of the houses that sat on the slope off to my right. There were fabulous rocky outcrops that rose up on one side of the path. The rocks were hidden a lot by lush bushes and trees, a green belt between strollers and homes. The other side of the path drops away to the rocky shoreline and offers one photo opportunity after another. There is a sea water pool that has been made from rocks and concrete that has water circulating from a pump house at one end and flowing out over a waterfall at the other. This provides a safe place to swim where currents are not worried about.

I love the way that art just seems to pop out of nowhere! A small mother penguin with her chick tucked between her feet was sitting on a rocky ledge to my right. It was one of a series of cast metal sculptures that adorn the walkway. I loved them all: a diving female snorkeler, a blue octopus, a long-nosed bandicoot, two scuba divers rising out of the rock so only their heads and upper torsos were apparent, a snail and a surfer lying on his board on a rock so that his upper legs disappeared into the rock and his feet protruded from the other side of the rock as if he were in a wave.

We all stood aside at one point to let a number of teachers and parents herd a group of students past us. There were about a hundred of them all decked out in navy blue shorts, bright green polo shirts and navy baseball style hats.

I noticed a group of surfers across the bay gathered in a special area. This is Fairy Bower, a spot that produces a long wave breaking over a reef. This is a very popular surfing spot. They would ride in, paddle out, ride in and paddle out. It reminded me a bit of my days skiing in the Rocky Mountains. My friends and I would ride up the lift and ski down, ride up and ski down. I'm pretty sure I would have grown up a surfer girl had I lived in Australia.

We reached our destination of Shelly Beach to find a wedding reception taking place. The couple had been married on the beach and now families and friends were gathered in formal wear, walking around barefoot with glasses of champagne. It didn't look out of place at all to me. Shelly Beach is at the end of Cabbage Tree Bay and is protected by a headland which results in an area of calm seas instead of the usual wave-pounded shorelines. This makes it a great place for families to go swimming and snorkelling. It is also a good place to get in the water to go scuba diving as the rocky shoreline and reefs make it an interesting place to dive. Shelly Beach actually faces inland, the only beach doing so on the eastern coast of Australia.

The return trip was like a whole new walk with the change of direction and I enjoyed it just as much. We came back to Manly Beach where I stopped to talk with two of the life savers who work there. They were volunteers and loved the job. Lyn pointed out a male kayaker who was coming in to shore. My, oh my, this guy was incredibly fit looking! Lyn told me I was looking at iron man legend, Guy Leech, winner of many races in the '80's and 90's. I didn't manage to get a picture but I went in to the kayak rental place and got a postcard of him in a kayak. Good enough for me.

We were headed to the ferry terminal when I saw two familiar faces. It was one of the holidaying English couples that I had spent an evening with at the Yulara resort at Uluru! I mean what were the chances that we would ever run into each other again?

At this point, Tom made his way home while Lyn, Roni and I caught the Manly Ferry to Sydney Harbour. As a tourist I elected to spend the trip out on the front deck while Lyn and Roni stayed in the warmth of the inside seating area. I was enjoying being outside on the deck and just soaking in the sights of the harbour and watching the fish swimming around the dock and ferry.

"Look, that's a predator fish!" I looked to my right where there stood a good-looking man who pointed out another large predator and the smaller fish he was after. "That is a school of Angel fish," Tony said, pointing off to where they were gathered. "There's another predator fish." I could now see the much larger fish bombing along after the smaller ones again and again, and then they would slow down as if to catch a second wind before pursuing their prey.

It was great to have Tony's insight, he was very personable and we quickly eased into a conversation that was to last the entire trip. We were immediately in sync and bantered back and forth of heroes, our childhoods, natural science and classic rock tunes, even singing together. We created songs and poems on the spot of our time together and the sights around us. It was just one of those perfect meetings of two people enjoying each other's company and not afraid of being a little weird in front of another person. Tony's son, Josh had taken a fall during ANZAC Day celebrations the previous week and Tony had been at the local hospital with him when he had his stitches removed from his forehead. On his cell phone, Tony showed me a picture of Josh proudly displaying his new scar.

The ferry ride from Manly to Circular Quay in downtown Sydney is quite spectacular and it was wonderful to have Tony to provide information as to what I was looking at. "There are some very nice homes along the shore over there on our left. The treed area along the shore on our right is part of the Grotto Point Reserve. There are a lot of reserves around Sydney that provide green space. Over there on the left, you see the cliffs? That's North Head."

"Yes, my friends took me out there yesterday and we had a nice walk there. I loved the views."

"There, just to the right of North Head we are looking out at the Pacific. That is the entrance to Sydney Harbour. On our right now is Cobblers Reserve. Out to the left is Watson's Bay, a very beautiful and popular place. That finger of land sticking out on the right is Aston Park. If you want to go to Taronga Zoo, you can catch a ferry from downtown Sydney to get over there."

Now we were about twenty minutes into the half hour ride. We made a gentle turn to the right and the view made me grin from ear to ear. There it was - the skyline of downtown Sydney, the Harbour Bridge and the Opera House. The Opera House, that iconic building that lets you know you are in Sydney, Australia - just as the Eiffel Tower says Paris, France, the Empire State building says New York City, the Tower Bridge says London, England. I was blown away by the beauty of it all. Many pictures were taken.

"Tony, what's that island?" I was looking at a small island that was basically flat with several low-lying buildings on it. The most interesting feature was an impressive circular tower built of sandstone. It was about ten meters tall and had several open windows spaced around its circumference; they looked like places for large guns to be fired from.

"That's Pinchgut Island. It was used as a prison of sorts in the late 1700's then a fort was made on it about fifty years after that. The tower has very thick walls to withstand artillery fire. There was never a shot fired from it to defend the harbour. Now, you can visit it by taking a ferry from the docks downtown."

On the right I noticed a large sandstone mansion, beigy-brown with a grey roof. It was rectangular with many arches running along the lower level and a wrap around covered deck on the upper level. It stood on the tip of the rocky foreshore about ten meters above the water. There were hedges along the top of the natural rock wall then manicured lawns to the building. Tony told me that was the Governor General's House. It would be a wonderful place to live. The views of the harbour with the Opera House, Harbour Bridge and skyline would be amazing!

We passed very close by the Opera House, slowing down on the far side of it for docking. A few minutes later we pulled into our berth and my first ferry ride into Sydney was over. What a great bargain that ferry ride is. Just imagine, for under ten dollars, spending a half hour passing by all that gorgeous scenery and docking next to one of the most recognized buildings in the world! Blows my mind – yes it does.

Tony was now on his way to mark papers at the College he taught at in Sydney. His commute took him through the Botanic Gardens and he asked us if we wanted to join him and he would be our unofficial guide. The Botanic Gardens occupy a spectacular position in Sydney on the edge of the harbour next to the Opera House. It provides a garden oasis of thirty hectares for people to wander through. The gardens have a fantastic collection of plants from both Australia and from overseas. They were first used as a buffer between the governor's home and the penal colony that was once Sydney. In the mid eighteen hundreds roads and paths were built to allow public access and it has been a refuge for the public since then. Tony pointed out a lot of works of art, statues and memorials that even Lyn and Roni weren't aware of. He had obviously spent a lot of time in the park and it was wonderful to have this personally guided mini tour with him.

"Look, a fox!" Sure enough there was a beautiful red fox sleeping in the sun, just tucked away under a tree. Tony managed to snap a picture on his cell phone, but I missed the shot with my camera before the fox ran and jumped over a wall into heavier foliage. I had never thought of seeing a fox in Australia, let alone in downtown Sydney. Then again, back home in Victoria there have been cougars seen a few times in the downtown core.

The last memorial he showed us brought tears to my eyes, then to his. It is a memorial to the troops and their horses that fought in northern Africa and the Middle East during the First World War. The soldiers and their tough horses were used to the extreme heat and harsh conditions of Australia and were suited to the type of territory they now had to fight in. Three horses are shown in bronze bas-relief, ammunition carried around their necks, eyes wide, reins held by a short-sleeved trooper. These brumbies that had travelled so far from home were either killed in battle or left behind when the troops went home to Australia – "for them, no homecoming." I was fortunate enough to have had two horses in my life, Blaze and Cinnabar and I loved them with a passion. I could tell when they were unsure about a situation. Nostrils would flare, their eyes would become wide and worry lines would form above their brows. So it was hard for me to think of the very tough conditions of war that the horses had been put through: taken away from home, travelled on a ship, thrust into terrifying battle conditions – no explanation or understanding, no choice of their own. Then to be left behind . . . .

That was the end of our time with Tony. We gave each other a hug, he continued on his way to work and Lyn, Roni and I turned and headed back into the park.

Ten minutes later I was delighted to see a camp of Grey-headed Flying Foxes, otherwise known as fruit bats, in some trees. These cute fox-faced mammals can have a wing span of up to a meter and weigh up to one kilogram. Unlike smaller insect-eating bats that use echolocation to find their food these bats use sight and smell to find their food of pollen, nectar and rainforest fruits such a figs and lilly pilly berries. While most were sleeping, others were active and flying between the trees or hanging around grooming themselves. These bats found in Australia, can be found in the Botanic Gardens year round at this permanent camp. Flying foxes are a very social animal and can be found roosting together in groups of hundreds or even thousands.

We were heading back in the direction of the Opera House. It sits at the tip of a narrow peninsula beautifully surrounded by blue water on three sides and the green of the Botanic Gardens on the fourth. It is simply beauty surrounded by more beauty. With its striking roof line of 'sails', it is in a perfect location – absolutely mind boggling.

As we got closer I was surprised at what I saw on the roof. From a distance and in pictures I have seen, the roof looks simply white. It's not. The concrete roof sections have been laid with just over a million tiles that were made in Sweden! They are white with some having a glossy finish while others have a matte finish which looks very cool close-up. They seemed to take on different colors as the light changed. In one picture some are a glossy blue, in another they are light pink. There is no grouting between the tiles, just millions of tiny U shaped channels separating them from one another.

I took pictures of Roni and Lyn. Lyn took pictures of Roni and me. Roni took pictures of Lyn and me. Lyn took pictures of me. Lyn and Roni sat down on one of the benches on the harbour side of the Opera House while I walked around it. A little girl, about three years old, dressed in blue, caught and held my attention for about five minutes. She was there with her young Asian parents and she had control of the camera. I watched as they tried to get the camera from her, but she just said "No, mine" walked away from them and took her own pictures.

I took great delight in shooting pictures of the Opera House from angles I had never seen before. From the ferry deck I had taken pictures of both sides and the front of the building. Now, I had pictures of: the back of it, massive stairs, doors, handles, flags, the base, the supporting structures and visitors, lots of visitors. Sitting at number three of my favourite pictures of the Opera House is a close-up of a soaring conglomerate of tiles – thousands of them. The tiles are arranged in chevron patterns so the roof has hundreds of wonderful 'ziggity-zaggity' paths, like a Charlie Brown shirts pattern, all over it. My eyes scanned all over the roof. There was something magical about standing at the base of the wall and just being able to reach out and touch it. I walked between the two large sections of the complex. It was like walking through a tiled canyon of brightness. I loved it – it was amazing!

I stopped in the 'canyon' and I could feel time pause as I slipped into a moment of wonder. I was really here - this was no mere picture, but a three dimensional example of extraordinary architecture and construction; a building whose architect received the Pritzker Prize, architecture's highest honour. The Opera House is on the World Heritage List for the following criterion; "The Sydney Opera House is a great architectural work of the 20th century. It represents multiple strands of creativity, both in architectural form and structural design, a great urban sculpture carefully set in a remarkable waterscape and a world famous iconic building."

The Opera House sits on an enormous sandstone platform, part of which is a wide pedestrian concourse. The Opera House itself is just a tad larger than five football fields. The extraordinary roof is made of many pre-fabricated concrete sections which were all cast from the same hemisphere. Construction was begun in 1959 and was scheduled to be completed in 1963 but it was completed ten years later in 1973 and at one hundred and two million dollars had a budget over run of fourteen times the original estimate! But, I think it's worth every penny. I was just one of the seven million who visit here each year. It must add a lot to Sydney's economy.

Finished taking pictures for awhile, I joined Lyn and Roni. We found a place to have lunch and ate outside on the concourse with one of the most scenic backdrops in the world. I had a big burst of contentment going on. Lyn and Roni told me that the Opera House is home to Opera Australia, the Australian Ballet, the Sydney Theatre Company and the Sydney Symphony. I hadn't really thought much about what performances take place here – operas are only one facet of the site. At the back of the building are the Monumental Steps. These are often used as a performance space for large outdoor performances and free community events. There are also a recording studio, cafes, bars, restaurants and retail outlets in the building.

After lunch it was time for Roni to catch her train that would take her south to her home. Lyn and I saw her to the station then we walked to the dock where we boarded Charlotte, our ferry, for the return trip to Manly. I got to experience the voyage of the morning in reverse now which gave me a whole new perspective on everything. It was all stunning once again and was somewhat changed in the late afternoon light. When we got to the Manly terminal I spent time looking over the side as the ferry's thrusters guided the boat to the dock; just watching the water turn into a most beautiful, frothy, turquoise and white.

The last part of our trip was on the bus to Dee Why from in front of the Manly ferry terminal. Lyn and I got home around five thirty where we had a barbeque dinner of lamb and pork chops. We spent a quiet evening chatting and watching television.

On this, my last Saturday in Australia I would be a real tourist and take a bus tour around Sydney. Tom and Lyn were busy with a grandson's soccer game in the morning and a big family reunion in the evening. I headed off on the now familiar route from Dee Why to Sydney Harbour. I had already figured out which bus route I wanted to follow and walked the short distance from the ferry to the ticket booth where I bought my day pass.

The Bondi Explorer is a bus service which travels south of Sydney, stopping at nineteen points of interest along its route. Not that I could ever do that many in any one day. I began my trip at Circular Quay, gateway to

Sydney Harbour, which is the bus, ferry and rail transport hub. Beginning at 8:40 am the buses run at half hour intervals with the last bus returning to Circular Quay at 6:15 pm. I would be able get off the bus, take in the sights then re-board at any of the stops along the thirty kilometre route. The route would take me through Sydney's eastern suburbs to Watson's Bay, Bondi, Tamarama, Bronte and Coogee beaches. The ticket was thirty- nine dollars for the day. This also allows travel on the Sydney Explorer and on regular Sydney blue buses until midnight of the same day. The Sydney Explorer offers twenty-seven stops including the Opera House, Luna fun Park, Queen Victoria Building, Chinatown, the fish market and several museums. There was an ongoing commentary about the area and sites, including historic lessons, announced through the speaker system.

We left the terminus and made our way southeast past Woolloomooloo Bay, an area of five star restaurants and home to the stars. We continued through King's Cross, the Cruising Yacht Club and Rose Bay, home of the Royal Sydney Golf Club. The bus stopped for a five minute photo opportunity at Rose Bay Convent as it did at several other locations. I think this is a great idea as this was all I wanted to do at these stops – I couldn't really see myself hanging around for a half hour until the next bus came by! There were a lot of beautiful vistas and people enjoying the many harbour side parks on the way. We passed Watson's Bay then rather than get out here and climb the path up to the next stop, The Gap, I rode up the hill and got off at the top. The Gap is the opening to Sydney Harbour, which has spectacular coastal views from the rocky cliff side. Camera in hand, I made my way downhill, back to Watson's Bay, taking photos along the way then got on the next bus up the hill and beyond. This knee saving manoeuvre was a good idea!

Stop number twelve is Bondi Beach and was the stop of most interest to me. It is a world famous beach, an iconic sweep of sand that is the closest surfing beach to downtown Sydney. Eighty-five percent of visitors to Australia make it to Bondi. The one kilometre long sun-swept beach was backdropped on the ocean side by dark rainclouds making the sand and surroundings more striking. While tens of thousands may occupy Bondi on a summer weekend, the activity level was relatively calm with only a few hundred people there. They were walking, swimming, surfing, and playing in the sand and water, relaxing - just living in the moment. I soon joined them, first walking along the concrete promenade where I took a picture of a couple then had my picture taken with the Bondi Beach sign; yes, I was really here! One of the ramps took me down to beach level, where my sandals were removed and I made my way over the sand to the water.

This is Bondi Beach. Bondi is an Aboriginal word meaning "water breaking over rocks". The water is a palette of hues of blues. A color of Apple computers 'imac' is Bondi Blue. It was an Olympic site where in 2000, both the men's and women's beach volleyball had been contested.

The Guinness World Record for largest swimsuit photo taken was at Bondi Beach in 2007 when one thousand ten women posed in bikinis. Movies have been shot here. A large saltwater swimming pool at one of the world's oldest Surf Life Saving clubs is at the south end of the beach. No smoking is allowed on the beach. There is a reality series, Bondi Rescue that takes us into the world of the lifeguards as they do patrols and rescues. In 2008, Bondi Beach was added to the National Heritage List.

The south end of the beach is more hazardous for swimming because of a strong rip tide called The Backpacker's Express. It is so named because the bus drops passengers off at the south end of Bondi and many people swim at this more dangerous area because they are just too lazy to walk to the north end where it is much safer for swimming. Red and yellow flags mark where it is safe to swim and you are strongly advised to stay between them.

The waves at the south end are usually reserved for surfing. Light weight wetsuits were the surfers' attire on this day. The surfers were having such a good time. They paddled out then waited for the right wave enjoying varying levels of success as they rode toward the beach then repeated this many times over. At one point, I noticed that a lot of surfers were sitting on their boards, all facing out to sea and looking in the same direction. I followed their gaze and saw the grey dorsal fins cutting through the water some fifty yards from the surfers. There is probably nothing that gets the attention of people in the water more than the sight of rapidly approaching dorsal fins. As the animals surfaced there was a tiny puff of water from first one, then the others. The puffs of water were from blowholes; these were not sharks, but dolphins. Within seconds the dolphins were surfing alongside their human counterparts and shared several waves over the next few minutes before they moved on.

There had been five or six shark attacks in 2009 in the Sydney area by the time I arrived in late April. No fatalities, but one cost a Sydney Harbour diver a hand and a leg. There is a shark net that is in place during the summer months at Bondi Beach. I didn't know much about shark nets. I have found out that: they do not touch shorelines and they ride some four to eight meters below the surface of the water so as not to interfere with boats. Sharks are free to swim around or over the nets. Their purpose is to entangle and thus drown the sharks, not just to keep sharks from swimming in to an area. Just as many sharks get tangled in the nets from the beach side as from the ocean side.

Bondi Beach was everything I had imagined it would be and so much more. My only disappointment was not being able to find a burgundy, Bondi Beach tee shirt with a simple surfer logo on it in my size. I left Bondi Beach heading south to take a six kilometre coastal walk to Coogoo Beach. I spent quite some time above the swimming pool watching as waves crashed over the sea wall and into the swimmers paths. Just a really cool place to be. The walk goes along sea sculptured sandstone cliffs and offers amazing coastal views. You may recall that there was a bank of storm clouds off shore and I was keeping an eye on these. I noticed that the squall line was getting closer at a rapid pace and I increased the speed of my limping walk as my knee would allow, hoping to get to Bronte Beach and its bus shelter before the rain hit. Nope, it didn't quite work out for me. The rain wasn't too cold but it was very persistent and soon I was wet through to the skin. I took shelter in a bus stop with others who were also seeking a dry place. Oops, it was not the Bondi Express bus shelter and I saw my bus go past me and stop about a kilometre down the road. When the rain let up a little bit I made my way to the Express stop where I had about a twenty minute wait. This stop was simply a sign, no shelter, and the rain was cat and dogging furiously once again. I took the liberty of crossing the road and sitting on a neighbour's step which had a bit of an overhang so managed to keep out of the worst of it. I was glad to see the blue bus come around the corner and I made it back across the street in time to enter its' sheltered interior.

It was getting late and I didn't have time to get off at any more stops but I enjoyed driving past the Royal Randwick Racecourse, the Cricket Grounds, football stadium and Hyde Park. By the time I got back to Circular Quay I was pretty warm and dry. This late afternoon ferry ride gave me some of the most spectacular images of my trip. Imagine the Opera House lit by warm, soft rays from a sun low in the sky – it isn't white in this light, but the softest coral pink you can think of. Add some blue sky when you look almost straight up. Now as you bring your gaze downward you see storm clouds in the background. Clouds that are dark, shark grey on the bottom and a soft, glowing orangey-pink on their puffy tops. The clouds darken as you look down, until just above the horizon they are almost black with storm activity. It was a perfectly dramatic lighting situation – I have pictures! It was another incredibly beautiful ferry trip back to Manly. When I got off the ferry the street lights had come on. The lights, as do a row of tall pines, follow the curve of the shoreline and it was quite striking to see them lit up in the evening. When I got back to Dee Why I walked to a pizza place and got a personal sized pepperoni pie which I took back to Lyn and Toms and had for my dinner. 'Easy, peasy, nice and easy' as they say down here – at least I had never heard that expression before New Zealand. It had been a most wonderful day.

Today was the last day of my adventure – other than travelling home the next day. I would go into Sydney and meet Susan, my couch surfing hostess from Wollongong seven and a half weeks ago. We would have a lot to talk about. I was very familiar with my commute now and I enjoyed all its dramatic scenery once more. From Circular Quay I caught a bus to the Maritime Museum where we had agreed to meet. I was meandering around, not very mindful of people, which I should have been and I looked right past Susan before I pulled my brain into focus and recognized her – I felt a bit dense at missing her smiling face. We greeted each other with smiles and hugs and started talking and walking. That went on pretty much for the length of our visit together. Being with Susan is like being with a lifelong friend and we were comfortable in each other's company. She drove me around the downtown area until lunch time when somehow she managed to find a parking spot on the street. I treated her to a scrumptious lunch in a small Chinese restaurant. After another bit of driving it was time to part company and I did so with some reluctance. It is my hope that Susan or her daughters will make it to Canada to surf with me some time.

Sydney Tower would be my last tourist stop of my trip. As you know, I usually like to head to these tall attractions at the beginning of my stay but the timing just wasn't right for a visit until now. I liked the tower from my first glimpse of it. The design has some very interesting differences from other towers I have visited. The observation deck is just one of four stories in the turret that sits near the top of the tower. The turret looks like a huge flower pot, that is to say it is cylindrical and tapered out at the top – this 'flower pot' is as tall as a nine story building. The tower rises from the roof of a shopping center built at its base. It is stabilized by a lattice work of fifty-six cables that rise from the building at the tower's base which seemed to give it an almost delicate appearance. The cables gradually taper inward to just below the turret before flaring out ever so slightly and disappearing into the base of the turret.

It was a three block walk from where Susan had dropped me off and took only a few minutes to get to the tower. Lyn had given me a two-for-one admission coupon so I began to look for someone I could pair up with. I saw a dad with his young son and daughter so walked over to them and introduced myself. That is how we became a temporary 'family' at the tower. I picked up an information pamphlet along with my ticket in the lobby then headed over to one of the three elevators. It took only forty seconds to be carried up to the observation deck two hundred fifty meters above the ground. I stepped out of the elevator onto rich blue carpet then on to red carpet next to the windows. The red carpet is a few meters wide and makes a circle around the observation deck. I spent a lot of time on this red carpet circling the deck several times and sharing it with the other visitors. The windows slant gently upwards and outwards so I was able to put my head out 'over the edge' so to speak. The views are perfect panorama postcard opportunities. Built around the harbour, Sydney is simply gorgeous – I loved being able to see all the ins and outs of water against land. I was now able to get a much better appreciation of the scenery I had passed by so many times on the ferry and I was able to see almost everywhere I had visited. It was easy to trace the ferry route from Manly to Circular Quay. The tower looks almost directly down over the Botanic Gardens, the Domain and Hyde Park, and its shadow rolled across the treetops and lawns down below. I loved seeing the different architecture from short copper-domed older buildings and the spires of

St. Mary's Cathedral to the modern skyscrapers that now surround them. I now saw sports stadiums and playing fields, kids playing cricket, people walking in the park and on the beaches. It was incredible to have so much information about Sydney spread out below me.

Looking out towards North Head I saw dozens of white sails contrasting against the blue waters as sailors vied for wind and position in Sunday races. In one of my pictures of the harbour I counted one hundred twenty-nine sailboats, fourteen power boats and the Manly-Sydney ferry. Only from the tower did I become aware of the hundreds of boats alongside docks or moored just off shore. Water is just a magical element; necessary for life, habitat for thousands of species, creator of natural beauty and a plaything for animals of the world.

From my vantage point I got an appreciation for the size of the Harbour Bridge. I was able to pick out some vertical irregularities along the uppermost arch – a group of people climbing. They looked most insignificant from this far away. The Opera House could be seen between the buildings although it was a limited view. It looked like two white Conquistador helmets that had been laid down on the waterfront.

Then there was the traffic, vehicles and pedestrians going about their daily business while I was up here watching them go by. They were in a different world of hustle and bustle and noise. I was in a quiet world of jaw-dropping vistas and peace. Looking west, away from the water I could see the thousands of red tiled roofs of the suburbs. I had seen the same suburbs while flying into Sydney a few days before.

The turret also houses a coffee bar, two restaurants and a small gift shop. I never thought that I'd be buying souvenirs up here on my last day, but that's exactly what I did. The prices were the same as in other shops which was nice to see. I found three pieces of aboriginal art that I could roll up and fit in my duffle bag. I mean, what are the chances of making a find of three pieces that I loved, all in one place on my last tourist stop? (Travel Luck) I bought pens for my children and Australia themed pencils for students at my school. Fridge magnets were added to the list; colourful, non-breakable, small, all good qualities for a souvenir. Armed with pictures and trinkets, I took one last look at the sweeping views and then turned and walked off the red carpet, onto the blue and back into an elevator.

I got off the elevator on another level of the turret where I met back up with my 'family.' Our tickets included admission to OzTrek, a virtual reality tour across Australia. I took my seat and clicked my seatbelt together. Yes, a seatbelt. This was no ordinary seat, but a motion seat. I immersed myself in the simulated flight and was instantly transferred out of the tower to fly effortlessly over the nearby Opera House and the Harbour Bridge. Next I got to see Bondi Beach as the birds do. I was having a great time in just the opening seconds of this fifteen minute adventure across Australia. The six meter high, one hundred eighty degree screen and moving seat let me plant myself firmly in the co-pilots' seat as we left Sydney and headed further afield. I was so delighted to re-visit the places I had been over the last two months and see new things as well. Here, I got to go white water rafting in Queensland, fly over Barron Falls, climb Uluru, get up close and personal with a salt-water crocodile, get on the field during an Aussie Rules football game and herd buffalo by helicopter. It was a blast and I thought a perfect summary to my journey. I am so glad that I experienced OzTrek, a one of a kind ride in Australia.

Back out to the elevators again, a rapid descent, the doors opened and I was back at ground level. I walked around the downtown area enjoying the old and new architecture of the buildings. We have a very similar building situation home in Victoria, being a Commonwealth country too. The Strand on George Street was like a piece of candy plunked down between walls of grey neighbours with her pink walls and borders of light-colored stones around windows and doors. One of the tenants is Haigh's Chocolates where I stopped and bought some yummy treats for Lyn and Tom. Another building with perfectly pink sandstone walls and columns and bold, grey blocks on the bottom story housed a McDonald's – they seemed to me an odd match - it appears that Mickie Dees has invaded everywhere. The four and a half story Bank of Australasia stood proudly on a street corner surrounded by modern skyscrapers.

I was amused by two simple words and an arrow stencilled on the one-way streets at many crosswalks, a warning for pedestrians; ← LOOK LEFT. Of course I have a picture of that. Near Circular Quay there is a gathering of metal sculptures that occupy a wide strip of the pedestrian walkway. This would be my last series of pictures in Australia. The collection is just marvellous and is in part a water feature. The whole group of art flows down the walkway just as the water flows. The theme is one of nature: plants rising from ponds, a turtle on a giant lily pad, lizards on rocks, a bird with wings outstretched drying its feathers, snakes curling along rocks, two frogs playing tag, a toad, an echidna, insects and a pelican hovering over two chicks in a nest. I loved it all!

I passed along the walkway and went to the ferry terminal. Seated on the concourse a short distance away sat an Aborigine, artistically made up in white paint, legs crossed; the iconic sound of the didgeridoo vibrated through the harbour. As I listened and watched, I was taken back to that night on the west coast when Capes had played for us in front of the fire, under the stars. It seemed a fitting end to my adventure in Australia.

It was early evening when I boarded the ferry. The lighting was spectacular once again and it sent a surreal glow over the harbour. The Opera House stood as always, an unforgettable landmark of Sydney. I have a glorious picture of the Harbour Bridge silhouetted with golden orange rays of sunshine radiating through soft clouds. I stood on deck and watched Sydney Harbour until the ferry turned gently to starboard and the scene disappeared. I was a bit sad at its passing but tossed my mind into the sunset that was happening all around me. Everything was lit with a soft glowing of the fading day. It was absolutely beautiful.

I caught the bus back to Dee Why and walked up the road then the steep driveway to Lyn and Tom's place. "Hi, I'm home." I told them about my day in Sydney and presented them with the chocolates which they immediately shared with me – yummy all around.

SYDNEY TO SIDNEY

Monday, the final day; I would leave Sydney and travel home to Sidney. It was hard to believe that three months had passed, but here I was at seven fifteen in the morning walking down the driveway to the airport shuttle. Hugs and goodbyes to Lyn and Tom and I was on my way home.

I was the first one on the shuttle so had my choice of seats. We stopped and picked up more passengers until it was quite crowded with people and luggage; then one last stop where four more people boarded. I think we must have hit an illegal number of people on board as all the seats were taken and one little girl found a berth sitting wedged on a suitcase in the aisle between her parents. It's so easy to meet people!

We were all happy to disembark at the departure terminal, the shuttle doors opening and its passengers almost tumbling to the sidewalk. I had plenty of time to check in and go through the security process. I had remembered to pack my Swiss army knife in my checked luggage and didn't have any liquids to be confiscated. Once through security I passed the time having breakfast and strolling through the shops. My eye was attracted by a sale sign in the last store I visited. I walked over and started going through the bargains. There it was – the tee shirt I had been looking for. It was a rich burgundy color and had the perfect small logo of two surfers walking along the beach with their boards tucked under their arms, the sun low on the horizon. In tidy print it said Bondi Beach. The clincher was that it was my size! Imagine that! The final store I would visit in Australia, in the airport, on a sale shelf! I grabbed my prize, clutched it to my chest and went to the cashier, a smile plastered on my face! (Travel Luck) Every time I put it on I am taken back to Bondi Beach, I can even smell the sunscreen!

The now familiar flight over the endless blue ocean passed with ease and I was once again back in Auckland, New Zealand where I had a five hour layover. I headed out to the front of the terminal where I waited for Heather and Mike; we had arranged to have dinner together. It was so wonderful to see their car approach and pull up in front of me.

"Hi Joan! O my gosh, it's so good to see you! You look great. Can't wait to hear all about your trip in Australia." Heather and I gave each other a quick hug then got into the car. We were soon at a nearby restaurant and had placed our orders. They asked me all about my trip so I was the last one to finish my meal as I ended up talking a lot. They were very interested in all that had happened in the past two months and made a good audience of two. Soon it was time for me to get back to the airport. We stopped in front of the departures terminal and got out of the car. With hugs and smiles we said our goodbyes not knowing if and when we might ever see each other again. I think we will.

Passing through security and wandering around the stores inside the terminal was now very familiar territory and I found it was easy to pass the time while waiting for my flight to be called. A national icon for New Zealand is the fern. I had looked, unsuccessfully, for a pair of silver fern earrings during my stay in New Zealand but of the hundreds of pairs I had seen, none were what I was looking for. So I here I was in the last New Zealand store I would be in where good old travel luck came my way again! There on the last side of the last rotating rack of jewellery, down near the bottom were the fern earrings I had been searching out! They were silver with mother of pearl showing between the leaves of the fern. I had them off the rack in quick time and made my way to the cashier with a smile for this little treasure I had found!

The flight to Los Angeles passed by fairly quickly. We departed in the early evening and I was able to pass the greatest part of the trip in sleep or at least semi-conscious rest – that wonderful time when you teeter on the edge of consciousness and sleep and you can feel your mind slipping away to a special place of dreamtime. I also got to watch a few new movies which I enjoyed. The layover was only two hours in Los Angeles so went fairly quickly with walking outside and browsing through the stores in the terminal. With the time change and passing over the International Dateline I gained back the day I had 'lost' and somehow landed in Vancouver the same evening I had left Auckland. I was careful to gather my belongings from the plane and waited patiently at my seat until the aisle had cleared in front of me and it was my turn to walk to the front of the plane. I followed my fellow passengers out of the jet then along one corridor an another as we found our way to the empty baggage carousel. It was exciting when the baggage began to appear. Black is the most popular color for suitcases - there were probably about forty or so similar to mine. But there were no other suitcases with green, gold and red, curly Christmas ribbon attached to them. Bam! I saw them coming at me from a distance and was able to squiggle forward through the other people and grab the handles as first my suitcase then my duffle bag arrived beside me. Now with my possessions safely loaded on a luggage cart I made my way towards the Customs line. I was lucky to have only five others in front of me so I made it to this final checkpoint pretty quickly. I handed my completed customs form to the officer, she read it over. "Welcome home." "Thank you. It's nice to be back."

Having passed through customs I immediately knew I was back home in Canada when upon rounding a corner I looked up at a huge television screen to see a hockey game in full stride – Welcome Home! I took my luggage and checked it in for my final flight to Victoria. Back through security one last time then I had two hours in the terminal. I love the Vancouver terminal as it has a distinguished collection of artwork throughout.

Inspiration for the artwork in the Vancouver air terminal was inspired by the outdoors. The art shows British Columbia's mountains, forests, rivers, seas, wildlife and First Nations heritage. The pieces vary from weavings, glass works, water pieces, totem poles, sculptures both large and small, to paintings.

The First Nations art in the Vancouver airport is just amazing. Two, seventeen foot tall, carved cedar welcoming figures stretch their arms forward in greeting to international travellers. Suspended above them is "Hugging the World", a carving of eagle and raven that has a wingspan of forty feet. Probably the most admired and photographed sculpture is The Spirit of Haida Gwaii, The Jade Canoe, by world renowned First Nations sculptor, Bill Reid. Situated in the entrance to the main terminal, the magnificent bronze and jade statue is almost twenty feet long and twelve feet high. It is paddled by creatures from Haida legends. Looking at it just envelops me in the scene it portrays and I imagine myself as being in this mystical canoe with the other paddlers. Its image was used on the Canadian twenty dollar bill.

I spent my two hours looking in the terminal's stores, getting a late supper and reading. Soon it was time to head to my departure gate (once again the most distant one) for the final flight over to Vancouver Island. It was eleven forty-five when we got our boarding call. The plane holds about forty passengers and is powered by propellers. These small planes are regularly tossed around on this low-altitude flight.

We were just settled into our seats when the stewardess made the first announcement to us. "Welcome aboard. Please make sure that you find your airsick bags and move them to a handy location." There was a collective groan. Never before had I heard such an early flight turbulence warning. The door hadn't even been closed yet, most of us hadn't clicked our seatbelts. Well, let me tell you, I tried to lose all close ties I had with my supper as I thought we'd be parting company somewhere over the Strait of Georgia. Apparently the weather had been nasty all day. Was it saving the worst for the last flight of the day? What fate awaited us?

"Good evening ladies and gentlemen. This is your captain speaking. We have had turbulent weather here all day and we ask you to keep your seat belts firmly fastened at all times. There will be no in-flight service as the flight attendants will remain fastened in their seats too."

Basically, it was hang on to your loved ones, say goodbye to your meals and be glad it would be over in twenty-three minutes. So it was with great upchuck anticipation and extra nervousness for many passengers that we taxied to the runway, turned into the straightaway and felt the powerful thrust of the engines lift us into the air. True to the warnings we hit a little pocket of uneasy air almost immediately, dropped down and slid a bit sideways - but it was just a small bump to start things. I must say that I have never experienced such a flight as that one from Vancouver to Victoria.

We waited on guard for something that just never materialized. It was the smoothest flight I have ever had on that route, just the one bump on takeoff and then exceptionally calm skies for the remainder of the trip. The pilot performed a near perfect touchdown to cap it all off. We all clapped for our pilot and crew. What can I say? (Travel Luck)

We de-planed down the stairs onto the tarmac and walked the short distance to the terminal. Just through the doors I saw my daughter, Jenna, standing there with a smile to match mine. It was so good to be greeted by a loved one! Huge hugs and we walked and talked our way to the luggage claim area. I had my two bags pretty quickly. We made our way out in to the parking lot and were soon squared away in my little white Toyota. Jenna drove us home which took only a few minutes. We pulled into the driveway and we could hear my dog, Emma start to howl, something she does whenever we come home. Jenna and I got my gear out of the car, unlocked the front door and stepped inside. It was so good to walk into my home and see Emma. Jenna and I talked for about an hour before she went to bed and then I had a shower before falling into my own bed – my long lost friend. I knew I'd have a great sleep that night.

The adventure was just awesome!

Don't regret the things you didn't do.

Go ahead – plan something – go somewhere!

Surf's ups